AF773576

State Accountability for Environmental Damage in International Armed Conflict

The book comprehensively analyses whether a State may be held responsible for environmental damage resulting from its wrongful conduct in international armed conflict.

Focusing on elements of State responsibility's main elements, obligations, damage and standard of conduct, under the law of armed conflict and international environmental law, the book covers war and occupation and other relevant applicable laws. This extends to international water and human rights law. It presents techniques to resolve conflicts of norms from different law branches, when simultaneously applied, and incorporates latest legal developments and potential impact on the subject. Engaging with detailed analysis of legal rules, the book highlights weaknesses within the law alongside proposing new interpretations of outdated notions. Practical application of the rules is illustrated by two cases of damage to land, Mediterranean Sea and air pollution in the Israel-Hezbollah war in Lebanon (2006) and to the Occupied Palestinian Territory's natural resources, mainly land, water and quarries. It concludes by examining mechanisms to enforce State responsibility.

The book will be of interest to graduate law students, researchers and practitioners in the field of international law, the law of armed conflict international environmental and water law and human rights law.

Aïda Tamer Chammas is an independent international law researcher. After graduating from University Paris II, Panthéon-Assas and further studies at the Fletcher School, Boston, she practiced as a finance lawyer in Paris, before moving to London in 1996. Her current research interests, developed during an LLM and PhD at the University of London, SOAS Law School, cover mainly international environmental law, the law of armed conflict including war and occupation and public international law issues. She was an alternate member of the International Law Association Committee on Participation in Global Cultural Heritage Governance between 2018 and 2022.

Routledge Research in International Environmental Law

Marine Conservation and International Law
Legal Instruments for Biodiversity Beyond National Jurisdiction
Sarah Louise Lothian

Nature Law and Policy in Europe
Edited by Andrew L.R. Jackson

Environmental Liability and the Interplay between EU Law and International Law
Dr Emanuela Orlando

Implementing International Environmental Law and Policy
An Interactive Approach to Environmental Regulation
Joanna Miller Smallwood

Environmental Law and Governance in India
Sairam Bhat and Centre for Environmental Law, Education, Research, and Advocacy (CEERA)

Environmental Law and Policy in India
Sairam Bhat and Centre for Environmental Law, Education, Research, and Advocacy (CEERA)

Protection of the Environment under International Law during Occupation
International Humanitarian, Human Rights and Environmental Law
Waad Abualrob

State Accountability for Environmental Damage in International Armed Conflict
Aïda Tamer Chammas

www.routledge.com/Routledge-Research-in-International-Environmental-Law/book-series/INTENVLAW

State Accountability for Environmental Damage in International Armed Conflict

Aïda Tamer Chammas

Routledge
Taylor & Francis Group
LONDON AND NEW YORK

First published 2025
by Routledge
4 Park Square, Milton Park, Abingdon, Oxon OX14 4RN

and by Routledge
605 Third Avenue, New York, NY 10158

Routledge is an imprint of the Taylor & Francis Group, an informa business

© 2025 Aïda Tamer Chammas

The right of Aïda Tamer Chammas to be identified as author of this work has been asserted in accordance with sections 77 and 78 of the Copyright, Designs and Patents Act 1988.

All rights reserved. No part of this book may be reprinted or reproduced or utilised in any form or by any electronic, mechanical, or other means, now known or hereafter invented, including photocopying and recording, or in any information storage or retrieval system, without permission in writing from the publishers.

Trademark notice: Product or corporate names may be trademarks or registered trademarks, and are used only for identification and explanation without intent to infringe.

British Library Cataloguing-in-Publication Data
A catalogue record for this book is available from the British Library

ISBN: 978-0-367-41482-5 (hbk)
ISBN: 978-1-041-02432-3 (pbk)
ISBN: 978-0-367-82328-3 (ebk)

DOI: 10.4324/9780367823283

Typeset in Times New Roman
by Apex CoVantage, LLC

Contents

Acknowledgements *vi*
List of Abbreviations *vii*

1 General context 1

2 State responsibility for environmental war damage under the law of armed conflict 33

3 State responsibility for environmental damage during occupation under the law of occupation 68

4 State responsibility under international environmental law for environmental damage in international armed conflict 110

5 Environment under war: Israel and Hezbollah, Lebanon, 2006 150

6 Environment under occupation: Occupied Palestinian Territory 187

7 In the aftermath of international armed conflicts 237

Index *246*

Acknowledgements

I would like to thank the persons who accompanied me during the process of elaborating this book.

I first presented the idea as a subject for PhD research to Philippe Cullet, renowned for his vast international environmental law expertise. Philippe did not hesitate to give his approval and he would become my PhD supervisor, in a supportive role that I greatly appreciated. Mid-way through the PhD, Iain Scobbie graciously accepted my request to be parachuted on the project to lend me his critical eye on international humanitarian law. His suggestion to turn the PhD thesis into a manuscript for publication would prove invaluable. I would pick on it much later, having put the thesis aside for some time.

At Routledge, Siobhan Poole, my first law editor, backed my book proposal and was consistent in her encouragement, before moving on to a new role. In a nice twist of fate, Nicola Sharpe, who had also been involved when I first approached Routledge, would be the new law editor who would oversee the publication of the monograph assisted by Diksha Bhugra, the editorial assistant. I am grateful for their patience in giving me the space I needed to significantly overhaul the previous version of the manuscript.

Last but not least, the unwavering support of my immediate family members who steadfastly believed in the book was instrumental in getting me to persevere and see it through. I owe them my gratitude. Emile, my husband, has been a tireless advocate of my endeavours from early days to the final dot of this monograph.

Abbreviations

A.F.L. Rev.	Air Force Law Review
Am. J. Comp. L.	American Journal of Comparative Law
Am. U. L. Rev.	American University Law Review
AJIL	American Journal of International Law
A.D.I.L.	Annual Digest and Reports of Public International Law Cases
Am. U. Int'l L. Rev.	American University International Law Review
Am. U. L. Rev.	American University Law Review
Amsterdam U. Int'l L. Rev.	Amsterdam University International Law Review
Annals Am. Acad. Pol. & Soc. Sci.	Annals of the American Academy of Political and Social Science
Ann. Surv. Int'l & Comp. L.	Annual Survey of International and Comparative Law
ARIJ	Applied research Institute in Jerusalem
Ariz. L. Rev.	Arizona Law Review
Austl Y.B. Int'l L.	Australian Yearbook of International Law
Austrian Rev. Int'l & Eur. L.	Austrian Review of International & European Law
ASIL	American Society of International Law
Baltic Y. B. Int'l L.	Baltic Yearbook of International Law
Berkeley J. Int'l L.	Berkeley Journal of International Law
B.C. Int'l & Comp. L. Rev.	Boston College International and Comparative Law Review
BIICL	British Institute of International and Comparative law
B.C. Envt'l. Aff. L.Rev.	Boston College Environmental Affairs Law Review
BGR	Bundesanstalt für Geowissenschaften und Rohstoffe (Institute for Geosciences and Natural Resources, Germany)
Brit. Ency Int'l L.	British Encyclopedia of International Law
BJPIR	British Journal of Politics and International Relations
Brit. Y.B. Int'l L.	British Yearbook of International Law

Can. Y.B. Int'l L.	Canadian Yearbook of International Law
Cardozo L. Rev.	Cardozo Law Review
Case W. Res. J. Int'l L.	Case Western Reserve Journal of International Law
Chinese JIL	Chinese Journal of international Law
Colo. J. Int'l Env. L. & Pol'y	Colorado Journal of Environmental Law and Policy
Colum. J. Envtl L.	Columbia Journal of Environmental Law
Colum. J. Transnat'l L.	Columbia Journal of Transnational Law
Colum. L. Rev.	Columbia Law Review
Cornell Int'l L.J.	Cornell International Law Journal
CUP	Cambridge University Press
Denv. J. Int'l L. & Pol'y	Denver Journal of International law and policy
Duke J. Int'l & Comp. L.	Duke Journal of comparative and international law
Dick. J.	Int'l L. Dickinson Journal of International Law
Ecology L.Q.	Ecology Law Quarterly
EC	European Commission
ECHR	European Convention on Human Rights
ECtHR	European Court of Human Rights
ECR	European Court Reports
Env. L. Rev.	Environmental Law Review
Env. Pol'y & L.	Environmental Policy and Law
ECHO	European Commission Humanitarian Aid Department
EJIL	European Journal of International Law
EC	European Commission
E.H.R.L.R.	European Human Rights Law Review
Emory Int'l L. Rev.	Emory International Law Review
EU	European Union
FAO	Food and Agriculture Organisation of the United Nations
Fla. J. Int'l L.	Florida Journal of international Law
Geo. Wash. Int'l L.	Rev. George Washington International Law Review
German Y.B. Int'l L.	German Yearbook of International Law
Goettingen J. Int'l L.	Goettingen Journal of International Law
HRW	Human Rights Watch
Harv. Int'l L. J.	Harvard International Law Journal
Harv. Int'l Rev.	Harvard International Review
Harv. L. Rev.	Harvard Law Review
Hous. J. Int'l L.	Houston Journal of International Law
IDI	Institut de Droit International
IDI Y.B.	Institut de Droit International Yearbook (Institute of International Law)
IAEA	International Atomic Energy Agency
IAEA	Int'l L. Series IAEA International Law Series
ICC	International Criminal Court
ICCPR	International Covenant on Civil and Political Rights

ICESCR	International Covenant on Economic, Social and Cultural Rights
ICJ	International Court of Justice
ICJ	Rep. International Court of Justice Reports
ICLQ	International and Comparative Law Quarterly
Int. C.L. Rev.	International Community Law Review
ICRC	International Committee of Red Cross
ICTR	International Criminal Tribunal for Rwanda
ICTY	International Criminal Tribunal for the Former Yugoslavia
IDF	Israël Defence Forces
IHL	International Humanitarian Law
IISD	International Institute for Sustainable Development
Int'l J. Env. Stud.	International Journal of Environmental Studies
Int'l J. Marine & Coastal L.	International Journal of Marine & Coastal Law
Int'l J. Mid. E. Stud.	International Journal of Middle East Studies,
ILA	International Law Association
ILC	International Law Commission
ILC Y.B.	Yearbook of the International Law Commission
ILM	International Legal Materials
ILSA J. Int'l & Comp. L.	ILSA Journal of International and Comparative Law
IMO	International Maritime Organisation
IMT	Nuremberg International Military Tribunal Nuremberg
IRRC	International Review of the Red Cross
Israël L. Rev.	Israël Law Review
Israël	Yearbook on Human Rights
ITLOS	International Tribunal for the Law of the Sea
IUCN	International Union for Conservation of Nature
JEL	Journal of Environmental Law
J.C.& S.L.	Journal of Conflict & Security Law
J. Int'l Hum Leg. Stud	Journal of International Humanitarian Legal Studies
J. Palestine Stud.	Journal of Palestine Studies
Law & Hist. Rev.	Law and History Review
LJIL	Leiden Journal of International Law
La. L. Rev.	Louisiana Law Review
Law & Soc'y Rev.	Law & Society Review
McGill L.J.	McGill Law Journal
Macquarie J. Int'l & Comp. Envt'l. L.	Macquarie Journal of International and Comparative Environmental Law
MUP	Manchester University Press
Maryland J. Int'l L.	Maryland Journal of international law
Max Planck Y.B. UN L.	Max Planck Yearbook of United Nations Law
Melbourne J. Int'l L.	Melbourne Journal of International Law
MEMO	Middle East Monitor

Mich. L. Rev.	Michigan Law Review
Middle E. J.	Middle East Journal
Middle E. Stud.	Middle Eastern Studies
MENA	Middle East and North Africa
MAE	Ministère des Affaires Etrangères (France)
Minnesota J Int'l L.	Minnesota Journal of International Law
MPEPIL	Max Plank Encyclopaedia of International Law
MEAE	Ministère de l'Europe et des Affaires étrangères (France)
Mich. J. Int'l L.	Michigan Journal of International Law
Military L. Rev.	Military Law Review
Nat. Resources J.	Natural Resources Journal
Naval L.	Rev. Naval Law Review
Nordic J. Int'l L.	Nordic Journal of International Law
N.C. J. Int'l L.	North Carolina Journal of International Law
N.Y. Int'l L.	Netherlands Yearbook of International Law
N.Y.U. J. Int'l L. & Pol.	New York University Journal of International Law & Politics
NMT	Nuremberg Military Tribunal
Palestine Y.B. Int'l L.	Palestine Yearbook of International Law
PCA	Permanent Court of Arbitration
PCBS	Palestinian Central Bureau of Statistics
PNUE	Programme des Nations Unies pour l'Environnement
RIIA	Report of International Arbitral Awards
RECIEL	Review of European Community & International Environmental Law
Rev. ICR	Revue Internationale de la Croix-Rouge
Rev. Hist. Dr. F. & Etran.	Revue Historique de Droit Français et Etranger
Scandinavian Studies in Law	Scandinavian Stud. L.
Stanford J. Int'l L.	Stanford Journal of International Law
Stanford J. Int'l Stud.	Stanford Journal of International Studies
The Modern L. Rev.	The Modern Law Review
UK	United Kingdom
UK MoD	United Kingdom Ministry of Defence
UKHL	UK House of Lords
UN	United Nations
UN Audiovisual Library of Int'l L.	United Nations Audiovisual Library of International Law
UNCC	United Nations Compensation Commission
UNCC	GV United Nations Compensation Commission Governing Council
UNCED	United Nations Conference on Environment and Development
UNCESCR	United Nations Committee on Economic, Social and Cultural Rights
UNCHE	Conference on the Human Environment

UNCHS	United Nations Centre for Human Settlements (Habitats)
UNCLOS	United Nations Convention on the Law of the Sea
UNCLOS	III Third United Nations Conference on the Law of the Sea, 1973–1982
UNDP	United Nations Development Programme
UNECE	United Nations Economic Commission for Europe
UNEP	United Nations Environment Programme
UNESC	United Nations Economic and Social Council
UNESCWA	United Nations Economic and Social Commission for Western Asia
UNGA	United Nations General Assembly
UNHR Com.	United Nations Human Rights Committee
UNHRC	United Nations Human Rights Council
UNHCHR	UN High Commissioner for Human Rights
UNOCHA	United Nations Office for the Coordination of Humanitarian Affairs
UNRWA	United Nations Relief and Works Agency for Palestine Refugees in the Near East
UNSC	United Nations Security Council
UNCSD	United Nations Conference on Sustainable Development
UNTS	United Nations Treaty Series
U. Pa. J. Intl L.	University of Pennsylvania Journal of International Law
U. St Thomas J.L. & Pub. Pol'y	University of St Thomas Journal of Law and Public Policy
US	United States
US DoD	United States Department of Defense
US MTN	United States Military Tribunal Nuremberg
Vand. J. Transnat'l L.	Vanderbilt Journal of Transnational Law
VCLT	Vienna Convention on the Law of Treaties
WHO	World Health Organisation
WZO	World Zionist Organisation
Windsor Y.B. Access Just.	Windsor Yearbook Access to Justice
Yale L.J.	Yale Law Journal
Y.B. Int'l H.L.	Yearbook of International Humanitarian Law
Y.B. Int'l Env. L.	Yearbook of International Environmental Law

1 General context

Armed conflicts and environmental crises are omnipresent in our world, separate or intertwined. Environmental threats linked to climate change, ocean pollution or waste issues are looming. Natural disasters are wreaking havoc on the planet and its people, from volcanic eruptions to floodings, tsunamis, earthquakes and typhoons.

"Many of us are now bored by the increasingly frequent news of environmental destruction and impending ecological disasters. After all, it is old news that we are messing up the planet. Increasingly shocking stories or images are required to maintain our attention."[1]

As if such events are not devastating enough, humanity is engaged in armed conflicts unfolding humanitarian tragedies and destroying the environment. Images of military strikes and their resulting deaths, injuries and ruins are relayed relentlessly on our screens. At its most outrageous, environmental annihilation results from "scorched earth" policy used as military strategy.[2] Once the spotlight of the news is diverted from a country at – or emerging from – war or occupation to some other story, the armed conflict's environmental legacy endures for many years. The consequences of environmental degradation reverberate in terms of social impact, economic costs and political impediment to post-conflict peace and security, putting at risk sustainable development – all reasons making it pressing to acknowledge the disastrous effect of armed conflicts on the environment, increase environmental protection during conflicts and hold States accountable for environmental damage.

I. Historical perspective

The international community has woken up to confront this reality. Wars and their terrible human and environmental consequences have existed since time immemorial and will always be part of the human condition. What has changed is an

1 Cormac Cullinan, *Wild Law, a Manifesto for Earth Justice* (Green Books 2003) 38

2 Steve Bloomfield and Katherine Butler, 'Darfur's Return to Hell, "Scorched Earth" Unleashed on Darfur, despite UN Presence' The Independent, 12 March 2008, 3

DOI: 10.4324/9780367823283-1

increased public awareness and environmental consciousness fuelled by a growing flow of information, a leap in scientific knowledge and international environmental law ("IEL") reaching maturity since the emergence of the legal concept of environment in the 1960s.

International reporting on environmental effects of armed conflicts has grown.[3] Since 1994, the United Nations Environment Program ("UNEP") Post-Conflicts and Disasters Management branch has operated in about 50 countries emerging from armed conflict or natural disaster to respond to the need for high-level environmental expertise.[4] It supports States in reducing risks and preparing for natural disasters, provides assessments of post-conflicts[5] or of disasters' environmental impacts on human health, livelihoods and security and helps in establishing environmental recovery programmes.[6]

Interest in the issue of environmental protection during armed conflicts has surged in reaction to these, leading to development of a range of legal tools. In June 1972, an Emergency Conference against Environmental Warfare in Indochina, held in Stockholm, discussed a proposal for a Convention on Ecocide and the adoption of a Draft Protocol on Environmental Warfare.[7] The same month, the UN Conference on the Human Environment ("UNCHE") Declaration stipulated: "man and his environment must be spared from the effects of nuclear weapons and all other means of mass destruction" and States must strive to agree on the elimination and destruction of nuclear weapons.[8] The Vietnam War was the impetus for the adoption, on 10 December 1976, of a Convention.on the Prohibition of Military or any other Hostile Use of Environmental Modification Techniques, ("ENMOD"). It was negotiated to address international concern for large scale destruction of vegetation through chemical and physical means, such as those used by the US in Vietnam and its attempt to modify climate and induce rain through "cloud-seeding" to flood and muddy the supply routes for the North Vietnamese forces.[9] Two Protocols Additional to the 1949 Geneva Conventions Relating to the Protection of Victims of International Armed Conflicts ("AP/I") and Non-International Armed Conflicts ("AP/II")

3 Conflict and Environment Observatory, *Report: Investigating the Environmental Dimensions of the 2020 Nagorno-Karabakh Conflict* (2021); UNEP, *The Environmental Impact of the Conflict in Ukraine, A Preliminary Review* (2022)

4 UNEP, 'World Environment Situation Room, Disasters and Conflicts'

5 UNEP, *Afghanistan, Post-Conflict Environmental Assessment* (2003); UNEP, *UNEP in Iraq, Post-Conflict Assessment, Clean-up and Reconstruction* (2007); UNEP, *Desk Study on the Environment in Liberia* (2004); UNEP, *Post-Conflict Environmental Assessment – FYR of Macedonia* (2000)

6 UNEP, 'World Environment Situation Room, Disasters and Conflicts'

7 Michael Schmitt, 'Green War: An Assessment of the Environmental Law of International Armed Conflict' 22 Yale J Int'l L (1997) 1, 11–12
Richard Falk, 'Environmental Warfare and Ecocide-Facts, Appraisal, and Proposals' Bull Peace Proposals 4 (1973) 80

8 UNCHE, Stockholm, 5–16 June 1972, *Report (A/CONF.48/14/Rev.1)* Declaration 3, Principle 26

9 Erik Koppe, *The Use of Nuclear Weapons and the Protection of the Environment during International Armed Conflict* (Hart Publishing Ltd. 2008) 124

of 1977 were negotiated at a diplomatic conference concomitant to the ending on 30 April 1975 of the Vietnam war.[10] Clauses included in AP/I prohibit the use of warfare methods that may damage the environment above some threshold and the destruction of objects indispensable to the survival of the population, such as livestock, water installations or agricultural crops, as issues of extensive use of herbicides – essentially Agent Orange – and land ploughing during the Vietnam War weighed on the discussions.[11] The use of cluster bombs during the 2006 Israeli war in Lebanon prompted calls for negotiation of a convention banning the use of cluster bombs, which was duly signed on December 2008.[12] An environmental war crime was introduced in the legal sanctions' apparatus under the 1998 Statute of the International Criminal Court ("ICC Statute").[13] No investigations or prosecutions for such crime happened. A stated policy to prosecute war crimes related to environmental destruction, illegal exploitation of natural resources or dispossession of land[14] was followed by another initiative to advance accountability for such crime under the ICC Statute.[15] The International Law Commission ("ILC") elaborated draft principles that sought to enhance environmental protection prior to, during and after armed conflicts ("ILC Environment Protection Principles").[16]

The bombing and burning of oil fields by Iraq during the first Gulf War[17] renewed scrutiny of armed conflicts' environmental impacts, triggering academic discussions and involvement of international organizations. The World Charter for Nature stated that "nature shall be secured against degradation caused by warfare or other hostile activities," a general principle that "shall be reflected in the law and practice of each state, as well as at the international level," including through the avoidance of "military activities damaging to nature."[18] International conferences were organized in 1991 in London, Ottawa and Munich to address the subject, including a proposal for a new environmental protection convention.[19] The Second Review of the Conference

10 The Diplomatic Conference on the Reaffirmation and Development of International Humanitarian Law Applicable in Armed Conflicts met for four sessions between 1974 and 1977; ICRC, *Commentary on the Additional Protocols of 8 June 1977 to the Geneva Conventions of 12 August 1949* (Yves Sandoz, Christophe Swinarski and Bruno Zimmermann eds, Martinus Nijhoff Publishers 1987) Introduction

11 Schmitt 9–11

12 Convention on Cluster Munitions (CCM), Dublin, 30 may 2008, Oslo 3–4 December 2008, entry into force 1 August 2010

13 Rome Statute of the ICC art.8(2)(b)(iv)

14 ICC Office of the Prosecutor, *Policy Paper on Case Selection and Prioritisation* (2016) par.41

15 ICC, *The Office of the Prosecutor Launches Public Consultation on a New Policy Initiative to Advance Accountability for Environmental Crimes under the Rome Statute* (16 February 2024)

16 ILC, *Draft Principles on Protection of the Environment in Relation to Armed Conflicts, with Commentaries, A/77/10* (ILC YB 2022, vol II (2), 2022)

17 The war took place between 2 August 1990 when Iraq invaded Kuwait and 28 February 1991. An international coalition of forces authorized by the UNSC fought the Iraqi forces between 17 January and 28 February 1991.

18 UNGA, *World Charter for Nature, A/Res/37/7* (1982) principles 5, 14, 20

19 (i) The London Round Table Conference on "a 'fifth Geneva' Convention on the protection of the environment in time of armed conflict" organized by Greenpeace, the London School of Economics

on ENMOD held in Geneva in 1992 addressed the question of environmental protection during conflicts. At the 1992 UN Conference on Environment and Development ("UNCED"), the Rio Declaration Principle 24 provided that "[w]arfare is inherently destructive of sustainable development. States shall therefore respect international law providing protection for the environment in times of armed conflict and co-operate in its further development, as necessary."[20] UNCED Action Plan (Agenda 21) called for the United Nations General Assembly ("UNGA") to consider measures in accordance with international law to address, in times of armed conflict, large-scale destruction of the environment that cannot be justified under international law.[21] The International Committee of the Red Cross ("ICRC") submitted reports to the UN Secretary-General[22] and issued guidelines on environmental protection during armed conflicts, revised in 2020,[23] that were not formally adopted by the UNGA, though it urged the international community to incorporate them in its domestic laws.[24]

Doctrinal debates on adequacy and effectiveness of rules related to environmental protection during armed conflict, under the Law of Armed Conflict ("LOAC"), revealed a chasm between two major trends.[25] The first opinion considered existing legal rules adequate, though in need of further dissemination for information and improved compliance or requiring improved enforcement.[26] The second line of thought lamented their ineffectiveness and inadequacy and called for their modification to achieve major improvement.[27] Despite critical appraisals of these rules

---

and the British Centre for Defence Studies, June 1991 (Glen Plant, environmental protection and the law of war, Belhaven Press, 1992); (ii) Ottawa Conference on the use of the environment as a tool of conventional warfare, organized by the Canadian Ministry of External Affairs, July 1991 and (iii) Munich Conference co-sponsored by the International Council of Environmental Law (IECL) and the Commission on Environmental Law of the International Union for the Conservation of Nature and Natural Resources and financed in part by the Dutch government, December 1991 (IECL, Law concerning the protection of environment in times of armed conflict, final report of consultation of December 13–15, 1991)

20 UNCED, Rio de Janeiro, 3–14 June 1992, *Report, A/CONF.151/26/Rev.1 (Vol. I)* Rio Declaration 3

21 Ibid, Agenda 21, par.39.6

22 UNGA, *Protection of the Environment in Times of Armed Conflict: Report of the Secretary General, A/47/328* (1992); UNGA, *Report of the Secretary General on the Protection of the Environment in Times of Armed Conflict, A/48/269* (1993)

23 ICRC, *Guidelines for Military Manuals and Instructions on the Protection of the Environment in Times of Armed Conflict (UN Doc. A/49/323, Annex)* (1994); ICRC, *Guidelines on the Protection of the Natural Environment in Armed Conflict* (2020)

24 UNGA, *UN Decade of International Law, A/Res/49/50* (1995) par.11

25 It is impossible to list all relevant articles. A few examples: Christopher Joyner and James Kirhope, "The Persian Gulf War Oil Spill: Reassessing the Law of Environmental Protection and the Law of Armed Conflict" 24 Case West Reserve J Int'l L 1, Winter (1992) 29; Wil D. Verwey, "Protection of the Environment in Times of Armed Conflict: In Search of a New Legal Perspective" 8 Leiden J Int'l L 1 (1995) 7 Luan Low and David Hodgkinson, "Compensation for Wartime Environmental Damage: Challenges to International Law after the Gulf War" 35 Va J Int'l Law (1994–1995) 405

26 ICRC Report, Doc. A/47/328 (1992)

27 Schmitt 4; Verwey 30; Hans Wassgren, 'The UN Compensation Commission: Lessons of Legitimacy, State Responsibility and War Reparations' Leiden J Int'l L (1998) 473

and submission of proposals to remedy their perceived deficiencies, the international normative documents remained untouched.

Conflict-related environmental damage came under judicial examination. For the first time, following the first Gulf war, liability for environmental damage caused during armed conflict was attributed to a belligerent State and financial compensation awarded for such damage. The UN Security Council ("UNSC") found that "Iraq . . . is liable under international law for any direct loss, damage, including environmental damage and the depletion of natural resources, or injury to foreign Governments, nationals and corporations, as a result of Iraq's unlawful invasion and occupation of Kuwait."[28]

In 2000, the Office of the Prosecutor of the International Criminal Tribunal for the former Yugoslavia ("ICTY") decided to assess allegations that NATO may have committed war crimes during its air campaign against Yugoslavia, including environmental damage caused by the bombing of the Pancevo chemical factory during the Kosovo conflict.[29] In 2007, Darfur victims, internally displaced persons and international organizations such as Human Rights Watch urged the ICC to charge Sudanese officials with environmental war crimes, for burning fields, contaminating water supplies and raiding cattle and livestock committed by its allied militias.[30] The International Commission of Inquiry on Darfur found as an "irrefutable fact" that large scale destruction and burning of villages occurred, together with destruction of water pumps, wells and implements for food processing and destruction and burning of trees and crops.[31] There was no prosecution following allegations of environmental war damage in both Kosovo and Darfur cases; however, these instances reflect the beginning of a more assertive environmental litigation voice.

The questions previously debated remain relevant today. Though the UNSC decision on Iraq's liability for environmental damage could be seen as a leap forward, it resulted from the convergence of the political will of its members. It left the question of violation of the rules on conduct of armed conflict (*jus in bello*) unanswered, as it based Iraq's liability on its unlawful invasion and occupation of Kuwait, violating rules on the legality of war (*jus ad bellum*).[32] The issue, then, is whether it is possible, under the current international legal regime, to attribute liability to a belligerent State for environmental damage arising from breach of its obligations during an international armed conflict under the LOAC (*jus in bello*),

28 UNSC, *Resolution 687, 3 April 1991, S/RES/687* (1991)

29 Prosecutor, *Report on the Nato Bombing Campaign, 13 June 2000, ICTY Doc. PR/P.I.S./510-e* (2000). The Committee Established to Review the NATO Bombing Campaign against the Federal Republic of Yugoslavia, *Final Report to the Prosecutor* (2000) par.3

30 Katy Glassborow, 'Sudan, Court Urged to Consider Environmental Crimes, 4 September 2007' Institute for War and Peace Reporting

31 International Commission of Inquiry on Darfur, *Report to the UN Secretary-General, 25 January 2005, S/2005/60* par.225

32 Low and Hodgkinson 414. Eliana Cusato, 'Overcoming the "Logic of Exception": A Critique of the UN Security Council's Response to Environmental Damage from the 1990–91 Gulf War' 9 Asian J Int'l L (2019) 75 82, 86

applicable IEL or international human rights law ("IHRL"). That is the question this book proposes to examine.

II. Legal framework

The subject is under the umbrella of public international law, at the crossroad of the LOAC and IEL, each briefly presented. Are equally applicable IHRL constituted by multilateral treaties incorporating human rights standards and international water law ("IWL") related to shared water resources. IHRL is addressed in Chapter 3 as its application is most discussed in occupations and IWL in Chapter 4 on IEL.

1. The Law of Armed Conflict

The Lieber Code promulgated during the American civil war was the first binding code of conduct for armed forces in modern times,[33] based on what was then deemed accepted practice, many countries following suit.[34] Rules included in these national codes or written by international law authorities constitute customary international LOAC and are deemed international law binding rules, unless they have been expressly overruled by treaty or rejected by a military power.[35] An 1868 St Petersburg Declaration prohibiting use of projectiles, explosive or charged with inflammable substances, deemed to cause unnecessary suffering and "contrary to the laws of humanity,"[36] was the basis of the prohibition to use weapons of a nature to cause unnecessary suffering or superfluous injury in the Hague Regulations, article 23(e).[37] In 1874 a Conference in Brussels of 15 European States issued a Declaration calling for revision of the general usages of war.[38] In 1880, the Institute of International Law adopted a Manual of the Laws of War on Land.[39] They were the first codifications of the laws of war and the basis of the Hague Conventions.[40]

The Hague Peace Conferences convened in 1899 and 1907, to revise the 1874 Declaration, adopted Convention (IV) respecting the Laws and Customs of War on Land and its annex: Regulations concerning the Laws and Customs of War on

33 *Instructions for the Government of Armies of the United States in the Field (Lieber Code)* (1863).

34 Burrus M. Carnahan, 'Lincoln, Lieber and the Laws of War: The Origins and Limits of the Principle of Military Necessity' 92 AJIL April (1998) 213

35 Leslie C. Green, *The Contemporary Law of Armed Conflict* (3rd edn, MUP 2008) 37

36 Declaration Renouncing the Use in Time of War of Explosive Projectiles Under 400 Grammes Weight, St Petersburg, 1868, Preamble

37 Green 41. ICRC, *Commentary on the Declaration Renouncing the Use, in Time of War, of Explosive Projectiles under 400 Grammes Weight, Saint Petersburg, 1868*

38 *Projet d'une Déclaration Internationale Concernant les Lois et Coutumes de la Guerre* (*Bruxelles* 1874).

39 IDI, *The Laws of War on Land, Oxford* (9 September 1880). The International Law Institute was founded in 1873 in Belgium by 11 renowned international lawyers as an institution independent of any governmental influence to contribute to the development of international law and to act for its implementation.

40 ICRC, *Commentary on Project of an International Declaration concerning the Laws and Customs of War, Brussels, 27 August 1874*

Land, (1907) ("Hague Regulations" or "Regulations"), replacing and amending the 1899 Convention.[41] This Convention and Regulations constitute customary international law as they were "recognised by all civilised nations and regarded as "being declaratory of the laws and customs of war" at the Nuremberg trials, re-affirmed by the International Court of Justice ("ICJ").[42] Together with two declarations banning the use of certain weapons adopted at the Hague in 1899, the 1907 Hague Convention constitutes what is known as the Hague Law.[43] Ten other Conventions adopted in 1907 at the Hague are equally considered to represent, or have developed into, customary law.[44]

The Geneva Law is constituted by four conventions adopted in Geneva on 12 August 1949 replacing two 1929 conventions: Convention (I) for the Amelioration of the Condition of the Wounded and Sick in Armed Forces in the Field; Convention (II) for the Amelioration of the Condition of Wounded, Sick and Shipwrecked Members of Armed Forces at Sea; Convention (III) relative to the treatment of prisoners at war and Convention (IV) relative to the treatment of civilian persons in time of war ("GC I", "GC II", "GC III" and "GC IV" respectively). They are supplemented by two 1977 Additional Protocols and one on the Adoption of an Additional Distinctive Emblem (2005). The four GC are universally adhered to, while AP/I on IAC benefits from near universal adhesion with 174 States that are party out of 196.[45]

Traditionally, Hague Law, focusing on means and methods used during war, was distinguished from Geneva Law dealing with humanitarian concern, protection of wounded armed forces, prisoners and civilian populations caught in armed conflicts. The difference is less pronounced today with the two strands forming one complex legal system, since the adoption of the Additional Protocols.[46] International humanitarian law ("IHL") is a term used to cover both Hague and Geneva law and is today synonymous with the LOAC,[47] which is used in this book. Occupation law is the part of IHL that applies specifically to occupation, a specific type of armed conflict.

Additionally, the LOAC includes ENMOD and conventions prohibiting the use or development, production and stockpiling of certain non-conventional weapons such as gases, biological or chemical weapons, a convention regulating conventional weapons that can cause excessive injury or indiscriminate effects and

41 Convention (II) with Respect to the Laws and Customs of War on Land and its annex: Regulations concerning the Laws and Customs of War on Land, The Hague, 29 July 1899

42 *Trial of the Major War Criminals, 14 November 1945–1 October 1946,* Vol I, IMT Nuremberg 254; *Legality of the Threat or Use of Nuclear Weapons, Advisory Opinion* ICJ Rep 1996, 226 par.81, 82

43 See ICRC website for database of LOAC treaties. The two 1899 Declarations are: Declaration (IV.2) concerning asphyxiating gases, 29 July 1899 and Declaration (IV.3) concerning expanding bullets, 29 July 1899.

44 Green 39

45 ICRC, 'States Party to the Following International Humanitarian Law and Other Related Treaties, as of 3rd September 2024'

46 Emily Crawford, 'Armed Conflict, International' MPEPIL, online edition par.29. *Nuclear Weapons* par.75

47 Yoram Dinstein, *The Conduct of Hostilities under the Law of International Armed Conflict* (CUP 2022) par.68, 78

conventions on anti-personnel mines and cluster bombs.[48] There is also a convention on protection of cultural property during armed conflict.[49]

2. *International environmental law*

IEL is the corpus of law related to environmental issues,[50] ranging widely from pollution of marine life, freshwater, soil and air; ozone layer depletion; desertification; deforestation; nuclear energy; oil regime; conservation and protection of nature, endangered species and marine resources and toxic and hazardous waste. It "comprises those substantive, procedural and institutional rules of law that have as their primary objective the protection of the environment."[51]

IEL has developed through three major international environmental conferences. The 1972 UNCHE aimed to answer "the need for a common outlook and common principles to inspire and guide the peoples of the world in the preservation and enhancement of the human environment."[52] One hundred and thirteen States participated to the conference, apart from the USSR and States from the Eastern or socialist bloc, because East Germany was not invited to the conference, though the USSR later would participate in the new UN environment programme ("UNEP") organization. The UNCHE recommended the establishment of the UNEP around four main constituents: a Declaration of 26 principles on the human environment ("Stockholm Declaration"), an Action Plan for environmental policy consisting of 106 recommendations, an Environment Fund to be financed from States' voluntary contributions and a new UNEP body.[53]

In 1992, UNCED ("the Earth Summit") took place in Rio, attended by 176 States, about 50 international organizations and two thousand non-governmental organizations ("NGOs"). With the emergence of sustainable development concern, the Conference adopted Agenda 21, a comprehensive plan of action to address environment and development goals in the twenty-first century and a declaration based on the principles of the 1972 Stockholm Declaration ("Rio Declaration").[54] While the Rio Declaration transposed and amended some of these principles, it constituted a progressive development of international "soft" law on environment and development. The Stockholm and Rio Declarations are considered to have provided a basis for the development of national and international environmental law and policy in the years ensuing.

48 See Chapter 2, the Weapons Conventions

49 The Hague Convention for the Protection of Cultural Property in the Event of Armed Conflict, 14 May 1954 and its First Protocol, 14 May 1954, and Second Protocol 26 March 1999

50 Alan Boyle and Catherine Redgwell, *Birnie, Boyle and Redgwell's International Law and the Environment* (4th edn, OUP 2021) 3

51 Philippe Sands, Jacqueline Peel, Adriana Fabra, and Ruth MacKenzie, *Principles of International Environmental Law* (4th edn, CUP 2018) 13

52 UNCHE Declaration, 3, Preamble

53 Ibid, Action Plan 6, Resolution on Institutional and Financial Arrangements 30

54 UNCED Rio Declaration 3, Agenda 21 9

A Commission on Sustainable Development was established, in 1992, by the UNGA as a functional commission of the United Nations Economic and Social Council ("ECOSOC") to ensure the follow up on UNCED.[55] In 2002, a World Summit on Sustainable Development took place in Johannesburg, South Africa, to assess the progress made since UNCED, reaffirm the commitment to implementation of Agenda 21 and identify areas for improvement. The resulting Johannesburg Declaration focused on issues of development and poverty eradication that were of concern to developing countries, barely mentioning the environment. Environmentalists were disappointed with NGOs, denouncing the summit as a failure.[56]

In 2012, the UN Conference on Sustainable Development (UNCSD or Rio+20), convened to examine the development of global environmental governance, recognized "the need to strengthen international environmental governance within the context of the institutional framework for sustainable development, in order to promote a balanced integration of the economic, social and environmental dimensions of sustainable development."[57] It committed to "strengthening the role of the . . . UNEP as the leading global environmental authority that sets the global environmental agenda, promotes the coherent implementation of the environmental dimension of sustainable development within the United Nations."[58] The conference also decided to establish the UN High-level Political Forum on Sustainable Development and to launch a process to develop a set of Sustainable Development Goals (SDGs) after 2015, building upon the eight Millennial Development Goals agreed on, in 2000, to reduce extreme poverty by 2015.[59] It led to the adoption of the 2030 Agenda for Sustainable Development.[60] At the midpoint through the 2030 Agenda, progress is very slow – 12 percent of SDG on track – or has regressed below the 2015 baseline.[61]

The development of IEL based on UN Conferences explains the reliance of such a branch of law on principles and "soft" law documents that are policy guidelines at most, though a few represent "milestones in IEL."[62] Some principles have attained a customary international law status or have been included in treaties and morphed

55 UNGA, *Institutional Arrangements to Follow Up UNCED, A/RES/47/191* (1992)

56 Dinah Shelton, 'Stockholm Declaration (1972) and Rio Declaration (1992)' in *MPEPIL*; Elli Louka, *International Environmental Law, Fairness, Effectiveness, and World Order* (CUP 2006) 35–36

57 UNCSD, Rio de Janeiro 20–22 June 2012, *Report, A/CONF.216/16* (2012) Annex the Future We Want, par.87

58 Ibid, par.88

59 Ibid, par.248–249

60 UNGA, *Transforming Our World: The 2030 Agenda for Sustainable Development (A/RES/70/1)* (2015)

61 UNGA, *Political Declaration of the High-Level Political Forum on Sustainable Development Convened under the Auspices of the General Assembly, 29 September 2023, A/RES/78/1* (2023) par.8; The previous draft of June 2023 mentions 12 percent, par.6

62 Alexandre Kiss and Dinah Shelton, *International Environmental Law* (3rd ed. edn, Transnational Publishers 2004) 54–58; Alice Louise Bunker, 'Protection of the Environment during Armed Conflict: One Gulf, Two Wars' 13 RECIEL 2 (2004) 201, 204

into opposable legal obligations.[63] Furthermore, IEL has seen an explosion of treaties, generally in the form of framework agreements establishing an institutional regime, stating general obligations and procedures for adoption of subsequent protocols containing more detailed obligations.[64]

III. Notions affecting applicability of the law

1. Determination of armed conflict under the LOAC and its effect

The applicability of the LOAC rules depends first on the existence of an armed conflict – distinct from a low-level violence situation – and second on whether it qualifies as international ("IAC") or non-international armed conflict ("NIAC").[65] It is therefore important to examine the different types of conflict.

1.1 Evolution from war to armed conflict

Before World War I, the several-hundred-years-old concept of war in international law was used to differentiate between the effects of war proper and other measures short of war, such as reprisals, armed interventions and blockades[66] and to trigger applicability of laws of war to the conduct of hostilities.[67] The 1919 Covenant of the League of Nations outlawed resort to war. Concepts of war varied from abstract legal concepts to those concerned with sociological and factual perspectives, considering the intention of the parties. A conflict could not be qualified as war under international law if belligerents did not recognize that they were at war, for example the Italy and Ethiopia war (1935–1936).[68] The 1949 GC introduced the notion of armed conflict to surmount some of these difficulties. The UN Charter avoids reference to war, mentioning an obligation of Member States to refrain from the threat or use of force in their international relations,[69] except for self-defence or under UNSC authorization.[70]

63 See Chapter 4

64 Sands 106

65 ILA Use of Force Committee, 'Final Report on the Meaning of Armed Conflict in International Law' 8; *Prosecutor v. Dusko Tadic, IT-94-1-T, Decision on the Defence Motion for Interlocutory Appeal on Jurisdiction, 2 October 1995* ICTY Appeals Chamber par.96–127

66 Karl Josef Partsch, 'Armed Conflict' in Rudolf Bernhardt (ed), *Encyclopedia of Public International Law* (Elsevier North-Holland 1990) 250 Meng Werner, 'War' in Rudolf Bernhardt (ed), *Encyclopedia of Public International Law* (Elsevier North-Holland 1982) 1336

67 Christopher Greenwood, 'The Concept of War in Modern International Law' 36 ICLQ (1987) 283, 284

68 Werner 1337

69 UN Charter art.2(4)

70 Ibid, art.51

1.2 International armed conflict

Under their common article 2, the GC apply to all cases of (i) declared war or any other armed conflict which may arise between parties to the Conventions – even if the state of war is not recognized by one of them – or (ii) partial or total occupation of the territory of a party to the Convention, even if there is no armed resistance to the occupation. The subjective element of intent of the parties, prevalent until after World War II, has been replaced by objective factual criteria.[71] Accordingly, an IAC is a conflict between States, since only States can be parties to the GC. The LOAC rules reflect the historical development of international law since the Westphalia treaty and its focus on States as subjects of international law.[72]

AP/1 article 1(4) added to the scope of IAC "armed conflicts in which people are fighting against colonial domination and alien occupation and against racist regimes in the exercise of their right of self-determination." The Conference for its adoption debated whether these armed conflicts are of "international character" or are international conflicts.[73] Countries harbouring such conflicts at the time, Portugal, Zimbabwe and South Africa,[74] adhered to AP/1 from 1992, while others such as Israel, India and the US have not yet joined, as they oppose the inclusion of non-State armed groups under the umbrella of the LOAC.[75]

1.3 Non-international armed conflict

GC common article 3 applies to "armed conflict not of an international character occurring in the territory of one of the High Contracting Parties." It covers internal armed conflict of relatively low-level violence – where at least one party is not a State – or conflict between different armed groups.[76] It provides a legal basis for relief work by the ICRC or other international organization and ensures that States are legally bound to grant fundamental protection to victims in all NIAC and respect rules on conduct of hostilities.[77]

AP/II applies to conflicts "which take place in the territory of a High Contracting Party [to the GC] between its armed forces and dissident armed forces or other

71 Partsch 250

72 Dapo Akande, 'Classification of Armed Conflicts: Relevant Legal Concepts' in Elizabeth Wilmhurst (ed), *International Law and the Classification of Conflicts* (OUP 2012) 32; Green 66

73 ICRC, *Commentary on the Protocol Additional to the Geneva Conventions of 12 August 1949, and relating to the Protection of Victims of International Armed Conflicts (Protocol I), 8 June 1977* (Yves Sandoz, Christophe Swinarski and Bruno Zimmermann eds, Martinus Nijhoff 1987) art.1(4) par.66

74 David E. Graham, 'Defining Non-International Armed Conflict: A Historically Difficult Task' 88 Int L Stud Ser US Naval War Col (2012) 43, 46

75 Andreas Paulus and Mindia Vashakmadze, 'Asymmetrical War and the Notion of Armed Conflict – a Tentative Conceptualization' 91 IRRC 873 (2009) 95, 103

76 ICRC, *Commentary on the Third Geneva Convention* (2020) art.3, par.427–428

77 Ibid, par.422, 816

organized armed groups which, under responsible command, exercise such control over a part of its territory as to enable them to carry out sustained and concerted military operations and to implement this Protocol."[78]

The territorial State must be engaged in conflict with one or more armed groups on its territory.[79] AP/II focuses on NIAC of a higher threshold of violence (large-scale civil wars) than GC common article 3.[80] It excludes from its scope "situations of internal disturbances and tensions, such as riots, isolated and sporadic acts of violence and other acts of a similar nature."[81]

Determination of the existence of a NIAC, specifically the threshold at which the violence becomes armed conflict, based on GC common article 3 proved challenging, as there was no internationally agreed definition.[82] The ICTY elaborated that notion in its decision on *Tadic*, a Bosnian Serb charged with crimes against humanity, grave breaches of GC and violations of laws and customs of war.[83] Before the ICTY Appeals Chamber, the defence contested the existence of "a legally cognizable armed conflict – either internal or international – at the time and place that the alleged offences were committed," because the conflict in the region where the crimes were alleged to have taken place was limited to a political assumption of power by the Bosnian Serbs and did not involve armed combat.[84] The tribunal defined a NIAC "whenever there is . . . protracted armed violence between governmental authorities and organized armed groups or between such groups within a State."[85] The definition was used by the ICTY and other international courts, included in the ICC Statute article 8.2(f), reflected in State practice and is expressed similarly by the ICRC.[86] Two main elements are necessary: intensity of the armed conflict and organization of the parties.[87] They are established by different objective factors identified by jurisprudence, such as command structure, discipline to implement and ensure respect for IHL and control of a determined

78 AP/II, article 1 (1)

79 ICRC, *Commentary on Protocol II* (Yves Sandoz, Christophe Swinarski and Bruno Zimmermann eds, Martinus Nijhoff 1987), art.1 par.4339

80 Ibid, art.1, par.4457

81 AP/II, article 1 (2)

82 ILA Use of Force Committee 4. Mary Ellen O'Connell, 'Defining Armed Conflict' 13 JC& SL (2008) 393, 393; ICRC, *Commentary on GC III*, art.3, par.449

83 *Prosecutor v. Dusko Tadic, IT-94–1-A, Second Amended Indictment, 14 December 1995* ICTY Appeals Chamberpar.4–5

84 *Tadic Decision on Defence Motion* par.66

85 Ibid, par.70; *Prosecutor v. Dusko Tadic, IT-94–1-A, Opinion and Judgement, 7 May 1997*; ICTY Trial Chamber II par.562

86 Anthony Cullen, *The Concept of Non-international Armed Conflict in International Humanitarian Law* (CUP 2010) 117; ICRC, *How Is the Term "Armed Conflict" Defined in International Humanitarian Law? Opinion Paper, March 2008* 5; ICRC, *Commentary on GC III*, art.3, par.457–458; *Situation in the Central African Republic in the Case of the Prosecutor v. Jean-Pierre Bemba Gombo, ICC-01/05–01/08, 21 March 2016* ICC, Trial Chamber III par.128

87 *Prosecutor v. Dusko Tadic, IT-94–1-A, Opinion and Judgement, 7 May 1997, par.562*; *Prosecutor v. Akayesu, Judgment, 2 September 1998, ICTR-96–4-T par.619–627*; ILA Use of Force Committee 32. ICRC, Commentary on GC III art.3, par.455

territory.[88] There seems to be no practical difference between the two thresholds of conflict intensity under Common Article 3 and AP/II or a distinction as a matter of customary international law.[89]

1.4 Disputed classification

Classification of contemporary armed conflicts is complicated by the so-called "war on terror" waged by the US against al Qaeda since 9/11, outside the remit of this book,[90] by the proliferation of non-State armed groups – such as the Islamic State of Iraq and Syria and Wagner group in Ukraine – and by foreign States' interventions in NIAC supporting one of the parties to the conflict.

An armed conflict in which a foreign State acts in support of the government of the territorial State, remains a NIAC between a State and a non-State armed group.[91] There is no IAC if the territorial State gives its consent to the foreign State intervention,[92] though lack of consent may relate to *jus ad bellum* issues and not to conflict classification.[93] The armed conflict in Afghanistan from 7 October 2001 between the US-led coalition and the Taliban, who were the government of Afghanistan at the time, was international. After the adoption of UNSC Resolution 1386 (2001) or the creation of an Afghan Interim Authority in December 2001 and the installation of Karzai as President or, according to the ICRC, the establishment of a new Afghan government in June 2002, the Taliban became a non-State armed group; the conflict between the government of Afghanistan and the international coalition forces acting effectively on its behalf and with its consent, on one side, and the Taliban, on the other, was deemed NIAC.[94]

By contrast, if the foreign State supports a non-State armed group, then it is engaged in an IAC with the territorial State, in parallel to the original NIAC conflict between the latter and the non-State armed group.[95] The tribunal in Tadic judged

88 ICRC, *Commentary on GC III* par.462–469; *Prosecutor v. Boškoski and Tarčulovski, IT-04-82-T*, ICTY, Trial Chamber II par.199–203; *ICC Bemba Judgement* par.137–141

89 Elizabeth Wilmshurst, 'Conclusions' in Elizabeth Wilmshurst (ed), *International Law and the Classification of Conflicts* (OUP 2012) 482

90 See George W. Bush, Address to the Nation (11 September 2001); *Hamdan v. Rumsfeld, Secretary of Defense et al., 2006, No. 05–184, 548 U.S. 557*; Natasha Balendra, 'Defining Armed Conflict' 29 Cardozo L Rev (2007–2008) 2461; Noam Lubell, 'The War (?) against Al-Qaeda' in Elizabeth Wilmhurst (ed), *International Law and the Classification of Conflicts* (OUP 2012) 437; Matthew C. Waxman, 'The Structure of Terrorism Threats and the Laws of War' 20 Duke J Int'l Comp L (2010) 431, 456

91 ICRC, Commentary on GC III

92 Sylvain Vité, 'Typology of Armed Conflicts in International Humanitarian Law: Legal Concepts and Actual Situations' 91 IRRC 873, March (2009) 69, 89; Akande 55

93 Lubell 432, 433

94 Francoise J. Hampson, 'Afghanistan 2001–2010' in Elizabeth Wilmshurst (ed), *International Law and the Classification of Conflicts* (OUP) 251–252, 276; ICRC, Commentary on GC III par.434; Marko Milanovic, 'What Exactly Internationalizes an Internal Armed Conflict? May 7, 2010' EJIL: Talk!

95 ICRC, *Commentary on GC III*, par.436, 438–439

that the conflicts had mixed character, with internal and international aspects, of which the UNSC was well aware in its decision.[96] To avoid such potentially incoherent situations, it was suggested as a matter of policy to consider the conflict "internationalized,"[97] which is not widely accepted.

A different situation is that of an armed conflict taking place on the territory of a State, without its consent, between a foreign State and a non-State armed group. Qualification of such conflict is disputed.[98] It has been named "extraterritorial,"[99] "hybrid," or "transnational" conflict.[100] Though the applicability of the LOAC rests on the traditional opposition of international versus non-international conflict reflecting the paradigm of the GC Common Articles 2 and 3,[101] classification of such conflict "does not, *prima facie*, fit [this] traditional understanding."[102] A minority view arguing that it falls within a regulatory gap, requiring recognition of a new legal category,[103] would be problematic as relying on subjective choice of rules.[104] The majority finds the current classification sufficient to accommodate the challenges of contemporary conflicts.[105]

Since classification relies on the nature of the parties, an armed conflict between a State and a non-State armed group that is not within the overall or effective control of – or related to – another State cannot be an IAC and is a NIAC, even if it occurs extraterritorially,[106] as "the geographical element should not determine whether a conflict is qualified as international."[107] The issue of control is unsettled.[108] The ICJ had to determine in *Nicaragua* whether the relationship of the *contras* armed group with the US was one of dependence and control such as to consider them as an organ of the US or acting on its behalf.[109] It required complete dependence of the non-State armed group on the foreign State to attribute all of the armed group's activities to the foreign State and general control to attribute specific LOAC violations committed by the armed group to the foreign State.[110] The ICTY

96 *Tadic Decision on Defence Motion par.74, 77*
97 ICRC, Commentary on GC III par.437 and n.92 doctrine cited Milanovic
98 Akande 59
99 Lubell 30
100 Paulus and Vashakmadze 110
101 Geoffrey S. Corn, 'Hamdan, Lebanon, and the Regulation of Hostilities: The Need to Recognize a Hybrid Category of Armed Conflict' 40 Vand J Transnat Law (2007) 305, 300; Lubell 451
102 Lubell 451; Paulus and Vashakmadze 111
103 Corn 326
104 Dr Tristan Ferraro, 'The ICRC's Legal Position on the Notion of Armed Conflict Involving Foreign Intervention and on Determining the IHL Applicable to this Type of Conflict' 97 IRRC 900 (2015) 1227, 1229
105 Wilmshurst 484
106 Hampson 256; Wilmshurst 484; Lubell 451; Iain Scobbie, 'Lebanon 2006' in Elizabeth Wilmhurst (ed), *International Law and the Classification of Conflicts* (OUP 2012) 410
107 Paulus and Vashakmadze 112
108 ICRC, *Commentary on GC III*, par.440
109 *Military and Paramilitary Activities in and against Nicaragua (Nicaragua v. United States of America). Merits, Judgment.* ICJ Rep 1986, p. 14, par.109
110 Ibid, par.110–116

Appeals Chamber considered in *Tadic* an "overall control" test, which may be suitable to classify the conflict as international or non-international according to the ICJ but not to determine State responsibility for the acts of armed groups that are not its official organs under State responsibility law.[111]

In contrast, some scholars have relied on the notion of use of force against a State's territory to infer that an armed conflict against a non-State entity from another State is international. As such, "[a]ny use of armed force by one state *against* the territory of another"[112] or "the use of force by the intervening foreign state *on* the territory of the territorial state, without the consent of the latter, is a use of force *against* the territorial state"[113] and will trigger the applicability of the GC.[114] It does not matter whether or not the State attacked resists[115] or if the use of force is "directed against non-state groups" or if it "is not directed against the governmental structures of the territorial state, or the purpose of the use of force is not to coerce the territorial state in any particular way."[116] Fenrick recognizes that "at a minimum, AP/1 applies wherever regular armed forces engage the regular armed forces of a foreign state or enter the territory of a foreign state without permission."[117] Similarly, the legal effect of imposing aerial and maritime blockade on the territory of the State where the conflict takes place is to render the conflict international,[118] as blockade is a warfare means.[119]

Under general international law, the "exclusive attributes" or "classical" criteria of a State are "(a) a permanent population; (b) a defined territory; (c) a government; and (d) a capacity to enter into relations with the other States."[120] Attacks against a government, such as assassination of government members or

111 *Prosecutor v. Dusko Tadic, IT-94–1-A, Judgement, 15 July 1999* ICTY Appeals Chamber par.115–145; *Application of the Convention on the Prevention and Punishment of the Crime of Genocide (Bosnia and Herzegovina v. Serbia and Montenegro), Judgment* ICJ Rep 2007, 43 par.404

112 ICRC, How is the Term "Armed Conflict" Defined in International Humanitarian Law? Opinion Paper, March 2008 2 Hans-Peter Gasser, 'International Humanitarian Law: An Introduction' in H. Haug (ed), *Humanity for All: The International Red Cross and Red Crescent Movement* (Paul Haupt 1993) 510

113 Akande 59

114 ICRC, How is the Term "Armed Conflict" Defined in International Humanitarian Law? Opinion Paper, March 2008 2; Gasser 510

115 Gasser 510

116 Akande 59; Contra: Paulus and Vashakmadze 123–124 qualify the armed conflict between Israel and Hezbollah (2006) as international only after the attacks by Israel on Lebanon's government and public facilities.

117 William J. Fenrick, Lieutenant Colonel, 'The Rule of Proportionality and Protocol I in Conventional Warfare' 98 Mil L Rev (1982) 91, 98

118 Scobbie 402 For a discussion of the requirements of blockade under the San Remo Manual, see Matthew L. Tucker, 'Mitigating Collateral Damage to the Natural Environment' 57 Naval L Rev (2009) 161

119 L. Oppenheim, *International Law, Vol. II Disputes, War and Neutrality* (H. Lauterpacht ed, 7th edn, Longmans, Green and Co. 1952) 768, par.368

120 James Crawford, *State* (2011) par.11; Montevideo Convention on the Rights and Duties of States, 1933 art.1

cyber-attacks, may not be considered, on their own, armed conflicts under the LOAC. The fact that the government of a State whose territory and population are under military attacks chooses not to defend itself and participate actively in the armed conflict on its territory between a non-State armed group and a foreign State does not negate that acts of war are committed against the territorial State without its consent. I would submit that not only use of force against a State's territory amounts to an international armed conflict, based on the doctrine cited, but equally use of force against a State's population amounts to an attack on that State and renders the conflict international.

1.5 Effect of classification

A practical example of classification of an armed conflict shall be studied in Chapter 5. Applicable rules depend on classification. The Hague Regulations, GC and AP/I apply to IAC. Regarding NIAC, civil wars are governed by AP/II, while low-level violence situations fall under GC common article 3. Although few rules cover specifically NIAC, jurisprudence suggests an extension of the applicability of some customary international law rules governing IAC to NIAC.[121] The Court found in *Tadic* that IHL applies from the initiation of armed conflict – however classified – and extends beyond the cessation of hostilities until a general conclusion of peace is reached.[122] Equally, customary international law rules would apply to States or non-State entities that are not parties to the Conventions or Additional Protocols, whether a conflict is international or not.[123] Consequently, the issue of classification may become less central, at least regarding certain LOAC customary rules. However, it is still relevant as there are LOAC rules applicable to IAC that do not exist for NIAC.[124] For example, captured combatants in an IAC are considered war prisoners under GC III, while in a NIAC their treatment obeys domestic law, which might comply with IHRL or Additional AP/II.[125] IHRL's applicability was first examined in the context of a NIAC, recently extending to IAC.

Laws governing both types of conflicts apply in parallel to conflicts having dual IAC-NIAC aspects.[126] The ICJ judged that the conflict between the *contras*

121 *Tadic Decision on Defence Motion* par.70, 96–99, 126–127; Major Ian G. Corey, 'The Fine Line between Policy and Custom: Prosecutor v. Tadic and the Customary International Law of Internal Armed Conflict' 166 Mil L Rev (2000) 145, 152; Dinah PoKempner, 'The "New" Non-State Actors in International Humanitarian Law' 38 Geo Wash Int'l L Rev (2006) 551, 553–554; Scobbie 410; Paulus and Vashakmadze 112

122 *Tadic Decision on Defence Motion* par.70 (n.45)

123 Frederic L. Kirgis, 'Some Proportionality Issues Raised by Israel's Use of Armed Force in Lebanon' 10 ASIL Insights 20

124 ICRC, Commentary on GC III par.425

125 Iain Scobbie, 'Human Rights Protection during Armed Conflict: What, When and for Whom?' in Erika de Wet and Jann Kleffner (eds), *Convergence and Conflicts of Human Rights and International Humanitarian Law in Military Operations*, vol 1 (Pretoria University Law Press 2014) 8

126 Ferraro 1229–1230; Dinstein par.110–115 on this duality

and Nicaragua armed forces was "not of an international character" governed by the law relating to such conflict while the US actions in and against Nicaragua were an international conflict under IHL rules.[127] Under the LOAC, environmental protection during armed conflict is covered directly by two specific provisions of AP/I. Their status as customary law being uncertain, they may not apply to internal armed conflict. A State bound by customary obligation under IEL to prevent harm to the environment remains bound by such obligation, whether the conflict is international or not. As to its conventional obligations to protect the environment under IEL, this requires prior analysis of the effect of armed conflict on IEL treaties, examined in Chapter 4. A non-State entity cannot be bound by an IEL treaty it has not signed, though its members could be prosecuted under international criminal law for LOAC violations.

2. *Notion of environment*

The LOAC refers to "natural environment," without definition, to grant it protection from widespread, long-term and severe damage.[128] According to the ICRC, natural environment should be understood widely, as our understanding constantly evolves, to cover the biological environment in which a population is living.[129] It constitutes a system of relations between living organisms and inanimate environment, comprising natural resources and natural elements that may be products of human action, such as drinking water, agricultural areas, foodstuff and livestock.[130]

Under IEL, the concept of environment needs to be defined as it affects the notion of environmental damage and applicable liability rules.[131] Environment means

> "(a) the complex of physical, chemical and biotic factors (such as climate, soil, and living things) that act upon an organism or an ecological community and ultimately determine its form and survival; (b) the aggregate of social and cultural conditions that influence the life of an individual or community."[132]

An early European Community regulation combined these two, defining environment as "the combination of elements whose complex inter-relationships make up the settings, the surroundings and the conditions of life of the individual and of

127 *Military and Paramilitary Activities in and against Nicaragua (Nicaragua v. United States of America). Merits, Judgment.* par.219

128 Protocol Additional to the Geneva Conventions of 12 August 1949, relating to the Protection of Victims of International Armed Conflicts (Protocol I), 8 June 1977 art.35.3, 55

129 ICRCAP/I Commentary Commentary on Protocol I, art.55 par.2126, art.35.3 par.1441

130 ICRC, Guidelines par.9

131 Sands 14

132 Merriam-Webster Dictionary online, Environment

society as they are and as they are felt."[133] An often-cited environment definition in the Lugano Convention includes: "natural resources both abiotic and biotic, such as air, water, soil, fauna and flora and the interaction between the same factors; property which forms part of the cultural heritage; and the characteristic aspects of the landscape."[134] Referred to by some as an emerging universal reference,[135] the definition is considered progressive as the Lugano Convention is not yet in force. Generally, a definition of environment cannot be found under the existing IEL corpus, whether treaties and conventions or "soft law" instruments, such as declarations, codes of conduct, guidelines and others.[136] IEL conventions define broadly the environment[137] in definitions intended only for the different purposes of each treaty.[138]

"Natural" being defined as "found in nature and not involving anything made or done by people,"[139] natural environment under AP/I may arguably refer to characteristic aspects of the landscape which is part of nature but cannot, in a literal interpretation, include man-made cultural heritage property. The link between environment and cultural heritage is, however, recognized in some instances, such as sites constituting cultural heritage defined as "combined works of nature and man" under the World Heritage Convention,[140] the American Bison deemed ecologically important and culturally significant,[141] or effects on the environment including historical monuments and cultural heritage, in the transboundary watercourses convention.[142] The ILC used "environment" in its principles on environmental protection in relation to armed conflicts, in line with IEL terminology, instead of "natural environment," noting that it is without incidence on that notion under the LOAC.[143] It included areas of cultural importance into areas of environmental importance that States could designate unilaterally or by common

133 Council (EEC), *Regulation No 1872/84 of 28 June 1984 on Action by the Community Relating to the Environment*

134 Convention on Civil Liability for Damage resulting from Activities Dangerous to the Environment, Lugano, 21 June 1993 art.2.10, as out

135 Karine Mollard-Bannelier, *La Protection de l'Environnement en Temps de Conflit Armé* (Editions A. Pedone 2001) 22

136 Boyle and Redgwell 4–5; Sands 15

137 Sands 14

138 Boyle and Redgwell 6

139 Cambridge Dictionary, natural meaning. ICRCAP/I Commentary commentary on Protocol I, art.35 par.1450–1452

140 UNESCO Convention for the Protection of the World Cultural and Natural Heritage, 23 November 1972, art.1

141 Cymie R. Payne, 'Chapter 2, Defining the Environment, Environmental Integrity' in Carsten Stahn, Jens Iverson, and Jennifer S. Easterday (eds), *Environmental Protection and Transitions from Conflict to Peace, Clarifying Norms, Principles, and Practices* (OUP 2017) 65

142 UNECE Convention on the Protection of Transboundary Watercourses and International Lakes, 1992 art.1(2)

143 ILC Environment Protection Principles, Part Three, Principles applicable during armed conflict, Commentary par.(5), p. 136

agreement as protected zones in case of armed conflict.[144] The principle, however, does not apply to "cultural objects *per se*," which would imply viewing the environment as including cultural heritage property, but "cultural" indicates a close link to the environment, such as ancestral lands of indigenous people.[145] Therefore, though a cultural aspect attaches to some environmental areas, this does not warrant, according to the ILC, an extension of the definition of natural environment to include cultural heritage property. Future research could elaborate on what is considered "important" culturally as the notion seems subjective and could analyse whether protection of cultural heritage under existing international conventions[146] would be enhanced if considered part of the environment under the LOAC.

An argument could be made, however, that perennial cultural monuments, such as Rome's Colosseum (AD 80), Egypt's pyramids (2700–1500 BC) and Afghanistan's Bamiyan Buddhas (sixth century), destroyed by the Taliban in 2001, are part of the "characteristic aspects of the landscape" of these places, in view of their immemorial presence and since landscape means "all the visible features of an area of land, often considered in terms of their aesthetic appeal."[147] They are "objects . . . by which one is surrounded"[148] and consequently are elements forming part of the environment. The difficulty is where to trace the line between those perennial cultural monuments and others that should not be considered characteristically part of the landscape.

Considering cultural heritage part of the environment is supported by the United Nations Compensation Commission ("UNCC") adjudicated claims and recent doctrine. Regarding claims of "environmental damage and natural resources depletion" caused by Iraq invasion and occupation, the Working Group of Experts concluded that environment includes natural resources (air, water, soil, fauna and flora) and the ecosystem formed by their interaction and might include cultural heritage and landscape features.[149] The UNCC Panel assessing environmental damage claims considered that "environmental damage" included both environmental damage that encompasses human health and cultural heritage issues and natural resources' depletion,[150] although this may have been for

144 Ibid, Principles 4, 18

145 Ibid, Principles 4, Commentary par.(9)

146 Hague Convention for Cultural Property Protection; UNESCO Convention for the Protection of the World Cultural and Natural Heritage, 23 November 1972

147 Oxford Dictionary, landscape meaning

148 Merriam-Webster Dictionary online, Environment

149 'Conclusions by the Working Group of Experts on Liability and Compensation for Environmental Damage Arising from Military Activities' in Alexandre Timoshenko (ed), *Liability and Compensation for Environmental Damage, Compilation of Documents* (UNEP 1998) par.31 cited in Payne 41

150 Julia Klee, 'Chapter 2: The Process' in Cymie R. Payne and Peter H. Sand (eds), *Gulf War Reparations and the UN Compensation Commission, Environmental Liability* (OUP 2011) (Gulf War and the UNCC), 29 n.1, 37 n.28; UNCC, *Reports and recommendations made by the Panel of Commissioners concerning the fifth instalment of "F4" claims, S/AC.26/2005/10* (2005) par.4

"procedural convenience."[151] Payne proposes to define the environment through a broad notion of environmental integrity, including services affecting it (waste, disease, water quality), cultural services that it provides and other parameters, to address the confusion around which environmental components are legally protected and how to characterize them, leading to failures to bring environmental claims in post-conflict settings.[152]

As the issue is unsettled, this book retains the working definition of "natural environment" common to IEL and LOAC as including natural resources, both abiotic and biotic, such as air, water, soil, fauna and flora and the interaction between them and the characteristics of the landscape, adopted by international law authorities.[153]

IV. Relevant public international law issues

1. Sources of international law

International law offers a framework of norms for the conduct of interstate relations.[154] Its traditional sources are treaties, customary international law, general principles of law and, as subsidiary sources, judicial decisions and teachings of the most highly qualified publicists.[155]

Although there is no formal hierarchy between the main international law sources, in practice, legal reasoning subjects them to an informal hierarchy whereby treaties will be consulted first, then custom, then general principles.[156]

1.1 Customary international law

Customary international law is general State practice accepted as law.[157] Two elements are necessary for its formation: settled general practice and "acceptance as law" (*opinio juris)*, which is the belief that this practice is rendered obligatory by a rule requiring it.[158] Practice must be substantially uniform, though no specific duration is determined.[159] Universal acceptance is not required, as some rules may be

151 Payne 55

152 Payne 62–63, 68–70

153 ILC, *Special Rapporteur Marie G. Jacobsson, Preliminary Report on the Protection of the Environment in Relation to Armed Conflicts, A/CN.4/674* (2014) 24; Institut de Droit International, *Resolution on Environment* (1997) art.1

154 James Crawford, *Brownlie's Principles of Public International Law* (9th edn, OUP 2019) 18

155 ICJ Statute art.38(1)

156 ILC, *Fragmentation of International Law: Difficulties Arising from the Diversification and Expansion of International Law, Report of the Study Group of the ILC, A/CN.4/L.682* (2006) par.85

157 The ICJ Statute, art.38.1(c)

158 Michael Wood, Special Rapporteur, *Third Report on Identification of Customary International Law, A/CN.4/682* (2015) par.13; ILC, *Draft Conclusions on Identification of Customary International Law (A/73/10, par.66)* (2018) Conclusions 2, 4, 9

159 Crawford, *Brownlie's Principles of Public International Law* 22

considered customary international law, without being universally accepted, though practice of States affected by a rule is important; in addition, regional or bilateral customs exist.[160] A State that objects persistently to a rule, during or subsequently to its formation, exempts itself from the application of the rule.[161]

Evidence of customs is found in material acts of State and various documents, such as diplomatic correspondence, policy statements, opinions of government legal advisers, official manuals, governments' comments on ILC drafts, legislation, international and national jurisprudence and resolutions by international bodies, though circumstances will determine the value of these sources.[162] UNSC Resolutions, Statements from the EC and Commonwealth Heads of Governments rejecting a declaration of establishment of the Turkish Republic of Northern Cyprus as legally invalid and recognizing only the Cypriot government as the government of the Republic of Cyprus were considered, together with international practice, as evidence of the international community position by the European Court of Human Rights.[163]

International organizations have come to play a significant role in international law. As a forum to formulate and debate rules, they participate in development and making of customary international law, based on specific legislative powers and their substantive authority representing the collective expression of the practice of Member States.[164] It is particularly true for the UN where States' practice demonstrated by their votes and views on UNGA Resolutions, when repeated and acquiesced by sufficient numbers, may translate over time as reflecting customary law[165] or potentially indicating its development.[166] UNGA Resolutions are not binding but exceptionally may have a normative value, depending on the content and conditions of their adoption and whether *opinio juris* exists in relation thereto;[167] for example, its resolution on permanent sovereignty over natural resources was a "landmark instrument in the development of international law."[168] The ILC is a body devoted to clarification and progressive development of international law. Its reports, based on extensive research and analysis, submitted for debate at the UNGA, are valuable indicators of the state of international law.

Custom is an important component of the LOAC. The 1907 Hague Convention IV and its Regulations, GC IV, the 1948 Genocide Convention and the 1945 Charter

160 Ibid, 25–28; Jan Klabbers, *International Law* (3rd edn, CUP 2021) 30; *North Sea Continental Shelf* ICJ Rep 1969, p. 3, par.73

161 Crawford, *Brownlie's Principles of Public International Law* 27–28; *Fisheries case (UK v. Norway), Judgement* ICJ Reports 1951, p. 116.

162 Klabbers 31–32; Crawford, *Brownlie's Principles of Public International Law* 21–22

163 *Loizidou v Turkey, Judgment (18 December 1996), (Application no. 15318/89)* ECtHR par.22, 23, 44

164 Klabbers 23, 24; Crawford, *Brownlie's Principles of Public International Law*; ILC, Draft Conclusions on Identification of Customary International Law (A/73/10, par.66) Conclusion 4(2)

165 Crawford, *Brownlie's Principles of Public International Law* 182

166 Jean Combacau and Serge Sur, *Droit International Public* (13th edn, LGDJ 2019) 131

167 Rosalyn Higgins, 'The UN at 70 Years: The Impact Upon International Law' 65 ICLQ (2016) 1 2–3

168 Sands 61

of the Nuremberg Tribunal[169] are customary international law.[170] In its study on customary IHL ("ICRC Study"), the ICRC attempts to determine which of its provisions is customary law and could be considered binding on all States.[171] That does not necessarily grant a customary cloak on these rules since a few States – such as the US – and scholars have objected to the methodology chosen regarding the formation of customary international law.[172] Criticisms centred on the reference to Kirgis' proposition that humanitarian considerations may trump the balance between State practice and *opinio juris*, the conclusion drawn from widespread or universal treaty ratification to formation of a customary norm and the practice and official acts relied upon to conclude on the formation of a custom.[173] Nonetheless, the ICRC Study involved considerable research into, and assessment of national legislation and practice of 150 States collected within the framework of international organizations, case law and ICRC sources, submitted to governmental and academic experts; it is then a reference in discussion about the LOAC customary law or at least regarding "implementation, clarification and possible development of the law."[174] International courts and tribunals tend to cite the study as a source of customary international law without independent analysis, based on its rigour and for pragmatic reasons, conceding it an authority likely to grow.[175] A few IEL principles have also become part of customary international law, examined in Chapter 4.

1.2 General principles of law

There is no clear definition of general principles of law.[176] It is a broad category, not specifically determined.[177] Characterized by their generality, they are abstract and universal – though universality is variable and was not accepted as a necessary

169 Convention on the Prevention and Punishment of the Crime of Genocide of 9 December 1948; Charter of the International Military Tribunal of 8 August 1945

170 *Trial of the Major War Criminals, 14 November 1945–1 October 1946,* 254; *Report of the Secretary-General pursuant to paragraph 2 of Security Council resolution 808 (1993) (S/25704)* par.35; *Nuclear Weapons* par.81

171 ICRC, *Customary International Humanitarian Law, Vol. I Rules, 3rd. 2009, Vol. II Practice, 2005* (Jean-Marie Henckaerts and Louise Doswald-Beck eds, CUP)

172 Michael Schmitt, '21st Century Conflict: Can the Law Survive?' 8 Melb J Int'l L (2007) 443, 459; John B. Bellinger III, Legal Adviser, U.S. Department of State and William J. Haynes, General Counsel, U.S. Department of Defense, *Letter of November 3, 2006 to Dr. Jakob Kellenberger, President of the International Committee of the Red Cross*

173 Iain Scobbie, 'The Approach to Customary International Law in the Study' in Elizabeth Wilmshurt and Susan Breau (eds), *Perspectives on the ICRC Study on Customary International Humanitarian Law* (1st edn, Chatham House and BIICL 2007) 26

174 Jean-Marie Henckaerts, 'The ICRC Study on Customary International Humanitarian Law: Characteristics, Conclusions and Practical Relevance' 6 Slov L Rev (2009) 225–276 229–230, 256

175 Marko Milanovic and Sandesh Sivakumaran, 'Assessing the Authority of the ICRC Customary IHL Study, How Does IHL Develop?' 104 ICRC 920–921 (2022) 1856, 1897

176 Kirsten Stefanik, 'The Environment and Armed Conflict, Employing General Principles to Protect the Environment' in Carsten Stahn, Jens Iverson, and Jennifer S. Easterday (eds), *Environmental Protection and Transitions from Conflict to Peace* (OUP 2017) 95

177 'General Principles of Law in International Commercial Arbitration' 101 Harv L Rev 8, June (1988), 1819

requirement by the ICJ – and represent essential notions that form part of, or all of, most legal systems,[178] such as the notion of good faith and the idea that people cannot be judged twice for the same act. They were included as a subsidiary source of law, to allow the ICJ to rely on municipal law principles, insofar as they are generally applicable to State relations, to fill a gap in international law, in the absence of treaty or customary international law.[179] Arbitral tribunals have shown considerable discretion in using them, while the ICJ has relied sparingly on them, including them in judicial reasoning without necessarily labelling them.[180] They are not a more authoritative source than contrary custom or treaties.[181] As to general principles of international law, such as *pacta sunt servanda*, they are derived from international law, whether customary international law or elements of judicial reasoning based on existing international law.[182] Both the LOAC and IEL contain general principles of law.

1.3 Treaties

A treaty is a written international agreement governed by international law, embodied in a single or more related instruments, whatever its designation.[183] "Law-making" treaties creating general universal norms that govern the conduct of the parties (such as the Hague and Geneva Conventions) are distinct from treaties related to a joint single enterprise, where fulfilment of the treaty's object discharges the parties' obligation. Treaties are binding on the parties only, though some create a law effect, due to the number of parties, States' acceptance of the rules and their declaratory character.[184]

Rules on treaty interpretation are embodied in the Vienna Convention on the Law of Treaties (VCLT) articles 31 to 33, which have codified principles of interpretation.[185] They represent customary international law and are applied as such by international judiciary bodies.[186] A treaty shall be interpreted in good faith and its terms given their ordinary meaning according to the context, object and purpose of the treaty, taking into account other elements, such as subsequent agreement of the

178 Combacau and Sur 140; Stefanik 95–96; *South West Africa, Second Phase, Judgment,* ICJ Reports 1966, p. 6

179 Crawford, *Brownlie's Principles of Public International Law* 32; Klabbers 37; Sands 125–126

180 Ibid, 33; Natalie Kaufman Hevener and Steven A. Mosher, 'General Principles of Law and the UN Covenant on Civil and Political Rights' 27 ICLQ 3, July (1978) 599; *Factory at Chorzow, Merits, 1928* PCIJ Ser A No 17, 29; *North Sea Continental Shelf* 26

181 Howard S. Schrader, 'Custom and General Principles as Sources of International Law in American Federal Courts' 82 Colum L Rev 4 (1982) 756

182 Crawford, *Brownlie's Principles of Public International Law* 34; Combacau and Sur 143

183 VCLT art.2(1)

184 Crawford, *Brownlie's Principles of Public International Law* 29

185 UN Conference on the Law of Treaties, *Official Records, First and Second Sessions Vienna, 26 March–24 May 1968 and 9 April–22 May 1969* 38

186 Ibid, 38, par.5; Anthony Aust, 'Vienna Convention on the Law of Treaties (1969)' *MPEPIL* (2006) par.14–16; *Arbitral Award of 31 July 1989 (Guinea-Bissau v. Senegal)* ICJ Rep 1991, 53, par.48; *ITLOS, Responsibilities and Obligations of States Sponsoring Persons and Entities with Respect to Activities in the Area, Advisory Opinion, 2011* ITLOS Reports 2011, 10 150

parties or practice related to the treaty.[187] If the meaning is not clear, recourse may be had to the preparatory work (*travaux préparatoires*) recorded in diplomatic conferences preceding the signature of international treaties and their circumstances,[188] to supplement or confirm the interpretation of the ordinary meaning of the treaty's terms.[189] As such, *travaux préparatoires* are analysed when necessary for our purposes.

When a treaty has been authenticated in two or more languages, each text is equally authoritative, unless the treaty provides otherwise.[190] If the texts reveal different meanings, they should be interpreted in accordance with the VCLT rules, failing which, the meaning that best reconciles the texts, having regard to the object and purpose of the treaty, shall be adopted.[191] The reconciliation of both authentic texts has been a feature of treaty interpretation by the courts, before the adoption of the VCLT.[192] For those LOAC conventions authenticated in French and English, both texts are analysed when necessary.

2. *Responsibility and liability*

The framework of State responsibility is established and some of its elements codified in the ILC States' Responsibility Articles[193] are deemed customary international law.[194] This ILC's work during about half a century (1955–2001) is "part of a process of customary law articulation."[195]

State responsibility is raised in case of an international wrongful act, whether action or omission attributable to a State under international law, constituting a breach of its international obligation in force at that moment.[196] Content of the obligation, any required standard of conduct (fault, culpability, negligence or want of due diligence) and notion of damage are determined by the rules related to that

187 VCLT, 23 May 1969 (in force 27 January 1980) art.31
188 Ibid, art.32
189 UN Conference on the Law of Treaties 42
190 VCLT, 23 May 1969 (in force 27 January 1980) art.33.1
191 Ibid, art.33.4
192 Jean Hardy, 'The Interpretation of Plurilingual Treaties by International Courts and Tribunals' 37 Br Y.B. Int'l Law 72, 1961, 150
193 ILC, *Articles on Responsibility of States for Internationally Wrongful Acts, with Commentary, A/56/10* (ILC YB 2001, vol II (2))
194 Jutta Brunnée, 'Sense and Sensibility: Reflections on International Liability Regimes as Tools for Environmental Protection' 53 ICLQ (2004) 351, 353; ILC, States' Responsibility Articles 31, par. (1); Peter Malanczuk, *First Report of the ILA Study Group on the Law of State Responsibility, Submitted by the Chair of the Study Group to the Special Rapporteur and the Chair of the UN ILC and the ILA Director of Studies* (2000) 30
195 James Crawford, 'The ILC's Articles on Responsibility of States for Internationally Wrongful Acts: A Retrospect' 96 AJIL, 890; Crawford was ILC's Special Rapporteur on State Responsibility between 1997 and 2001.
196 ILC, States' Responsibility Articles Commentary 34 art.2

obligation under customary or conventional international law ("primary" rules).[197] The primary substantive rules governing obligations of environmental protection in armed conflict, whether war or occupation, that will raise State responsibility in case of breach, are found under the LOAC, IEL or IHLR.[198] Liability, meaning the legal consequences of a breach of primary obligation, such as cessation of wrongful conduct and reparation for any resulting injury, are determined under the "secondary rules" of State responsibility law,[199] dealt in the ILC State Responsibility Articles.[200]

Separating general rules and secondary rules in the ILC State responsibility Articles appears problematic, as an abstract idea that dissociates responsibility from tangible obligation, especially compared to common law systems lacking usually a general theory of responsibility; these Articles are inspired, however, by civil law responsibility theory.[201] Equally, it may seem impossible to determine State responsibility for environmental damage arising out of armed conflict in view of the imprecision of the doctrine. However uncertainties "depend essentially on the method of study that has nearly always been adopted," the legal literature having dealt with the subject "in dogmatic terms, or, at least in very theoretical terms, placing the relative legal discourse at the general level of theory of law or theory of the state."[202] This book does not discuss State responsibility in the abstract but examines its application through analysis of the elements (standard of conduct and notion of damage, if any) characterizing State obligations under the rules of the LOAC, IEL and IHRL in order to ascertain whether their breach could give rise to accountability, encompassing State responsibility and liability.

V. Scope of the study

There have been attempts to hold accountable States manufacturing or selling arms, based on States' obligations to respect and ensure respect for the GC, State responsibility law, or States' obligations under the UN Arms Trade Treaty (2013) to assess risk of use of exported arms in violations of LOAC or war crimes.[203] Equally, individual members of a State's armed forces or of belligerent non-State armed groups could be held accountable under international criminal law for environmental

197 Ibid, art.2 par. (3), (4)

198 ILC, Environment Protection Principles,121, Commentary on principle 9, par.(3)

199 ILC, States' Responsibility Articles 343(f)

200 Pierre-Marie Dupuy, 'Reviewing the Difficulties of Codification: On Agos' Classification of Obligations of Means and Obligations of Result in Relation to State Responsibility' 10 EJIL 2 (1999) 371, 373

201 Katja 187

202 Riccardo Pisillo-Mazzeschi, 'The Due Diligence Rule and the Nature of the International Responsibility of States' in *State Responsibility in International Law* (Ed. Rene Provost 2002)

203 Kimberley N. Trapp and Edmund Robinson, 'Extra-territorial "Fiducuary" Obligations and Ensuring Respect for International Humantarian Law' 63 McGill L J 3&4 (2018) 677

damage.[204] The book focuses solely on State's accountability for environmental damage in IAC. NIAC is not covered.

Considering the historical context of international law and its evolving nature, the book adopts a traditional perspective of positive law while proposing novel interpretations of notions that have become outdated, particularly the threshold of environmental damage under LOAC. State responsibility for environmental damage in IAC is engaged by violation of its environmental obligations during war (Chapter 2) or occupation (Chapter 3), both defined as IAC and under IEL (Chapter 4). The analysis is complemented by a pragmatic approach based on two case studies assessing practical application of the rules in war (Chapter 5) and occupation (Chapter 6). Few IAC cases provide environmental damage issues that have been well documented. The Israel-Hezbollah conflict in Lebanon in 2006 was chosen as exemplifying environmental damage caused by war reported on by numerous international organizations, including the largest oil-pollution event in the Eastern Mediterranean Sea at the time.[205] The Russia-Ukraine war could be an interesting case study of IAC presenting potential instances of environmental damage, though not included herein for reasons of timing. Contemporary occupations range from Northern Cyprus, Crimea, Western Sahara to Nagorno-Karabakh. The Israeli occupation of Palestinian Territory was retained as the most prominent,[206] longest running occupation, featuring well-documented environmental damage.

Bibliography

Treaties

Convention (II) with Respect to the Laws and Customs of War on Land and Its Annex: Regulations Concerning the Laws and Customs of War on Land, The Hague, 29 July 1899

Convention on Civil Liability for Damage Resulting from Activities Dangerous to the Environment, Lugano, 21 June 1993

Convention on Cluster Munitions (CCM), Dublin, 30 may 2008, Oslo 3–4 December 2008, entry into force 1 August 2010

Convention on the Prohibition of Military or any Other Hostile Use of Environmental Modification Techniques, 10 December 1976

Declaration Renouncing the Use in Time of War of Explosive Projectiles Under 400 Grammes Weight, St Petersburg, 1868

ICJ Statute

Montevideo Convention on the Rights and Duties of States, 1933

204 Amnesty International, *Dead Land, Islamic State's Deliberate Destruction of Iraq's Farmland* (2018)

205 Giovanni Coppini and others, 'Hindcast of Oil-spill Pollution during the Lebanon Crisis in the Eastern Mediterranean, July – August 2006' 62 Marine Pollution Bulletin 1, January (2011) 140, Conclusions

206 ILC, *Special Rapporteur Marja Lehto, First Report on Protection of the Environment in Relation to Armed Conflicts, A/CN.4/720* (2018) par.26

Projet d'une Déclaration Internationale Concernant les Lois et Coutumes de la Guerre (Bruxelles 1874)
Protocol Additional to the Geneva Conventions of 12 August 1949, and relating to the Protection of Victims of International Armed Conflicts (Protocol I), 8 June 1977
Rome Statute of the ICC
The Hague Convention for the Protection of Cultural Property in the Event of Armed Conflict, 14 May 1954
UN Charter
UNECE Convention on the Protection of Transboundary Watercourses and International Lakes, 1992
UNESCO Convention for the Protection of the World Cultural and Natural Heritage, 23 November 1972
VCLT

International organizations documents

Amnesty International, *Dead Land, Islamic State's Deliberate Destruction of Iraq's Farmland* (2018)
Conflict and Environment Observatory, *Report: Investigating the Environmental Dimensions of the 2020 Nagorno-Karabakh Conflict* (2021)
Council (EEC), *Regulation No 1872/84 of 28 June 1984 on Action by the Community Relating to the Environment*
ICRC, *Commentary on the Additional Protocols of 8 June 1977 to the Geneva Conventions of 12 August 1949* (Sandoz Y, Swinarski C and Zimmermann B eds, Martinus Nijhoff Publishers 1987)
———, *Commentary on the Declaration Renouncing the Use, in Time of War, of Explosive Projectiles under 400 Grammes Weight, Saint Petersburg* (1868)
———, *Commentary on the Project of an International Declaration Concerning the Laws and Customs of War, Brussels* (27 August 1874)
———, *Commentary on the Protocol Additional to the Geneva Conventions of 12 August 1949, and relating to the Protection of Victims of International Armed Conflicts (Protocol I), 8 June 1977* (Sandoz Y, Swinarski C and Zimmermann B eds, Martinus Nijhoff 1987)
———, *Commentary on the Protocol Additional to the Geneva Conventions of 12 August 1949, and relating to the Protection of Victims of* Non-*International Conflicts (Protocol II), 8 June 1977* (Sandoz Y, Swinarski C and Zimmermann B eds, Martinus Nijhoff 1987)
———, *Commentary on the Third Geneva Convention* (2020)
———, *Customary International Humanitarian Law, Vol. I Rules, 3rd. 2009, Vol. II Practice* (Henckaerts J-M and Doswald-Beck L eds, CUP 2005)
———, *Guidelines for Military Manuals and Instructions on the Protection of the Environment in Times of Armed Conflict (UN Doc. A/49/323, Annex)* (1994)
———, *Guidelines on the Protection of the Natural Environment in Armed Conflict* (2020)
———, *How Is the Term "Armed Conflict" Defined in International Humanitarian Law? Opinion Paper*, March 2008
———, 'States Party to the Following International Humanitarian Law and Other Related Treaties, as of 3rd September 2024'
ILA Use of Force Committee, 'Final Report on the Meaning of Armed Conflict in International Law' (2010)
ILC, *Articles on Responsibility of States for Internationally Wrongful Acts, with Commentary, A/56/10* (ILC YB 2001, vol II (2))

———, *Draft Conclusions on Identification of Customary International Law, A/73/10, par.66* (2018)
———, *Draft Principles on Protection of the Environment in Relation to Armed Conflicts, with commentaries, A/77/10* (ILC YB 2022, vol II, (2), 2022)
———, *Fragmentation of International Law: Difficulties Arising from the Diversification and Expansion of International Law, Report of the Study Group of the ILC, A/CN.4/L.682* (2006)
———, *Protection of the Environment in Relation to Armed Conflicts, Draft Principles Provisionally Adopted on First Reading, A/CN.4/L.937* (2019)
———, *Special Rapporteur Marie G. Jacobsson, Preliminary Report on the Protection of the Environment in Relation to Armed Conflicts, A/CN.4/674* (2014)
———, *Special Rapporteur Marja Lehto, First Report on Protection of the Environment in Relation to Armed Conflicts, A/CN.4/720* (2018)
Institut de Droit International, *Resolution on Environment* (1997)
International Commission of Inquiry on Darfur, *Report to the UN Secretary-General, 25 January 2005, S/2005/60*
Malanczuk P, *First Report of the ILA Study Group on the Law of State Responsibility, Submitted by the Chair of the Study Group to the Special Rapporteur and the Chair of the UN ILC and the ILA Director of Studies* (2000)
UN Conference on the Law of Treaties, *Official Records, First and Second Sessions Vienna*, 26 March–24 May 1968 and 9 April–22 May 1969
UNCC, *Reports and Recommendations Made by the Panel of Commissioners Concerning the Fifth Instalment of "F4" Claims, S/AC.26/2005/10* (2005)
UNCED, Rio de Janeiro, 3–14 June 1992, *Report, A/CONF.151/26/Rev.1 (Vol. I)*
UNCHE, Stockholm, 5–16 June 1972, *Report, A/CONF.48/14/Rev.1*
UNCSD, Rio de Janeiro 20–22 June 2012, *Report, A/CONF.216/16* (2012)
UNEP, *Afghanistan, Post-Conflict Environmental Assessment* (2003)
———, *Desk Study on the Environment in Liberia* (2004)
———, *Post-Conflict Environmental Assessment – FYR of Macedonia* (2000)
———, *The Environmental Impact of the Conflict in Ukraine, A Preliminary Review* (2022)
———, *UNEP in Iraq, Post-Conflict Assessment, Clean-up and Reconstruction* (2007)
———, 'World Environment Situation Room, Disasters and Conflicts'
UNGA, *Institutional Arrangements to Follow Up UNCED, A/RES/47/191* (1992)
———, *Political Declaration of the High-Level Political Forum on Sustainable Development Convened under the Auspices of the General Assembly, 29 September 2023, A/RES/78/1* (2023)
———, *Protection of the Environment in Times of Armed Conflict: Report of the Secretary General, A/47/328* (1992)
———, *Report of the Secretary General on the Protection of the Environment in Times of Armed Conflict, A/48/269* (1993)
———, *Transforming Our World: the 2030 Agenda for Sustainable Development, A/RES/70/1* (2015)
———, *UN Decade of International Law, A/Res/49/50* (1995)
———, *World Charter for Nature, A/Res/37/7* (1982)
UNSC, *Resolution 687, 3 April 1991, S/RES/687* (1991)
UN Secretary-General, *Report of the Secretary-General Pursuant to Paragraph 2 of Security Council Resolution 808 (1993) (S/25704)*
Wood M, Special Rapporteur, *Third Report on Identification of Customary International Law, A/CN.4/682* (2015)

National legislation and documents

Bellinger JB III, Legal Adviser, U.S. Department of State and William J. Haynes, General Counsel, U.S. Department of Defense, *Letter of November 3, 2006 to Dr. Jakob Kellenberger, President of the International Committee of the Red Cross*

Instructions for the Government of Armies of the United States in the Field (Lieber Code) (1863)

International tribunal decisions and documents

Application of the Convention on the Prevention and Punishment of the Crime of Genocide (Bosnia and Herzegovina v. Serbia and Montenegro), Judgment ICJ Rep 2007
Arbitral Award of 31 July 1989 (Guinea-Bissau v. Senegal) ICJ Rep 1991, p. 53
Factory at Chorzow, Merits, 1928, PCIJ Ser A No 17
Fisheries case (UK v. Norway), Judgement ICJ Rep 1951, p. 116
Hamdan v. Rumsfeld, Secretary of Defense et al., 2006, No. 05–184, 548 U.S. 557
ICC, *The Office of the Prosecutor Launches Public Consultation on a New Policy Initiative to Advance Accountability for Environmental Crimes under the Rome Statute* (16 February 2024)
———, Office of the Prosecutor, *Policy Paper on Case Selection and Prioritisation* (2016)
ITLOS, Responsibilities and Obligations of States Sponsoring Persons and Entities with Respect to Activities in the Area, Advisory Opinion, 2011, ITLOS Reports 2011
Legality of the Threat or Use of Nuclear Weapons, Advisory Opinion ICJ Rep 1996
Loizidou v. Turkey, Judgment (18 December 1996), (Application no. 15318/89) (ECtHR)
Military and Paramilitary Activities in and against Nicaragua (Nicaragua v. United States of America). Merits, Judgment ICJ Rep 1986, p. 14
North Sea Continental Shelf ICJ Rep 1969, p. 3
Prosecutor v. Akayesu, Judgment, 2 September 1998, ICTR-96–4-T (ICTR Trial Chamber)
Prosecutor v. Boškoski and Tarčulovski, IT-04–82-TIT-04–82-T (ICTY, Trial Chamber II)
IT-94–1-T, Decision on the Defence Motion for Interlocutory Appeal on Jurisdiction, 2 October 1995 (ICTY Appeals Chamber)
Prosecutor v. Dusko Tadic, IT-94–1-A, Judgement, 15 July 1999 (ICTY Appeals Chamber)
———, IT-94-1-T, *Opinion and Judgement, 7 May 1997* (ICTY Trial Chamber II)
———, IT-94-1-T, *Second Amended Indictment, 14 December 1995* (ICTY Appeals Chamber)
Prosecutor's Report on the Nato Bombing Campaign, 13 June 2000, ICTY Doc. PR/P.I.S./510-e (2000)
Situation in the Central African Republic in the Case of the Prosecutor v. Jean-Pierre Bemba Gombo, ICC-01/05–01/08, 21 March 2016 (ICC, Trial Chamber III)
South West Africa, Second Phase, Judgment ICJ Rep 1966
———, The Committee Established to Review the NATO Bombing Campaign against the Federal Republic of Yugoslavia, *Final Report to the Prosecutor* (2000)
Trial of the Major War Criminals, 14 November 1945–1 October 1946, vol I (IMT Nuremberg)

Journal articles

Balendra N, 'Defining Armed Conflict' 29 Cardozo L Rev 2007–2008 2461
Bloomfield S and Butler K, 'Darfur's Return to Hell, "Scorched Earth" Unleashed on Darfur, despite UN Presence' The Independent, 12 March 2008 1
Brunnée J, 'Sense and Sensibility: Reflections on International Liability Regimes as Tools for Environmental Protection' 53 ICLQ 2004 351
Bunker AL, 'Protection of the Environment during Armed Conflict: One Gulf, Two Wars' 13 RECIEL 2 2004 201
Carnahan BM, 'Lincoln, Lieber and the Laws of War: The Origins and Limits of the Principle of Military Necessity' 92 AJIL April 1998 213
Coppini G and others, 'Hindcast of Oil-spill Pollution during the Lebanon Crisis in the Eastern Mediterranean, July – August 2006' 62 Marine Pollution Bulletin 1, January 2011 140

Corey MIG, 'The Fine Line between Policy and Custom: Prosecutor v. Tadic and the Customary International Law of Internal Armed Conflict' 166 Military L Rev 2000 145
Corn GS, 'Hamdan, Lebanon, and the Regulation of Hostilities: The Need to Recognize a Hybrid Category of Armed Cconflict' 40 Vand J Transnat L 2007 305
Crawford J, 'The ILC's Articles on Responsibility of States for Internationally Wrongful Acts: A Retrospect' 96 AJIL 2002 874
Cusato E, 'Overcoming the "Logic of Exception": A Critique of the UN Security Council's Response to Environmental Damage from the 1990–91 Gulf War' 9 Asian J Int'l L 2019 75
Dupuy P-M, 'Reviewing the Difficulties of Codification: On Agos' Classification of Obligations of Means and Obligations of Result in Relation to State Responsibility' 10 EJIL 2 1999 371
Falk R, 'Environmental Warfare and Ecocide-Facts, Appraisal, and Proposals' Bull Peace Proposals 4 1973 80
Fenrick WJ, Lieutenant Colonel, 'The Rule of Proportionality and Protocol I in Conventional Warfare' 98 Military L Rev 1982 91
Ferraro DT, 'The ICRC's Legal Position on the Notion of Armed Conflict Involving Foreign Intervention and on Determining the IHL Applicable to This Type of Conflict' 97 IRRC 900 2015 1227
'General Principles of Law in International Commercial Arbitration' 101 Harv L Rev No. 8, June 1988 1816
Graham DE, 'Defining Non-International Armed Conflict: A Historically Difficult Task' 88 Int'l L Stud Ser US Naval War Col 2012 43
Greenwood C, 'The Concept of War in Modern International Law' 36 ICLQ 1987 283
Hardy J, 'The Interpretation of Plurilingual Treaties by International Courts and Tribunals' 37 Br Y B Int'l Law 1961 72
Henckaerts J-M, 'The ICRC Study on Customary International Humanitarian Law: Characteristics, Conclusions and Practical Relevance' 6 Slovenian L Rev 2009 225–276 225
Hevener NK and Mosher SA, 'General Principles of Law and the UN Covenant on Civil and Political Rights' 27 ICLQ 3, Jul. 1978 596
Higgins R, 'The UN at 70 Years: The Impact upon International Law' 65 ICLQ 2016 1
Joyner C and Kirhope J, 'The Persian Gulf War Oil Spill: Reassessing the Law of Environmental Protection and the Law of Armed Conflict' 24 Case W Res J Int'l L 1, Winter 1992 29
Kirgis FL, 'Some Proportionality Issues Raised by Israel's Use of Armed Force in Lebanon' 10 ASIL Insights 20
Low L and Hodgkinson D, 'Compensation for Wartime Environmental Damage: Challenges to International Law after the Gulf War' 35 Va J Int'l L 1994–1995 405
Milanovic M and Sivakumaran S, 'Assessing the Authority of the ICRC Customary IHL Study, How Does IHL Develop?' 104 ICRC 920–921 2022 1856
O'Connell ME, 'Defining Armed Conflict' 13 JC& SL 2008 393
Paulus A and Vashakmadze M, 'Asymmetrical War and the Notion of Armed Conflict – a Tentative Conceptualization' 91 IRRC 873 2009 95
PoKempner D, 'The "New" Non-State Actors in International Humanitarian Law' 38 Geo Wash Int'l L Rev 2006 551 551
Schmitt M, 'Green War: An Assessment of the Environmental Law of International Armed Conflict' 22 Yale J Int'l L 1997 1
———, '21st Century Conflict: Can the Law Survive?' 8 Melb J Int'l L 2007 443
Schrader HS, 'Custom and General Principles as Sources of International Law in American Federal Courts' 82 Colum L Rev 4 1982 751
Trapp KN and Robinson E, 'Extra-territorial "Fiducuary" Obligations and Ensuring Respect for International Humantarian Law' 63 McGill LJ 3&4 2018 677
Tucker ML, 'Mitigating Collateral Damage to the Natural Environment' 57 Naval L Rev 2009 161

Verwey WD, 'Protection of the Environment in Times of Armed Conflict: In Search of a New Legal Perspective' 8 Leiden J Int'l L 1 1995 7
Vité S, 'Typology of Armed Conflicts in International Humanitarian Law: Legal Concepts and Actual Situations' 91 IRRC 873, March 2009 69
Wassgren H, 'The UN Compensation Commission: Lessons of Legitimacy, State Responsibility and War Reparations' Leiden J Int'l L 1998 473 473
Waxman MC, 'The Structure of Terrorism Threats and the Laws of War' 20 Duke J Int'l Comp L 2010 431

Electronic articles

Crawford E, 'Armed Conflict, International' MPEPIL 2015, online edition 2015
Crawford J, 'State', MPEPIL online edition 2011
Glassborow K, 'Sudan, Court Urged to Consider Environmental Crimes, 4 September 2007' Institute for War and Peace Reporting
Milanovic M, 'What Exactly Internationalizes an Internal Armed Conflict? May 7, 2010' EJIL: Talk!

Books

Boyle A and Redgwell C, *Birnie, Boyle and Redgwell's International Law and the Environment* (4th edn, OUP 2021)
Brooke-Holland L, *Research Briefing, UK Arms Export to Israel, 22 May 2024, Number 9964 (House of Commons Library)*
Combacau J and Sur S, *Droit International Public* (13th edn, LGDJ 2019)
Crawford J, *Brownlie's Principles of Public International Law* (9th edn, OUP 2019)
Cullen A, *The Concept of Non-international Armed Conflict in International Humanitarian Law* (CUP 2010)
Cullinan C, *Wild Law, a Manifesto for Earth Justice* (Green Books 2003)
Dinstein Y, *The Conduct of Hostilities under the Law of International Armed Conflict* (CUP 2022)
Fleck D (ed) *The Handbook of International Humanitarian Law* (4th edn, OUP 2021)
Green LC, *The Contemporary Law of Armed Conflict* (3rd edn, MUP 2008)
IDI, *The Laws of War on Land, Oxford* (9 September 1880)
Kiss A and Shelton D, *International Environmental Law* (3rd ed. edn, Transnational Publishers 2004)
Klabbers J, *International Law* (3rd edn, CUP 2021)
Koppe E, *The Use of Nuclear Weapons and the Protection of the Environment during International Armed Conflict* (Hart Publishing Ltd. 2008)
Louka E, *International Environmental Law, Fairness, Effectiveness, and World Order* (CUP 2006)
Mollard-Bannelier K, *La Protection de l'Environnement en Temps de Conflit Armé* (Editions A. Pedone 2001)
Oppenheim L, *International Law, Vol. II Disputes, War and Neutrality* (Lauterpacht H ed, 7th edn, Longmans, Green and Co. 1952)
Sands P and others, *Principles of International Environmental Law* (4th edn, CUP 2018)

Book chapters

Akande D, 'Classification of Armed Conflicts: Relevant Legal Concepts' in Wilmhurst E (ed), *International Law and the Classification of Conflicts* (OUP 2012)
Aust A, 'Vienna Convention on the Law of Treaties (1969)' in *MPEPIL* (2006)

'Conclusions by the Working Group of Experts on Liability and Compensation for Environmental Damage Arising from Military Activities' in Timoshenko A (ed), *Liability and Compensation for Environmental Damage, Compilation of Documents* (UNEP 1998)
Gasser H-P, 'International Humanitarian Law: An Introduction' in Haug H (ed), *Humanity for All: The International Red Cross and Red Crescent Movement* (Paul Haupt 1993)
Hampson FJ, 'Afghanistan 2001–2010' in Wilmshurst E (ed), *International Law and the Classification of Conflicts* (OUP 2012)
Klee J, 'Chapter 2, the Process' in Payne CR and Sand PH (eds), *Gulf War Reparations and the UN Compensation Commission, Environmental Liability* (OUP 2011)
Lubell N, 'The War (?) against Al-Qaeda' in Wilmhurst E (ed), *International Law and the Classification of Conflicts* (OUP 2012)
Partsch KJ, 'Armed Conflict' in Bernhardt R (ed), *Encyclopedia of Public International Law* (Elsevier North-Holland 1990)
Payne CR, 'Chapter 2, Defining the Environment, Environmental Integrity' in Stahn C and others (eds), *Environmental Protection and Transitions from Conflict to Peace, Clarifying Norms, Principles, and Practices* (OUP 2017)
Pisillo-Mazzeschi R, 'The Due Diligence Rule and the Nature of the International Responsibility of States' in *State Responsibility in International Law* (Ed. Rene Provost 2002)
Scobbie I, 'Human Rights Protection during Armed Conflict: What, When and for Whom?' in de Wet E and Kleffner J (eds), *Convergence and Conflicts of Human Rights and International Humanitarian Law in Military Operations*, vol 1 (Pretoria University Law Press 2014)
———, 'Lebanon 2006' in Wilmhurst E (ed), *International Law and the Classification of Conflicts* (OUP 2012)
———, 'The Approach to Customary International Law in the Study' in Wilmshurt E and Breau S (eds), *Perspectives on the ICRC Study on Customary International Humanitarian Law* (1st edn, Chatham House and BIICL 2007)
Shelton D, 'Stockholm Declaration (1972) and Rio Declaration (1992)' in *MPEPIL*
Stefanik K, 'The Environment and Armed Conflict, Employing General Principles to Protect the Environment' in Stahn C and others (eds), *Environmental Protection and Transitions from Conflict to Peace* (OUP 2017)
Werner M, 'War' in Bernhardt R (ed), *Encyclopedia of Public International Law* (Elsevier North-Holland 1982)
Wilmshurst E, 'Conclusions' in Wilmshurst E (ed), *International Law and the Classification of Conflicts* (OUP 2012)

2 State responsibility for environmental war damage under the law of armed conflict

The chapter focuses on State responsibility for environmental damage in war caused by its wrongful act,[1] under the LOAC. A State is generally responsible for acts committed by its organs, acting in that capacity, even if the actions are unauthorized (*ultra vires*) or in breach of the rules; it is not liable for wholly private acts committed by its organs that are not imputable to it.[2] Under the LOAC, a party to an armed conflict is responsible for all acts committed by individuals of its armed forces.[3] The State is therefore liable for acts committed *ultra vires* by its soldiers, even if acting in their private capacity, though it is debatable whether such responsibility extends to acts breaching rules not included under LOAC conventions.[4] Environmental obligations during armed conflict which breach is a wrongful act, standard of conduct, where applicable, and environmental damage, under the LOAC principles and conventions, are examined.

I. LOAC principles under customary law and conventional rules

The LOAC principles of distinction, proportionality, military necessity and humanity that purport to restrain military action are accepted as customary law[5] and codified

1 ILC, *Draft Principles on Protection of the Environment in Relation to Armed Conflicts, with commentaries, A/77/10* (ILC YB 2022, vol II (2), 2022) Principle 9, par.1 (ILC Environment Protection Principles)

2 ILC, *Articles on Responsibility of States for Internationally Wrongful Acts, with Commentary, A/56/10* (ILC YB 2001, vol II (2)) commentary on art.7 par.(7)

3 *Armed Activities on the Territory of the Congo (DRC v. Uganda), Judgment* ICJ Rep 2005, p. 168, ICJ par.214. Convention (IV) Respecting the Laws and Customs of War on Land and its annex: Regulations Concerning the Laws and Customs of War on Land, the Hague, 18 October 1907 art.3 (Hague Regulations). Protocol Additional to the Geneva Conventions of 12 August 1949, and relating to the Protection of Victims of International Armed Conflicts (Protocol I), 8 June 1977 Art.91 (AP/I)

4 Christopher Greenwood, 'State Responsibility and Civil Liability for Environmental Damage Caused by Military Operations' in John King, Ronald McCain, and Richard Grunawalt (eds), *Protection of the Environment during Armed Conflict*, vol 69 (US Naval War College 1996) 400, 402; Marco Sassoli, 'State Responsibility for Violations of International Humanitarian Law' 84 IRRC 846, June (2002) 405–406

5 A.P.V. Rogers, *Law on the Battlefield* (3rd edn, MUP 2012) 3

DOI: 10.4324/9780367823283-2

under the LOAC conventions. The distinction between customary principles and conventional rules is not sharp; the relation between them is one of mutual influence.

1. Distinction principle

1.1 Customary status

The customary distinction (or discrimination) principle means that "war is to be waged against the enemy's armed forces, not against its civilian population. Attacks are to be directed at military targets, not at civilian objects."[6] It was mentioned in the Lieber Code, the Preamble to the St Petersburg Declaration and article 24 of the 1923 Draft Hague Air Rules of Aerial Warfare that reflected emerging customary rules prior to WWI.[7] Undermined by WWII State aerial bombardments "taken to horrifying excesses" by the German side and the Allied Powers and use of new "barbarized" technological warfare, the principle was consigned to oblivion.[8] A UNGA resolution (1968) affirmed the prohibition of launching attacks against civilians and the obligation of distinction between civilians and combatants at all times.[9] The Institute of International Law adopted a resolution on the distinction between military and non-military objectives, qualifying objectives as military if they make an effective contribution to military action or exhibit a generally recognized military significance.[10] The US did not view it "as an accurate statement of international law relating to armed conflict," though it considered the UNGA resolution "declaratory of existing customary international law."[11] This "cardinal" principle is an "intransgressible principle of international customary law."[12]

6 Rogers 11

7 *Instructions for the Government of Armies of the United States in the Field (Lieber Code)* (1863) art.22; Declaration Renouncing the Use in Time of War of Explosive Projectiles Under 400 Grammes Weight, St Petersburg, 1868; UK MoD, *The Joint Service Manual of the Law of Armed Conflict, JSP 383* (2004) par.1.26.3; Marcus Hanke, 'The 1923 Hague Rules of Air Warfare – A Contribution to the Development of International Law Protecting Civilians from Air Attack' IRRC No. 292 March (1993) 28, 36

8 Stefan Oeter, 'Methods of Combat' in Dieter Fleck (ed), *The Handbook of International Humanitarian Law* (4th edn, OUP 2021) Introductory Remarks par.3; Rogers 17, 20. Kenneth Watkin, '21st Century Conflict and International Humanitaria Law: Status Quo or Change?' in Michael Schmitt and Jelena Pejic (eds), *International Law and Armed Conflict: Exploring the Faultlines* (Martinus Nijhoff Publishers 2007) 276; H. Lauterpacht, 'The Problem of the Revision of the Law of War' 29 Brit YB Int'l L (1952), 360 The UK Manual, par.1.26.3.

9 UNGA, *Respect for Human Rights in Armed Conflicts* (Resolution 2444 (XXIII), 1968) par.1 Vienna International Conference of the Red Cross, *Resolution XXVIII, Protection of Civilian Populations against the Dangers of Indiscriminate Warfare* (1965)

10 IDI, 'The Distinction between Military Objectives and Non-Military Objectives in General and Particularly the Problems Associated with Weapons of Mass Destruction'

11 General Counsel, Department of Defense, *Letter, 22 September 1972, to Senator Edward Kennedy, Chairman, Subcommittee on Refugees of Committee on Judiciary* (67 AJIL 122 1973)

12 *Legality of the Threat or Use of Nuclear Weapons, Advisory Opinion* ICJ Rep 1996, 226 par.78–79

1.2 Conventional rules

Incorporated in Additional Protocols to the Geneva Conventions, distinction is required in warfare between civilians and combatants and civilian objects and military objectives.[13] Civilian populations, individuals and objects cannot be object of attacks, nor objects of attacks which sole purpose is spreading terror or reprisals.[14] Attacks must be directed at military objectives.[15] These are customary law rules applicable in international and non-international conflicts.[16]

Indiscriminate attacks striking military objectives and civilians or civilian objects are prohibited.[17] An attack is indiscriminate when:

(i) It is not directed at a military objective,[18]
(ii) Warfare methods or means used cannot be directed at a military objective,[19]
(iii) Its effects cannot be limited as required by AP/I,[20] including regarding environmental protection (art.35(3) and 55), attacks releasing dangerous forces (art.56) or breaching proportionality (art.51(5)(b) and 57 (2)(a)(iii)),[21]
(iv) It treats distinct military objectives, within a rural or urban area where civilians or civilian objects are concentrated, as one military objective,[22]
(v) It breaches the proportionality principle, examined later.[23]

Consequently, weapons or methods used in an indiscriminate manner (i.e. poisoning wells) or weapons that are inherently indiscriminate (i.e. bacteriological weapons) breach the prohibition on indeterminate attacks[24] and must never be used by States.[25]

13 AP/I art.48; Protocol Additional to the Geneva Conventions of 12 August 1949, and relating to the Protection of Victims of Non-International Armed Conflicts (Protocol II), 8 June 1977 art.13 (AP/II)
14 AP/I art.51(2), 51(6), 52(1)
15 AP/I art.52(2)
16 ICRC, *Customary International Humanitarian Law, Vol. I Rules* (Jean-Marie Henckaerts and Louise Doswald-Beck eds, 3rd. edn, CUP 2009) Vol. I, Rule 1, Rule 7 (ICRC, Customary IHL Rules); *Prosecutor v. Kordic & Cerkez, IT-95–14/2-PT,* Decision on the Joint Defense Motion to Dismiss the Amended Indictment for Lack of Jurisdiction Based on the Limited Jurisdictional Reach of Articles 2 and 3, 2 March 1999, ICTY Trial Chamber par.31
17 AP/I art.51.4; ICRC, *Commentary on the Protocol Additional to the Geneva Conventions of 12 August 1949, and relating to the Protection of Victims of International Armed Conflicts (Protocol I), 8 June 1977* (Yves Sandoz, Christophe Swinarski and Bruno Zimmermann eds, Martinus Nijhoff 1987) par.1418 (ICRC AP/I Commentary)
18 AP/I art.51.4(a)
19 AP/I art.51.4(b)
20 AP/I art.51.4(c)
21 Oeter 7.16, par.4; Michael Bothe, Karl Joseph Partsh, Waldemar A. Solf with the collaboration of Martin Eaton, *New Rules for Victims of Armed Conflicts, Commentary on the Two 1977 Protocols Additional to the Geneva Conventions of 1949* (Martinus Nijhoff Publishers 1982) 305–306, par.2.5.2.3.
22 AP/I art.51.5(a)
23 AP/I art.51.5(b)
24 Karen Hulme, *War Torn Environment: Interpreting the Legal Threshold* (Martinus Nijhoff 2004) 171; Bothe par.1963, 1965
25 *Nuclear Weapons* par.78

The military objective notion has evolved from military objects, such as establishments, depots of arms and warships in the harbour,[26] to objects which destruction would constitute a distinct military advantage[27] and a broader customary understanding during the two World Wars.[28] Under AP/I, article 52.1, civilian objects are objects which are not military objectives. Military objectives are objects (i) which make an effective contribution to military action by their nature, location, purpose or use and (ii) whose total or partial destruction, capture or neutralization, in the circumstances ruling at the time, offers a definite military advantage (article 52.2). "'Purpose' means the future intended use of an object while 'use' means its present function."[29] The definition may not be opposable to States that are not AP/I signatories. The US has replaced the term military action with "war sustaining capability," allowing interpretation of every civilian activity as participating in the war,[30] widening considerably the range of military targets.[31] Rogers posits that AP/I did not apply in the Gulf War and the less clear customary understanding applied.[32] However, the definition is deemed customary international law in IAC and NIAC, as it was accepted at the conference for the adoption of AP/I without reservations, recognized in military manuals and official statements from States that are not or were not, at the time, signatories to AP/I.[33]

AP/I definition is hotly debated. As it does not list "objects" to allow flexibility of implementation, it is open to wide interpretation, subject to belligerents' interests.[34] Difficulties revolve around objects that may have "dual" civilian and military uses (i.e. bridges, means of communication and transport, industrial facilities, power stations). Military commanders may not rely on abstract categories of specific objects to decide they constitute military objectives; the military advantage must be evaluated in the current circumstances.[35] In case of doubt on its use, an object is presumed not to contribute to military action. As there are no general rules applicable, objects should be examined on a case-by-case basis. Russian bakeries fabricating military drones[36] could be regarded as military objectives, because of

26 Convention (IX) concerning Bombardment by Naval Forces in Time of War, the Hague, 18 October1907, art.2

27 1923 Draft Hague Air Warfare Rules, art.24

28 Rogers 100

29 UK MoD par.5.4.4(e); ICRC AP/I Commentary art.51 par.2022; Oeter 7.02, par.5

30 US Naval Manual 1997 par.8.1.1. Oeter 7.02 par.6, 7.03 par.8

31 Rogers 119–120

32 Ibid, 112

33 ICRC Customary IHL Rules, Rule 8, 29–32; ICRC, *Customary International Humanitarian Law, Vol. II Practice* (Jean-Marie Henckaerts and Louise Doswald-Beck eds, CUP 2005) 181–190 par.316–369 (ICRC Customary IHL Practice); Francoise Hampson, 'Proportionality and Necessity in the Gulf Conflict' 86 Am Soc Int'l L Proc (1992) 45, 50

34 Oeter 7.02, par.5, 8

35 Frits Kalshoven, 'Reaffirmation and Development of International Humanitarian Law Applicable in Armed Conflicts: The Diplomatic Conference, Geneva, 1974–1977, Part II' 8 NY Int'l L (1978) 107, 111

36 Max Seddon and Polina Ivanova, 'Russian Bakery Rises to Putin's Call by Making Killer Drones' Financial Times (6/7 January 2024) 5

their effective contribution to military action in the Russia-Ukraine war and their destruction providing a military advantage.

Examples illustrate the difficulties. NATO bombing of Serbia State television in 1999 and the US attack on a Baghdad television station in 2003 were controversial.[37] Bridges have been variously considered not being military objectives per se,[38] deemed military objects to be attacked only when supplies destined for the front pass over them[39] or when used for troop movements,[40] to a maximalist approach approving the destruction of "all bridges – however minor in themselves-spanning a wide river . . . to effect a fragmentation of enemy land forces."[41] The Eritrea-Ethiopia Claims Commission found that the Hirgigo power station, not yet in service, was a military objective; as power stations are important for wartime needs, Hirgigo was going to replace power generating facilities next to a port and naval base, and its destruction would eliminate a potential power source.[42] The analysis was wrong, as a definite military advantage must be evaluated considering actual circumstances[43] and cannot be based on speculative effect from destruction.[44] Whereas caution is required for assumptions,[45] the Commission made assumptions about Eritrea's future intended use of the power station,[46] without even considering Eritrea's assertion that the military had their own power-generating facilities.[47]

AP/I also prohibits attacks and reprisals on specific civilian objects, comprising cultural objects (article 53), objects indispensable to survival of the population (article 54), natural environment (article 55) and works and installations containing dangerous forces (article 56), unless used in support of military action. Oeter finds these prohibitions absolute as constituting peremptory fundamental safeguards for the population.[48] Others are more sceptical about the exclusion of civilian objects from reprisals under treaty rules, though as a principle it should apply.[49] Protection

37 Oeter 7.03 par.6

38 Hampson 49

39 Michael Bothe, 'The Protection of the Civilian Population and NATO Bombing on Yugoslavia: Comments on the Report to the Prosecutor of the ICTY' 12 EJIL (2001) 531, 531, 534

40 Rogers 123

41 Yoram Dinstein, *The Conduct of Hostilities under the Law of International Armed Conflict* (CUP 2022) par.382

42 *Eritrea-Ethiopia Claims Commission, Partial Award, Western Front, Aerial Bombardment and Related Claims, Eritrea's Claims 1, 3, 5, 9–13, 14, 21, 25 & 26, 19 December 2005* 45 ILM 396 (2006), par.117 (EECC Western Front)

43 Elliot Winter, 'The Compatibility of Autonomous Weapons with the Principle of Distinction in the Law of Armed Conflict' 69 ICLQ October (2020)

44 *EECC Western Front Separate opinion, par.4,5,9,10 (n.38)*

45 J. Romesh Weeramantry, Ed. Daniel Bodansky, 'International Decisions, the Eritrea-Ethiopia Claims Commission Awards' 101 AJIL, 625.

46 *EECC Western Front par.120*

47 Weeramantry 625–626

48 Oeter 7.12 par.3

49 Dinstein par.1045, 1059

of the environment from reprisal attacks is contentious.[50] Based on the customary prohibition of reprisal attacks on "property" of protected persons (GC IV article 33) and AP/I articles, the ILC concludes it applies to the environment as a civilian object – unless it becomes a military objective – and retains it in its principles.[51] It appears it is a progressive development of the law by the ILC, as States were opposed to the qualification of customary status of this rule,[52] and the customary status of AP/I article 55(2) containing the prohibition is unsettled.[53] Additionally, States could designate areas of environmental importance as protected zones in the event of armed conflict,[54] as recommended by scholars and international organizations.[55] Environmental concerns, though, are not the most urgent priority during armed conflicts, except for environmental disasters necessitating immediate coordinated responses; mediation primarily focuses on humanitarian relief, evacuation of civilians or safe passage of food and medical supplies.

1.3 Application to the environment

The distinction principle applies to the environment.[56] Applying the military objective definition to the environment raises questions as to whether (i) it is an "object" (ii) that is "civilian" and (iii) can become a "military objective." The environment is constituted of tangible natural resources (fauna, flora, water, soil) and intangible components (air and light). An "object" "is not usually a living animal [or] plant."[57] It is traditionally a "material" thing.[58] Not only does air constituted by gases not fit that description, but being res communes, its inclusion under "civilian objects" is controversial.[59] Yet, as AP/l I was adopted when the environment concept was emerging, "object" is assumed to include environmental resources, air, water, soil, fauna and flora, in accordance with its current interpretation under IEL.

The environment is "civilian" by nature.[60] None of its parts can be attacked, unless it becomes a military objective fulfilling the requirements of AP/I article

50 Matthew Gillett, 'Criminalizing Reprisals against the Natural Environment' 105 IRRC, Protecting the Environment in Armed Conflict, 924 (2023) 1463, 1480

51 ILC, Environment Protection Principles, Principle 15, Commentary par(4); AP/I art.51(6), art.52(1)

52 Gillett 1480

53 ICRC, Customary IHL Rules Rule 147, Commentary p. 525; ICRC, *Guidelines on the Protection of the Natural Environment in Armed Conflict* (2020) par.93 ILC, Environment Protection Principles, Principle 15, Commentary par(3)

54 ILC, Environment Protection Principles Principles 4, 18

55 Michael Bothe and others, 'International Law Protecting the Environment during Armed Conflict: Gaps and Opportunities' 92 IRRC 879 (2010) 569 577

56 ICRC, *Customary IHL Rules Customary IHL Rules*, Rule 43.A, Commentary, pp. 143–144

57 Cambridge Dictionary, "object."

58 Merriam-Webster, Cambridge and Oxford online dictionaries, "object."

59 Michael Schmitt, 'Green War: An Assessment of the Environmental Law of International Armed Conflict' 22 Yale J Int'l L (1997) 1 64, 106. Karine Mollard-Bannelier, *La Protection de l'Environnement en Temps de Conflit Armé* (Editions A. Pedone 2001) 179

60 Eric Talbot Jensen, 'The International Law of Environmental Warfare: Active and Passive Damage during Armed Conflict' 38 Vand J Transnat Law (2005) 169; ILC, Environment Protection Principles Commentary on Principle 14, par.(3); ICRC, Guidelines par.18

52(2).[61] The US disagrees, considering that not all its parts are necessarily civilian, without clarifying which ones are.[62] Natural resources would have to contribute to military action through their use, as contribution through purpose, although possible,[63] seems difficult to envisage[64] and their destruction must provide a definite military advantage. During the Vietnam War, the US military considered mangroves and crops, used by the Vietcong for cover and sustenance in South Vietnam, military objectives.[65] They cleared vegetation by ploughing the land extensively[66] and used 19 million gallons of herbicide containing dioxin for defoliation and crop destruction between 1961 and 1971, covering entire forests in Vietnam's military zones.[67] The "scorched earth" land[68] covered whole areas stripped of vegetation affecting animal habitats and others unsuitable for agriculture for decades.[69]

The environment may suffer harm indirectly, as collateral damage from attacks on military objectives. Water pollution may result from destruction of bridges leading to debris falling in the water or from attack on industrial facilities, power stations or oil platforms at sea. Air pollution could be caused by the release of toxic substances into air by attack on chemical facilities. Navigation on watercourses can be affected, such as interruption of navigation on the Danube between 1999 and 2002, following the Kosovo conflict, because of risks associated with unexploded munitions and debris from destruction of bridges.[70] "Denial of use [of the environment] is the functional equivalent of damage."[71]

2. *Proportionality principle*

2.1 *Customary principle*

Proportionality underlies and guides the application of the LOAC.[72] It refers to attempts at balancing achievements of military goals and humanitarian costs in terms of lives (necessity and humanity) by reducing collateral damage from military

61 ILC, Environment Protection Principles Principle 13.3 h; ICRC, Guidelines Rule 5; ICRC, Customary IHL Rules

62 W. Casey Biggerstaff and Michael N. Schmitt, 'Protecting the Environment in Armed Conflict: Evaluating the US Perspective' 105 IRRC 924 (2023) 1267, 1277, 1290

63 Jensen 170

64 Rogers 106

65 Benjamin B. Ferencz, 'War Crimes Law and the Vietnam War' 17 Am U L Rev 3 (1967–1968) 403, 413; Marco Roscini, 'Targeting and Contemporary Aerial Bombardment' 54 ICLQ 2 (2005) 411, 437

66 Schmitt 10

67 Department of Veterans Affairs, Environmental Agents Service, *Agent Orange, Information for Veterans Who Served in Vietnam* (2003) 2

68 Richard Falk, 'United States Foreign Policy and the Vietnam War: A Second American Dilemma' Stanf J Int'l Stud 3 (1968) 78, 87

69 UNEP, *From Conflict to Peacebuilding, The Role of Natural Resources and the Environment* (2009) 15

70 Mara Tignino, *L'eau et la Guerre, Eléments pour un Regime Juridique* (Bruylant 2011) 46

71 Schmitt 5

72 Judith Gail Gardam, *Necessity, Proportionality and the Use of Force by States* (CUP 2004) 3

operations.[73] Accordingly, means of attack and amount of destruction permitted should be proportionate to anticipated ends and the military objective importance.[74] Considered customary international law rule today, the principle gained acceptance in the 1970s.[75]

2.2 *Conventional application*

The principle has been codified in

(i) the prohibition of an indeterminate attack defined as expected to cause "excessive" incidental loss of civilian life, injury, or damage to civilian objects, "in relation to the concrete and direct military advantage anticipated"[76] – "excessive" was considered less subjective than "disproportionate" – but the provision refers to the customary proportionality rule;[77] and

(ii) precautions in attacks, AP/I articles 57(2)(a)(iii) and 57(2)(b). "Collateral damage" from attacks on lawful military targets is prohibited if excessive.

First, assessing proportionality involves weighing anticipated military advantage from destruction or capture of a military objective and projected estimates of civilians dead or injured and civilian objects or environment damaged or destroyed. Comparing heterogeneous values impossible to quantify provides no clear guidance to military commanders on the weight of each side of the equation. It is subjective.[78] Subjectivity is best illustrated by an example. For Dinstein, "destruction of a whole village with scores of civilian casualties and immense destruction of property" to eliminate an entire artillery battery operating from that village may be deemed not excessive.[79] This comment seems to justify disproportionate military operations and disregard for distinction principle. If razing a village with massive destruction and casualties is not excessive, compared to the destruction of an artillery battery, what would be? Others find excessive loss difficult to avoid when belligerents do not separate military objectives from their civilian population, which

73 Rogers 21; Judith Gail Gardam, 'Proportionality and Force in International Law' 87 AJIL 3 (1993) 391

74 Bernard L. Brown, 'The Proportionality Principle in the Humanitarian Law of Warfare: Recent Efforts at Codification' 10 Cornell Int'l L J (1976–1977) 134, 136; ICRC Commentary on AP/I art.51 par.1979, art.57 par.2200; Douglas P. Lackey, *The Ethics of War and Peace* (Prentice-Hall 1989) 59 Larry May, *War Crimes and Just War* (CUP 2007) 159

75 Rogers 21; ICRC, Customary IHL Rules Rule 14

76 AP/I art.51.5(b)

77 William J. Fenrick, 'Applying IHL Targeting Rules to Practical Situations: Proportionality and Military Objectives' 27 Windsor YB Access Just (2009), 277; ICRC, Guidelines par.114; ICRC, Customary IHL Rules Rule 14

78 Mollard-Bannelier 165; Schmitt 55; Richard Falk, 'The Environmental Law of War: An Introduction' in Glen Plant (ed), *Environmental Protection and the Law of War: A fifth Geneva Convention on the Protection of the Environment in Time of Armed Conflict* (Belhaven Press 1992) 86; ICRC AP/I Commentary art.57, par.2187

79 Dinstein par.527

is the case of the artillery battery in the village. However, even in such case where the use of civilians as human shields is in violation of the LOAC, precautionary obligations must be observed.[80] Common sense and moral judgement developed by military experience and training should inform military commanders' decision to avoid blatant disproportionality.[81]

Proportionality must be assessed when attacking "dual use" objects necessary for civilians' survival, such as power infrastructures.[82] Experts consider that destroying power stations would provide no concrete and direct military advantage, when generators can substitute the destroyed infrastructure, and destruction is disproportionate compared to the chance to disrupt the command centre capacity.[83] Yet attacks against power infrastructures remain frequent. During the 1990–1991 Persian Gulf conflict, the US air campaign targeted Iraqi electricity production facilities and telecommunication systems, which destruction was deemed necessary to isolate and incapacitate the Iraqi regime.[84] Although "smart" weapons were used, "investigations revealed that the Coalition's systematic destruction of Iraq's infrastructure . . . resulted in catastrophic damage to civilian lives and property," and about 100,000 Iraqi civilians dead a year after the war.[85] Russian attacks on Ukraine energy infrastructures caused "extensive damage to energy facilities, compromising water supply in certain areas and disrupting electricity access for millions of civilians" leaving them temporarily without power, water, or gas.[86]

A second issue is whether the impact of an attack should be evaluated on a cumulative assessment of the campaign or for each attack.[87] Some consider that the anticipated military advantage relates to the operation "as a whole," as interpreted by States ratifying AP/I, because a single attack is part of integrated operation;[88] however, such terms do "not provide useful guidance as to what limits there are to aggregating these incidences."[89] This approach allows attackers to balance greater collateral damage from some attacks with less collateral damage

80 Oeter 7.17, par.3. AP/I art.51(8)
81 Oeter, 7.17, par.2–6
82 Francesca Capone, 'The Wave of Russian Attacks on Ukraine's Power Infrastructures: An Opportunity to Infuse Meaningfulness into the Notion of 'Dual-use Objects'?' European Papers 21 November (2023) 743
83 ICRC and Université Laval, *International Experts Meeting, The Principle of Proportionality in the Rules Governing the Conduct of Hostilities under International Humanitarian Law* (2016) 20, 39
84 Ruth Wedgwood and Fred Green, 'Proportionality and Necessity in American National Security Decision Making' 86 ASIL Proceedings April 1–4, 67
85 Mollard-Bannelier 160; Jochnick Normand, 'The Legitimation of Violence: A Critical Analysis of the Gulf War' 35 Harv Int'l L J (1994)
86 UN, *Escalating Attacks on Ukraine's Civilian, Energy Infrastructure Making Humanitarian Aid Delivery Even More Dangerous, Relief Chief Tells Security Council, SC/15695, 14 May 2024*
87 Hampson 46; Hamutal (Mutal) Esther Shamash, 'How Much Is Too Much? An Examination of the Principle of Jus in Bello Proportionality' 2 IDF L Rev (2005–2006) 103, 119; Brown 141
88 Leslie C. Green, *The Contemporary Law of Armed Conflict* (3rd edn, MUP 2008) 150. Schmitt 55. Oeter 7.03 par.9, 7.17 par.2 ICRC, Customary IHL Rules Rule 14 ICRC and Université Laval 17 UK MoD par.54.4.(j)
89 Ryan Christian Else, 'Proportionality in the Law of Armed Conflict – The Proper Unit of Analysis for Military Operations' 5 U St Thomas J L Pub Policy (2010–2011) 205

of others.[90] Adopted by the US in the Vietnam war, it led to wide condemnation as civilian losses vastly exceeded guerrillas' losses during specific military operations.[91] A contrasting view is that the language "concrete and direct" means that each attack should be assessed individually,[92] as argued by the Prosecutor in the *Galic* case and judged by the ICTY, regarding a shelling of a gathering of about 200 persons.[93] Others interpret "concrete" as meaning real as opposed to hypothetical.[94] Hanson considers that qualification of target as military objective – and not proportionality – is the issue, if the cumulative impact of an attack is a concern. A "consequential" effects approach should be adopted,[95] though proportionality debate could be wrongly evaded by shifting the focus on targeting.[96] Considering the Diplomatic Conference's aim to increase civilian protection, a case-by-case analysis is more appropriate.[97]

The timeframe to assess the damage is debated. If long-term casualties of the attack from starvation, diseases, unexploded weapons and environmental damage are taken into account,[98] despite a remote causality link between attacks and civilian damage,[99] then damage assessment would outweigh the military advantage.[100] For some, as long as both elements of the equation are assessed on the same time scale, that should not cause a problem.[101]

Finally, there is a gap between what States recognize as national practice recorded in their military manuals and legislations and actual conduct during armed conflicts. Historical research on the application of the proportionality principle during past armed conflicts and judicial decisions that compare military advantage and civilian losses are practically non-existent.[102] A few analyses reveal "blindness" of States towards the proportionality rule during WWII[103] and "scant attention" paid to it in the Persian Gulf War and the Kosovo conflict.[104] States' conduct during armed conflicts (Bosnia-Herzegovina, Iraq/Kuwait, SFRY (FRY)/Croatia, Nigeria,

90 Shamash 119
91 Brown 142
92 Gardam, 'Proportionality and Force in International Law' 407
93 *Prosecutor v. Stanislav Galic, Judgement and Opinion, 5 December 2003* ICTY Tribunal Chamber par.37, 387; ICRC and Université Laval 14
94 ICRC and Université Laval 17
95 Hampson 46
96 Shamash 136
97 Brown 142. Hampson 47
98 Roscini 441
99 Alexander Breitegger, 'Preventing Human Suffering during and after Conflict? The Complementary Case for a Specific Convention on Cluster Munitions' 10 Austrian Rev Int'l Eur L (2005) 3, 16
100 Shamash 20
101 Rogers 26
102 William J. Fenrick, Lieutenant Colonel, 'The Rule of Proportionality and Protocol I in Conventional Warfare' 98 Mil L Rev (1982) 91, 124
103 Fenrick 118, 124
104 Judith Gail Gardam, 'Proportionality as a Restraint on the Use of Force' 20 Aust YB Int'l L (1999) 161, 173

Russia/Chechnya, Rwanda) allegedly breached proportionality, despite the principle being incorporated into national legislation.[105] Current conflicts seem to ignore equally the rule.[106]

2.3 Application to the environment

The principle applies to the environment during armed conflict,[107] though adding the notion of harm to the environment in the value-balancing exercise creates more confusion.[108] The ICJ judged that States must take environmental considerations into account when assessing the conformity of military actions to necessity and proportionality.[109] The committee established to review the NATO bombing campaign against the Federal Republic of Yugoslavia concluded that, even when targeting legitimate military objectives compatible with AP/I article 52, attacks should be avoided if their anticipated long-term environmental damage, resulting in adverse effect on civilian populations, would be excessive compared to expected direct military advantage, though what is excessive is not clear under the customary proportionality rule.[110] However, introducing this "long-term" qualification of environmental damage, corresponding to AP/I articles 35.3 and 55, into the application of the proportionality rule is questionable, as it is required neither under the customary proportionality principle nor its codification in AP/I article 51.5(b). Attacks assumed to cause "grave environmental harm" may need to confer a "very substantial military advantage" to be considered legitimate.[111] The principle implies at least a duty to minimize environmental damage in warfare conduct or planning,[112] such as listing targets and those to be avoided[113] and estimating collateral damage including environmental, based on computer simulation, geospatial and human analysis.[114]

105 ICRC, Customary IHL Practice Proportionality in attack

106 The Independent International Commission of Inquiry, *Report on the Occupied Palestinian Territory, including East Jerusalem, and Israel, A/HRC/56/26, (Advance unedited version)* (2024) par.45, 79, 83, 98

107 ICRC, Guidelines Rule 7, par.114; ICRC, Customary IHL Rules Rule 43C; ILC, Environment Protection Principles Principle 14

108 Schmitt 56

109 *Nuclear Weapons* par.30

110 The Committee Established to Review the NATO Bombing Campaign against the Federal Republic of Yugoslavia, *Final Report to the Prosecutor* (2000) par.18, 20; AP/I art.51.5(b), art.55

111 The Committee Established to Review the NATO Bombing Campaign against the Federal Republic of Yugoslavia, *Final Report to the Prosecutor* (2000) par.22

112 Richard Desgagné, 'The Prevention of Environmental Damage in Time of Armed Conflict: Proportionality and Precautionary Measures' 3 YB Int'l H L (2000) 117

113 GardamNecessity, Proportionality and the Use of Force by States 21, Colin Kahl, 'How We fight' 85 Foreign Affairs 6 (2006) 86

114 Kahl 90; Helen Obregón Gieseken and Vanessa Murphy, 'The Protection of the Natural Environment under International Humanitarian Law: The ICRC's 2020 Guidelines' 105 IRRC 924 (2023) 1180, 1183

3. Military necessity

Military necessity requires that belligerents apply only the amount of force and use combat methods or means necessary to achieve the purpose of war which is "to weaken the military forces of the enemy,"[115] as quickly as possible and with the least cost to lives and property.[116] Therefore, belligerents' right to choose warfare methods or means is not unlimited.[117] This is deemed a "conceptual basis for environmental prescriptions."[118] Military necessity cannot be used to derogate from a formal prohibition or norm under the LOAC or to seek a military advantage using forbidden means,[119] unless expressly provided in the norm itself[120] or to justify use of warfare methods in violation of AP/I provisions.[121] Destruction of property, including the environment, is prohibited unless required by military necessity,[122] though the prohibition regarding environmental damage that reaches AP/I's threshold is absolute and cannot be overcome by military necessity considerations.[123]

The Nuremberg Military Tribunal scrutinized the scorched earth policy conducted in a Norwegian province by Rendulic, a German army commander, under orders for civilians evacuation and total destruction of the area, including homes, food supplies, livestock and natural resources.[124] Rendulic was found not guilty of the charge of wanton destruction of private and public property under the Hague Regulations article 23(g), the tribunal concluding that his decision that there was "military necessity" for the decision of evacuation to be taken may have been faulty but not criminal.[125]

4. Humanity principle

In cases not covered by AP/I or by other international agreements, the Martens clause provides that "civilians and combatants remain under the protection and

115 St Petersburg Declaration Preamble
116 Oeter Introductory remarks, par.2. Fenrick 93. ICRC AP/I Commentary art.35.1 par.1389
117 Hague Regulations art.22; AP/I art.35.1
118 Schmitt 63
119 Christopher Greenwood, 'Historical Development and Legal Basis' in Dieter Fleck (ed), *The Handbook of International Humanitarian Law* (2nd edn, OUP 2008) section 132
120 Fenrick 82; Green 147 ICRC AP/I Commentary art.35.1 par.1390
121 Mollard-Bannelier 82; Jensen 178; Schmitt 72
122 Hague Regulations art.23(g); GC VI article 53; ICRC, Customary IHL Rules Rule 43.B
123 Michael Bothe, 'Protection of the Environment in Relation to Armed Conflicts' in Dieter Fleck (ed), *The Handbook of International Humanitarian Law* (4th edn, OUP 2021) 10.06 par.3
124 *The Hostage Case, Indictment, Nuremberg Trial Transcripts* (The University of North Dakota, Chester Fritz Library, Centre for Human Rights and Genocide Studies Collections)Indictment, Count 2, par.9a
125 *United States v. Wilhelm List et al., (the Hostages Trial), 8th July 1947 to 19th February 1948* UN War Crimes Commission, Law Reports of Trials of War Criminals, vol VIII, 34 (US MTN)

authority of the principles of international law derived from established custom, from the principles of humanity and from the dictates of public conscience."[126] This humanitarian principle aims to ensure that populations and belligerents engaged in armed conflicts are not submitted to arbitrary judgement of military commanders, in cases of unforeseen circumstances or unwritten rules, but they remain protected by international law principles.[127]

Sands advances that "in modern international law, there is no reason why these [humanitarian principles] should not encompass environmental protection."[128] It seems a step too far to englobe the environment under a concept "understood in terms of humane treatment and mercy" for people.[129] However, considerations of health and survival of the population weigh on environmental protection.[130] In 2000, a recommendation to UN Member States to endorse a "Martens clause for environmental protection" applicable during peacetime and armed conflicts[131] was adopted by consensus at the International Union for Conservation of Nature ("IUCN") World Conservation Congress, composed of about a thousand NGOs and more than 200 States and Government Agencies, with only the United States and its Agency Members abstaining.[132] In a "progressive development,"[133] the ILC and doctrine consider the Martens Clause applicable to environmental protection during armed conflicts,[134] even including IEL "soft law" within established custom.[135]

Cynics might wonder whether "principles of humanity" and "dictates of public conscience" have ever existed during armed conflicts or are just lofty ideals inserted in the LOAC to give it some moral veneer. Though these notions enshrined in the Hague Regulations of 1899[136] were reiterated in the text of 1907,[137] historians would be hard pressed to find "humanity" in the armed conflicts that have punctuated the past century since the adoption of the Regulations, whether in the horrors of the two world wars, the Vietnam War, the Korean war or the conflict

126 AP/I art.1.2 Hague Regulations Preamble Convention (II) with Respect to the Laws and Customs of War on Land and its annex: Regulations concerning the Laws and Customs of War on Land, The Hague, 29 July 1899 Preamble.

127 Green 20

128 Philippe Sands, Jacqueline Peel, Adriana Fabra, and Ruth MacKenzie, *Principles of International Environmental Law* (4th edn, CUP 2018) 792

129 May 53.

130 AP/I art.55

131 IUCN World Conservation Congress, Amman, Jordan, 4–11 October 2000, *Resolutions and Recommendations* 105

132 IUCN, 'Who Are Our Members?' accessed 28 April 2015

133 Daniëlla Dam-de Jong and Britta Sjöstedt, 'Enhancing Environmental Protection in Relation to Armed Conflict: An Assessment of the ILC Draft Principles' 44 Loy LA Int'l Comp L Rev 2 (2021) 129, 144

134 ILC, Environment Protection Principles, Principle 12

135 Bothe par.10.10

136 Hague Regulations 1899, Preamble

137 Hague Regulations 1907, Preamble

in Afghanistan, to name but a few. It seems grossly indecent to speak of environmental protection under public conscience when it does not manifest itself regarding human beings, in armed conflicts conducted in violation of the LOAC. Today there are 110 armed conflicts around the world, most of them NIAC,[138] leaving the international community powerless or unable to intervene, despite their devastating impact on the population.[139] Such is the nature of the subject of LOAC. Other States' obligations under diverse LOAC conventions may help to strengthen environmental protection in armed conflict.

II. LOAC treaties environmental obligations

1. ENMOD

Under ENMOD, each signatory "undertakes not to engage in military or any other hostile use of environmental modifications techniques having widespread, long-lasting or severe effects as the means of destruction, damage or injury to any other state Party."[140] Any technique used for changing the environment "through the deliberate manipulation of natural processes" is prohibited. The environment is defined in a wide sense: "the dynamics, composition or structure of the Earth, including its biota, lithosphere, hydrosphere and atmosphere, or of outer space."[141] Despite ENMOD's unsettled customary status, there is sufficient widespread State practice for the ICRC to conclude that destruction of the natural environment may not be used as a weapon, a principle recognized by the ILC.[142]

"Widespread, long-lasting, or severe" are not cumulative. They mean:

> "(a) "widespread": encompassing an area on the scale of several hundred square kilometres (km^2); (b) "long-lasting": lasting for a period of months, or approximately a season; (c) "severe": involving serious or significant disruption or harm to human life, natural and economic resources or other assets."[143]

This interpretation is intended exclusively for ENMOD and does not prejudice the interpretation of the same or similar terms used in AP/I.[144] However, participants

138 Geneva Academy online, Today's Armed Conflicts

139 International Organization for Migration, 'Sudan Internal Displacement Set to Top 10 Million as Famine Looms, 6 June 2024'

140 Convention on the Prohibition of Military or Any Other Hostile Use of Environmental Modification Techniques, 10 December 1976 ("ENMOD") art.I

141 ENMOD art. II

142 ICRC, Customary IHL Rules Rule 45, Commentary, pp. 155–156; ILC, Environment Protection Principles

143 ENMOD, Understandings regarding the Convention

144 UNGA, *Report of the Conference of the Committee on Disarmament, 1976, A/31/27*, Vol. I, 91–92

at the Conference negotiating the Additional Protocols ("CDDH"),[145] the Conference of the Committee on Disarmament ("CDD") on ENMOD Convention and the Ad Hoc Committee on Conventional Weapons[146] deemed important harmonization efforts on the notion of environmental damage under ENMOD and draft AP/I articles 33.3 (current article 35.3), 48bis and 49bis (current article 55).[147] At the CDDH, it was considered that an amendment to article 49bis prohibiting any action detrimental to the environment, in international armed conflicts,[148] "embodied the same concept" as the proposed ENMOD Convention.[149] It could suggest that the same interpretation applies.

2. *Additional protocol I*

AP/I article 35.3 (section methods and means of warfare), prohibits

> "to employ methods or means of warfare which are intended, or may be expected, to cause widespread, long-term and severe damage to the natural environment."

Article 55.1 (section civilian objects) provides that

> "care shall be taken in warfare to protect the natural environment against widespread, long-term and severe damage. This protection includes a prohibition of the use of methods or means of warfare which are intended or may be expected to cause such damage to the natural environment and thereby to prejudice the health or survival of the population."

Reflecting the division within the Working Group at the CDDH,[150] the environment is protected for itself (intrinsic approach) in AP/I article 35.3, while being protected insofar as its damage affects the population (anthropocentric perspective) in article 55.1 (second sentence).[151]

Under the intrinsic perspective adopted by the ICRC, there is no "grey zone" where parts of the environment, such as a bush in a desert, are neither military

145 Diplomatic Conference on the Reaffirmation and Development of International Humanitarian Law Applicable in Armed Conflicts (1974–1977)

146 Its work led to the adoption of the Convention on Prohibitions or Restrictions on the Use of Certain Conventional Weapons which may be deemed to be Excessively Injurious or to have Indiscriminate Effects of 10 October 1980 ("CCW")

147 UNGA Report of the Conference of the Committee on Disarmament, 1976, A/31/27, Vol. II, 12

148 *Official Records CDDH*, Vol. XIV, 171, par.2 (CDDH/III/SR.20)

149 Ibid, 171 par.3, 172 par.5, 173 par.10 and 15 (CDDH/III/SR.20)

150 Ibid, 358–359 (CDDH/III/275)

151 Schmitt 70; Wil D. Verwey, 'Protection of the Environment in Times of Armed Conflict: in Search of a New Legal Perspective' 8 Leiden J Int'l L 1 (1995) 7, 13; Mollard-Bannelier 81; David Guillard, *Les armes de guerre et l'environnement naturel* (L'Harmattan 2006) 59; Jensen 169 Stephanie N. Simonds, 'Conventional Warfare and Environmental Protection: A Proposal for International Legal Reform' 29 Stanf J Int'l L (1992–1993) 165, 173

objective nor civilian because they are not used by civilians.[152] Yet, given the complex links between environment and human health, it would be "scientifically unsound" not to consider that environmental damage will not foreseeably impact health or survival of the population.[153] According to the anthropocentric view, areas not used by civilians are not necessarily civilian objects and therefore cannot benefit from protection under IHL principles.[154] However, nothing in the definition of civilian objects under AP/I requires the use of part of the environment by civilians for it to be considered a civilian object protected as such. Civilian objects are defined negatively as "all objects which are not military objectives."[155]

The status of these provisions has evolved. In 1996, the ICJ found that the obligation of environmental protection and prohibition related to warfare means "are powerful constraints for all the States having subscribed to these provisions,"[156] though they have not replaced general customary rules applicable to all means and methods of combat.[157] The final report to the Prosecutor of the ICTY, in 2000, noted that though the USA and France have not signed AP/I, article 55 "may nevertheless reflect current customary law."[158] Yet while including the prohibition on environmental damage in their military manuals,[159] the USA, UK and France deny that the rule has customary status,[160] with the USA characterizing the provisions as "overly broad and ambiguous."[161] As the ICC adopted its Statute in 1998 which includes a war crime of environmental damage in similar terms to AP/I and France acceded to the latter in 2001, obligations under articles 35.3 and 55 "may now reflect a rule of customary international law."[162] The ICRC considers this rule "as a norm of customary international law applicable in international, and arguably also in non-international, armed conflicts."[163] At the least, State practice in its Customary IHL Study "demonstrates wide acceptance of the prohibition,"[164] though some find that practice has

152 ICRC, Guidelines par.19, 21
153 Helen Obregón Gieseken and Murphy 1190
154 ICRC, Guidelines par.19, 21
155 AP/I art.52.1, 52.2
156 *Nuclear Weapons* par.31
157 Ibid, par.84
158 The Committee Established to Review the NATO Bombing Campaign against the Federal Republic of Yugoslavia par.15
159 ICRC, Customary IHL Practice Chap. 14, 880, par.170 (France) and 882, par.184 (UK)
160 Iain Scobbie, 'The Approach to Customary International Law in the Study' in Elizabeth Wilmshurt and Susan Breau (eds), *Perspectives on the ICRC Study on Customary International Humanitarian Law* (1st edn, Chatham House and BIICL 2007) 35; John B. Bellinger III, Legal Adviser, U.S. Department of State and William J. Haynes, General Counsel, U.S. Department of Defense, *Illustrative Comments on Specific Rules in the Customary International Humanitarian Law Study, Annex to the Letter of November 3, 2006 to Dr. Jakob Kellenberger, President of the International Committee of the Red Cross* 7 ICRC, Customary IHL Practice Chap.14
161 U.S. DoD, *Law of War Manual, June 2015, updated December 2016* p. 378, par.6.10.3.1
162 Sands 835
163 ICRC, Customary IHL Rules Rule 45; ICRC, Guidelines Rule 2, par.47
164 ICRC, Customary IHL Practice Chap. 14; Karen Hulme, 'Natural Environment' in Elizabeth Wilmshurt and Susan Breau (eds), *Perspectives on the ICRC Study on Customary International Humanitarian Law* (1st edn, Chatham House and BIICL 2007) 232

not codified into a legally binding rule and the regime is still evolving.[165] Finally, the ILC has coopted both articles in its Principle 13.[166]

Under the AP/I section on civilian objects, those indispensable to survival of the population or releasing dangerous forces are protected from attacks unless they become military objectives.[167] As the environment is not subject to a similar exception under article 55, protection from attacks is unconditional even if the environment is deemed a military object.[168] However, the *travaux préparatoires* discussed the threshold of environmental damage under AP/I resulting from attacks, therefore implying that attacks are permissible when damage is below it. Environmental resources can sustain collateral damage.[169] The standard of conduct and notion of environmental damage need analysis.

2.1 Standard of conduct

It is determined from the terms "which are intended, or may be expected to." "Intent,"[170] "hostile intent"[171] or "intention or expectation to cause damage"[172] seem obvious meanings. Depending on the case, criminal intent (*mens rea*) will be either intent or "constructive intent," with reference to be made to the notion of intent under UK criminal law and its definition in article 30 of the ICC Statute.[173] Boisson de Chazournes notes that proof of intent to cause environmental damage is required for a war crime under ICC Statute article 8(2)(b)(iv) "intentionally launching an attack in the knowledge that such attack," in addition to AP/I articles 35.3 and 55 and ENMOD requirements.[174] A contrario, the notion of intent is absent thereunder.

Alternatively, the terms mean "which are known to cause damage"[175] or imply some prior knowledge of possible detrimental effects of means and methods

165 Cymie R. Payne, 'Chapter 2, Defining the Environment, Environmental Integrity' in Carsten Stahn, Jens Iverson, and Jennifer S. Easterday (eds), *Environmental Protection and Transitions from Conflict to Peace, Clarifying Norms, Principles, and Practices* (OUP 2017) 46

166 ILC, Environment Protection Principles Principle 13

167 AP/I art.54, 56

168 Erik Koppe, *The Use of Nuclear Weapons and the Protection of the Environment during International Armed Conflict* (Hart Publishing Ltd. 2008) 151; Michael Bothe, 'The Protection of the Environment in Times of Armed Conflict; Legal Rules, Uncertainty, Deficiencies and Possible Developments' 34 German YB Int'l L (1991) 54, 56.

169 Oeter Introductory remarks, par.6

170 Christopher Joyner and James Kirhope, 'The Persian Gulf War Oil Spill: Reassessing the Law of Environmental Protection and the Law of Armed Conflict' 24 Case W Res J Int'l L 1, Winter (1992) 39

171 Huston Meredith DuBarry, 'Wartime Environmental Damages: Financing the Cleanup' 23 Univ Pa J Int'l Econ L (2002) 899

172 Dinstein par.822

173 Hulme, *War Torn Environment* 73–80

174 Laurence Boisson de Chazournes, *La Protection Internationale de l'Environnement* (Ed. Pedone 2005) 642–643

175 Verwey 11; Desgagné 117

chosen.[176] "NATO's knowledge as to the nature of the industrial targets, the likelihood of environmental damage" was a relevant element on which the ICTY did not have enough information.[177] However, a knowledge standard is doubtful, given the scientific uncertainty surrounding interactive natural processes; an apparently short-term environmental damage may result in future harmful effects previously unrecognized or unexpected.[178] "May be expected" leads to a subjective "should have known" standard that will be used to judge commanders for war crime of excessive collateral environmental damage.[179] If a commander knew (or reasonably could have known) that an attack on a legitimate military target would result incidentally in the burning of a nearby forest but in no way desired this outcome, it is "an unintended yet foreseeable consequence of his military decision."[180] "Mere foreseeability of this type of harm resulting, but not the intent to cause that harm, is required for an action to constitute a violation of the prohibition" of AP/I article 35.3.[181]

Finally, "the issue here is the effect an act has on the environment, not the means or methods or even the intention of the actors."[182] Protecting the environment "from the effects of hostilities" is the concern of AP/I and the effects of attacking certain types of military objectives such as nuclear submarines or super tankers, or of using certain warfare means, such as herbicides or chemical agents, should be considered.[183] The type of environment should be considered. More vulnerable environments may require additional protection, such as rare or fragile marine ecosystems.[184] A mine exploding in the desert has a different environmental impact than an explosion in the Artic.[185]

Interpretations are confusingly diverse. As both AP/I English and French texts are authentic,[186] the French version can be referred to.[187] The original French text of the ICRC Commentary on Additional Protocols was translated into English.[188] Under its commentary on articles 35.3 and 55, "*toute méthode et tout moyen de guerre conçus pour causer ou, même si ce n'est pas leur but,*" is translated as

176 Koppe 152
177 Desgagné 117
178 Verwey 12
179 Schmitt 72
180 Gregory Reichberg and Henrik Syse, 'Protecting the Environment in Wartime: Ethical Considerations from the Just War Tradition' 37 J Peace Res 4 (2000) 449, 459
181 David E. Mosher and others, *Green Warriors, Army Environmental Considerations for Contingency Operations from Planning Through Post-Conflict* (2008) iii
182 Jensen 161–162
183 UK joint manual par.5.29.1 and 5.29.3
184 Michaela S. Halpern, 'Protecting Vulnerable Environments in Armed Conflict: Deficiencies in International Humanitarian Law' 51 Stanf J Int'l L 2 (2015) 123–124; *San Remo Manual on International Law Applicable to Armed Conflicts at Sea, 1994* Part I, section IV, art.11
185 Halpern 123
186 AP/I art.102
187 See Chapter 1 paragraph on interpretation of treaties
188 ICRC AP/I Commentary, Editors' note

"any method or means of warfare which are planned to cause, or may be expected (albeit without the intention),"[189] and "*l'arme géophysique, exclusivement destinée à agir . . . sur le climat*" as "geophysical weapons, exclusively intended to affect . . . the climate."[190] *Conçus*, *leur but* and *destinée* qualify the design and purpose of the weapons and not the intention of belligerents. When authentic texts differ, interpretation should reconcile them,[191] failing which the clearer text should be used to interpret the more obscure version.[192] As such the French version of AP/I, and its Commentary should be given prominence. The word "*conçu*" in the French Civil Code, when used to qualify work or equipment,[193] is translated as "designed" in the English version published by the French State. The translations have no legal value and are for informational purposes,[194] yet, emanating from official authority, they carry weight. Therefore, warfare means and methods "*conçus pour causer*" mean weapons "designed" to cause damage. Doctrine agrees, finding that articles 35.3 and 55.1 refer to "rather less conventional modes of warfare, such as the use of herbicides or other methods or means specifically designed to damage the environment,"[195] including geophysical and chemical means.[196] The clause "care shall be taken" of article 55.1 addresses "situations involving methods or means not designed to damage the environment."[197] "Expected" relates to collateral environmental damage caused by large scale use of conventional weapons, affecting vast land areas, whether populated or not.[198] According to the US, France and the UK the rule does not apply to nuclear weapons.[199]

Though the use of non-conventional warfare means, under AP/I articles 35.3 and 55.1 (second sentence), may support an intention to cause environmental damage, intent is not a requirement characterizing the standard of conduct for violation of obligations. The ICRC views article 35.3 as a prohibition of result, as the "prohibition relating to the results produced, though not directly a prohibition on the means" under article 35.2.[200] Nonetheless, it is advanced that obligations under both provisions are obligations of conduct, meaning that States have an obligation not to use certain warfare means that will lead to a foreseeable environmental

189 ICRC AP/I Commentary, Editors' note par.1440
190 Ibid, Editors' note, par.1458
191 VCLT art.33.4
192 Jean Hardy, 'The Interpretation of Plurilingual Treaties by International Courts and Tribunals' 37 Brit YB Int'l L 1961 150–151
193 République Française, Code Civil art.1792–4
194 République Française, Légifrance, le Service Public de la Diffusion du Droit
195 Kalshoven 130. Rogers 57
196 ICRC AP/I Commentary, art.35.3, par.1458, 1462
197 Schmitt 73
198 ICRC par.1458, 1462
199 ICRC, Customary IHL Practice Chap.14, 882–883, par.185,896, par.269 (US), 882, par.184, 894, par.262 (UK); See France's reservation, deposited on 11 April 2001, paragraph 2 and United Kingdom's declaration, deposited on 28 January 1998 paragraph (a), on ratification of AP/I (ICRC website).
200 ICRC AP/I Commentary, art.35.2, par.1430

damage. It is similar to the due diligence obligation under IEL requiring States to take measures to prevent transboundary environmental damage. Equally, obligations requiring care to be taken to protect the environment under AP/I article 55.1 (first sentence), overlapping with the obligation to spare the environment as civilian object under AP/I article 57.1, are obligations of conduct.[201] A duty of care, which is a legal obligation to adhere to a reasonable care standard while performing acts that could foreseeably harm others or to act with prudence and vigilance to prevent any risk of foreseeable damage, is an obligation of means (or of conduct) as opposed to obligations of result.[202]

2.2 *Environmental damage*

2.2.1 NOTION OF ENVIRONMENTAL DAMAGE

Different terms were suggested under AP/I article 33.3, to prohibit warfare means and methods, which destroy the natural conditions of the human environment[203] or "disturb or alter the ecological balance of the human environment,"[204] and amendments to article 48bis included prohibition "to despoil the natural environment,"[205] "to impair or destroy" it[206] or introduce "irreparable damage."[207] "Harm to the environment disturbing the stability of the ecosystem," suggested by the "Group Biotope" set up to assist the Working Group[208] and the Committee III's Rapporteur,[209] was rejected, as the meaning of ecosystem was unclear.[210] At the next CDDH session, the Rapporteur would submit a completely different proposal, identical to the current prohibition of article 55,[211] influenced by the US-USSR joint submission of a draft ENMOD Convention.[212]

2.2.2 THRESHOLD OF ENVIRONMENTAL DAMAGE

"Widespread, long-term and severe" are not defined and have generated much debate. The threshold's requirements seem almost impossible to attain, due to its

201 Karen Hulme, 'Taking Care to Protect the Environment against Damage' 92 IRRC 879 (2010) 675, 679, 687
202 ICRC, 'ICRC Duty of Care: Elements of Definition'
203 *Official Records CDDH,* Vol. III, 155 (CDDH/III/108), 157 (CDDH/III/238)
204 Ibid, Vol. III, 156 (CDDH/III/225)
205 Ibid, Vol. III, 220 (CDDH/III/60)
206 Ibid, Vol. III, 221 (CDDH/III/64)
207 Ibid, Vol. XIV, 173 par.18 (CDDH/III/SR.20)
208 Howard S. Levie, *Protection of War Victims: Protocol 1 to the 1949 Geneva Conventions* (Oceana Publications 1979–1985), vol. III, 268, CDDH/III/GT/35
209 Ibid
210 *Official Records CDDH*, Vol. XV, 359
211 Levie 270
212 *Official Records CDDH*, Vol. III, xiv comparative table of titles of articles; UNGA, Vol. I, 61 (A/31/27); ICRC AP/I Commentary art.35, par.1447, n.99

cumulative conditions and imprecision of its terms.[213] No environmental damage from armed conflict was deemed to have reached it. In the first Gulf War, "a case involving near-universal condemnation of the resulting environmental destruction,"[214] the issue proved difficult to resolve.[215] Despite the release in the Gulf of between seven and nine million barrels of oil and the sabotage of 590 oil well heads and setting of 508 oil wells on fire,[216] "the consensus is that Iraq would not have violated it" (the threshold).[217] Assuming oil spills were widespread and severe, they would not "be long-term in the sense of their effects lasting decades."[218] Equally, NATO's attacks on a petrochemical complex at Pancevo, Kosovo, releasing stored toxic chemicals into the air and water causing pollution threatening human health, did not attain the threshold of environmental damage required because of the difficulty of building a prima facie case under articles 35.3 and 55,[219] in "a step back to a pre-Gulf standard" and away from greater accountability for environmental damage during wartime.[220] The US does not accept "this absolute ceiling of permissible destruction" and follows a traditional proportionality analysis, balancing military necessity and expected military advantage,[221] which would better serve the environment.[222] Scholars question the classical interpretation of the threshold. It is unclear whether it lost its relevance.[223] It needs to be determined.

The intertemporal character of international law requires interpretation of rules according to contemporaneous law as it existed when they were established, accounting for non-retroactivity of international law norms and unavoidably an evolutionary interpretation of international law rules that must adapt to ever-changing societies.[224] When a treaty refers to a concept without defining it, its interpretation according to international law applicable between the parties must determine whether the concept should be understood at the time it was drawn

213 Schmitt 4; Mara Tignino, *Water during and after Armed Conflicts: What Protection under International Law?* (Brill 2016) 20, 22
214 Schmitt 108
215 Mollard-Bannelier 94
216 Schmitt 18 and 19 Mollard-Bannelier 94
217 Luan Low and David Hodgkinson, 'Compensation for Wartime Environmental Damage: Challenges to International Law after the Gulf War' 35 Va J Int'l L (1994–1995) 429
218 Glen Plant, 'Legal Aspects of Marine Pollution during the Gulf War' 7 IJECL 3 (1992) 217, 226
219 The Committee Established to Review the NATO Bombing Campaign against the Federal Republic of Yugoslavia par.15 and 17
220 Aaron Schwabach, 'NATO's War in Kosovo and the Final Report to the Prosecutor of the ICTY' 9 Tul J Int'l Comp L (2001) 167, 175
221 National Security Law Department, The Judge Advocate General's Legal Center and School, *The Operational Law Handbook* (2021) 444, par.7a
222 Schmitt 108
223 Bothe and others 576
224 Mieke van der Linden, 'The Inextricable Connection between Historical Consciousness and International Law: New Imperialism, the International Court of Justice and Its Interpretation of the Inter-temporal Rule, Conference Paper No. 2/2014' (ESIL) 5–6

up or at the time of its application.[225] Terms in a treaty which are "evolutionary" and description of obligations in general terms point out that parties intended that future developments be taken into account.[226] Since adoption of AP/I, our understanding of the environment evolved, influenced by scientific and economic developments.[227] Constant increase in weapons' destructive powers and introduction of new forms of warfare lead to a reassessment of acceptable levels of environmental damage.[228] Rejecting the interpretation of the 1970s and viewing the text under an evolving interpretation, in light of current military capabilities and scientific and technical information, is a better-suited approach to environmental protection.[229]

Though the threshold was extensively discussed at the CDDH,[230] the reports contain little on the terms' intended meaning[231] or the Working Group discussions.[232] Some considered that duration should be measured in decades, referring to 20 or 30 years. For the Biotope Group, the intention was not to prohibit warfare acts, such as artillery bombardments which cause short-term environmental damage, and the period referred to may be ten years or more. The Committee noted that there was uncertainty about the period involved.[233] By contrast, the Rapporteur commented that "the population might be that of today or tomorrow, in the sense that both short-term and long-term survival was contemplated,"[234] in observations unapproved by the Working Group.[235] There is no other reference to a time period in the official records.[236] These few comments cannot constitute, as claimed, "*substantial* grounds, including from the *travaux préparatoires*, for interpreting long-term as decades."[237] Therefore, this interpretation "is not necessarily generally accepted nowadays," though admittedly parties to the treaty intended to establish a very high threshold.[238]

225 IDI, *The Intertemporal Problem in Public International Law* (Wiesbaden, 1975) par.4

226 ILC, *Fragmentation of International Law: Difficulties Arising from the Diversification and Expansion of International Law, Report of the Study Group of the ILC, (A/CN.4/L.682)* (2006) par.478; *WTO Appelate Body, United States – Import Prohibition of Certain Shrimp and Shrimp Products* WT/DS58/AB/R, DSR 1998:VII, 2793 par.130

227 Sands 13

228 Belt Walters, 'Missiles over Kosovo: Emergence, Lex Lata, of a Customary Norm Requiring the Use of Precision Munitions in Urban Areas' 47 Naval L Rev (2000) 157

229 Payne 62; Desgagné 112

230 Koppe 170; *Official Records CDDH*, Vol. XV, 268

231 Schmitt 71

232 *Official Records CDDH*, Vol. V, 343, par.34 (CDDH/SR.29)

233 Ibid, Vol. XV, 268–269, par.27 (CDDH/215/Rev.1); Levie, Vol. II, 276–277, par.27

234 Ibid, Vol. XV, 360 (CDDH/III/275)

235 Ibid, Vol. XV, 258 (CDDH/III/275)

236 Schmitt 71

237 Alexandre Kiss, 'Les Protocoles additionnels aux Conventions de Geneve de 1977 et la protection de biens de l'environnement' in Christophe Swinarski and International Committee of the Red Cross (eds), *Studies and Essays on International Humanitarian Law and Red Cross Principles in Honour of Jean Pictet* (Martinus Nijhoff Publishers 1984) 189

238 Bothe and others 576

The UNCC granted Kuwait, in 2001, compensation for monitoring programmes to assess long-term impacts from damaged oil wells on its marine environment during five years[239] and on groundwater aquifers for ten years.[240] It considered these periods of 15 and 20 years respectively, after the end of the war, "long-term," though no reference was made to AP/I articles 35.3 or 55.[241] That does not mean that long-term should be minimum 15 or 20 years, as the UNCC was unable to decide on these compensation claims earlier. Requiring that the environment remains damaged during decades before acknowledging it is damaged is a curious way to protect it. Given that damage to natural resources used by the civilian population, such as water and land, affects its health and survival, that a fundamental human right to water is protected under IHRL and that a right to a healthy environment was recognized by UN institutions,[242] long-term cannot be anymore interpreted as decades, ignoring such considerations. Consequently, it could be understood as in ENMOD or relatively higher.

There is no indication concerning the meaning of "severe" and "widespread" in the CDDH reports.[243] Severe may refer to "damage that is of great intensity in a small confined area" or "damage of a lower intensity over a large area."[244] It could be interpreted in accordance with the understandings of ENMOD[245] or "explained by Article 55's reference to any act that 'prejudices the health or survival of the population.'"[246] Plant proposed the adoption of a harm threshold that "might usefully reflect variations in the susceptibility of different regional marine ecologies to pollution."[247] Severity of damage depends on the environment, biotic or abiotic – and environmental resources damaged – as the rate of potential recovery differs accordingly. Military activities affect differently each environment; the threshold should be then viewed in the context of the environment damaged,[248] which was the idea behind a proposal for a Geneva Convention with different Protocols.[249]

"Widespread" was considered higher under AP/I than under ENMOD. Regarding its lower limit, "the minimum definition possible" should be adopted to avoid arbitrariness and "widespread" interpreted as "a minimum of "X hundred km^2"

239 UNCC, *Report and Recommendations made by the Panel of Commissioners Concerning the First Installment of "F4" Claims, S/AC.26/2001/16* (2001) par.411
240 Ibid, *S/AC.26/2001/16* (2001) par.396–398
241 Ibid, *S/AC.26/2001/16* (2001) par.40, 412
242 UNHRC, *Res. 48/13* (2021). UNGA, *Res. 76/300, 28 July* (2022)
243 Mollard-Bannelier 91; Schmitt 71
244 Hulme, *War Torn Environment* 98.
245 Schmitt 108
246 National Security Law Department 444, par.7b
247 Plant 230
248 Desgagné 112; ICRC, *Contributions to the Rio Conference, Protection of the Natural Environment in Time of Armed Conflict* (1992); Halpern 123
249 Michael A. Meyer, 'A Definition of the "Environment"' in Glen Plant (ed), *Environmental Protection and the Law of War: A Fifth Geneva Convention on the Protection of the Environment in the Time of Armed Conflict* (Belhaven Press 1992) App.6

where X is above ENMOD's "several hundred km^2."[250] As the US and USSR proposed together an identical draft ENMOD Convention which influenced the terms of AP/I threshold,[251] their intention should be considered. The US interprets "widespread" under AP/I as probably meaning several hundred km^2 as in ENMOD.[252] Therefore an area of 999 km^2, which is the maximum of "several hundred km^2," could be considered as the maximum of the lower limit of widespread. Multiple countries party to AP/I have a territory of an area inferior to one thousand km^2.[253] The criterion of several hundred km^2 cannot apply to them, or they will disappear into oblivion. A treaty's clauses should be interpreted in view of its purposes. Provisions on an environmental damage threshold cannot mean that countries may be annihilated. Whatever number of square metres is retained, many countries will be adversely affected in a significant way, while others will sustain an insignificant damage. Therefore, "widespread" cannot correspond to a specified area of damage applicable to all. It could be interpreted in a relative sense, in proportion to the area of the country concerned.

An estimate of what 999 km^2 means for Russia today (previously USSR) and the US is useful. Compared to their geographical areas, 999 km^2 corresponds to 0.0044 percent of Russia's territory (17.09 million km^2) and 0.011 of the USA's (9 million km^2) and to 38.63 percent of Luxemburg's territory (2,586 km^2).[254] In that sense, Witteler argues that damage that would obliterate Luxemburg would hardly be noticed in Russia.[255] The lower limit of a permissible damaged area should then be less than one percent of any country's territory, as that was the intent of both proponents of ENMOD threshold. As to its higher limit, the 20,200 km^2 of environmental damage in Vietnam caused by the war corresponding approximately to 6 percent of the total area of the country (331,689 km^2) was considered a maximum area of permissible damage during the *travaux préparatoires*. That 6 percent could be retained as a maximum threshold, though it is not without complications. It is a relatively important area for a small country and it is unapplicable to flowing water resources that are not restricted to a specific area. Alternatively, the US interpretation could be adopted meaning that a widespread area should be under 1 percent of a country's territory.

250 Hulme, *War Torn Environment* 92–93

251 UN Audiovisual Library of International Law, 'ENMOD, procedural history'; UNGA, Report of the Conference of the Committee on Disarmament, 1976, A/31/27 Vol. I, 61 (A/31/27); ICRC AP/I Commentary art.35

252 National Security Law Department 444, par.7b

253 Examples: Antigua and Barbuda, Bahrain, Cook Islands, Dominica, Grenada, Liechtenstein, Maldives, Malta, Micronesia, Monaco Nauru, Palau, San Marino, Sao Tome and Principe, Seychelles, Singapore, St Lucia, Tonga; ICRC, 'States Party to the Following International Humanitarian Law and Other Related Treaties, as of 3rd September 2024'; UN Statistics Division, *Population by sex, rate of population increase, surface area and density*

254 UN Statistics Division; USSR was about 22.4 million km^2, John C. Dewdney and Robert Conquest, 'Soviet Union, Historical State, Eurasia' Encyclopedia Britannica

255 Rogers 219, citing Witteler, Der Krieg im Golf 51

III. LOAC treaties obligations indirectly related to environment

1. Pillage, destruction and seizure

Pillage of a town or place is prohibited.[256] Illegal natural resources exploitation or plunder could be covered under the war crime of pillage, causing economic damage to the country and harm to the environment.[257] Equally, destruction or seizure of property, including the environment and natural resources constituting it, is prohibited unless required by military necessity.[258] There must be a link between destruction of property and overcoming of enemy forces.[259] This prohibition covers public and private property situated in all territory involved in war.[260] Extensive destruction of property unjustified by military necessity and carried out unlawfully and wantonly is a grave breach under GC IV article 147[261] and a violation of the LOAC.[262]

2. Objects indispensable to survival of the population

Scorched earth strategy and population starvation, as warfare methods, are outlawed. AP/I prohibits attack or destruction of objects indispensable to survival, "such as food-stuffs, agricultural areas for the production of food-stuffs, crops, livestock, drinking water installations and supplies and irrigation works" to deny them for sustenance to the civilian population.[263] The liability standard is intent to deny sustenance to population[264] or to harm the population, whether direct intent or recklessness in disregarding the consequences of military actions.[265] The provision indirectly protects "particular ecosystems and any wildlife dependent upon the crops."[266] Objects used solely as sustenance by enemy armed forces or in direct

256 Hague Regulations art.28, GC IV art.33

257 Olivia Radics and Carl Bruch, 'Chapter 6, The Law of Pillage, Conflict Resources, and Jus Post Bellum,' in Carsten-Stahn, Jens Iverson, and Jennifer S. Easterday (eds), *Environmental Protection and Transitions from Conflict to Peace* (OUP 2017) 145–146

258 Hague Regulations art.23(g); ICRC, Customary IHL Rules Rule 50

259 *United States v. Wilhelm List et al., (the Hostages Trial), 8th July 1947 to 19th February 1948*; UN War Crimes Commission, Law Reports of Trials of War Criminals, Vol VIII, 34, US MTN

260 Schmitt 63; Daniëlla Dam-de Jong, *International Law and Governance of Natural Resources in Conflict and Post-Conflict Situations, Doctoral Thesis* (Open Access edn, Meijers 2013) 222; ICRC, *Commentary on the Fourth Geneva Convention* (1958) 301; U.S. DoD 806 par.11.18.2; UK MoD par.11.75, 15.17

261 Also GC I art.50, GC II art.51.

262 ICRC, Guidelines Specific rules on protection of the environment (8)

263 AP/I art.54.1 and Art.54.2

264 Schmitt

265 Daniëlla Dam-de Jong, 'From Engines for Conflict into Engines for Sustainable Development: The Potential of International Law to Address Predatory Exploitation of Natural Resources in Situations of Internal Armed Conflict' 82 Nordic J Int'l L (2013) 155, 163, analysing AP/II art.14 on internal armed conflict, which is the same provision than AP/I article 54

266 Hulme, *War Torn Environment* 117

support of military actions are excluded.[267] The article is customary law applicable to IAC, occupied and non-occupied territory and NIAC.[268] It should be interpreted considering article 1(2) of ICESCR and ICCPR under which a people may not be deprived of its subsistence means. Therefore, valuable natural resources offering an income to the population, such as mines or forests, should be covered under AP/I article 54(2).[269]

Water resources in harsh climate countries, such as rivers, lakes or groundwaters and power plants generating electricity necessary for pumping and purification of drinking water, could arguably be considered indispensable to survival of the population. Attacks on these installations would result in depriving the population of indispensable drinking water and could be included in drinking water installations.[270] They are unlikely to be used solely by armed forces or in support of military operations;[271] even so, attacks should not compel the population to move or starve.[272] Iraqi attacks on Saudi desalination plants may have violated article 54.[273]

The Eritrea Ethiopia Claims Commission held that Ethiopia's targeting, during four days in the Ethiopia-Eritrea armed conflict 1999–2000, a water reservoir situated in a harsh desert region about 17 kilometres from Assab, on the Eastern Front, with the purpose to deprive the city of its water for sustenance, knowing that the reservoir was a vital water source, breached AP/I article 54(2). Eritrea indicated the reservoir served civilians only, was the sole drinking water source for the town and Eritrean armed forces in the area had their own wells and underground storage tanks. AP/I article 54(2) had become customary international law consistent with State practice, even recognized as such by the US who is not a party to AP/I.[274]

The warfare method is exceptionally admitted, if carried out within the territory under its control, by a party to the conflict, if military necessity requires it in defence against invasion.[275] The exception does not exist for a NIAC,[276] where effectiveness of the prohibition is even more dubious, given that international pressure on belligerents is less important and media's access more restricted than in

267 AP/I art.54.3

268 ICRC AP/I Commentary art.54, par.2091, 2097, 2120, 2121; ICRC, Customary IHL Rules Rule 54; *Eritrea-Ethiopia Claims Commission, Partial Award, Western Front, Aerial Bombardment and Related Claims, Eritrea's Claims 1, 3, 5, 9–13, 14, 21, 25 & 26, 19 December 2005* 45 ILM 396 (2006), par.105

269 Daniëlla Dam-de Jong, 'From Engines for Conflict into Engines for Sustainable Development' 163–164

270 Mara Tignino, 'Water, International Peace, and Security' 92 IRRC 879, September (2010) 647 659; Henry Shue and David Wippman, 'Limiting Attacks on Dual-use Facilities Performing Indispensable Civilian Functions' 35 Cornell Int'l L J 2002 573

271 Tignino, *Water during and after Armed Conflicts: What Protection under International Law?* 7; ICRC AP/I Commentary art.54 par.2010

272 ICRC Commentary on AP/I, art.54, par.2107, 2110–2112

273 Laura Edgerton, 'Eco-terrorist Acts during the Persian Gulf War: Is International Law Sufficient to Hold Iraq Liable?' 22 Ga J Int'l Comp L (1992) 151

274 *EECC Western Front* par.98–100, 103–105

275 AP/I art.54.5

276 AP/II art.14

an IAC. Examples abound from Sudan[277] to Sierra Leone where armed groups targeted water supply systems and destroyed crops.[278]

3. *Works and installations containing dangerous forces*

AP/I article 56 prohibits attacks against "works or installations containing dangerous forces, namely dams, dykes and nuclear electrical generating stations, even where these objects are military objectives, if such attack may cause the release of dangerous forces and consequent severe losses among the civilian population." Destruction of dams and dykes by German troops to cause flooding by seawater of agricultural lands and prevent advance of the enemy in the Netherlands during WWII[279] could now breach this article. The list of installations is exhaustive, as it would have not been agreed upon, otherwise.[280] Proposals to include oil production installations and storage facilities were rejected.[281] Consequently, destruction by Iraq and setting alight oil installations in the first Gulf war was not prohibited thereunder but subject to other LOAC provisions including article 55.[282]

The provision was ignored during the Ukraine-Russia armed conflict. At its start, more than 1,000 experts and organizations warned of the "war's potentially catastrophic environmental impacts, which themselves pose both immediate and long-term threats to human rights, health, welfare, and livelihoods" in a country with 15 active nuclear reactors.[283] The Khakova dam in Ukraine was hit by an explosion in June 2023, causing collapse of its wall, destruction of the adjacent hydroelectric plant and flooding that lasted about 14 days, emptying the total volume of the reservoir's water (18km^3) over an area of 630 km^2 later reduced to 40km^2.[284] Russian forces took control of two civil nuclear power plants, Chernobyl and Zaporizhzhia, after attacking them in 2022.[285] Missile strikes hit two radioactive waste facilities in Kiev and Kharkiv.[286]

4. *Precautions in attacks*

Constant care in the conduct of military operations is required to spare civilians and civilian objects.[287] Those planning or deciding on an attack have precautionary duties to ensure that the proposed target is a legitimate military object without any special

277 Steve Bloomfield and Katherine Butler, 'Darfur's Return to Hell, "Scorched Earth" Unleashed on Darfur, despite UN Presence' The Independent (12 March 2008) 1

278 UNEP, *Sierra Leone, Environment, Conflict and Peacebuilding Assessment* (February 2010) 45

279 Schmitt 8

280 ICRC Commentary on AP/I, art.56, par.2147

281 Ibid, art.56, par.2149–2150

282 Ibid, art.56, par.2150

283 Environmental Peacebuilding Association, *Open Letter on the Environmental Dimensions of the Russian Invasion of Ukraine, 3 March 2022*

284 UNEP, *Rapid Environmental Assessment of Kakhovka Dam Breach, Ukraine, 2023* par.2.3, 3.1.1, 3.1.2

285 World Nuclear Association, 'Ukraine: Russia-Ukraine War and Nuclear Energy'

286 IAEA, *IAEA Director General Statement on Situation in Ukraine, 27 Febryary 2022*

287 AP/I art.57.1; ICRC, Customary IHL Rules Rule 15

protection status and to avoid or minimize incidental damage to civilian objects through the choice of means and methods of attack[288] and of military objectives.[289] The rule is considered customary international law,[290] such status being questioned, as it is refused by the US, a most powerful military player.[291] Precautions apply to the environment. The ICRC replaced constant care by "due regard" to environmental protection and preservation, when using warfare means and methods, in its customary study.[292] Though some questioned the status of this new formulation,[293] due regard is a customary law obligation,[294] which threshold is unclear.[295] Practice will tell whether it differs from the "care" obligation of AP/I article 55.1 (first sentence), requiring steps to be taken to protect the environment, such as undertaking impact assessment of attacks.[296]

When considerations regarding the proposed target cannot be respected or attacks are expected to cause excessive environmental damage compared to the anticipated military advantage, they must be cancelled or suspended.[297] Precautions must be "feasible" or practicable in view of existing circumstances.[298] Belligerents may not rely on scientific uncertainty regarding the extent of environmental damage from military operations to absolve themselves from taking precautions in their operations. By introducing the notion of scientific uncertainty, a core element of IEL precautionary principle, to assess potential damage, the ICRC has integrated it with an IHL rule.[299]

5. *Weapons conventions*

To protect civilians from unnecessary suffering, different conventions concerning gases,[300] biological[301] and chemical weapons[302] and anti-personnel mines[303] include obligations prohibiting use of certain weapons or their development, production and stockpiling, which could result indirectly in environmental protection. A convention

288 AP/I art.57(2)(a) (i) and (2)(a)(ii)
289 AP/I art.57.3
290 ICRC, Customary IHL Rules Rule 15, Commentary p. 53 ILC, Environment Protection Principles Principle 14, Commentary par.(8)
291 Biggerstaff and Schmitt 1279
292 ICRC, Customary IHL Rules Rule 44; ICRC, Guidelines Rule 8; ILC, Environment Protection Principles Principle 14
293 Hulme 686
294 Bothe, 'Protection of the Environment in Relation to Armed Conflicts' 10.02, par.1
295 ICRC, Customary IHL Rules Rule 44; Bothe, 'Protection of the Environment in Relation to Armed Conflicts' 10.02 par.1; Hulme 686
296 Hulme 679–680 Bothe, 'Protection of the Environment in Relation to Armed Conflicts' 10.02, par.1
297 AP/I art.57(2)(a)(iii) and (2)(b); ILC, Environment Protection Principles Principle 14, commentary par.(5)
298 ICRC, Customary IHL Rules Rule 15, Commentary p. 54, Rules 16–19
299 Ibid Rule 44, Commentary p. 150
300 Protocol for the prohibition of the use in war of asphyxiating, poisonous or other gases and of bacteriological methods of warfare, Geneva, 17 June 1925.
301 Convention on the prohibition of the development, production and stockpiling of bacteriological (biological) weapons and toxic weapons and on their destruction, 10 April 1972, (in force 26 March 1975).
302 Convention on the prohibition of the development, production and stockpiling and use of chemical weapons and on their destruction, 13 January 1993, (in force 29 April 1997).
303 Convention on the prohibition of the use, stockpiling, production and transfer of anti-personnel mines and on their destruction, 18 September 1997 (in force 1 March 1999).

on cluster munitions contains similar obligations.[304] The prohibition on the use of mines, aimed at protecting civilians, benefits agricultural lands and spares them from being rendered unusable. The Convention on Conventional Weapons ("CCW"), signed in 1980 with three protocols,[305] reiterates in its Preamble the prohibition of AP/I article 35.3. Its third protocol contains a prohibition to attack forests or other plants by incendiary weapons except when such natural elements are used to cover, conceal or camouflage combatants or other military objectives or are themselves military objectives.[306] Of the two protocols adopted later,[307] one focuses on explosive remnants of war, such as land mines legally banned today but still present in many countries' soils. It contains a general obligation of the parties to the conflict to remove or render harmless all mines to protect a UN force sent to the area.[308]

IV. Conclusion

The framework of conduct of hostilities is well established. Despite the imprecision of some of the norms leading to different interpretations by belligerent States, customary principles and conventional obligations related to the environment are constraints regulating military operations during armed conflict that States must respect. They are sufficiently defined to constitute a basis for atttribution of State liability in case of breach and have been clarified by international bodies. A State responsible for violations of its LOAC obligations is under obligation to make reparation,[309] which could be compensation in case of damage to the environment and natural resources composing it. Enforcement of State liability for violations of its obligations related to the conduct of hostilities remains an issue, as it is the case for violations of occupation law, which will be examined in chapter 7. The next chapter examines States' obligations pertaining to environment and natural resources in occupation under the LOAC.

Bibliography

Treaties

Convention (II) with Respect to the Laws and Customs of War on Land and Its Annex: Regulations Concerning the Laws and Customs of War on Land, The Hague, 29 July 1899

304 Eitan Barak, 'Doomed to Be Violated? The US-Israeli Clandestine End-User Agreement and the Second Lebanon War: Lessons for the Convention on Cluster Munitions' 38 Denver J Int'l L Policy (2009) 1, 33; The Convention on Cluster Munitions, Dublin, 30 May 2008, (in force 1 August 2010)

305 Convention on prohibitions or restrictions on the use of certain conventional weapons which may be deemed to be excessively injurious or to have indiscriminate effects, 10 October 1980, (in force 2 December 1983), amended 21 December 2001 (in force 18 May 2004) with three original annexed protocols: (i) Protocol I on Non-Detectable Fragments, (ii) Protocol II on Prohibitions or Restrictions on the Use of Mines, Booby Traps and Other Devices, (amended 3 may 1996, in force 3 December1998) and (iii) Protocol III on Prohibitions or Restrictions on the Use of Incendiary Weapons.

306 Protocol III, art.2.4

307 Protocol IV on Blinding Laser Weapons, 13 October 1995, (in force on 30 July 1998) and Protocol V on Explosive Remnants of War, 28 November 2003 (in force 12 November 2006)

308 Karl Jose Partsch, 'Remnants of War as a Legal Problem in the Light of the Libyan Case' 78 AJIL 2, April (1984) 386, 391

309 Hague Regulations art.3; AP/I art.91

Convention (IV) Respecting the Laws and Customs of War on Land and Its Annex: Regulations Concerning the Laws and Customs of War on Land, the Hague, 18 October 1907
Convention on the Prohibition of Military or Any Other Hostile Use of Environmental Modification Techniques, 10 December 1976
Declaration Renouncing the Use in Time of War of Explosive Projectiles under 400 Grammes Weight, St Petersburg, 1868
Protocol Additional to the Geneva Conventions of 12 August 1949, and relating to the Protection of Victims of International Armed Conflicts (Protocol I), 8 June 1977
Protocol Additional to the Geneva Conventions of 12 August 1949, and relating to the Protection of Victims of Non-International Armed Conflicts (Protocol II), 8 June 1977
San Remo Manual on International Law Applicable to Armed Conflicts at Sea, 1994

International organizations documents

Environmental Peacebuilding Association, *Open Letter on the Environmental Dimensions of the Russian Invasion of Ukraine, 3 March 2022*
IAEA, *IAEA Director General Statement on Situation in Ukraine* (27 February 2022)
ICRC, *Commentary on the Fourth Geneva Convention* (1958)
———, *Commentary on the Protocol Additional to the Geneva Conventions of 12 August 1949, and relating to the Protection of Victims of International Armed Conflicts (Protocol I), 8 June 1977* (Sandoz Y, Swinarski C and Zimmermann B eds, Martinus Nijhoff 1987)
———, *Contributions to the Rio Conference, Protection of the Natural Environment in Time of Armed Conflict* (1992)
———, *Customary International Humanitarian Law, Vol. II Practice* (Henckaerts J-M and Doswald-Beck L eds, CUP 2005)
———, *Customary International Humanitarian Law, Vol. I Rules* (Henckaerts J-M and Doswald-Beck L eds, 3rd edn, CUP 2009)
———, *Guidelines on the Protection of the Natural Environment in Armed Conflict* (2020)
ICRC and Université Laval, *International Experts Meeting, The Principle of Proportionality in the Rules Governing the Conduct of Hostilities under International Humanitarian Law* (2016)
IDI, 'The Distinction between Military Objectives and Non-Military Objectives in General and Particularly the Problems Associated with Weapons of Mass Destruction'
———, *The Intertemporal Problem in Public International Law* (Wiesbaden, 1975)
ILC, *Articles on Responsibility of States for Internationally Wrongful Acts, with Commentary, A/56/10* (ILC YB 2001, vol II (2))
———, *Fragmentation of International Law: Difficulties Arising from the Diversification and Expansion of International Law, Report of the Study Group of the ILC, A/CN.4/L.682* (2006)
———, *Draft Principles on Protection of the Environment in Relation to Armed Conflicts, with Commentaries, A/77/10* (ILC YB 2022, vol II, (2), 2022)
International Conference of the Red Cross V, *Resolution XXVIII, Protection of Civilian Populations against the Dangers of Indiscriminate Warfare* (1965)
IUCN, 'Who Are Our Members?' accessed 28 April 2015
IUCN World Conservation Congress, Amman, Jordan, 4–11 October 2000, *Resolutions and Recommendations*
Levie HS, *Protection of War Victims: Protocol 1 to the 1949 Geneva Conventions* (Oceana Publications 1979–1985)
The Independent International Commission of Inquiry, *Report on the Occupied Palestinian Territory, including East Jerusalem, and Israel, A/HRC/56/26 (Advance unedited version)* (2024)
UN, *Escalating Attacks on Ukraine's Civilian, Energy Infrastructure Making Humanitarian Aid Delivery Even More Dangerous, Relief Chief Tells Security Council, SC/15695* (14 May 2024)

UN Audiovisual Library of International Law, 'ENMOD, Procedural History'
UN Statistics Division, *Population by Sex, Rate of Population Increase, Surface Area and Density*
UNCC, *Report and Recommendations Made by the Panel of Commissioners Concerning the First Installment of "F4" Claims, S/AC.26/2001/16* (2001)
UNEP, *From Conflict to Peacebuilding, The Role of Natural Resources and the Environment* (2009)
———, *Rapid Environmental Assessment of Kakhovka Dam Breach, Ukraine* (2023)
———, *Sierra Leone, Environment, Conflict and Peacebuilding Assessment* (February 2010)
UNGA, *Report of the Conference of the Committee on Disarmament, 1976, A/31/27*
———, *Respect for Human Rights in Armed Conflicts* (Resolution 2444 (XXIII), 1968)
———, *Res. 76/300, 28 July* (2022)
UNHRC, *Res. 48/13* (2021)
World Nuclear Association online, 'Ukraine: Russia-Ukraine War and Nuclear Energy'

National legislation and documents

General Counsel, Department of Defense, *Letter, 22 September 1972, to Senator Edward Kennedy, Chairman, Subcommittee on Refugees of Committee on Judiciary* (67 AJIL 122 1973)
Instructions for the Government of Armies of the United States in the Field (Lieber Code) (1863)
John B. Bellinger III, Legal Adviser, U.S. Department of State and William J. Haynes, General Counsel, U.S. Department of Defense, *Illustrative Comments on Specific Rules in the Customary International Humanitarian Law Study, Annex to the Letter of November 3, 2006 to Dr. Jakob Kellenberger, President of the International Committee of the Red Cross*
Mosher DE and others, *Green Warriors, Army Environmental Considerations for Contingency Operations from Planning Through Post-Conflict* (Rand Arroyo Corporation 2008)
National Security Law Department, The Judge Advocate General's Legal Center and School, *The Operational Law Handbook* (2021)
République Française, Code Civil
UK MoD, *The Joint Service Manual of the Law of Armed Conflict, JSP 383* (2004)
U.S. Department of Veterans Affairs, Environmental Agents Service, *Agent Orange, Information for Veterans Who Served in Vietnam* (2003)
U.S. DoD, *Law of War Manual, June 2015, updated December 2016*

International tribunals decisions and documents

Armed Activities on the Territory of the Congo (DRC v. Uganda), Judgment ICJ Rep 2005, p. 168 (ICJ)
Eritrea-Ethiopia Claims Commission, Partial Award, Western Front, Aerial Bombardment and Related Claims, Eritrea's Claims 1, 3, 5, 9–13, 14, 21, 25 & 26, December 19, 2005 45 ILM 396 (2006)
Legality of the Threat or Use of Nuclear Weapons, Advisory Opinion ICJ Rep 1996
Prosecutor v. Kordic & Cerkez, IT-95–14/2-PT, Decision on the Joint Defense Motion to Dismiss the Amended Indictment for Lack of Jurisdiction Based on the Limited Jurisdictional Reach of Articles 2 and 3, 2 March 1999, (ICTY Trial Chamber)
Prosecutor v. Stanislav Galic, Judgement and Opinion, 5 December 2003 (ICTY Tribunal Chamber)
Statement of ICC Prosecutor Karim A.A. Khan KC: Applications for Arrest Warrants in the Situation in the State of Palestine, 20 May 2024

The Committee Established to Review the NATO Bombing Campaign against the Federal Republic of Yugoslavia, *Final Report to the Prosecutor* (2000)

The Hostage Case, Indictment, Nuremberg Trial Transcripts (The University of North Dakota, Chester Fritz Library, Centre for Human Rights and Genocide Studies Collections)

United States v. Wilhelm List et al., (the Hostages Trial), 8th July 1947 to 19th February 1948 UN War Crimes Commission, Law Reports of Trials of War Criminals, vol VIII, 34 (US MTN)

WTO Appelate Body, United States – Import Prohibition of Certain Shrimp and Shrimp Products WT/DS58/AB/R, DSR 1998:VII

Journal articles

Barak E, 'Doomed to Be Violated? The US-Israeli Clandestine End-User Agreement and the Second Lebanon War: Lessons for the Convention on Cluster Munitions' 38 Denv J Int'l L Policy 2009 1 1

Biggerstaff WC and Schmitt MN, 'Protecting the Environment in Armed Conflict: Evaluating the US Perspective' 105 IRRC 924 2023 1267

Bloomfield S and Butler K, 'Darfur's Return to Hell, "Scorched Earth" Unleashed on Darfur, Despite UN Presence' The Independent, 12 March 2008 1

Bothe M, 'The Protection of the Environment in Times of Armed Conflict; Legal Rules, Uncertainty, Deficiencies and Possible Developments' 34 German YB Int'l L 1991 54 54

———, 'The Protection of the Civilian Population and NATO Bombing on Yugoslavia: Comments on the Report to the Prosecutor of the ICTY' 12 EJIL 2001 531

Bothe M and others, 'International Law Protecting the Environment during Armed Conflict: Gaps and Opportunities' 92 IRRC 879 2010 569

Breitegger A, 'Preventing Human Suffering during and after Conflict? The Complementary Case for a Specific Convention on Cluster Munitions' 10 Austrian Rev Int'l Eur L 2005 3 3

Brown BL, 'The Proportionality Principle in the Humanitarian Law of Warfare: Recent Efforts at Codification' 10 Cornell Int'l L J 1976–1977 134 134

Capone F, 'The Wave of Russian Attacks on Ukraine's Power Infrastructures: An Opportunity to Infuse Meaningfulness into the Notion of 'Dual-use Objects'?' European Papers 21 November 2023

Dam-de Jong D, 'From Engines for Conflict into Engines for Sustainable Development: The Potential of International Law to Address Predatory Exploitation of Natural Resources in Situations of Internal Armed Conflict' 82 Nordic J Int'l L 2013 155

Dam-de Jong D and Sjöstedt B, 'Enhancing Environmental Protection in Relation to Armed Conflict: An Assessment of the ILC Draft Principles' 44 Loy LA Int'l Comp L Rev 2 2021 129

Desgagné R, 'The Prevention of Environmental Damage in Time of Armed Conflict: Proportionality and Precautionary Measures' 3 YB Int'l H L 2000 109

DuBarry HM, 'Wartime Environmental Damages: Financing the Cleanup' 23 U Pa J Int'l Econ L 2002 899 899

Edgerton L, 'Eco-terrorist Acts during the Persian Gulf War: Is International Law Sufficient to Hold Iraq Liable?' 22 Ga J Int'l Comp L 1992 151 151

Else RC, 'Proportionality in the Law of Armed Conflict – the Proper Unit of Analysis for Military Operations' 5 U St Thomas J L Pub Policy 2010–2011 195

Falk R, 'United States Foreign Policy and the Vietnam War: A Second American Dilemma' Stanford J Int'l Stud 3 1968 78 78

Fenrick WJ, 'Applying IHL Targeting Rules to Practical Situations: Proportionality and Military Objectives' 27 Windsor YB Access Just 2009 271

Fenrick WJ, Lieutenant Colonel, 'The Rule of Proportionality and Protocol I in Conventional Warfare' 98 Military L Rev 1982 91

Ferencz BB, 'War Crimes Law and the Vietnam War' 17 Am U L Rev 3 1967–1968 403 403

Gardam JG, 'Proportionality and Force in International Law' 87 AJIL 3 1993 391 391

———, 'Proportionality as a Restraint on the Use of Force' 20 Austl YB Int'l L 1999 161 161
Gieseken HO and Murphy V, 'The Protection of the Natural Environment under International Humanitarian Law: The ICRC's 2020 Guidelines' 105 IRRC 924 2023 1180
Gillett M, 'Criminalizing Reprisals against the Natural Environment' 105 IRRC, Protecting the Environment in Armed Conflict 924 2023 1463
Halpern MS, 'Protecting Vulnerable Environments in Armed Conflict: Deficiencies in International Humanitarian Law' 51 Stanf J Int'l L 2 2015
Hampson F, 'Proportionality and Necessity in the Gulf Conflict' 86 Am Soc Int'l L Proc 1992 45 45
Hanke M, 'The 1923 Hague Rules of Air Warfare – A Contribution to the Development of International Law Protecting Civilians from Air Attack' IRRC No. 292 March 1993
Hardy J, 'The Interpretation of Plurilingual Treaties by International Courts and Tribunals' 37 Br Year B Int Law 1961 72
Hulme K, 'Taking Care to Protect the Environment against Damage' 92 IRRC 879 2010 675 675
Jensen ET, 'The International Law of Environmental Warfare: Active and Passive Damage during Armed Conflict' 38 Vand J Transnat L 2005 145
Joyner C and Kirhope J, 'The Persian Gulf War Oil Spill: Reassessing the Law of Environmental Protection and the Law of Armed Conflict' 24 Case W Res J Int'l L 1, Winter 1992 29
Kahl C, 'How We Fight' 85 Foreign Affairs 6 2006
Kalshoven F, 'Reaffirmation and Development of International Humanitarian Law Applicable in Armed Conflicts: The Diplomatic Conference, Geneva, 1974–1977, Part II' 8 NY Int'l L 1978 107 107
Lauterpacht H, 'The Problem of the Revision of the Law of War' 29 Brit YB Int'l L 1952
Linden Mvd, 'The Inextricable Connection between Historical Consciousness and International Law: New Imperialism, the International Court of Justice and Its Interpretation of the Inter-temporal Rule, Conference Paper No. 2/2014' ESIL
Low L and Hodgkinson D, 'Compensation for Wartime Environmental Damage: Challenges to International Law after the Gulf War' 35 Va J Int'l L 1994–1995 405
Normand J, 'The Legitimation of Violence: A Critical Analysis of the Gulf War' 35 Harv Int'l L J 1994 35
Partsch KJ, 'Remnants of War as a Legal Problem in the Light of the Libyan Case' 78 AJIL 2, April 1984 386
Plant G, 'Legal Aspects of Marine Pollution during the Gulf War' 7 Int'l J Estuarine Coastal L 3 1992 217 217
Reichberg G and Syse H, 'Protecting the Environment in Wartime: Ethical Considerations from the Just War Tradition' 37 Journal of Peace Research 4 2000 449
Roscini M, 'Targeting and Contemporary Aerial Bombardment' 54 ICLQ 2 2005 411 411
Sassoli M, 'State Responsibility for Violations of International Humanitarian Law' 84 IRRC 846, June 2002
Schipani A, 'ICC Prosecutor Seeks Information about Possible Sudan Conflict War Crimes' Financial Times, 13 June 2024
Schmitt M, 'Green War: An Assessment of the Environmental Law of International Armed Conflict' 22 Yale J Int'l L 1997 1
Schwabach A, 'NATO's War in Kosovo and the Final Report to the Prosecutor of the ICTY' 9 Tul J Int'l Comp L 2001 167 167
Seddon M and Ivanova P, 'Russian Bakery Rises to Putin's Call by Making Killer Drones' Financial Times, 6/7 January 2024 5
Shamash HME, 'How Much is Too Much? An Examination of the Principle of Jus in Bello Proportionality' 2 IDF L Rev 2005–2006 103 103
Shue H. and Wippman D. 'Limiting Attacks on Dual-use Facilities Performing Indispensable Civilian Functions' 35 Cornell Int Law J 2002

Simonds SN, 'Conventional Warfare and Environmental Protection: A Proposal for International Legal Reform' 29 Stanf J Int'l L 1992–1993 165 165
Tignino M, 'Water, International Peace, and Security' 92 IRRC 879, September 2010 647
Verwey WD, 'Protection of the Environment in Times of Armed Conflict: in Search of a New Legal Perspective' 8 Leiden J Int'l L 1 1995 7
Walters B, 'Missiles over Kosovo: Emergence, Lex Lata, of a Customary Norm Requiring the Use of Precision Munitions in Urban Areas' 47 Naval L Rev 2000 115
Wedgwood R and Green F, 'Proportionality and Necessity in American National Security Decision Making' 86 ASIL Proceedings April 1–4 58
Weeramantry JR and Bodansky ED, 'International Decisions, the Eritrea-Ethiopia Claims Commission Awards' 101 AJIL 616
Winter E, 'The Compatibility of Autonomous Weapons with the Principle of Distinction in the Law of Armed Conflict' 69 ICLQ October 2020 845

Electronic articles

Dewdney JC and Conquest R, 'Soviet Union, Historical State, Eurasia' Encyclopedia Britannica
ICRC, 'ICRC Duty of Care: Elements of Definition'
———, 'States Party to the Following International Humanitarian Law and Other Related Treaties, as of 3rd September 2024'
International Organization for Migration, 'Sudan Internal Displacement Set to Top 10 Million as Famine Looms, 6 June 2024'
Mednick S and Knickmeyer E, 'The UN Says There's "Full-Blown Famine" in Northern Gaza. What Does That Mean?' AP, 6 May 2024

Books

Boisson de Chazournes L, *La Protection Internationale de l'Environnement* (Ed. Pedone 2005)
Bothe M, Partsh KJ, Waldemar A. Solf with the collaboration of Martin Eaton, *New Rules for Victims of Armed Conflicts, Commentary on the Two 1977 Protocols Additional to the Geneva Conventions of 1949* (Martinus Nijhoff Publishers 1982)
Dam-de Jong DA, *International Law and Governance of Natural Resources in Conflict and Post-Conflict Situations, Doctoral Thesis* (Open Access edn, Leiden: Meijers 2013)
Dinstein Y, *The Conduct of Hostilities under the Law of International Armed Conflict* (CUP 2022)
Gardam JG, *Necessity, Proportionality and the Use of Force by States* (CUP 2004)
Green LC, *The Contemporary Law of Armed Conflict* (3rd edn, MUP 2008)
Guillard D, *Les armes de guerre et l'environnement naturel* (L'Harmattan 2006)
Hulme K, *War Torn Environment: Interpreting the Legal Threshold* (Martinus Nijhoff 2004)
Koppe E, *The Use of Nuclear Weapons and the Protection of the Environment during International Armed Conflict* (Hart Publishing Ltd. 2008)
Lackey DP, *The Ethics of War and Peace* (Prentice-Hall 1989)
May L, *War Crimes and Just War* (CUP 2007)
Mollard-Bannelier K, *La Protection de l'Environnement en Temps de Conflit Armé* (Editions A. Pedone 2001)
Rogers APV, *Law on the Battlefield* (3rd edn, MUP 2012)
Sands P and others, *Principles of International Environmental Law* (4th edn, CUP 2018)
Tignino M, *L'eau et la Guerre, Eléments pour un Regime Juridique* (Bruylant 2011)
———, *Water during and after Armed Conflicts: What Protection under International Law?* (Brill 2016)

Book chapters

Bothe M, 'Protection of the Environment in Relation to Armed Conflicts' in Fleck D (ed), *The Handbook of International Humanitarian Law* (4th edn, OUP 2021)

Falk R, 'The Environmental Law of War: An Introduction' in Plant G (ed), *Environmental Protection and the Law of War: A Fifth Geneva Convention on the Protection of the Environment in Time of Armed Conflict* (Belhaven Press 1992)

Greenwood C, 'State Responsibility and Civil Liability for Environmental Damage Caused by Military Operations' in King J and others (eds), *Protection of the Environment during Armed Conflict*, vol 69 (US Naval War College 1996)

———, 'Historical Development and Legal Basis' in Fleck D (ed), *The Handbook of International Humanitarian Law* (2nd edn, OUP 2008)

Hulme K, 'Natural Environment' in Wilmshurt E and Breau S (eds), *Perspectives on the ICRC Study on Customary International Humanitarian Law* (1st edn, Chatham House and BIICL 2007)

Kiss A, 'Les Protocoles additionnels aux Conventions de Geneve de 1977 et la protection de biens de l'environnement' in Swinarski C and Cross ICotR (eds), *Studies and Essays on International Humanitarian Law and Red Cross Principles in Honour of Jean Pictet* (Martinus Nijhoff Publishers 1984)

Meyer MA, 'A Definition of the "Environment"' in Plant G (ed), *Environmental Protection and the Law of War: A Fifth Geneva Convention on the Protection of the Environment in the Time of Armed Conflict* (Belhaven Press 1992)

Oeter S, 'Methods of Combat' in Fleck D (ed), *The Handbook of International Humanitarian Law* (4th edn, OUP 2021)

Payne CR, 'Chapter 2, Defining the Environment, Environmental Integrity' in Stahn C and others (eds), *Environmental Protection and Transitions from Conflict to Peace, Clarifying Norms, Principles, and Practices* (OUP 2017)

Radics O and Bruch C, 'Chapter 6, The Law of Pillage, Conflict Resources, and Jus Post Bellum,' in Stahn C and others (eds), *Environmental Protection and Transitions from Conflict to Peace* (OUP 2017)

Scobbie I, 'The Approach to Customary International Law in the Study' in Wilmshurt E and Breau S (eds), *Perspectives on the ICRC Study on Customary International Humanitarian Law* (1st edn, Chatham House and BIICL 2007)

Watkin K, '21st Century conflict and International Humanitaria Law: Status Quo or Change?' in Schmitt M and Pejic J (eds), *International Law and Armed Conflict: Exploring the Faultlines* (Martinus Nijhoff Publishers 2007)

3 State responsibility for environmental damage during occupation under the law of occupation

This chapter focuses on State responsibility for environmental damage during occupation under the LOAC. It presents the legal regime applicable to occupation, its general principles and reviews rules governing occupant's obligations towards natural resources constituting the environment. It introduces IHRL that may strengthen protection of civilians and their environment in occupied territory.

I. Legal framework

1. Occupation law

Occupation law is constituted by the 1907 Hague Regulations, (the "Regulations"), 1949 GC IV and AP/I and conventions devised for specific protection during armed conflicts.[1] Belligerent occupations taking place during armed conflict, *flagrante bello*, are governed by the Regulations, whether the government is military, civil or a mixed administration.[2] Occupations that follow an armistice agreement are subject to the Regulations, unless the agreement contains provisions departing from them, that take precedence.[3] In a dispute over exploitation of new oil fields in the Sinai and Gulf of Suez following the 1967 war, the argument that the Regulations were inapplicable during the armistice period – or after hostilities ended following a cease-fire[4] – was contested.[5]

1 The Hague Convention for the Protection of Cultural Property in the Event of Armed Conflict, 14 May 1954 art.5, 18

2 F. Llewellyn Jones, 'Military Occupation of Alien Territory in Time of Peace' 9 Transactions of the Grotius Society, Problems of Peace and War, Papers Read before the Society in the Year 1923 149, 150. U.S. DoD, *Law of War Manual, June 2015, updated December 2016* par.11.8.6

3 Brice Clagett, O. Thomas Johnson, and Thomas Johnson Jr., 'May Israel as a Belligerent Occupant Lawfully Exploit Previously Unexploited Oil Resources of the Gulf of Suez?' 72 AJIL No. 3, July (1978) 558, 561; Adam Roberts, 'What Is Military Occupation' 50 Brit YB Int'l L (1984) 249, 267; E.H. Feilchenfeld, *The International Economic Law of Belligerent Occupation* (Carnegie Endowment for International Peace 1942) 111

4 Israel Ministry of Foreign Affairs, *Memorandum of Law on the Right to Develop New Oil Fields in the Sinai and the Gulf of Suez, 1 August 1977* (1978) 432, 433

5 Clagett, Johnson, and Johnson Jr. 561. Ando Nisuke, *Surrender, Occupation and Private Property in International Law, an Evaluation of US Practice in Japan* (Clarendon Press 1991) 42–43

DOI: 10.4324/9780367823283-3

"Mixed" occupations, such as the occupation of Rhineland, Germany, in World War I ("WWI") result from armistice and occupation agreements that may deviate from the Regulations.[6] A surrender declaration signals the end of hostilities, even if technically the state of war is not ended.[7] The imposition of unconditional surrender, actual surrender and disintegration of German government were circumstances justifying the assumption and exercise of power by the Allied, rendering the Regulations inapplicable to Germany's occupation during World War II ("WWII").[8]

UNSC Resolutions under UN Charter's Chapter VII, such as those concerning Iraq, modify occupation law.[9] If a UNSC Resolution on occupation leads to conflict of obligations for the State concerned with its obligations under international LOAC conventions, the former should prevail by application of the UN Charter, article 103.[10] However, courts should interpret UNSC Resolutions with reference to customary international law rules, including those under LOAC.[11] Finally, whether resistance to occupation is a right or misconception, the situation can degenerate in fully fledged hostilities, where *jus in bello* and occupation law are both applicable.[12]

2. *Hague Regulations relevance*

The customary status of the Regulations is established since the judgement of the Nuremberg Military Tribunal,[13] confirmed by the Wall advisory opinion of the ICJ[14]

6 Armistice Agreement of 11 November 1918 and Agreement among the United States of America, Belgium, the British Empire, France and Germany with regard to the Military Occupation of the Territories of the Rhine, signed at Versailles, 28 June 1919 adopted on the basis of article 432 of the Versailles Peace Treaty.

7 Curtis C. Shears, 'Some Legal Implications of Unconditionnal Surrender' 39 ASIL Proceedings April 13–14 (1945) 44, 45, 50–51; *Rex v. Bottrill, ex parte Kuechenmeister* LR [1947] KB 41; R.Y. Jennings, 'Government in Commission' 23 Brit YB Int'l L (1946) 112, 120

8 Charles Fahy, 'Legal Problems of German Occupation' 47 Mich L Rev 1 (1948) 11, 13 *United States v. Altstoetter et al., (Case 3), 960* Trials of War Criminals, Military Tribunal Nuremberg III, 954, US MTN U.S. DoD 11.1.3.4

9 UNSC, *Resolution1483, S/RES/1483, 22 May 2003* (2003) and UNSC Res 1511 (2003); Kaitan Homi Kaikobad, 'Problems of Belligerent Occupation: The Scope of Powers Exercised by the Coalition Provisional Authority in Iraq, April/May 2003-June 2004' 54 ICLQ (2005) 253, 264 Rudiger Wolfrum, 'The Adequacy of International Humanitarian Rules on Belligerent Occupation: To What Extent May Security Council Resolution 1483 Be Considered a Model for Adjustment?' in M.N. Schmitt and J. Pejic (eds), *International Law and Armed Conflict: Exploring the Faultlines, Essays in Honour of Yoram Dinstein* (Martinus Nijhoff 2007) 508

10 Dennis Mandsager, Joshua L. Dorosin, and Jean-Philippe Lavoyer, 'Jus in Bello: Occupation Law and the War in Iraq' 98 ASIL Proceedings March 31–April 3 (2004) 117, 119. UN Charter, Chapter VI: Actions with respect to the peace, breaches of peace and acts of aggression, articles 39–51

11 Anthony E. Cassimatis, 'International Humanitarian Law, International Human Rights Law, and Fragmentation of International Law' ICLQ (2007) 636

12 Yoram Dinstein, *The International Law of Belligerent Occupation* (2nd edn, CUP 2019) par.307, 311; Dapo Akande, 'Classification of Armed Conflicts: Relevant Legal Concepts' in Elizabeth Wilmhurst (ed), *International Law and the Classification of Conflicts* (OUP 2012) 47

13 *IMT (Nuremberg) Judgement and Sentences, October 1, 1946* AJIL Jan, 1947, Vol 41, No 1, 172, 248–249

14 *Legal Consequences of the Construction of a Wall in the Occupied Palestinian Territory, Advisory Opinion* ICJ Rep 2004, 136 par.89 (the Wall)

and recognized in military manuals.[15] GC IV is also part of customary international law.[16] Meant to supplement the Regulations, they both apply if GC IV is applicable.[17] Yet, a review of multiple occupations concluded in a systematic failure to apply the Regulations during the two World Wars and occupants' refusal to acknowledge occupations since the 1970s.[18] There is "a trend of denying the applicability of occupation law," as States refuse its constraints or do not see themselves as occupants.[19] So, what is the legal relevance of these Regulations? If they are systematically put aside by States, one may question whether they have fallen in desuetude, defined as the rejection of rule through non-enforcement or non-compliance.[20] Desuetude may represent a factual cause for termination of a treaty, but its legal basis is the implied consent of the parties.[21]

Occupations present diverse regulatory regimes implemented by occupants, without common emerging rules consistently applied, that could constitute a nascent developing custom replacing the Regulations. Absent another applicable legal framework, the occupation regime is considered in force, as shown by its revival for Iraq's occupation.[22] If occupation law is deemed applicable, while not being applied effectively, it is an enforcement issue. The Regulations should be interpreted according to their purposes: protection of sovereign rights of the legitimate government of occupied territory and its inhabitants from exploitation for the pursuit of the occupant's war,[23] by providing a minimum humanitarian standard[24] and ensuring respect of private property[25] and to developments in international law and practice moving away from short occupations that were the norm pre-WWI.[26]

15 U.S. DoD par.11.1.2.2

16 Ardi Imseis, 'On the Fourth Geneva Convention and the Occupied Palestinian Territory' 44 Harvard Int'l L J 1, 90

17 GC IV, art.154; ICRC, *Commentary on the Fourth Geneva Convention* (1958) art.154

18 Eyal Benvenisti, *The International Law of Occupation* (2nd edn, OUP 2012) 8–9, 120–121, 129, 140–141, 164, 201; Dinstein par.27–29

19 Dr Knut Dörmann, 'Foreword' in Tristan Ferraro (ed), *Expert Meeting, Occupation and Other Forms of Administration of Foreign Territory* (ICRC 2012) 4

20 Antonios Tzanakopoulos and Sotirios-Ioannis Lekkas, 'Chapter 11, Pacta Sunt Servanda versus Flexibility in the Suspension and Termination of Treaties' in Christian J. Tams, Antonios Tzanakopoulos, and Andreas Zimmermann (eds), *Research Handbook on the Law of Treaties* (Elgar 2014) 11

21 ILC, *Draft Articles on the Law of Treaties with commentaries* (1966) Commentary on art.39, 237, (5); Jean Combacau and Serge Sur, *Droit International Public* (13th edn, LGDJ 2019) 184

22 Eyal Benvenisti, 'Water Conflicts during the Occupation of Iraq' 97 AJIL 4, October (2003) 860, 864

23 Adam Roberts, 'Transformative Military Occupation: Applying the Laws of War and Human Rights' in *Law and Armed Conflict: Exploring the Faultlines, Essays in Honour of Yoram Dinstein* 468; Benvenisti, *The International Law of Occupation* 159; Jennings 135

24 Christine Chinkin, *Laws of Occupation* (2008) 201

25 Deuxième Conférence Internationale de la Paix 1907/MAE, *Documents Diplomatiques* (Imprimerie Nationale, Paris 1908) 76; E. Lauterpacht, 'The Hague Regulations and the Seizure of Munitions de Guerre' 32 Brit YB Int'l L (1955) 218, 218

26 Benvenisti, *The International Law of Occupation* 10; Antonio Cassese, 'Powers and Duties of an Occupant in Relation to Land and Natural Resources' in Emma Playfair (ed), *International Law and the Administration of Occupied Territories, Two Decades of Israeli Occupation of the West Bank and Gaza Strip* (OUP 1992) 425–426; *Legal Consequences for States of the Continued Presence of South Africa in Namibia notwithstanding Security Council Resolution 276 (1970), Advisory Opinion* ICJ Rep 1971, p. 16 par.53; ILC, *Special Rapporteur Marja Lehto, First Report on Protection of*

3. *Other applicable laws*

IEL is considered applicable during armed conflict including occupation,[27] and general IEL issues must be considered in the occupied territory's administration.[28] IEL principles relevant during occupation, such as permanent sovereignty over natural resources and prevention of environmental damage, are analysed in Chapter 4 on IEL and IWL rules. IHRL equally applies during wars and occupations, at least regarding specific issues,[29] provided it does not conflict with the LOAC, the *lex specialis* applicable to armed conflicts.[30]

II. Occupation concept and principles

1. *Occupation and effective control*

Occupation triggers the application of occupation law.[31] It is a fact[32] from which the occupant derives its power.[33] Under the Regulations, article 42

> "territory is considered occupied when it is *actually* placed under the authority of the hostile army. The occupation extends only to the territory where such authority has been established and can be exercised"

the Environment in Relation to Armed Conflicts, A/CN.4/720 (2018) par.33, 36 (Lehto Environment and Armed Conflict, 2018)

27 ILC, *Draft Principles on Protection of the Environment in Relation to Armed Conflicts, with commentaries, A/77/10* (ILC YB 2022, vol II, (2), 2022)Principle 19, 159–160, par.(3), (4); ILC, Lehto Environment and Armed Conflict (2018) par.51–62, 77–80; Daniëlla Dam-de Jong, 'From Engines for Conflict into Engines for Sustainable Development: The Potential of International Law to Address Predatory Exploitation of Natural Resources in Situations of Internal Armed Conflict' 82 Nordic J Int'l L (2013) 155, 160; *Legality of the Threat or Use of Nuclear Weapons, Advisory Opinion* ICJ Rep 1996, 226 par.29–30

28 Benvenisti, 'Water Conflicts' 864; ILC, Environment Protection Principles, Principle 19 and its Commentary par.(1)

29 Benvenisti, 'Water Conflicts' 862

30 UNGA, *Basic Principles for Protection of Civilian Population in Armed Conflicts, A/Res/2675 (XXV)* (1970); Jann K. Kleffner, 'Human Rights in Armed Conflict' in Dieter Fleck (ed), *The Handbook of International Humanitarian Law* (4th edn, OUP 2021) 14.01 par.4–5; Benvenisti, *The International Law of Occupation* 13; Dinstein par.223; ILC, Lehto Environment and Armed Conflict (2018) par.14; *Armed Activities on the Territory of the Congo (DRC v. Uganda), Judgment* ICJ Rep 2005, p. 168, ICJ par.216–217; *The Wall* par.106; *Prosecutor v. Dragoljub Kunarac, Radomir Kovac and Zoran Vukovic, Case Nos. IT-96–23-T and IT-96–23/1-T, Judgment of 22 February 2001* ICTY, Trial Chamber par.467–471

31 Tristan Ferraro, 'Determining the Beginning and End of an Occupation under International Humanitarian Law' 94 IRRC 885, Spring (2012) 133, 138; Mandsager, Dorosin, and Lavoyer 121

32 *United States v. Wilhelm List et al., (the Hostages Trial), 8th July 1947 to 19th February 1948* UN War Crimes Commission, Law Reports of Trials of War Criminals, Vol VIII, 34, US MTN 55. U.S. DoD par.11.2.1

33 Conférence Internationale de la Paix 1899/MAE, *Documents Diplomatiques* (Imprimerie Nationale, Paris) 24; Edmund H. Schwenk, 'Legislative Power of the Military Occupant under Article 43, Hague Regulations' 54 Yale L J 395; Mandsager, Dorosin, and Lavoyer 118; Roberts

and article 43.

> "the authority of the legitimate power having *in fact* passed into the hands of the occupant" (article 43).

The Regulations only authentic text being French, terms should be interpreted according to their ordinary meaning in French, under international treaty interpretation rules. "*De fait*" translated as "actually" and "in fact"[34] refers to de facto power, which actually exists without being legally recognized.[35]

Territory is occupied "only when it is actually under the control and administration of an Occupant."[36] Doctrine generally considers occupants' potential exercise of authority sufficient, provided the occupation army controls enemy territory.[37] Favouring potential exercise of authority,[38] the Nuremberg military tribunal found that "an occupation indicates the exercise of governmental authority." This presupposes "the establishment of an administration to preserve law and order. To the extent that the occupant's control is maintained and that of the civil government eliminated, the area will be said to be occupied."[39] Dinstein finds that a "theoretical capability to exercise" authority is not enough, as actual exercise is required under article 42,[40] though it is not borne out by the term "can" or the French text "*en mesure*." The UK military manual "appears undecided."[41] The ICJ judged in *Armed Activities* that, for a State to be an occupying power, sufficient evidence must demonstrate that its "authority was in fact established and exercised" in the occupied areas, meaning that Uganda military must be stationed in particular locations and have substituted their authority to the Congolese government, the establishment of a military administration being irrelevant.[42] It was criticized for its reference to actual direct authority over the population.[43] The controversy is not resolved.[44]

34 Hague Regulations, French version, article 42: « *Un territoire (. . .) occupé (. . .) se trouve placé de fait sous l'autorité de l'armée ennemie.* » art.43: « *L'autorité (. . .) ayant passé de fait entre les mains de l'occupant, [. . .]* ».

35 Larousse, 'Langue Francaise, Dictionnaire,' Fait, Expresssion; « *De fait, qui existe réellement sans être juridiquement reconnu: le pouvoir de fait* ».

36 Leslie C. Green, *The Contemporary Law of Armed Conflict* (3rd edn, MUP 2008) 285

37 L. Oppenheim, *International Law, Vol. II Disputes, War and Neutrality* (H. Lauterpacht ed, 7th edn, Longmans, Green and Co. 1952) Chap. XII occupation of enemy territory; Benvenisti, *The International Law of Occupation* 50. Ferraro 150

38 Aeyal Gross, *The Writing on the Wall, Rethinking the International Law of Occupation* (CUP 2017) 62

39 *United States v. Wilhelm List et al., (the Hostages Trial), 8th July 1947 to 19th February 1948 55–56*

40 Dinstein par.119, 147

41 Benvenisti, *The International Law of Occupation* 48; UK MoD, *The Joint Service Manual of the Law of Armed Conflict, JSP 383* (2004) par.11.3 and 11.3.2

42 *Armed Activities (2005) par.173, 177*

43 Tristan Ferraro (ed), *Expert Meeting, Occupation and Other Forms of Administration of Foreign Territory, Report* (ICRC 2012) 150; Gross 72; Benvenisti, *The International Law of Occupation* 50; Contra: Dinstein par.147

44 Dana Wolf, 'Transitional Post-Occupation Obligations under the Law of Belligerent Occupation' Minn J Int'l L 2018 8

According to the ICTY, guidelines to determine whether "the authority of the occupying power has been actually established" are:

- The occupant being able to substitute its own authority for that of the previous authorities unable to function,
- Having sufficient troops present or being able to require them,
- Having issued and enforced directions to the population, (actual exercise of authority),
- Having established a temporary military administration over the territory,
- Defeat of enemy forces.[45]

Alternatively, the notion of effective control over territory is used, based on similar criteria requiring absence of former governmental authority, occupant's ability to substitute its own authority and presence of foreign forces without the former local government's consent.[46] Whether Iraq's occupation was "effective" was questioned, given the scale, after its invasion, of looting, lawlessness and resistance in towns, such as Fallujah, where occupation forces were unwilling to enter and maintain order and their inability to assert authority and provide effective protection.[47] Nonetheless, even if it is not invoked,[48] occupation law applies whenever foreign troops find themselves "in control" of a territory and in contact with the inhabitants[49] – even if not invoked[50] and whatever claims the occupant raises about legitimacy or sovereignty of the occupied belligerent[51] or unclear status of its territory.[52] Gross suggests taking into account political and technological changes impacting control, when it shifts from "boots on the ground" to other forms, in order to strengthen occupants' accountability. A functional approach to occupation law should be adopted, where obligations follow from the exercise of power and control.[53]

45 *Prosecutor v. Naletilic et al. IT-98-34-T, 31 March 2003* ICTY, Trial Chamber par.217

46 Prof. Michael Bothe, 'First Meeting of Experts, the Beginning and End of Occupation, Appendix 1 "Effective Control": A Situation Triggering the Application of the Law of Belligerent Occupation, Background Document' in Tristan Ferraro (ed), *Expert Meeting, Occupation and Other Forms of Administration of Foreign Territory* (ICRC 2012) 37, 38; Dinstein par.136, 137, 144. Benvenisti, *The International Law of Occupation* 47, 50; U.S. DoD par.11.2.2.1 and 11.2.2.2; UK MoD par.11.3 Effectiveness of occupation; *Prosecutor v. Naletilic et al. IT-98-34-T, 31 March 2003* par.217; Adam Roberts, 'Occupation, Military, Termination of' MPEPIL, online edition, par.4; ICRC, *Commentary on the First Geneva Convention* (2016) art.2 par.303, 304.

47 Ben Clarke, 'Military Occupation and the Rule of Law: the Legal Obligations of Occupying Forces in Iraq' 10 Int'l Trade Bus L Rev (2006) 133, 156

48 ILC, Lehto Environment and Armed Conflict (2018) par.26; Armed Activities on the Territory of the Congo, p. 230, par.173; Prosecutor v. Naletilić par.211

49 Roberts, 'What Is Military Occupation' 250

50 Ibid

51 Suzanne Weaver and others, 'Territories Occupied by Israel: Settlements and Exploration of Oil Resources' 72 ASIL Proceedings April (1978) 124

52 ILC, Lehto Environment and Armed Conflict (2018) par.20

53 Gross 129–130, 135

Occupation ends when effective control ceases by military withdrawal from occupied territory – though withdrawal does not automatically signify loss of control[54] – major renewed fighting and change of status of occupant's forces remaining in occupied territory.[55] It is not clear when armed resistance and temporary loss of control during occupation lead to requalify it as armed conflict.[56] Sovereignty returns to the legitimate government that must control the territory at the end of the occupation.[57] The Geneva Conventions remain applicable until one year after the close of military operations.[58] The Regulations do not apply as a matter of law to post conflict situations but may be observed as universal custom.[59]

2. General principles

2.1 Inalienability of sovereignty and temporary character

A State's competence over its territory is described in terms of jurisdiction and sovereignty, which is the legal personality of statehood.[60] Inalienability of sovereignty and occupations' temporary character are major principles[61] underpinning the administration of occupied territory.[62] Sovereignty is not transferred to the occupant,[63] cannot be considered suspended[64] and is retained by the occupied belligerent prevented from exercising it.[65] Its legal personality continues to exist and territory is attributed to that legal person and not to its holders.[66]

The population of an occupied territory retains its right, inherent to its political sovereignty, to permanent sovereignty over its natural resources,[67] a customary international law principle.[68] The principle is subject to geopolitics. Following East Timor invasion by Indonesia in 1975, most States at the UN refused to recognize Indonesia's sovereignty claims over East Timor, while Australia and New Zealand recognized its de jure sovereignty. Australia signed with Indonesia in

54 Dinstein par.858
55 Roberts, 'Occupation, Military, Termination of' par.17
56 ILC, Lehto Environment and Armed Conflict (2018) par.21
57 Iain Scobbie, 'H2O after Oslo: Legal Aspects of Water in the Occupied Territories' 8 PYBIL (1994–1995) 79, 84
58 GC IV, art.6
59 U.S. DoD 762, par.11.1.3.4
60 James Crawford, *Brownlie's Principles of Public International Law* (9th edn, OUP 2019) 192
61 Dinstein par.161. Benvenisti, *The International Law of Occupation* 5; Wolf 29; UK MoD par.11.9, 11.10; U.S. DoD paras. 11.4.1 and 11.4.2
62 Chinkin 29
63 Dinstein 162; Jennings 133; Cassese 420; C. W. Wickersham and Archibald King, 'The Government of the Occupied Territory' 37 ASIL Proceedings April 30-May 1 (1943) 27, 29; IDI, *Bruges Declaration on the Use of Force, 3 September 2003*
64 Dinstein 163; Contra: Gerhard Von Glahn, *The Occupation of Enemy Territory* (The University of Minnesota Press 1957) 31
65 Shears 45
66 Crawford 193
67 Mara Tignino, *L'eau et la Guerre, Eléments pour un Regime Juridique* (Bruylant 2011) 203
68 See chapter 4

December 1989, the Timor Gap "Zone of Cooperation Agreement," for joint exploration of Timor Gap natural resources.[69] The people of East Timor lost their sovereign rights over their natural resources. Portugal, considered the administrative authority, brought a recourse before the ICJ. As Indonesia had not recognized the ICJ compulsory jurisdiction, the court upheld Australia's objections that it could not consider the rights and obligations of Indonesia as it was not a party to the proceedings.[70] In 2018 East Timor and Australia signed a maritime boundary agreement determining that the Greater Sunrise oil fields where Australia had been drilling would be managed jointly and revenues shared between them.

In a case about activities affecting wetlands of international importance under the Ramsar Convention, the ICJ had to satisfy itself that a link existed between sovereign rights over a disputed area claimed by Costa Rica and provisional environmental measures it requested.[71] It judged that Costa Rica's sovereignty was breached by Nicaragua's excavation of artificial river channels and establishment of a military presence, breaching its obligations under a previous Court order regarding provisional measures.[72]

Occupation being temporary, the occupant may not alter the status of the occupied territory[73] or undertake permanent changes, unless these result from military needs narrowly understood or for the benefit of the local population. Population changes through the arrival of settlers are thus prohibited.[74] Unilateral annexation is prohibited under customary international law and does not affect the status of the territory under international law,[75] and neither does its recognition by a third State.[76] The Golan Heights, East Jerusalem, Western Sahara and Crimea are contemporary illegal annexations.[77]

2.2 Administration of the territory

Under the Regulations article 43, the occupant "shall take all the measures in his power to restore, and ensure, as far as possible, public order and safety, while

69 Laura Southgate, *ASEAN Resistance to Sovereignty Violation, Interests, Balancing and the Role of the Vanguard State* (OUP, Policy Press Scolarship Online 2019) 120

70 Neil Deeley, *The International Boundaries of East Timor* (Boundary and Territory Briefing, 2001) 23

71 *Certain Activities Carried Out by Nicaragua in the Border Area (Costa Rica v. Nicaragua), Provisional Measures, Order of 8 March 2011* ICJ Rep 2011, p. 6, par.55, 59–62

72 *Certain Activities Carried Out by Nicaragua in the Border Area (Costa Rica v. Nicaragua) and Construction of a Road in Costa Rica along the San Juan River (Nicaragua v. Costa Rica), Judgment* ICJ Rep 2015, p. 665, 665 par.92–93

73 Imseis 91

74 Chinkin 208

75 Green 285; Christopher Greenwood, 'The Administration of Occupied Territory in International Law' in Emma Playfair (ed), *International Law and the Administration of the Occupied Territories* (OUP 1992) 244; Dinstein par.63,66

76 Georg Schwarzenberger, *International Law as Applied by International Courts and Tribunals, the Law of Armed Conflict*, vol II (Stevens & Sons Ltd 1968) 167

77 European Parliament, Directorate General for External Policy, *Occupation/Annexation of a Territory: Respect for International Humanitarian Law and Human Rights and Consistent EU Policy* (2015) 14

respecting, unless absolutely prevented, the laws in force in the country." Public order and safety are inadequate translations of "*l'ordre et la vie publics.*" "*Vie publique,*" meaning "social, commercial and economic life of the country,"[78] should be civil or public life.

The occupant must administer the territory for the benefit of the population and their property.[79] Its duties extend to environmental and human rights concerns.[80] According to the ICJ and ILC, the occupant must respect and protect the environment in accordance with applicable LOAC, IEL and IHRL and take environmental considerations into account in its administration of the territory.[81] This ILC principle clarifies occupation law that does not specifically refer to the environment.[82] The occupant must respect the IHRL non-discrimination principle when exercising his duties.[83]

The purpose of article 43 is to protect the population from acts of violence through security measures.[84] Uganda, as occupying power in Congo, had obligations under this article to take measures in the territory it occupied (Ituri) (i) to end ethnic conflicts following seizure of land from the Lendu by the Hema of Ugandan origin, supported by Uganda military; (ii) to respect and ensure respect for human rights and IHRL[85] and (iii) to prevent looting, plundering and exploitation of natural resources by private persons.[86] Uganda was judged liable and ordered to pay compensation for damage resulting from looting, plundering and exploiting gold, diamonds, coltan, coffee and timber by members of its own armed forces in Congo and by third parties in the territory it occupied.[87] Uganda was also liable to make reparation on the significant damage it inflicted to wildlife in Ituri.[88] Environmental damage resulting from deforestation was not supported by any basis provided to the Court to assess the damage, though environmental damage "in and of itself" and its impairment was recognized as compensable.[89]

78 Greenwood 246; Ferraro 57; Conférence de Bruxelles, *Actes de la Conférence de Bruxelles de 1874 sur le Projet d'une Convention Internationale Concernant la Guerre, Protocoles des séances plénières, Protocoles de la commission déléguée par la conférence, Annexes* (Librairies des Publications Legislatives, A. Wittersheim & Cie, Paris 1874) 23

79 A.P.V. Rogers, *Law on the Battlefield* (3rd edn, MUP 2012) 247

80 ILC, Lehto Environment and Armed Conflict (2018) par.28, 47

81 *Nuclear Weapons* par.33; *Armed Activities (2005)* par.178; ILC, Environment Protection Principles, Principles 13.1, 19.1 and Commentary on Principle 19.1 par.1–3

82 Karen Hulme, 'Enhancing Environmental Protection during Occupation Through Human Rights' 10 GOJIL1 (2020) 203, 213

83 Tignino 215–216; Iain Scobbie, 'Natural Resources and Belligerent Occupation: Mutation through Permanent Sovereignty' in Stephen Bowen (ed), *Human Rights, Self-Determination and Political Change in the Occupied Palestinian Territories* (Martinus Nijhoff 1997) 231

84 Dinstein par.281–286

85 *Armed Activities (2005)* par.206,209,211,345(3)

86 Ibid, par.248–250, 345 (4); *Armed Activities on the Territory of the Congo (DRC v. Uganda), Reparations, Judgement* ICJ Rep 2022, p. 13, par.79, 275

87 *Armed Activities (2022)* par.296, 308–310, 320–322, 331, 344

88 Ibid, par.361–362

89 Ibid, par.348

Ensuring public order must be balanced with "[t]he basic requirement to respect the existing legal framework of a territory."[90] Literally, the article suggests that the occupant may only legislate to ensure public law and order, but a de facto broader legislative power is recognized.[91] It is not a general legislative competence, as respect for existing local laws, including environmental protection, remains an important benchmark.[92] The extent of acceptable legislative change was discussed during the *travaux préparatoires* of the Regulations. At the 1874 conference, participants agreed that changes, exceptionally admitted in case of necessity, should be limited to political, administrative or public interest laws. Civil and private laws concerning family, successions, private properties, sales and purchases and other matters remain in force in the occupied territory and are considered immune to change,[93] including laws related to business and commercial activities, even during long-term occupation.[94] At the 1899 conference, the occupant's duty to maintain existing laws and modify them only in case of necessity[95] was replaced by a duty to respect the laws in force unless absolutely prevented ("*empêchement absolu*"),[96] interpreted as a case of "absolute necessity."[97]

Legislative change should be introduced primarily, even exclusively, in the interest of the population,[98] taking into account human rights, administration of justice[99] and environmental protection.[100] Long-term occupation may require amending laws to protect the population[101] and avoid leaving the occupied territory in a "legal vacuum whereby it becomes socially and economically underdeveloped."[102] In such case the occupant must have the right to revise legislation,[103] incompatible with IHRL, for example.[104] Delegates in 1874 considered that temporary and long-term occupations should be distinguished, as what is applicable to one is not applicable to the other, without elaborating.[105]

90 Roberts 448
91 Schwenk 395
92 Roberts 587; Greenwood 247; ILC, Environment Protection Principles, Principle 20.3
93 Conférence de Bruxelles 23
94 Scobbie, 'H2O after Oslo' 88. Von Glahn 99.
95 *Projet d'une Déclaration Internationale Concernant les Lois et Coutumes de la Guerre* (*Bruxelles* 1874), art. 3
96 Conférence Internationale de la Paix 1899/MAE, 33
97 Schwenk 397, 401
98 Ibid, 397, 401; Scobbie, 'H2O after Oslo' 87
99 Roberts 587; Clarke 144; Sylvain Vité, 'The Interrelation of the Law of Occupation and Economic, Social and Cultural Rights: the Examples of Food, Health and Property' 90 IRRC 871, September (2008) 629, 635
100 Knut Dörmann and Sylvain Vité, 'Occupation' in Dieter Fleck (ed), *The Handbook of International Humanitarian Law* (4th edn, OUP 2021) 9.20, par.2–3; ILC, Environment Protection Principles, Principle 19.3 and its Commentary par.(11)
101 Iain Scobbie, 'International Law and the Prolonged Occupation of Palestine' (UN Roundtable on Legal Aspects of the Question of Palestine, The Hague, 20–22 May 2015) 10
102 Chinkin 210
103 Dinstein par.354, 365
104 Dörmann and Vité 9.05, par.4
105 Conférence de Bruxelles 24

In practice, occupants have used their prescriptive powers widely, almost as full discretionary powers,[106] pretexting military, legal and material necessity.[107] During their occupation of Belgium in WWI, German authorities interpreted the transfer of authority as a licence to eliminate subsequent legislative powers of the sovereign.[108] After the liberation, the Belgian government and courts considered measures taken by the occupant devoid of legal effect under international law and applied retroactively decrees taken by King Albert I considered Belgian laws.[109] Exceptional circumstances have justified substantial changes. Occupants' objectives in Italy, Japan and Germany after WWII entailed reform of the political structure and system,[110] demobilization, demilitarization, disarmament and "re-education of the German people"[111] or "creating a more liberal society and democratisation"[112] in Japan.[113] UNSC Resolution 1483 established a broad unprecedented basis for American and British occupation of Iraq between 2003 and 2004.[114] Wide ranging reforms of governmental or administrative structures by occupants in Iraq would have been unlawful under Regulations article 43, without such UNSC authorization.[115] It called upon the occupants to promote the welfare of Iraqi people through effective administration of the territory, restoration of its security and stability and creation of conditions in which they can freely determine their political future.[116]

All legislation remains in force in the occupied territory, under the Regulations article 43,[117] except for specific provisions on penal and labour laws.[118] GC IV article 64(1) provides that penal laws of the occupied territory remain in force, though their suspension or repeal is exceptionally admitted in cases of threat to the occupying power's security or obstacle in applying the Convention, while article 64(2) provides that the occupant may adopt provisions essential to fulfil its

106 Benvenisti, *The International Law of Occupation* 77, 79

107 Ferraro 56

108 Benvenisti, *The International Law of Occupation* 109

109 Ibid, 118–120, 320–322

110 Roberts 468; Benvenisti, *The International Law of Occupation* 159

111 Shears 46

112 State-War-Navy Coordinating Committee, *Politico-Military Problems in the Far East: United States Initial Post-Defeat Policy Relating to Japan, Reference: a. SWNCC 150/4* (21 September 1945) Part I, Part III 1, 3, Part IV, 1

113 Pitman B. Potter, 'Legal Bases and Character of Military Occupation in Germany and Japan' 43 AJIL 2 (1949) 325

114 David J. Scheffer, 'Beyond Occupation Law' 97 AJIL (2003) 842, 844; Clarke 145; Wolfrum Rüdiger, 'Iraq – from Belligerent Occupation to Iraqi Exercise of Sovereignty: Foreign Power versus International Community Interference' 9 UNYB (2005) 16

115 Lord Goldsmith QC Attorney General, *Iraq: Authorisation for an Interim Administration, 26 March 2003* par.1, 2(a)

116 UNSC Resolution S/RES/1483 (2003), par.4

117 ICRC, Commentary on GC IV art.64(1), par.1.A, p. 335; Dörmann and Vité 9.19 par.2

118 Jose Alejandro Carballo Leyda, 'The Laws of Occupation and Commercial Law Reform in Occupied Territories: Clarifying a Widespread Misunderstanding' 23 EJIL no. 1 (2012) 179 185–186

conventional obligations, maintain order in the territory and ensure its own security.[119] There is broad doctrinal agreement confirmed in military manuals that occupant's legislative authority under the latter is restricted to "essential" measures listed in the article.[120] The issue is whether this legislative authority extends to any type of law[121] or is restricted to criminal law, as indicated by the article's title and interpretation.[122] The *travaux préparatoires* confirm undoubtedly the latter.

> "The cases where the Occupying Power could change the penal laws of the occupied territory . . . concerned the security of the occupying power and the application of the present Convention. The changes introduced were those . . . necessary . . . to maintain order . . . ensure security . . . and . . . that the provision of the Convention were applied."[123]

Security measures include banning possession of firearms, assigned residence, requirement to carry identity cards and movements restrictions.[124]

III. Rules on property and their application to natural resources

The Rio Declaration Principle 23 stipulates: "the environment and natural resources of people under oppression, domination and occupation shall be protected." Permanent sovereignty over natural resources is an IEL customary principle that is recognized in international human rights covenants[125] and in Principles 21 and 2 of Stockholm and Rio Declarations. Under the Regulations, natural resources (air, water, soil, fauna and flora) are not regulated per se, (except for a mention on agricultural resources and forests) but as "property" and civilian objects in occupied territory.[126] Property rights regime determines access to and control over natural resources, whether State, private or community.[127] As the legal concept of environment was non-existent in 1907 and emerging when the Geneva Conventions were negotiated, property included what was not a civilian object.[128]

119 GC IV, art.64(2)

120 Leyda 183–184; Ferraro 57; Scobbie, 'International Law and the Prolonged Occupation of Palestine' 13; Vité 635, n.24; ILC, Lehto Environment and Armed Conflict (2018) par.43; U.S. DoD par.11.9.2. UK MoD par.11.25 mentions the "exigencies of armed conflict"; République Française, Ministère de la Défense, *Manuel de droit des conflits armés* (2012) 89.

121 Benvenisti, *The International Law of Occupation* 95–96, 100–101; Dinstein par.339; Scobbie, 'International Law and the Prolonged Occupation of Palestine' 13.

122 Schwarzenberger 194; Leyda 188, 183–186 for a detailed rebuttal of Benvenisti

123 *Final Record of the Diplomatic Conference of Geneva of 1949, Vol. II-A,* 771, 833

124 Dinstein par.342–343; ICRC, Commentary on GC IV p. 207, art.27

125 Common article 1 par.2 of both Covenants: ICESCR (ICESCR); ICCPR (ICCPR)

126 Mara Tignino, *Water during and after Armed Conflicts: What Protection under International Law?* (Brill 2016) 23; ILC, Lehto Environment and Armed Conflict (2018) par.29

127 Maria Ojanen et al., 'What are the environmental impacts of property rights regimes in forests, fisheries and rangelands?' 6 Environ Evid 12 (2017) 1

128 Cassese 421

1. Natural resources classification

The Regulations' distinctions between public (State) or private, movable or immovable, determine property's legal regime and apply to natural resources.[129]

1.1 Movable and immovable

Land is immovable. Natural resources in the ground (in situ), water, minerals (metallic, non-metallic or gemstones) and hydrocarbon resources (natural gas, oil and coal) are classified as real estate appurtenances or immovable.[130] Natural resources already extracted from the ground, such as oil and gas, are generally classified movable property in legal systems worldwide.[131] Water can be included in both categories, though it seems established that freshwater resources in rivers, lakes, wetlands and aquifers are considered immovable property.[132] If lakes ("habitats with slow-moving water"),[133] wetlands (land areas covered by or saturated with water),[134] and aquifers (groundwater) should be considered immovable, it seems curious to consider continuously flowing rivers or streams as immovable.

The Regulations being based on civil law notions, such as article 55 usufruct, French civil law rules may help clarify the water regime. Depending on whether water is movable or immovable, it has a different relation with property right. A landowner has no property right over a stream or watercourse streaming between properties and running through his land but a usage right,[135] subject to reciprocal obligations between owners of upper and lower properties.[136] Riparian owners of watercourses' bed stream that are outside the public domain have a restricted usage right over its water.[137] When water is immovable, its legal regime follows the regime of the property where it is located.[138] An irrigation canal is a hydraulic

129 ILC, Lehto Environment and Armed Conflict (2018) par.13, 29

130 Clagett, Johnson, and Johnson Jr. 562; Weaver and others 124; Benvenisti, 'Water Conflicts' 869; Daniëlla Dam-de Jong, *International Law and Governance of Natural Resources in Conflict and Post-Conflict Situations, Doctoral Thesis* (Open Access edn, Leiden: Meijers 2013) 217; Monroe Leigh, US Department of State 'Memorandum of Law on Israel's Right to develop New Oil Fields in Sinai and the Gulf of Suez, October 1, 1976' 16 ILM 3, May (1997) 733, 735; Contra: Dinstein par.666

131 Clagett, Johnson, and Johnson Jr. 562; Weaver and others 124; Daniëlla Dam-de JongGovernance of Natural Resources 217; Contra: Dinstein par.666 questioning whether underground resources are different

132 ILC, Lehto Environment and Armed Conflict (2018) par.36. Mara Tignino, 'Water, International Peace, and Security' 92 IRRC 879, September (2010) 647, 663; Cassese 431; Harold Dichter, 'The Legal Status of Israel's Water Policies in the Occupied Territories' 35 Harv Int'l L J 2, Spring (1994) 565 582–583; Benvenisti, *The International Law of Occupation* 82

133 Hannah Anderson, *Back to Basics: What Is a Lake?* (IISD 2020)

134 National Geographic online, Education, Encyclopedic Entry, *Wetland*

135 République Française, Code Civil art.644 Conseil d'Etat, *L'Eau et son Droit* (Etude, 2010) 51, 56, 57

136 République Française, Code Civil art.640

137 République Française, Code Civil art.563; Conseil d'Etat 53, 57

138 Conseil d'Etat 51

system that conveys water from a source (dam and river) to different users at the right moment and in the right quantity.[139] Water flowing in pipes and irrigations canals should then be considered movable.[140]

1.2 Public and private

Depending on pre-occupation national legislation, natural resources can be private or public.[141] Classifying water as public or private property corresponds to recognizing existing rights of governments and individuals, respectively, to control and access water. Individual rights have been mostly linked to land rights worldwide and often conceptualized as usufructuary rights.[142] However, the "impossibility for anyone to own water" is accepted since the Romans who considered water, air and sea as common resources.[143] Water is part of a category of things that do not belong to anybody and whose usage is common to all, under the French Civil Code and the *Cour de Cassation* jurisprudence.[144] It is part of the nation's common heritage under French environmental law, its protection and development being of public interest and a right to drinking water recognized for everybody.[145] Globally considering water as common heritage of mankind is resisted.[146] Transboundary rivers, lakes, wetlands and aquifers are distinctive resources that are not usually privately owned but classified as public property.[147]

As to private rights under French civil law, a landowner has property right over rainwater on his land that he may use and dispose of[148] and property right attenuated by customs over a water source (spring) attached to his land[149] and over groundwater under his property.[150] He may use source and groundwater within the limits and needs of his heritage, subject to respecting any existing customary water

139 Enrique Bonet Gil, 'Introduction' in *Experimental Design and Verification of a Centralized Controller for Irrigation Canals* (2018)

140 Gamal Abouali, 'Natural Resources under Occupation: The Status of Palestinian Waters under International Law' 10 Pace Int'l L Rev (1998) 411, 472; Contra: Cassese 431

141 Tignino, 'Water, International Peace, and Security' 663. ILC, Lehto Environment and Armed Conflict (2018) par.36. Marco Longobardo, 'State Responsibility for International Humanitarian Law Violations by Private Actors in Occupied Territories and the Exploitation of Natural Resources' 63 Neth Int'l L Rev (2016) 251, 254

142 Philippe Cullet, 'Water Law in a Globalised World: the Need for a New Conceptual Framework' 23 J Environ L 2 (2011) 233, 236–238

143 Cullet 236; Conseil d'Etat 50

144 République Française, Code Civil art.714; Conseil d'Etat 52

145 République Française, Code de l'Environnement art. L210; Conseil d'Etat 50

146 Philippe Cullet, Lovleen Bhullar and Sujith Koonan, 'Water Security and International Law' 17 Ann Rev L Soc Sci (2021) 271

147 Tignino, 'Water, International Peace, and Security' 663; ILC, Lehto Environment and Armed Conflict (2018) par.36

148 République Française, Code Civil art.641

149 Conseil d'Etat 53

150 République Française, Code Civil art.552; Conseil d'Etat 55

right of inhabitants.[151] The landowner has thus property rights over rain and well water, source and groundwater that are incomplete and temporary, since water will regain its natural course as a watercourse subject to a restricted usage right for riparian areas.[152] Accordingly, privately owned wells and pumps and water installations owned by municipalities considered private property in occupied territory must be respected and cannot be confiscated.[153]

2. *Rules applicable to public and private property*

2.1 *Property destruction and seizure for military operations or necessity*

2.1.1 PROPERTY DESTRUCTION

GC IV, article 53 prohibits destruction of movable or immovable property, privately or publicly owned in occupied territory, unless "absolutely necessary by military operations."[154] It is a customary international law norm applicable in IAC and NIAC.[155] The *travaux préparatoires* discussion on article 53 cited Leningrad's devastation during WWII by German bombing as an example.[156] The Regulations article 23(g), applicable to hostilities, prohibits destruction of enemy property unless for "necessities of war." During its latter *travaux préparatoires*, the initial provision prohibiting destruction of private property in occupied territory, unless urgent necessity,[157] was considered covered by the article on war means (article 23(g)) suppressed in 1899,[158] implying then that property in occupied territory subject to war was included in the category that could be destroyed for war necessity. The intention at both conferences was then that destruction of property is justified in case of war or renewed hostilities in occupied territory, as opposed to military operations not reaching that level.

Dinstein advances that military operations may be used by occupants to counter violence from armed groups and individual saboteurs in occupied territory, apart from hostilities against the enemy.[159] It is difficult to justify military operations against individual saboteurs, house destructions for example, as that seems excessive and does not correspond to the intention of the participants at the *travaux*

151 Conseil d'Etat 56 République Française, Code Civil art.642

152 Conseil d'Etat 57

153 Tignino, 'Water, International Peace, and Security' 663

154 Geneva Convention IV Relative to the Protection of Civilian Persons in Time of War, 12 August 1949 art.53

155 ICRC, *Customary International Humanitarian Law, Vol. I Rules* (Jean-Marie Henckaerts and Louise Doswald-Beck eds, 3rd edn, CUP 2009) Rule 50, Commentary 176; ICRC, *Guidelines on the Protection of the Natural Environment in Armed Conflict* (2020) Rule 13, Commentary par.175

156 Final Record 720–721

157 *Conférence de Bruxelles* 6 par.51

158 Ibid, 35

159 Dinstein par.600

préparatoires mentioned earlier. In operations against armed groups, occupants must weigh military advantage with damage done,[160] though a deliberate pattern of destruction requires the occupant to prove military necessity.[161]

AP/I article 54 prohibiting destruction of objects indispensable for the survival of civilians, applies to occupation and is analysed in Chapter 2. It covers foodstuffs, agricultural areas for the production of foodstuffs, crops, livestock, drinking water installations and supplies and irrigation works. Broadly interpreted, it extends to protection of the environment, including water, soil, air and ecosystems on which the population depends.[162] Attacks against objects mentioned are prohibited if they are expected to leave civilians without adequate water or force their movement.[163] Power plants should be granted same protection, even though they could be used for military and civilian purposes, because the electricity supplied is essential for the functioning of water infrastructure, pumping and purifying drinking water.[164] In the *Eritrea-Ethiopia* case, Ethiopia claimed damage to objects indispensable to survival of the population and to environmental resources in Mereb Lekhe and Irob that were occupied by Eritrean troops.[165] The Commission found that evidence for both fell short of the requirement to establish liability under the LOAC and below the standard of widespread and long-lasting environmental damage for environmental resources claims.[166]

2.1.2 PROPERTY SEIZURE

There is no provision for seizure of property in occupied territory under GC IV for military operations. Seizure of enemy property is prohibited, unless imperatively demanded by "necessities of war," under the Regulations article 23(g) applicable to hostilities.[167] The issue is whether it applies to property "wherever situated,"[168] including occupied territory. For the ICRC it applies to property in territory involved in war.[169] The ICJ concluded the same, based on the article's place under the section on hostilities in the Regulations.[170] Doctrine discussed the relevance of this

160 ICRC, Commentary on GC IV art.63, par.3
161 Dinstein par.604, 606; ICRC, Commentary on GC IV art.53
162 ICRC Commentary on AP/I, par.2102–2103; ILC, Lehto Environment and Armed Conflict (2018) par.42
163 Protocol Additional to the Geneva Conventions of 12 August 1949, and relating to the Protection of Victims of International Armed Conflicts (Protocol I), 8 June 1977 art.54(3)(b)
164 Tignino, 'Water, International Peace, and Security' 659
165 *Eritrea-Ethiopia Claims Commission, Partial Award Central Front, Ethiopia's Claim 2* par.41, 75
166 Ibid, *Partial Award Central Front, Ethiopia's Claim 2* par.53, 100
167 ICRC, Customary IHL Rules Rule 50
168 Michael Schmitt, 'Green War: An Assessment of the Environmental Law of International Armed Conflict' 22 Yale J Int'l L (1997) 1, 63; Babalola Cole, 'Property and the Law of Belligerent Occupation' 137 World Aff 1 (1974) 66 69, applying the article to all aspects of warfare
169 ICRC, Commentary on GC IV Commentary on art.53, p. 301, par.2 Scope of the provision
170 *The Wall* par.185

article for an occupant to seize land in occupied territory.[171] The Special Rapporteur for the OPT found that Israel's Wall generally violates the LOAC principles, including prohibition of private property confiscation under the Regulations article 23(g) and 46,[172] though it is not conclusive as to whether article 23(g) specifically applies to immovable property or natural resources' seizure in occupied territory. For example, mines are specifically regulated under article 55 and are not covered under article 23(g).[173] An Israeli attempt to exploit oil fields under the Suez Gulf, by claiming that oil is militarily useful and therefore exempt from article 55 and subject to article 23(g), put "impossible strains" on the purpose of this article.[174]

Schwarzenberger considers that though the article "applies directly to fighting zones alone, it *can* be legitimately extended by analogy to occupied territories."[175] However, he finds it difficult to reconcile that interpretation with the intention behind the Regulations. First, the dichotomy between fighting zones and occupied territories was much clearer in the 1899 version that included article 23(g). Second, rules regarding property in occupied territory are sufficiently comprehensive to form a complete codification in this field.[176] Finally, since article 46 under occupation law is the applicable rule on interferences with private property, corresponding to article 23(g) under the law of war in the strict sense, the latter should not apply.[177] In conclusion, though Schwarzenberger contemplates the application of article 23(g) by analogy, he argues against it.

The US military manual stating that article 23(g) is applicable to occupations assesses military necessity in that case for property destruction only (despite a contrary heading), while analysing it for seizure and destruction in case of hostilities.[178] Arguably, seizure in occupied territory may not be justified by military necessity, especially as it follows specific occupation rules. Private immovable property may "under no circumstances" be seized, though it may be requisitioned.[179] Taking private property for military use should conform to requisitions rules,[180] despite contrary Israeli jurisprudence.[181] Regarding public immovable property, an occupant may take temporary possession of it for direct military use in military operations, such as forts, arsenal, bridges, magazines, docks and barracks, for purposes of war

171 David Kretzmer, 'The Advisory Opinion: The Light Treatment of International Humanitarian Law' 99 AJIL (2005) 88, 95

172 John Dugard, Special Rapporteur of the Commission on Human Rights, *Question of the Violation of Human Rights in the Occupied Arab Territories, including Palestine, E/CN.4/2004/6/Add.1* par.29

173 UK MoD 11.86; U.S. DoD 11.18.5.2

174 Weaver and others 125

175 Schwarzenberger 253

176 Ibid, 314

177 Ibid, 266

178 U.S. DoD par.11.18.2.1

179 Ibid, par.5.17.2.2, 11.18.6.3

180 Jr. William Gerald Downey, 'Captured Enemy Property: Booty of War and Seized Enemy Property' 44 AJIL 3, July (1950) 488, 488. U.S. DoD 11.18.2.2

181 Dinstein par.697

necessities, to house troops and look after the sick and wounded, until the close of hostilities and destroy or damage it, if necessary.[182] After cessation of hostilities, immovable public property in occupied territory must be used in accordance with usufruct rules in the Regulations, article 55,[183] though some consider that a piece of public land could be requisitioned during occupation, if necessary for military reasons, such as defence position or to build accommodation for the troops.[184] In conclusion, article 23(g) does not apply to seizure of immovable property in occupied territory that is not subject to renewed hostilities.

2.2 Seizure of property of military use

Under the Regulations, article 53, the occupation army may seize:

(i) Cash, funds, realizable securities strictly the property of the State, depots of arms, means of transport, stores and supplies and generally all movable property belonging to the State which may be used for military operations,[185]
(ii) Privately owned means of communication and transport, except for those covered by naval law, depots of arms and generally all kinds of munitions of war, that must be restored and compensation fixed when peace is made.[186]

The article is customary international law.[187] Despite railway infrastructure being immovable, article 53 applies strictly to movable property, *munitions de guerre* being considered as such, as confirmed by the *travaux préparatoires* at the Brussels and Hague Conferences, doctrine and international jurisprudence.[188] Case law examples concerned a motor taken out of a motor boat that was not *munitions de guerre*[189] and calculating machines belonging to the Polish State that were not movables usable for war operations.[190] Courts have examined whether natural resources and raw material may be legally seized under this article.

182 Oppenheim 398, par.136; Von Glahn 176. Wickersham and King 33. Cole 71–72; U.S. DoD 11.18.5.1; UK MoD 11.85
183 Dinstein par.653; Rogers 264
184 Dörmann and Vité 9.33 par.6
185 The Hague regulations art.53(1)
186 Ibid, Art.53(2)
187 ICRC, Customary IHL Rules Rule 51(a)
188 MAE, 'Conférence Internationale de la Paix' in *Archives Diplomatiques: Recueil de Diplomatie et d'Histoire, 2ème série, Tome LXXI, Juillet Août Septembre* (France, 1899) cinquieme seance, 37; Dinstein par.670, 719; William Gerald Downey 488–489, 490; Oppenheim 399, 404; Lauterpacht 226, 234; Richard A. Curry, 'Oil Rights in the Gulf of Suez' 38 La L Rev 4, Summer (1978) 991; Schwarzenberger 269; C.A. Singapore, Opinion of C.J. Whyatt, 'N.V. de Bataafsche Petroleum Maatschappij and Others v. the War Damage Commission (1956)' 51 AJIL 4, October (1957) 802, 809
189 *Johansen v. Gross* ADIL 1949, Case No176,
190 Lauterpacht 231, 232.

2.2.1 PRIVATE PROPERTY AS WAR MUNITIONS

"Munitions of war" has been translated to "war materials" that could include a wide range of ordinary objects.[191] Determination of the term is essential. In the Regulations' authentic text, *munitions* means:

> «(i) *Vieux. Ce qui était indispensable à l'approvisionnement des armées . . . (vivres, matériels d'habillement, de couchage, de campement, etc.); (ii) Ce qui est nécessaire à l'approvisionnement des armes à feu (cartouches, projectiles, charges de poudre, fusées, amorces, etc.).*»[192]

Munitions de guerre, in its old meaning, correspond to army supply covered by article 52, while its meaning as firearms' ammunitions falls under article 53(2). It would make no sense to regulate army supply under two different regimes.

In the Singapore oil stocks case, Japanese armed forces, during their occupation of Sumatra in WWII, seized oil installations of Dutch companies exploiting oil reservoirs held under concessions.[193] They continued oil exploitation, shipping crude oil or refined product to Singapore where it was stored in tanks belonging to companies associated with the claimants and worldwide, including Japan where it was used for civilian and military purposes. In September 1945, British armed forces re-occupied Singapore and seized the oil found in storage tanks. The Dutch corporations claimed compensation.[194] On appeal, parties argued about the application of Regulations article 53(2) to the oil seizure. Crude oil in the ground was an immovable raw material that was not *munitions de guerre*, for appellants. It was susceptible of, or had a sufficiently close connection with, direct military use, for respondents citing Oppenheim only as supporting authority.[195]

Oppenheim shifted his views of raw materials (cloth for uniforms and leather for boots) from public or "private movable property which can serve as war material" that may be seized and used for military purposes under article 53[196] to resources subject to requisitions for the occupation army's needs under article 52.[197] Schwarzenberger, on the basis of old military manuals, considered that potentially useful material, such as crude oil, requiring processing to be actually useful for military operations, may be covered by article 53(2).[198] Under the UK

191 Lauterpacht 219

192 Larousse Munitions, Approvisionnement

193 C.A. Singapore

194 Ibid, 810–812

195 Ibid, 870–808 respondents were the Crown though not appearing as such in the proceedings

196 Oppenheim p. 400 par.137, p. 404

197 Lauterpacht 234; James E. E., L. Oppenheim and Great Britain, War Office, *Land Warfare: An Exposition of the Laws and Usages of War on Land, for the Guidance of Officers of His Majesty's Army* (London: H.M.S.O. 1912) 90.

198 Schwarzenberger 298–299, referring to the 1914 UK manual of military law p. 297 par.415 and 1958 edition pp. 165–166 par.597 and the US manual 1956 p. 153.

manual, all kind of property that could serve as war material, including raw material such as crude oil, comes under the scope of article 53.[199] It is a minority view.[200]

The Singapore Appeals Court judged that, given the need for elaborate installations, civilian specialists' help and complicated refinery process, oil in the ground neither has a sufficient close connection with, nor is susceptible enough of, direct military use, at the time of seizure, to bring it within the meaning of *munitions de guerre.*[201] Referring to a jurisprudential dictum finding seizure of private property as *munitions de guerre* illegitimate, "unless it was "ammunition or arms which could be used . . . in fighting,"[202] the Court judged that it would be "startling . . . to say that it could include minerals *in situ.*"[203] The minority opinion (Whitton) considered that, had petrol been found ready for immediate use, its use by the Japanese for the purposes of their campaign would not have violated article 53 and, by that same logic, the occupant could be entitled to seize "the crude material out of which the finished products are created,"[204] an opinion supported by a few.[205] However, Whitton concluded that the seizure was illegal, breaching article 53, because crude oil would not "under any circumstances have been readily susceptible of direct military use" and it was used for purposes that were not military necessity.[206] Such seizure would empty article 52 of justification, flaunting its requirement subjecting requisitions to the occupation army's needs.[207] Though not clearly stated, considering the Regulations' aims to protect private property, case law and doctrine, private property seized must be susceptible of direct military use.[208] Crude oil not yet extracted is considered immovable, not susceptible of direct military use.[209]

International courts' decisions on occupants taking raw materials have analysed their legality under confiscation and requisitions rules, not seizure.[210] Cotton seized

199 UK MoD par.11.18.1

200 Dinstein par.723

201 C.A. Singapore 808–809

202 *Schiffahrt-Treuhand v. Procurator General* A.C. 232 262

203 C.A. Singapore 809

204 *C.A. Singapore, De Bataafsche Petroleum Maatschappij v. War Damage Commission* 1956 23 ILR 810, 847

205 'War. Belligerency. Original Owners Retain Title to Oil Resources Seized by Belligerent Occupant in Violation of Hague Regulations. N. V. De Bataafsche Petroleum Maatschappij v. War Damage Comm'n (C. A. Singapore 1956)' 71 Harv L Rev 3, January (1958) 568, 570.
Dinstein par.722–723

206 *C.A. Singapore, De Bataafsche Petroleum Maatschappij v. War Damage Commission* 847

207 Lauterpacht 236–240

208 *The Proceedings of the Hague Peace Conferences, Translation of the Official Texts, the International Peace Conference, 1907, Acts and Documents, Volume III, Second, Third and Fourth Commissions* 128; *Conférence de Bruxelles* 4 (initial art.6) and 49; Cassese 428; Lauterpacht 234; Philip C. Jessup, 'Editorial Comment, A belligerent Occupant's Power over Property' 38 AJIL (1944) 457, 458; Contra: Erik Castren, *The Present Law of War and Neutrality* (Suomalainev Tiedeakemia 1954) 230; Von Glahn 181

209 ILC, Lehto Environment and Armed Conflict (2018) par.38

210 Lauterpacht 233, cases cited ftnte 3

between 1914 and 1916 during the occupation of Belgium by German forces and sent to Germany's War Raw Material Department was found to be a requisition to satisfy other needs than the occupation's army, in violation of article 52.[211]

Obviously from the Regulations' authentic text, *munitions de guerre* means strictly arms and ammunitions, in addition to the *travaux préparatoires'* reference to these terms only, their ordinary and historical meanings under contraband laws and jurisprudence.[212] Consequently, raw materials and semi-manufactured products necessary for war cannot be regarded as munitions of war.[213]

2.2.2 PUBLIC PROPERTY OF MILITARY USE

Alternatively, the issue is whether natural resources could be considered public property of military use subject to seizure under article 53(1). In a case mentioned earlier, a contention that oil in the ground should "be regarded as movable property having military value," subject by analogy to article 53(1),[214] was rejected by doctrine and the US State Department.[215] Views differ as to whether natural resources that could have an indirect military use, for example when converted to money, come within the scope of article 53(1).[216] The *travaux préparatoires* intended to limit seizure to property that could have a direct military use, including privately owned property, as they restricted seizure to property used for the purpose of "military operations", instead of "the purpose of war."[217]

In cases of disputed ownership of bank deposits and stores and supplies obtained from contractors, the UK and US military manuals assume that property is publicly owned until ownership is established.[218] Scholars suggested expanding this rule to natural resources whose ownership is disputed and assuming that they are publicly owned.[219] However, applying this presumption to natural resources would remove the benefit of immunity of private property from confiscation and leave natural resources – assuming they are covered hereunder – vulnerable to seizure for military necessity, an objective that could be abused. Cassese finds a presumption of public ownership unjustifiable, except in case of sufficient evidence of abusive transfer of public property to private individuals by the previous government, prior

211 *Ralli Brothers v. German Government* Anglo-German Mixed Arbitral Tribunal: Annual Digest, 1923–1924, Case No 244,

212 Lauterpacht 225–226, 233; Jessup 458; *Conférence de Bruxelles*, 25–26, 44.

213 Castren 236; Lauterpacht 226

214 Israel Ministry of Foreign Affairs 432

215 Weaver and others 124; Leigh 735

216 ILC, Lehto Environment and Armed Conflict (2018) par.38

217 *Conférence de Bruxelles* 4 (initial art.6) and 49; *The Proceedings of the Hague Peace Conferences, Translation of the Official Texts, the International Peace Conference, 1907, Acts and Documents, Volume III, Second, Third and Fourth Commissions* 128; Wickersham and King

218 U.S. DoD 11.18.4.3; UK MoD 11.90

219 Von Glahn 179 Scobbie, 'Natural Resources and Belligerent Occupation: Mutation through Permanent Sovereignty' 6

to an impending occupation.[220] Natural resources were not envisaged in the debate on article 53 and discussion on disputed ownership focused on cash, funds or negotiable securities held in State or public institutions; the term "*appartenant en propre*" was introduced solely to clarify that private deposits held in State institutions were excluded.[221] Functional tests were used by international jurisprudence to determine the actual purposes of privately owned ships operated by public authorities and identity of the bearer of financial risk at the time of seizure.[222] These include the status of the property owner, the property function and economic risk assumed by a State in holding and management of property.[223]

Natural resources in occupied territory cannot be seized under the Regulations article 53. Publicly owned resources extracted from the ground and not yet processed are not susceptible to direct military use, while land and underground resources, including water, being immovable, cannot be seized. Privately owned natural resources are not munitions of war.

2.3 Prohibition of pillage

Pillage of public or private property, by individual or organized acts, is prohibited.[224] A war crime under the IMT Charter (Nuremberg) article 6(b) on plunder and the ICC Statute article 8(2)(b)(xvi), it is a customary international law rule.[225] Pillage is appropriation of property for personal use, while seizure is for public use.[226] The prohibition of pillage applies to natural resources and related exploitation rights such as concessions.[227] According to the Eritrea-Ethiopia Claims Commission, Ethiopia, as occupying power, was responsible during Eritrea's occupation for the maintenance of public order, respect of private property and prevention of pillage and consequently is liable for permitting breach of these obligations, whether or not Ethiopian military were involved.[228] This duty to prevent pillage applies also to private actors' illegal exploitation of natural resources during occupation, as looting, plundering and exploiting natural resources were judged to amount to pillage

220 Cassese 437–438. See also Schwarzenberger 309

221 *Conférence de Bruxelles* 25, 49, 50

222 *Cession of vessels and tugs for navigation on the Danube (1921)* 1 RIAA 97, *Lighthouses* Permanent Court of International Justice, Series C, No. 74, 49; Schwarzenberger 260, 262, 264

223 Schwarzenberger 265; U.S. DoD 11.18.4.1. and 11.18.4.2; Dichter 577; Von Glahn 179

224 The Hague Regulations art.47. GC IV art.33; ICRC, Commentary on GC IV Commentary on art.33.2

225 ICRC, Customary IHL Rules Rule 52

226 Daniëlla Dam-de Jong, 'From Engines for Conflict into Engines for Sustainable Development' 166; *The Prosecutor v. Moinina Fofana and Allieu Kondewa, Special Court for Sierra Leone* par.392

227 Ibid, 164 on pillage prohibition in NIAC. The same analysis applies to IAC

228 *Eritrea-Ethiopia Claims Commission, Partial Award: Central Front – Eritrea's Claims 2, 4, 6, 7, 8 and 22*

in *Armed Activities*.[229] Uganda violated its duty of vigilance by not taking adequate measures to ensure that its military forces did not engage in such activities.[230]

3. *Rules applicable to private property*

3.1 Prohibition of confiscation

The Regulations' prohibition of confiscation of private property, movable or immovable, is customary international law.[231] It is an "unqualified" prohibition that does not allow for any exception, whether on grounds of military exigencies or other.[232] Property of municipalities and institutions dedicated to religion, charity and education, arts and sciences, even when State property, is treated as private property.[233] Any confiscation by the occupier and sale of private land or building cannot result in transfer of title or to the buyer;[234] he "would acquire no right whatever to the property."[235] However, "the loose and discretionary practice" of requisitions and contributions deviate considerably from the principle.[236] Expropriation is exceptionally admitted, if it was provided under pre-occupation law, and implemented in the interest of the protected population subject to adequate compensation.[237]

3.2 Requisitions for army needs

Under the Regulations article 52, requisitions in kinds and services cannot be demanded by the occupation army from the population or municipalities, except for its own needs and in proportion to the country's resources, under the authority of the local commander and against cash remuneration or due receipt given for later payment. GC IV restricts requisition of foodstuffs, articles or medical supplies available in occupied territory, except for use by occupation forces and administration personnel and only after taking into account the requirements of the civilian population to whom the occupant has a duty to ensure provision of food and supplies.[238] Requisitions differ from confiscation by their temporary nature.[239]

229 Longobardo 265; *Armed Activities (2005)* par.245
230 *Armed Activities (2005)* par.245,246
231 Regulations art.46; ICRC, Customary IHL Rules Rule 51(c); *Prosecutor v. Tihomir Blaskic, Case No. IT-95–14-A, 29 July 2004* ICTY, Appeals Chamber par.148
232 *Legal Consequences Arising from the Policies and Practices of Israel in the Occupied Palestinian Territory, including East Jerusalem, ICJ Advisory Opinion, 19 July 2024* ICJ par.122
233 The Hague Regulations, art.56
234 Kretzmer 97; Scobbie, 'Natural Resources and Belligerent Occupation: Mutation through Permanent Sovereignty' 230
235 Oppenheim 403
236 E. M. B. 'Confiscation of Enemy Private Property' 28 Yale L J 5, March (1919) 478, 479
237 Schwarzenberger 245
238 GC IV, art.55
239 Kretzmer 98

Some consider that only movables may be requisitioned under the Regulations article 52, while immovable property may be subject to temporary use, if required by military necessity.[240] For the US, temporary military use of private immovable property for army needs, including billeting, should follow requisitions rules,[241] while the UK provides for requisitions of commodities and services only, allowing temporary use of immovable property for military use, without compensation, except for damage and accommodation of troops in private homes.[242] The accepted position is that, though article 52 concerns mainly movables, it extends to requisitions of immovable (houses, buildings, land for campsites)[243] strictly for the purpose of the army's accommodation and cannot extend to possession of immovable property generally.[244] The *travaux préparatoires* confirm this interpretation. Under the initial convention, the occupying army could request from the local population supply items, clothing, shoes and others necessary to its maintenance,[245] replaced by "*prestations et services*" related to war needs,[246] then by requisitions.[247] "*Prestations*" referred to services in kind, such as military lodging, food, clothing and transport[248] and "*services*" to personal work provided.[249]

"Needs of the occupation army" replacing the wider "needs of the war"[250] are narrower than – and clearly different from – war necessities (Regulations, art.23(g)) or military operations (GC IV art.53).[251] They are strictly "the need of the army of occupation for its own maintenance,"[252] which was the aim of the original draft convention,[253] "such as foodstuffs, clothing, horses, transportation and means of transportation, and buildings."[254] Seizure of private oil installations under the Japanese State's plan to secure oil resources, not merely for its occupation army's

240 Dinstein par.697–703, par.767; Scobbie, 'Natural Resources and Belligerent Occupation: Mutation through Permanent Sovereignty' 229–230; Cole 74

241 U.S. DoD 11.18.2.2, 11.18.7, 11.18.7.2, 11.18.6.3

242 UK MoD par.11.78, 11.79, 11.83

243 *Trial of Alfried Felix Alwyn Krupp Von Bohlen und Halbach and eleven others, 17th November1947–30th June, 1948* UN War Crimes Commission, Law Reports of Trials of War Criminals, Vol X, 69, US NMT 137; Oppenheim 411; Benvenisti, *The International Law of Occupation* 7; Franklin municipal property under occupation 393; Jessup 459; Wickersham and King 33; David Kretzmer and Yaël Ronen, *The Occupation of Justice, The Supreme Court of Israel and the Occupied Territories* (2nd edn, OUP 2021) 188. Schwarzenberger 246

244 Dinstein par.704, 767. Contra Schwarzenberger 288

245 *Conférence de Bruxelles* 6 art.53

246 Ibid, 36

247 Ibid, 39

248 Ibid, 35, 36

249 Ibid, 37

250 MAE 34

251 Schwarzenberger 245; Kretzmer 97; Kretzmer and Ronen 134

252 Jessup 459. Blaine Sloan, *Study of the Implications, under International Law, of the UN Resolutions on Permanent Sovereignty over Natural Resources, on the Occupied Palestinian and other Arab Territories and on the Obligations of Israel Concerning its Conduct in these Territories, Report of the Secretary-General, Annex, UNGA A/38/50/Rev.1* (1983) par.50

253 UK MoD 11.83; U.S. DoD 11.18.7.2; *Conférence de Bruxelles* 38.

254 Von Glahn 165

requirements but to supply its military and civilian needs during the war, violated the laws and customs of war.[255]

Though requisitions for army bases are probably lawful,[256] it seems highly doubtful that army maintenance extends to security needs. Israeli jurisprudence differs, considering that security needs could justify land requisition, equating military needs of the occupation army with security needs.[257] Military necessity is different from "imperative reasons of security" under GC IV article 78 allowing the occupant to take safety measures concerning protected persons.[258] Under GC IV, "security" of the State, of the Occupying or Detaining Power, is related to measures that the occupant may take concerning protected persons[259] or criminal legislation[260] or to Protecting Powers' duties,[261] security of the population under occupation[262] or of the installations on which a protected person is working[263] or to conformity of the work of organizations and faith ministers to security regulations.[264] "Security" never appears in the Regulations and does not justify requisition of private property in occupied territory under occupation law.

Requisitions being for maintenance needs of the occupying army, they would violate article 52 if articles seized were sent outside the occupied territory,[265] such as (i) removal of vast amounts of raw textile materials from occupied Belgium and France and their transport to Germany[266] and (ii) imposition of quotas, if not amounting to confiscation, would be termed requisitions that were not imposed strictly for the occupation army but also for general army needs and the benefit of the civilian economy in Germany.[267] Finally, requisitions should cover occupation expenses only and cannot exceed the cost that the economy can be reasonably expected to incur or the capabilities of the population or territory.[268]

4. *Administration of public immovable property*

Under the Regulations article 55, the occupier is considered administrator and usufructuary (usufruct right holder) only of State immoveable property, constituted of

255 C.A. Singapore 808

256 James Crawford SC, *Opinion, Third Party Obligations with respect to Israeli Settlements in the Occupied Palestinian Territories* (2012) par.3

257 Kretzmer 97–98; HCJ 606/78, Ayoub v Minister of Defense, 33(2) PD 113; *Beit Sourik Village Council v. Israel (30 June 2004)* HCJ 2056/04, 43 ILM 1099 (2004),

258 Kretzmer and Ronen 134

259 GC IV art.5,27, 36, 39, 42, 62, 74, 75, 78, 142

260 Ibid, art.64

261 Ibid, art.9

262 Ibid, art.49

263 Ibid, art.51

264 Ibid, art.26, 30, 63, 93

265 Jessup 459, 460

266 *Ralli Brothers v. German Government*

267 *United States v. Weizsaecker (Ministries Trial) US MTN, Judgment 13 April 1949,* WorldCourts online database, p. 340, 766

268 ILC, Lehto Environment and Armed Conflict (2018) par.37; Dörmann and Vité 9.31 par.2

public buildings, real estate, forests and agricultural estates, in occupied territory. He must safeguard their capital and administer them according to usufruct rules.[269] This role extends to "objects forming part of the natural environment."[270] Although common law stretching back to the Saxon era recognized customary usufructuary rights of the English peasantry to the commons,[271] usufruct is a civil law concept derived from Roman law, with few national laws' variations.[272] The ILC, adapting environmental protection in armed conflict to legal developments, replaced the notion of usufruct with sustainable use.[273] It is still necessary to analyse usufruct; French Civil Code usufruct rules are elaborated.

Usufruct is a temporary right to use the property of another and enjoy its fruits, subject to conserving its substance.[274] Exceptionally, despite the finite nature of products extinguishable by long-term extraction (i.e. minerals, quarry products, hydrocarbons), the usufructuary is entitled to products already under exploitation when the usufruct started, subject to observing the existing exploitation mode.[275] Civil codes differ in their definitions of fruits and products.[276]

The usufructuary must exercise reasonably his right to enjoy the property's fruits[277] and is prohibited from doing so negligently or in a wasteful manner.[278] A reasonable exploitation rate is the previous one for non-renewable resources – unless it was excessive – or the rate at which fruits renew themselves,[279] in accordance with sustainable use of natural resources.[280] The occupant's duty to safeguard the capital of non-renewable resources, interpreted according to its ordinary meaning, should lead to prohibiting their exploitation;[281] extracting oil is depletion, not safeguarding, of capital.[282] Oil extraction and production, in infancy in 1874, were unlikely to have been envisaged. Under an agreed interpretation, continued exploitation

269 The Hague Regulations, Art.55; ICRC, Customary IHL Rules Rule 51; *Administration of Waters and Forests v. Falck,* 4 ADIL 563 (1927–1928),

270 ICRC, Guidelines Rule 15.B

271 Connor Bartlett McDermott, 'Monopolizers of the Soil: The Commons as a Source of Public Trust Responsibilities' 61 Nat Resour J 1, Winter (2021) 125 129, 133, 135

272 Weaver and others 125; A.N. Yiannopoulos, 'Rights of the Usufructuary: Louisiana and Comparative Law' 27 La L Rev 4, June (1967) 668.

273 ILC, Environment Protection Principles, Commentary on Principle 20. par(8)

274 Encyclopaedia Britannica, 'Usufruct (law)' Benjamin Straumann, 'Ususfructus' The Wiley-Blackwell Encyclopedia of Ancient History; République Française, Code Civil art.578; François Terré and Philippe Simler, *Droit Civil, Les Biens* (10 edn, Dalloz 2018) par.775

275 Terré and Simler par.807(a); Yiannopoulos 685

276 Yiannopoulos 671–673, 680, 685

277 Terré and Simler par.821–822; French Civil Code art.601

278 Ibid, par.822(c), (d); Oppenheim 398, par.134; Wickersham and King 33

279 Ibid, par.821; Dichter 576–577; Dinstein par.662

280 ILC, Environment Protection Principles, Commentary on Principle 20. par(8)

281 Sloan par.32 Clagett, Thomas Johnson and Thomas Johnson Jr. 578

282 Weaver and others 125

at a reasonable rate is allowed,[283] if sustainable and not excessive.[284] Excessive exploitation could result from prolonged occupation[285] and amount to pillage.[286] Preserving the capital of freshwater resources requires occupation authorities to limit water exploitation to the annual renewable river flow, avoiding long-term damage to water storage and irrigation installation, rivers and ecosystems.[287] Roman law usufruct rules were elaborated on the erroneous belief that minerals were renewable or at least inexhaustible.[288] Civil codes based on these rules that allowed existing exploitations to continue, ignoring the necessity to preserve a property's capital, were deemed illogical and should be replaced by other regimes respecting such duty.[289]

Arguing that natural resources exploitation in occupied territory is prohibited only in case of wanton dissipation[290] breaches the intended meaning of the Regulations and its "reasonableness" and local needs' requirements.[291] In a case involving felling of France's forests, under the direction of German occupation authorities in WWII, the *Cour de Cassation* held that the accused could not use the contract he had with the Germans as defence for his excessive exploitation of forests, contrary to article 55 of the Regulations.[292] During the occupation of Timor-Leste by Indonesia, forests were exploited to such an extent that the population was deprived from its basic needs of food, medicinal plants, firewood and fodder, in addition to the erosion of soil affecting agriculture and water resources.[293]

The occupant does not acquire legal title to public immovable property, though he may lease or use it.[294] He has the right to exploit forests, mines and agricultural lands for purposes of selling or consuming crops and keep the proceeds of agricultural and mineral products sold.[295] In France, the principle that mines belong to the nation and their exploitation requires prior State's authorization or concession

283 Weaver and others 129; Jordan Paust, 'Oil Exploitation in the Occupied Territory: Sharpening the Focus on Appropriate Legal Standards' 1 Hous J Int'l L (1979) 147, 149

284 Emilia Pabian, 'Prolonged Occupation and Exploitation of Natural Resources, A Focus on Natural Gas off the Coast of Northern Cyprus' 12 J Int'l Hum Leg Stud 1 (2021) 20; Nico Schriver, *Sovereignty Over Natural Resources, Balancing Rights and Duties* (CUP 1997) 269; Daniëlla Dam-de Jong, *Governance of Natural Resources* 228, 381–382.

285 Lauterpacht 240

286 *Armed Activities (2005)* par.245

287 Benvenisti, 'Water Conflicts' 869; Cassese 422

288 Weaver and others 125; Sloan par.29

289 Leigh 739–740

290 Allan Gerson, 'Off-Shore Oil Exploration by a Belligerent Occupant: The Gulf of Suez Dispute' 71 AJIL N. 4, October (1977) 725, 731

291 Paust 149; Clagett, Johnson, and Johnson Jr. 574

292 *l'Etat Francais v. Lemarchand (1948)* ADIL No 198, Court of Appeals of Rouen, France

293 Vité 647

294 Oppenheim par.134

295 Terré and Simler par.806–808; Wickersham and King 33; Scobbie, 'Natural Resources and Belligerent Occupation: Mutation through Permanent Sovereignty' 44

has existed since 1791, strengthened in 1810.[296] Under the Mining Code, mineral substances and fossil fuels are administered by the State,[297] while quarries require the State's authorization to exploit.[298] Exploitation of existing mines or quarries held under concession cannot continue, unless the usufructuary is granted permission from the State, since an 1804 law,[299] meaning the occupant as usufructuary would need permission from the occupied territory's previous authorities that have permanent sovereignty over natural resources. It is therefore questionable, in the absence of any reference in the *travaux préparatoires*, whether delegates to the 1874 Brussels Conference intended that usufruct on public land implied automatic right to continue exploitation of mines or quarries, in view of contrary legislation such as the French one.

As usufructuary, the occupant is not entitled to start a new exploitation or intensify an existing one.[300] Increasing the rate or volume of oil production or using new technologies to that effect[301] would violate this rule. In the case of the Continental Shelf oil exploitation, Israel's contention that, should oil be considered immoveable property, the law of usufruct permits reasonable operations of new wells and granting of concessions by the occupant[302] was considered "inconceivable"[303] and rejected.[304] According to Dinstein, exploitation of new mines, quarries and oil wells enhances a property's value,[305] and, as judged by Israel's High Court of Justice (HCJ) in the *Na'ale* case, is not prohibited as it benefits local residents including Israeli settlers or local needs, even if "quarrying cannot be considered usufructing."[306] The first argument is unpersuasive, as the search for new resources will destroy the corpus of the land and diminish the value of the property while depleting its resources, particularly during long-term occupation, therefore breaching the obligation to safeguard their capital.[307] Furthermore, including settlers in the definition of protected population violates the Regulations.[308] The *Na'ale* ruling

296 Terré and Simler par.323; Lionel Latty, 'La Loi du 21 avril 1810 et le Conseil Général des Mines avant 1866' 16 Documents pour l'Histoire des Techniques 2ème semestre 2008 17 19, 21
297 République Française, Code Minier art.L100–3
298 Ibid, art.L331–1
299 Terré and Simler par.807; République Française, Code Civil art.598
300 République Française, Code Civil art.598; Terré and Simler par.807(a); Curry 990 note 73; ILC, Environment Protection Principles Commentary on Principle 20, par (8)
301 R. Dobie Langenkamp and Rex J. Zedalis, 'What Happens to the Iraqi Oil? Thoughts on Some Significant, Unexamined International Legal Questions Regarding Occupation of Oil Fields' 14 EJIL 3, June (2003) 417, 418; Dinstein par.662
302 Israel Ministry of Foreign Affairs 440
303 Clagett, Johnson, and Johnson Jr. 575
304 Leigh 736; Curry 990 note 73.
305 Gerson 732; Dinstein par.663.
306 *HCJ 9717/03, Na'ale v. Planning Council for the Judea and Samaria Region et al.* ILDC 70 (IL 2004) and 37 Israel Yearbook on Human Rights 332 (2007) 333
307 Curry 990 note 73; Clagett, Johnson, and Johnson Jr. 575; Leigh 736–737; David Kretzmer, 'The Law of Belligerent Occupation in the Supreme Court of Israel' 94 IRRC 885, Spring (2012) 222
308 Rogers 253

is "manifestly incorrect," as erasing article 55 violates article 43.[309] Similar judgements by the HCJ finding operation of new quarries by private concessionaire consistent with the Regulations[310] were criticized by Israeli scholars and NGOs.[311]

The occupant may only use natural resources of the occupied territory for the benefit of the protected population.[312] UNSC Resolution 1483 (par. 20) on occupants' duties in Iraq provided that natural resources may only be exploited for the benefit of the Iraqi people. It is the traditional interpretation of the Regulations that should inform discussions on the issue.[313] The protected population is the protected persons under GVC IV[314] or "indigenous" or "local population at the time the occupation is established, adjusted for subsequent natural growth."[315] Further, population transfer being prohibited under GC IV, article 49(6) and a war crime under ICC Statute, art.8.2(b)(viii), the use by settlers of natural resources, such as land and water, is illegal on both counts.[316] Consequently, the occupant may not use natural resources for its own domestic purposes, its economy or its civilian population in the occupied territory[317] or use usufruct proceeds at his discretion[318] on public administration, services and infrastructure to benefit settlers or their military protection[319] or outside occupied territory, as claimed,[320] as that would not benefit the protected population. During their occupation of Timor-Leste, Indonesian authorities' exploitation of natural resources such as coffee and sandalwood, for their own benefit and to fund military operations, violated their duties as occupant and the right to self-determination of Timor-Leste people.[321]

Generally, "property can only be taken for purposes of occupation itself," whatever provisions of the Regulations the taking is under.[322] The only "lawful purpose

309 Scobbie, 'International Law and the Prolonged Occupation of Palestine, 2015' 23

310 Dinstein par.664; *Yesh Din – Volunteers for Human Rights v. Commander of the IDF Forces in the West Bank et. al.* HCJ 2164/09

311 Kretzmer, 'The Law of Belligerent Occupation in the Supreme Court of Israel' 220–222; Guy Harpaz, Yuval Shany, Eyal Benvenisti, Amichai Cohen, Yael Ronen, Barak Medina, and Orna Ben-Naftali, *Expert Legal Opinion, HCJ 2164/09 Yesh Din – Volunteers for Human Rights v. Commander of IDF Forces in West Bank et. al. (26 December 2011)*

312 ILC, Environment Protection Principles Principle 20, Commentary par.(2), (3); IDI 3; Julius Stone, *Legal Controls of International Conflict* (1959) 697; Cassese 425.

313 Dörmann and Vité 9.33 par.5

314 ILC, Environment Protection Principles, Commentary on principle 20 par(3)

315 Ben Saul, 'The Status of Western Sahara as Occupied Territory under International Humanitarian Law and the Exploitation of Natural Resources' Sydney Law School, Legal Studies Research Paper No 15/81, September 2015, 30

316 Tignino, *L'eau et la Guerre* 206–207

317 ILC, Environment Protection Principles Principle 20, Commentary par.(2), (3); Tignino, *L'eau et la Guerre* 204; Dörmann and Vité 9.33 par.5; Chinkin 208; Pabian 24

318 Dieter Fleck (ed), *The Handbook of International Humanitarian Law* (4th edn, OUP 2021) par.9.33(5) Contra: Dinstein par.660

319 Saul 30

320 Dinstein par.660

321 The Timor-Leste Commission for Reception, Truth and Reconciliation, *The Final Report* (2013) 50, 71

322 Leigh 743

under the LOAC"[323] of the use by the occupant of an occupied territory's natural resources is to cover occupation expenses necessary for its current administration.[324] Reference to "army needs"[325] should be understood in that sense. Some scholars mention security needs as purpose of natural resources' use,[326] following the lead of the Israeli HCJ that has refused to rule on "security" issues when they are raised by the military.[327] Yet, natural resources may not be exploited or used for military operations in the occupied territory[328] or for security, as this term is mentioned in specific IHL provisions that do not relate to natural resources,[329] and it is not mentioned in the *travaux préparatoires* discussing usufruct.[330] Immovable public property required for military accommodation or defence needs must be requisitioned and does not fall under usufruct rules.[331] Exploitation of resources of occupied territories during WWII for the German war effort, involving agricultural products and raw materials, without consideration of and out of proportion to the local economy and in pursuance of a deliberate policy, was a systematic plunder of private or public property, a crime under the Nuremberg Charter and a violation of the laws and customs of war.[332]

Finally, adapting usufruct to IEL principles, the ILC finds that the occupant must administer natural resources in occupied territory "in a way that ensures their sustainable use and minimizes harm to the environment"[333] and take measures ensuring activities in occupied territory do not cause harm to other States' environment.[334] The IEL principle of equitable allocation of international resources and its corresponding obligation under IWL must be respected.[335]

323 ILC, Environment Protection Principles Principle 20, Commentary par(3), n.784

324 IDI 3; Stone 697; Cassese 425; Daniëlla Dam-de Jong, *Governance of Natural Resources* 228; *Trial of the Major War Criminals, 14 November 1945–1 October 1946,* Vol I, IMT Nuremberg 239; Vité 648

325 Weaver and others 119–120; Dörmann and Vité 9.33 par.5; Paust 149. Kretzmer and Ronen 189

326 Benvenisti, *The International Law of Occupation* 82; Cassese 422

327 Dinstein par.86

328 Daniëlla Dam-de Jong, *Governance of Natural Resources* 228–229 *Trial of Alfried Felix Alwyn Krupp Von Bohlen und Halbach and eleven others, 17th November1947–30th June, 1948* 1341

329 See Requisitions for army needs

330 *Conférence de Bruxelles* 27–28

331 Fleck par.9.33(6); Contra: Dinstein par.657

332 *Trial of the Major War Criminals, Proceedings 27 August 1946 –1 October 1946* Vol XXII, IMT Nuremberg 482–483; See also *Case No. 48, Trial of Friedrich Flick and five others, 20th April – 22nd December1947* UN War Crimes Commission, Law Reports of Trials of War Criminals, Vol IX, 1, US MTN; *Trial of Alfried Felix Alwyn Krupp Von Bohlen und Halbach and eleven others, 17th November1947–30th June, 1948*; *The I.G. Farben Trial. Trial of Carl Krauch and twenty-two others, 14th August,1947–29th July, 1948* UN War Crimes Commission, Law Reports of Trials of War Criminals, Vol X, 1, US MTN

333 ILC, Environment Protection Principles, Principle 20; Michael Bothe, 'Protection of the Environment in Relation to Armed Conflicts' in Dieter Fleck (ed), *The Handbook of International Humanitarian Law* (4th edn, OUP 2021) par.10.11

334 ILC, Environment Protection Principles, Principle 21

335 Convention on the Law on Non-Navigational Uses of International Watercourses (1997) art.5; ILA Water Resources Committee, *Helsinki Rules on the Uses of the Waters of International Rivers (1966), updated by Berlin Rules on Water Resources (2004)* art.12, 13

IV. International Human Rights Law

Under the Martens clause and treaty interpretation rules, IHRL applicable between the parties must be considered.[336] The European Convention on Human Rights (ECHR) and International Covenants on Economic, Social and Cultural Rights (ICESCR) and on Civil and Political Rights (ICCPR) are applicable, at least regarding specific issues, during occupations or when control is exercised outside national jurisdiction, except for derogation clauses under relevant treaties, taking into account the LOAC specificities.[337] Though national courts apply human rights extraterritorially, a few States contest the extension of the Covenants' territorial reach,[338] since the ICCPR covers States' obligations regarding rights of "individuals within *its* territory and subject to its jurisdiction" (article 2(1) emphasis added), while ICESCR is silent about its territorial applicability. The issue has been extensively debated regarding occupied territory where significant hostilities occur.[339] In the *Al-Skeini* case, the UK argued that it was not in effective control of Basra, in Iraq, for the purposes of establishing jurisdiction under the ECHR, desisting from this argument after a House of Lords decision.[340]

The ICJ found that issues may be subject either exclusively to the LOAC or to IHRL or to both, the LOAC being *lex specialis*.[341] Neither the ICJ nor human rights institutions clarified how to apply simultaneously norms from separate legal branches. Mechanisms provided under the LOAC for its implementation (designation of Protecting Powers,[342] formal enquiry procedure[343] or inquiry by the International Fact-Finding Commission)[344] lack relevance and their role regarding IHRL application is rarely, if ever, analysed.[345] The mandate of HR institutions (UNHR Committee, ECtHR, Inter-American Commission on Human Rights (IACHR), or investigative commissions set up by the UNHR Council) does not include LOAC

336 VCLT art.31(3)(c); Iain Scobbie, 'Principle or Pragmatics? The Relationship between Human Rights Law and the Law of Armed Conflict' J Confli Secur Law (2010) 449; Cassimatis 626, 634

337 *Nuclear Weapons* par.25; *Armed Activities (2005)* par.216; *The Wall par.107–113*; *Al-Skeini and others v. United Kingdom, Application No. 55721/07, Judgment of 7 July 2011* ECtHR par.94; *Loizidou v Turkey, Preliminary Objections Judgment (23 March 1995), (Application no. 15318/89)* ECtHR par.62–64; ILC, Lehto Environment and Armed Conflict (2018) par.52–55

338 Dinstein par.225; Kleffner 14.05 par.2; Cordula Droege, 'The Interplay between International Humanitarian Law and International Human Rights Law in Situations of Armed Conflict' 40 Israël L Rev 2 326 n.64, Israel, Netherlands, UK, US

339 Noam Lubell, 'Challenges in Applying Human Rights Law to Armed Conflict' 87 IRRC 860, December (2005) 740

340 *Al-Skeini and others v. Secretary of State for Defence, 14 December 2004* High Court of Justice, Queen's Bench Division par.284–285; *Opinions of the Lords of Appeal for Judgment in the Cause, Al-Skeini v. Secretary of State for Defence, 13 June 2007* UKHL 26, par.83

341 *The Wall* par.106; *Nuclear Weapons* par.25; *Armed Activities (2005)* par.178

342 GC common Art.8/8/8/9, AP/I art.5

343 Ibid, Art.52/53/132/149

344 AP/I art.90

345 Emilie Max, *Implementing International Humanitarian Law through Human Rights Mechanisms: Opportunity or Utopia? Working Paper* (Geneva Academy 2019) 4–6

examination, though it has been interpreted by the UNHR Council as allowing it to report on LOAC violations[346] and by the IACHR to use LOAC treaties to interpret human rights obligations during armed conflict.[347]

Different methods are used to resolve norms' conflict, the most relevant mentioned here. The *lex specialis derogare lex generali* maxim provides that a specific rule prevails over a general rule, either by setting it aside in case of rules' inconsistency or if a rule is more detailed than the other. Systemic integration requires obligations to be interpreted by reference to their normative environment ("system"), including applicable international law between the parties.[348] This reflects a "complementarity" principle.[349] *Lex specialis* may lack a general mechanism to characterize special and general laws and resolve conflict between norms from different legal fields.[350] However it is useful when a systemic interpretation of LOAC and IHRL norms is unhelpful, as they are fundamentally incompatible in their objectives, even though some of their norms may be complementary.[351] As such, the right not to be deprived arbitrarily of life under the ICCPR, applicable during armed conflict, shall be interpreted by reference to the LOAC.[352] The most potent area of divergence between human rights and occupation law concerns civil and political rights and liberties,[353] for example the conflict between preventive detention authorized by the UNSC during Iraq occupation and human rights.[354] The right to self-determination, recognized in article 1 of ICESCR and ICCPR, is viewed as a political or legal principle, affirmed in UNGA resolutions. It is "the right of peoples under colonial, foreign or alien domination to self-government."[355] Invoked by the ICJ and other courts,[356] it is an international customary law principle that is so fundamental as to be deemed peremptory, imposing "an obligation to the international community as a whole to permit and respect its exercise."[357] The difficulty

346 Max 8–11

347 Lubell 742

348 ILC, *Fragmentation of International Law: Difficulties Arising from the Diversification and Expansion of International Law, Report of the Study Group of the ILC, (A/CN.4/L.682)* (2006) par.413; VCLT art.31(3)(c)

349 Droege 337, 339

350 Anja Lindroos, 'Addressing Norm Conflicts in a Fragmented Legal System: The Doctrine of Lex Specialis' 74 Nordic J Int'l L (2005) 41–42; Droege 339

351 Scobbie, 'Principle or Pragmatics? The Relationship between Human Rights Law and the Law of Armed Conflict' 456; Droege 340

352 *Nuclear Weapons* par.25

353 Benvenisti, *The International Law of Occupation* 75

354 *R (In re Al-Jedda) v. Secretary of State for Defence (2007)* UKHL 58, *Al-Jedda v. United Kingdom, App. 27021/08, 7 July 2011* ECtHR

355 Crawford 621

356 South Africa in Namibia case, ICJ Advisory Opinion 1971, par. 52; *Western Sahara, Advisory Opinion* ICJ Reports, 12, 68; *The Wall 171–172*; *East Timor (Portugal v. Australia), Judgment* ICJ Reports, 90, 102; *Joined Cases C-779/21 P and C-799/21 P, Commission v. Front Polisario, Opinion of Advocate General Capeta* EU Ct of Justice par.69–71

357 ILC, *Articles on Responsibility of States for Internationally Wrongful Acts, with Commentary, A/56/10* (ILC YB 2001, vol II (2)) Commentary on art.40 par.(5)

is how to implement this obligation in the face of an occupant ignoring the right to self-determination of population under occupation.

Many non-derogable human rights are also protected under the LOAC.[358] IHRL and LOAC are then viewed as "complementary, not mutually exclusive,"[359] especially that the ICESCR overlaps substantially with the LOAC.[360] Obligations under both fields reinforce each other when they share the same objective of protection of civilian and civilian objects. Basic human rights to water, food and health are enhanced by natural resources' protection during occupation,[361] viewed as "environmental human rights."[362] Occupants' obligations to ensure hygiene and public health, food, water and relief to the protected population[363] can be enhanced through human rights detailed obligations, jurisprudence and UNCESCR comments.[364] A human right to a healthy environment was recognized at the UNGA.[365]

The right to water, covered under the right to an adequate standard of living, including food, clothing and housing and the right to be free from hunger are fundamental for survival.[366] Recognized in international agreements,[367] the right to water is essential for full enjoyment of life and all human rights.[368] It is inextricably linked to the right to attain the highest standard of health,[369] requiring food, water, shelter and sanitation.[370] It entitles everyone to have access to a minimum of sufficient, safe, acceptable, physically accessible and affordable water available for personal and domestic use, drinking and sanitation.[371] The right to food entails State responsibility to respect access to food, adopt relevant measures and strengthen access and use of resources and livelihood means.[372] The ICJ in the Navigational and Related Rights over the San Juan River recognized that the long-established

358 Yoram Dinstein, *The Conduct of Hostilities under the Law of International Armed Conflict* (CUP 2022) par.105

359 UNHRCom., *General Comment No. 31 [80], CCPR/C/21/Rev.1/Add. 13* (2004) par.11

360 ILC, Lehto Environment and Armed Conflict (2018) par.61

361 Ibid, par.14

362 Hulme 206, 211

363 GC IV art.55, 56, 59; ICRC, Commentary on GC IV art.55, 310

364 Hulme 210–211; ILC, Lehto Environment and Armed Conflict (2018) par.59, 66; Droege 342–343

365 UNGA, *The Human Right to a Clean, Healthy and Sustainable Environment, 28 July 2022, A/RES/76/300*

366 ICESCR art.11(a), (b); UNCESCR, *General Comment No. 15: The Right to Water (Arts. 11 and 12 of the Covenant), E/C.12/2002/11* (2002) par.3

367 UNCESCR General Comment No. 15 par.4; Convention on the Elimination of All Forms of Discrimination against Women, 18 December 1979 art.14.2(h); Convention on the Rights of Persons with Disabilities, 12 December 2006 art.28.2(a)15; Convention on the Rights of the Child, 1989 art.24.2(c)

368 UNGA, The Human Right to Water and Sanitation, 28 July 2010, A/Res. 64/292 par.1

369 ICESCR, art.12; UNCESCR General Comment No 15 par.3

370 UNCECSR, *General Comment No. 14, The Right to the Highest Attainable Standard of Health (ICESCR, Art.12), E/C.12/2000/4* par.12

371 Ibid, par.12 UNGA, *The Human Rights to Safe Drinking Water and Sanitation, A/Res.70/169* (2015) WHO, *Domestic Water Quantity, Service Level and Health* (2020)

372 UNCESCR, *General Comment, the Right to Adequate Food (art.11) E/C.12/1999/5* par.15–20; FAO, *Voluntary Guidelines to Support the Progressive Realization of the Right to Adequate Food in the Context of National Food Security* (2004)

practice of subsistence fishing by inhabitants of the Costa Rica bank of the river is a customary right that cannot be impeded by Nicaragua, though it would be subject to protection of resources and the environment.[373] Rights "to hold, access, use, manage or transact" a land are linked to right to property, food and freedom to manage natural resources.[374] Human rights jurisprudence connected land property right and livelihood of indigenous people to environmental protection.[375]

As human rights have entered the mainstream legal discourse, the focus has shifted to the need to ensure their effectiveness, through development of sanctions, control and strengthening of victims' rights.[376] The UNGA adopted in 2006 Basic Principles and Guidelines on the Right to a Remedy and Reparation for Victims of Gross Violations of International Human Rights Law and Serious Violations of International Humanitarian Law.

V. Conclusion

Populations living under the might of military authorities in occupied territory deserve more robust defence than lip service to their cause. They are living under occupants' boots, at least its military regime, and under the potential control of armed groups in occupied territory, even though part of the population may sympathize with their cause. The framework regarding occupants' conduct towards the environment and natural resources under occupation seems out-dated. Most rules, however, can withstand lapse of time, by adapting them to contemporary notions resulting from development of IEL, IWL and IHRL applicable between belligerents, since the adoption of the Regulations and GC. An occupant does not have a free ride in occupied territory and is constrained in its exploitation of the land and natural resources by occupation law rules. State responsibility attaches to violations of its LOAC obligations as occupant, and the State is liable to cease its wrongful act and make reparation in the form of restitution, compensation or satisfaction.[377] The issue is its enforcement, examined in Chapter 7, as it is common to liability for obligations breached during war. Accountability is paramount to redress the imbalance between occupants' powers and responsibilities. Diplomacy is the only path to achieve a fair and equitable arrangement respecting the rights of the people under occupation ultimately securing their self-determination and independence and the security of occupants.

373 *Dispute Regarding Navigational and Related Rights (Costa Rica v. Nicaragua), Judgement* ICJ Rep 2009, p. 213, par.134–136, 140–144

374 Lorenzo Cotula, 'Land' in Elisa Morgera and Kati Kulovesi (eds), *Research Handbook on International Law and Natural Resources* (Edward Elgar 2016) 140–141

375 ILC, *Special Rapporteur Marie G. Jacobsson, Second Report on the Protection of the Environment in Relation to Armed Conflicts, A/CN.4/685* (2015) par.99, 109–116; ILC, Lehto Environment and Armed Conflict (2018) par.28

376 Pierre d'Argent, 'Des reglements collectifs aux reglements individuels (collectivises)? La question des reparations en cas de violation massive des droits de l'homme' in *International law Forum du Droit International*, vol 5 (Kluwer Law International 2003) 1010

377 South Africa in Namibia, ICJ Advisory Opinion 1971, par.118; The Regulations, art.3 AP/I art.91; ILC, States' Responsibility Articles art.28, 30–37

Bibliography

Treaties

Agreement between the United States of America, Belgium, the British Empire and France, and Germany with regard to the Military Occupation of the Territories of the Rhine, signed at Versailles, 28 June 1919
Convention on the Elimination of All Forms of Discrimination against Women, 18 December 1979
Convention on the Law on Non-Navigational Uses of International Watercourses (1997)
Convention on the Rights of Persons with Disabilities, 12 December 2006
Convention on the Rights of the Child, 1989
Convention (IV) Respecting the Laws and Customs of War on Land and Its Annex: Regulations Concerning the Laws and Customs of War on Land, the Hague, 18 October, 1907
Geneva Convention IV Relative to the Protection of Civilian Persons in Time of War, 12 August 1949
ICCPR
ICESCR
Protocol Additional to the Geneva Conventions of 12 August 1949, and relating to the Protection of Victims of International Armed Conflicts (Protocol I), 8 June 1977
The Hague Convention for the Protection of Cultural Property in the Event of Armed Conflict, 14 May 1954
The Hague Regulations VCLT

International organizations documents

Conférence de Bruxelles, Actes de la Conférence de Bruxelles de 1874 sur le Projet d'une Convention Internationale Concernant la Guerre, Protocoles des séances plénières, Protocoles de la commission déléguée par la conférence, Annexes (Librairies des Publications Legislatives, A. Wittersheim & Cie, Paris 1874)
Conférence Internationale de la Paix 1899/MAE, *Documents Diplomatiques* (Imprimerie Nationale, Paris)
Deuxième Conférence Internationale de la Paix 1907/MAE, *Documents Diplomatiques* (Imprimerie Nationale, Paris 1908)
European Parliament, Directorate General for External Policy, *Occupation/Annexation of a Territory: Respect for International Humanitarian Law and Human Rights and Consistent EU Policy* (2015)
FAO, *Voluntary Guidelines to Support the Progressive Realization of the Right to Adequate Food in the Context of National Food Security* (2004)
Ferraro T (ed) *Expert Meeting, Occupation and Other Forms of Administration of Foreign Territory, Report* (ICRC 2012)
Final Record of the Diplomatic Conference of Geneva of 1949, Vol. II-A
ICRC, *Commentary on the First Geneva Convention* (2016)
———, *Commentary on the Fourth Geneva Convention* (1958)
———, *Customary International Humanitarian Law, Vol. I Rules* (Henckaerts J-M and Doswald-Beck L eds, 3rd edn, CUP 2009)
———, *Guidelines on the Protection of the Natural Environment in Armed Conflict* (2020)
IDI, *Bruges Declaration on the Use of Force* (3 September 2003)
ILA Water Resources Committee, *Helsinki Rules on the Uses of the Waters of International Rivers (1966), updated by Berlin Rules on Water Resources* (2004)
ILC, *Articles on Responsibility of States for Internationally Wrongful Acts, with Commentary, A/56/10* (ILC YB 2001, vol II (2))
———, *Draft Articles on the Law of Treaties with commentaries* (1966)

———, *Draft Principles on Protection of the Environment in Relation to Armed Conflicts, with commentaries, A/77/10* (ILC YB 2022, vol II, (2), 2022)
———, *Fragmentation of International Law: Difficulties Arising from the Diversification and Expansion of International Law, Report of the Study Group of the ILC, (A/CN.4/L.682)* (2006)
———, *Special Rapporteur Marie G. Jacobsson, Second Report on the Protection of the Environment in Relation to Armed Conflicts, A/CN.4/685* (2015)
———, *Special Rapporteur Marja Lehto, First Report on Protection of the Environment in Relation to Armed Conflicts, A/CN.4/720* (2018)
The Proceedings of the Hague Peace Conferences, Translation of the Official Texts, the International Peace Conference, 1907, Acts and Documents, Volume III, Second, Third and Fourth Commissions
The Timor-Leste Commission for Reception, Truth and Reconciliation, *The Final Report* (2013)
UNCESCR, *General Comment, the Right to Adequate Food (art. 11) E/C.12/1999/5*
———, *General Comment No. 14, The Right to the Highest Attainable Standard of Health (ICESCR, Art. 12), E/C.12/2000/4*
———, *General Comment No. 15: The Right to Water (Arts. 11 and 12 of the Covenant), E/C.12/2002/11* (2002)
UNGA, *Basic Principles for Protection of Civilian Population in Armed Conflicts, A/Res/2675 (XXV)* (1970)
———, *The Human Right to a Clean, Healthy and Sustainable Environment, 28 July 2022, A/RES/76/300*
———, *The Human Right to Water and Sanitation, A/Res. 64/292* (28 July 2010)
———, *The Human Rights to Safe Drinking Water and Sanitation, A/Res.70/169* (2015)
UNHR Com., *General Comment No. 31 [80], CCPR/C/21/Rev.1/Add. 13* (2004)
UNSC, *Resolution1483, S/RES/1483, 22 May 2003* (2003)
WHO, *Domestic Water Quantity, Service Level and Health* (2020)

National legislation

République Française, Code Civil
———, Code de l'Environnement
———, Code Minier

International and nationals tribunals decisions and documents

Administration of Waters and Forests v. Falck, 4 ADIL 563 (1927–1928)
Al-Jedda v. United Kingdom, App. 27021/08, 7 July 2011 (ECtHR)
Al-Skeini and others v. Secretary of State for Defence, 14 December 2004 (High Court of Justice, Queen's Bench Division)
Al-Skeini and others v. United Kingdom, Application No. 55721/07, Judgment of 7 July 2011 (ECtHR)
Armed Activities on the Territory of the Congo (DRC v. Uganda), Judgment ICJ Rep 2005, p. 168 (ICJ)
Armed Activities on the Territory of the Congo (DRC v. Uganda), Reparations, Judgement ICJ Rep 2022, p. 13
Beit Sourik Village Council v. Israel (30 June 2004) HCJ 2056/04, 43 ILM 1099 (2004)
C.A. Singapore, De Bataafsche Petroleum Maatschappij v. War Damage Commission 1956 23 ILR 810
Case No. 48, Trial of Friedrich Flick and five others, 20th April – 22nd December1947 UN War Crimes Commission, Law Reports of Trials of War Criminals, vol IX, 1 (US MTN)
Certain Activities Carried Out by Nicaragua in the Border Area (Costa Rica v. Nicaragua) and Construction of a Road in Costa Rica along the San Juan River (Nicaragua v. Costa Rica), Judgment ICJ Rep 2015, p. 665

Certain Activities Carried Out by Nicaragua in the Border Area (Costa Rica v. Nicaragua), Provisional Measures, Order of 8 March 2011 ICJ Rep 2011, p. 6
Cession of Vessels and Tugs for Navigation on the Danube (1921) 1 RIAA 97
Dispute Regarding Navigational and Related Rights (Costa Rica v. Nicaragua), Judgement ICJ Rep 2009, p. 213
East Timor (Portugal v. Australia), Judgment ICJ Rep
Eritrea-Ethiopia Claims Commission, Partial Award Central Front, Ethiopia's Claim 2
Eritrea-Ethiopia Claims Commission, Partial Award, Western Front, Aerial Bombardment and Related Claims, Eritrea's Claims 1, 3, 5, 9–13, 14, 21, 25 & 26, 19 December 2005 45 ILM 396 (2006)
Eritrea-Ethiopia Claims Commission, Partial Award: Central Front – Eritrea's Claims 2, 4, 6, 7, 8 and 22
Harpaz G and others, *Expert Legal Opinion, HCJ 2164/09 Yesh Din – Volunteers for Human Rights v. Commander of IDF Forces in West Bank et. al. (26 December 2011)*
IMT (Nuremberg) Judgement and Sentences, October 1, 1946 AJIL, January 1947, vol 41, no 1, 172
Israel HCJ 606/78, Ayoub v Minister of Defense, 33(2) PD 113
Israel HCJ 9717/03, Na'ale v. Planning Council for the Judea and Samaria Region et al. ILDC 70 (IL 2004) and 37 Israel Yearbook on Human Rights 332 (2007)
Johansen v. Gross ADIL 1949, Case No176
Joined Cases C-779/21 P and C-799/21 P, Commission v. Front Polisario, Opinion of Advocate General Capeta (EU Ct of Justice)
l'Etat Francais v. Lemarchand (1948) ADIL No 198 (Court of Appeals of Rouen, France)
Legal Consequences Arising from the Policies and Practices of Israel in the Occupied Palestinian Territory, including East Jerusalem, ICJ Advisory Opinion, 19 July 2024 (ICJ)
Legal Consequences for States of the Continued Presence of South Africa in Namibia Notwithstanding Security Council Resolution 276 (1970), Advisory Opinion ICJ Rep 1971 p. 16
Legal Consequences of the Construction of a Wall in the Occupied Palestinian Territory, Advisory Opinion ICJ Rep 2004
Legality of the Threat or Use of Nuclear Weapons, Advisory Opinion ICJ Rep 1996
Lighthouses (Permanent Court of International Justice, Series C, No. 74, 49)
Loizidou v Turkey, Preliminary Objections Judgment (23 March 1995), (Application no. 15318/89) (ECtHR)
Opinions of the Lords of Appeal for Judgment in the Cause, Al-Skeini v. Secretary of State for Defence, 13 June 2007 UKHL 26
Prosecutor v. Dragoljub Kunarac, Radomir Kovac and Zoran Vukovic, Case Nos. IT-96–23-T and IT-96–23/1-T, Judgment of 22 February 2001 (ICTY, Trial Chamber)
Prosecutor v. Naletilic et al. IT-98–34-T, 31 March 2003 (ICTY, Trial Chamber)
Prosecutor v. Tihomir Blaskic, Case No. IT-95–14-A, 29 July 2004 (ICTY, Appeals Chamber)
R (In re Al-Jedda) v. Secretary of State for Defence (2007) UKHL 58
Ralli Brothers v. German Government Anglo-German Mixed Arbitral Tribunal: Annual Digest, 1923–1924, Case No 244
Rex v. Bottrill, ex parte Kuechenmeister LR [1947] KB 41
Schiffahrt-Treuhand v. Procurator General (A.C. 232)
The I.G. Farben Trial, Trial of Carl Krauch and Twenty-two Others, 14th August, 1947–29th July, 1948 UN War Crimes Commission, Law Reports of Trials of War Criminals, vol X, 1 (US MTN)
The Prosecutor v. Moinina Fofana and Allieu Kondewa, Special Court for Sierra Leone
Trial of Alfried Felix Alwyn Krupp Von Bohlen und Halbach and Eleven Others, 17th November 1947–30th June, 1948 UN War Crimes Commission, Law Reports of Trials of War Criminals, vol X, 69 (US MTN)
Trial of the Major War Criminals, 14 November 1945–1 October 1946, vol I (IMT Nuremberg)

Trial of the Major War Criminals, Proceedings 27 August 1946 – 1 October 1946 vol XXII (IMT Nuremberg)
United States v. Altstoetter et al., 960 Trials of War Criminals, Military Tribunal Nuremberg III, 954 (US MTN)
United States v. Weizsaecker (Ministries Trial) (US MTN, Judgment 13 April 1949, World-Courts online database, p. 340)
United States v. Wilhelm List et al., (the Hostages Trial), 8th July 1947 to 19th February 1948 UN War Crimes Commission, Law Reports of Trials of War Criminals, vol VIII, 34 (US MTN)
Western Sahara, Advisory Opinion ICJ Rep
Yesh Din – Volunteers for Human Rights v. Commander of the IDF Forces in the West Bank et. al. (HCJ 2164/09)

Articles

Abouali G, 'Natural Resources under Occupation: The Status of Palestinian Waters under International Law' 10 Pace Int'l L Rev 1998 411 411
B EM, 'Confiscation of Enemy Private Property' 28 Yale LJ 5, March 1919 478
Benvenisti E, 'Water Conflicts during the Occupation of Iraq' 97 AJIL 4, October 2003 860
C.A. Singapore, Opinion of C.J. Whyatt, 'N.V. de Bataafsche Petroleum Maatschappij and Others v. the War Damage Commission (1956)' 51 AJIL 4, October 1957 802
Cassimatis AE, 'International Humanitarian Law, International Human Rights Law, and Fragmentation of International Law' ICLQ July 2007, vol. 56, 623
Chinkin C, *Laws of Occupation* (2008), Conference on Multilateralism and International Law with Western Sahara as a case study hosted by the South African Department of Foreign Affairs and the University of Pretoria
Clagett B and others, 'May Israel as a Belligerent Occupant Lawfully Exploit Previously Unexploited Oil Resources of the Gulf of Suez?' 72 AJIL 3, July 1978 558
Clarke B, 'Military Occupation and the Rule of Law: The Legal Obligations of Occupying Forces in Iraq' 10 Int'l Trade Bus L Rev 2006 133 133
Cole B, 'Property and the Law of Belligerent Occupation' 137 World Aff 1 1974 66
Cullet P, 'Water Law in a Globalised World: The Need for a New Conceptual Framework' 23 J Environ L 2 2011 233
Cullet P and others, 'Water Security and International Law' 17 Annu Rev L Soc Sci 2021 261
Curry RA, 'Oil Rights in the Gulf of Suez' 38 La L Rev 4, Summer 1978
Dam-de Jong DA, 'From Engines for Conflict into Engines for Sustainable Development: The Potential of International Law to Address Predatory Exploitation of Natural Resources in Situations of Internal Armed Conflict' 82 Nordic J Int'l L 2013 155
Dichter H, 'The Legal Status of Israel's Water Policies in the Occupied Territories' 35 Harv Int'l L J 2, Spring 1994 565
Droege C, 'The Interplay between International Humanitarian Law and International Human Rights Law in Situations of Armed Conflict' 40 Israël L Rev 2 310
Fahy C, 'Legal Problems of German Occupation' 47 Mich L Rev 1 1948 11
Ferraro T, 'Determining the Beginning and End of an Occupation under International Humanitarian Law' 94 IRRC 885, Spring 2012 133
Gerson A, 'Off-Shore Oil Exploration by a Belligerent Occupant: The Gulf of Suez Dispute' 71 AJIL 4, October 1977 725
Hulme K, 'Enhancing Environmental Protection during Occupation through Human Rights' 10 Goettingen J Int'l L 1 2020 203
Imseis A, 'On the Fourth Geneva Convention and the Occupied Palestinian Territory' 44 Harvard Int'l L J 1 65
Jennings RY, 'Government in Commission' 23 Brit YB Int'l L 1946 112
Jessup PC, 'Editorial Comment, A Belligerent Occupant's Power over Property' 38 AJIL 1944 457 457

Jones FL, 'Military Occupation of Alien Territory in Time of Peace' 9 Transactions of the Grotius Society, Problems of Peace and War, Papers Read before the Society in the Year 1923 149 149
Kaikobad KH, 'Problems of Belligerent Occupation: The Scope of Powers Exercised by the Coalition Provisional Authority in Iraq, April/May 2003-June 2004' 54 ICLQ 2005 253
Kretzmer D, 'The Advisory Opinion: The Light Treatment of International Humanitarian Law' 99 AJIL 2005 88
Kretzmer D, 'The Law of Belligerent Occupation in the Supreme Court of Israel' 94 IRRC 885, Spring 2012
Langenkamp RD and Zedalis RJ, 'What Happens to the Iraqi Oil? Thoughts on Some Significant, Unexamined International Legal Questions Regarding Occupation of Oil Fields' 14 EJIL 3, June 2003 417 417
Latty L, 'La Loi du 21 avril 1810 et le Conseil Général des Mines avant 1866' 16 Documents pour l'Histoire des Techniques 2ème semestre 2008 17
Lauterpacht E, 'The Hague Regulations and the Seizure of Munitions de Guerre' 32 Brit YB Int'l L 1955 218
Leigh M, 'US Department of State Memorandum of Law on Israel's Right to Develop New Oil Fields in Sinai and the Gulf of Suez, October 1, 1976' 16 ILM 3, May 1997 733
Leyda JAC, 'The Laws of Occupation and Commercial Law Reform in Occupied Territories: Clarifying a Widespread Misunderstanding' 23 EJIL no. 1 2012 179
Lindroos A, 'Addressing Norm Conflicts in a Fragmented Legal System: The Doctrine of Lex Specialis' 74 Nordic J Int'l L 2005 27
Longobardo M, 'State Responsibility for International Humanitarian Law Violations by Private Actors in Occupied Territories and the Exploitation of Natural Resources' 63 Neth Int'l L Rev 2016 251
Lubell N, 'Challenges in Applying Human Rights Law to Armed Conflict' 87 IRRC 860, December 2005
Mandsager D and others, 'Jus in Bello: Occupation Law and the War in Iraq' 98 ASIL Proceedings March 31–April 3 2004 117
McDermott CB, 'Monopolizers of the Soil: The Commons as a Source of Public Trust Responsibilities' 61 Nat Resour J 1, Winter 2021 125
Ojanen SM and others, 'What Are the Environmental Impacts of Property Rights Regimes in Forests, Fisheries and Rangelands?' 6 Environ Evid 12 2017 1
Pabian E, 'Prolonged Occupation and Exploitation of Natural Resources, A Focus on Natural Gas off the Coast of Northern Cyprus' 12 J Int'l Hum Leg Stud 1 2021
Paust J, 'Oil Exploitation in the Occupied Territory: Sharpening the Focus on Appropriate Legal Standards' 1 Houst J Int'l L 1979 147
Potter PB, 'Legal Bases and Character of Military Occupation in Germany and Japan' 43 AJIL 2 1949 323
Roberts A, 'What Is Military Occupation' 50 Brit YB Int'l L 1984 249
Rüdiger W, 'Iraq – from Belligerent Occupation to Iraqi Exercise of Sovereignty: Foreign Power versus International Community Interference' 9 Max Plank Yearbook of United Nations Law 2005 1
Saul B, 'The Status of Western Sahara as Occupied Territory under International Humanitarian Law and the Exploitation of Natural Resources' Sydney Law School, Legal Studies Research Paper No 15/81, September 2015
Scheffer DJ, 'Beyond Occupation Law' 97 AJIL 2003 842
Schmitt M, 'Green War: An Assessment of the Environmental Law of International Armed Conflict' 22 Yale J Int'l L 1997 1
Schwenk EH, 'Legislative Power of the Military Occupant under Article 43, Hague Regulations' 54 Yale L J 393
Scobbie I, 'H2O after Oslo: Legal Aspects of Water in the Occupied Territories' 8 PYBIL 1994–1995 79

———, 'International Law and the Prolonged Occupation of Palestine' UN Roundtable on Legal Aspects of the Question of Palestine, The Hague, 20–22 May 2015
———, 'Principle or Pragmatics? The Relationship between Human Rights Law and the Law of Armed Conflict' J Confli Secur L 2010 449
Shears CC, 'Some Legal Implications of Unconditionnal Surrender' 39 ASIL Proceedings April 13–14 1945 44
Tignino M, 'Water, International Peace, and Security' 92 IRRC 879, September 2010 647
Vité S, 'The Interrelation of the Law of Occupation and Economic, Social and Cultural Rights: the Examples of Food, Health and Property' 90 IRRC 871, September 2008 629
'War. Belligerency. Original Owners Retain Title to Oil Resources Seized by Belligerent Occupant in Violation of Hague Regulations. N. V. De Bataafsche Petroleum Maatschappij v. War Damage Comm'n (C. A. Singapore 1956)' 71 Harv L Rev No. 3 January 1958 568
Weaver S and others, 'Territories Occupied by Israel: Settlements and Exploration of Oil Resources' 72 ASIL Proceedings April 1978 118
Wickersham CW and King A, 'The Government of the Occupied Territory' 37 ASIL Proceedings April 30–May 1 1943 27
William Gerald Downey J, 'Captured Enemy Property: Booty of War and Seized Enemy Property' 44 AJIL 3, July 1950 488
Wolf D, 'Transitional Post-Occupation Obligations under the Law of Belligerent Occupation' Minn J Int'l L 2018, 354
Yiannopoulos AN, 'Rights of the Usufructuary: Louisiana and Comparative Law' 27 La L Rev 4, June 1967 668

Electronic articles

Anderson H, *Back to Basics: What Is a Lake?* (IISD 2020)
Encyclopaedia Britannica, 'Usufruct (law)'
Larousse, 'Langue Francaise, Dictionnaire,'
Roberts A, 'Occupation, Military, Termination of' MPEPIL, online edition
Straumann B, 'Ususfructus' The Wiley-Blackwell Encyclopedia of Ancient History

Books – reports

Benvenisti E, *The International Law of Occupation* (2nd edn, OUP 2012)
Castren E, *The Present Law of War and Neutrality* (Suomalainev Tiedeakemia 1954)
Combacau J and Sur S, *Droit International Public* (13th edn, LGDJ 2019)
Conseil d'Etat, *L'Eau et son Droit* (Etude 2010)
Crawford J, *Brownlie's Principles of Public International Law* (9th edn, OUP 2019)
Crawford SC J, *Opinion, Third Party Obligations with Respect to Israeli Settlements in the Occupied Palestinian Territories* (2012)
Dam-de Jong DA, *International Law and Governance of Natural Resources in Conflict and Post-Conflict Situations*, *Doctoral Thesis* (Open Access edn, Meijers 2013)
Deeley N, *The International Boundaries of East Timor* (Boundary and Territory Briefing, 2001)
Dinstein Y, *The International Law of Belligerent Occupation* (2nd edn, CUP 2019)
———, *The Conduct of Hostilities under the Law of International Armed Conflict* (CUP 2022)
Feilchenfeld EH, *The International Economic Law of Belligerent Occupation* (Carnegie Endowment for International Peace 1942)
Fleck D (ed) *The Handbook of International Humanitarian Law* (4th edn, OUP 2021)

Green LC, *The Contemporary Law of Armed Conflict* (3rd edn, MUP 2008)
Gross A, *The Writing on the Wall, Rethinking the International Law of Occupation* (CUP 2017)
Israel Ministry of Foreign Affairs, *Memorandum of Law on the Right to Develop New Oil Fields in the Sinai and the Gulf of Suez, 1 August 1977* (1978)
James EE, Oppenheim L and Great Britain, War Office, *Land Warfare: An Exposition of the Laws and Usages of War on Land, for the Guidance of Officers of His Majesty's Army* (H.M.S.O. 1912)
Dugard J, Special Rapporteur of the Commission on Human Rights, *Question of the Violation of Human Rights in the Occupied Arab Territories, Including Palestine, E/CN.4/2004/6/Add.1*
Kretzmer D and Ronen Y, *The Occupation of Justice, The Supreme Court of Israel and the Occupied Territories* (2nd edn, OUP 2021)
Lord Goldsmith QC Attorney General, *Iraq: Authorisation for an Interim Administration* (26 March 2003)
Max E, *Implementing International Humanitarian Law through Human Rights Mechanisms: Opportunity or Utopia? Working Paper* (Geneva Academy 2019)
Nisuke A, *Surrender, Occupation and Private Property in International Law, an Evaluation of US Practice in Japan* (Clarendon Press 1991)
Oppenheim L, *International Law, Vol. II Disputes, War and Neutrality* (Lauterpacht H ed, 7th edn, Longmans, Green and Co. 1952)
———, *Disputes, War and Neutrality*, vol II (Lauterpacht H ed, 7th edn, Longmans 1955)
République Française, Ministère de la Défense, *Manuel de droit des conflits armés* (2012)
Rogers APV, *Law on the Battlefield* (3rd edn, MUP 2012)
Schriver N, *Sovereignty Over Natural Resources, Balancing Rights and Duties* (CUP 1997)
Schwarzenberger G, *International Law as Applied by International Courts and Tribunals, the Law of Armed Conflict*, vol II (Stevens & Sons Ltd 1968)
Sloan B, *Study of the Implications, under International Law, of the UN Resolutions on Permanent Sovereignty over Natural Resources, on the Occupied Palestinian and other Arab Territories and on the Obligations of Israel Concerning Its Conduct in These Territories, Report of the Secretary-General, Annex, UNGA A/38/50/Rev.1* (1983)
Southgate L, *ASEAN Resistance to Sovereignty Violation, Interests, Balancing and the Role of the Vanguard State* (OUP, Policy Press Scolarship Online 2019)
State-War-Navy Coordinating Committee, *Politico-Military Problems in the Far East: United States Initial Post-Defeat Policy Relating to Japan, Reference: a. SWNCC 150/4* (21 September 1945)
Stone J, *Legal Controls of International Conflict* (1959)
Terré F and Simler P, *Droit Civil, Les Biens* (10 edn, Dalloz 2018)
Tignino M, *L'eau et la Guerre, Eléments pour un Regime Juridique* (Bruylant 2011)
———, *Water during and after Armed Conflicts: What Protection under International Law?* (Brill 2016)
U.S. DoD, *Law of War Manual* (June 2015, updated December 2016)
UK MoD, *The Joint Service Manual of the Law of Armed Conflict, JSP 383* (The Joint Doctrine and Concepts Centre 2004)
Von Glahn G, *The Occupation of Enemy Territory* (The University of Minnesota Press 1957)

Book chapters

Akande D, 'Classification of Armed Conflicts: Relevant Legal Concepts' in Wilmhurst E (ed), *International Law and the Classification of Conflicts* (OUP 2012)
Bothe M, 'First Meeting of Experts, the Beginning and End of Occupation, Appendix 1 "Effective Control": A Situation Triggering the Application of the Law of Belligerent Occupation, Background Document' in Ferraro T (ed), *Expert Meeting, Occupation and Other Forms of Administration of Foreign Territory* (ICRC 2012)

———, 'Protection of the Environment in Relation to Armed Conflicts' in Fleck D (ed), *The Handbook of International Humanitarian Law* (4th edn, OUP 2021)

Cassese A, 'Powers and Duties of an Occupant in Relation to Land and Natural Resources' in Playfair E (ed), *International Law and the Administration of Occupied Territories, Two Decades of Israeli Occupation of the West Bank and Gaza Strip* (OUP 1992)

Cotula L, 'Chapter 7 Land' in Morgera E and Kulovesi K (eds), *Research Handbook on International Law and Natural Resources* (Edward Elgar Publishing 2016)

d'Argent P, 'Des reglements collectifs aux reglements individuels (collectivises)? La question des reparations en cas de violation massive des droits de l'homme' in *International Law Forum du Droit International*, vol 5 (Kluwer Law International 2003)

Dörmann K, 'Foreword' in Ferraro T (ed), *Expert Meeting, Occupation and Other Forms of Administration of Foreign Territory* (ICRC 2012)

Dörmann K and Vité S, 'Occupation' in Fleck D (ed), *The Handbook of International Humanitarian Law* (4th edn, OUP 2021)

Gil EB, 'Introduction' in *Experimental Design and Verification of a Centralized Controller for Irrigation Canals* (Elsevier 2018)

Greenwood C, 'The Administration of Occupied Territory in International Law' in Playfair E (ed), *International Law and the Administration of the Occupied Territories* (OUP 1992)

Kleffner JK, 'Human Rights in Armed Conflict' in Fleck D (ed), *The Handbook of International Humanitarian Law* (4th edn, OUP 2021)

MAE, 'Conférence Internationale de la Paix' in *Archives Diplomatiques: Recueil de Diplomatie et d'Histoire, 2ème série, Tome LXXI, Juillet Août Septembre* (France, 1899)

National Geographic online, Education, Encyclopedic Entry, *Wetlands*

Roberts A, 'Transformative Military Occupation: Applying the Laws of War and Human Rights' in Michael Schmitt and Jelena Pejic (eds), *International Law and Armed Conflict: Exploring the Faultlines, Essays in Honour of Yoram Dinstein*, (Brill/Nijhoff 2007)

Scobbie I, 'Natural Resources and Belligerent Occupation: Mutation through Permanent Sovereignty' in Bowen S (ed), *Human Rights, Self-Determination and Political Change in the Occupied Palestinian Territories* (Martinus Nijhoff 1997)

Tzanakopoulos A and Lekkas S-I, 'Chapter 11, Pacta Sunt Servanda versus Flexibility in the Suspension and Termination of Treaties' in Tams CJ and others (eds), *Research Handbook on the Law of Treaties* (Elgar 2014)

Wolfrum R, 'The Adequacy of International Humanitarian Rules on Belligerent Occupation: To What Extent May Security Council Resolution 1483 Be Considered a Model for Adjustment?' in Schmitt MN and J. P (eds), *International Law and Armed Conflict: Exploring the Faultlines, Essays in Honour of Yoram Dinstein* (Martinus Nijhoff 2007)

4 State responsibility under international environmental law for environmental damage in international armed conflict

The chapter examines whether a State may be held accountable for environmental damage from armed conflict, based on breach of its obligations under IEL principles or treaties, analysing their applicability during armed conflicts. It presents briefly the legal regime of shared waters, a vital resource frequently affected during armed conflicts. Finally, it assesses requirements of environmental damage and standard of conduct under IEL rules that would give rise to State liability in case of violation of its obligations.

I. IEL principles

Some IEL principles elaborated in the 1972 Stockholm and 1992 Rio Declarations[1] have seen their status evolve, from principles to rights and obligations recognized in customary and conventional international law.

1. Applicability during armed conflict

In order to qualify as a source of international law creating legally binding obligations, applicable in armed conflict, principles should be recognized as customary international law principles or general principles of international law.[2] As IEL principles are distinct from general principles of law,[3] a judiciary authority will not necessarily find them to be part of such law category.[4] The status of a few is disputed under conflicting interpretation of State practice and the absence of

1 UNCHE, Stockholm, 5–16 June 1972, *Report (A/CONF.48/14/Rev.1)* (hereinafter Stockholm Declaration). UNCED, Rio de Janeiro, 3–14 June 1992, *Report, A/CONF.151/26/Rev.1 (Vol. I)* (hereinafter Rio Declaration)

2 ICJ Statute, art.36; ICRC, *Guidelines on the Protection of the Natural Environment in Armed Conflict* (2020) par.34

3 Philippe Sands, Jacqueline Peel, Adriana Fabra, and Ruth MacKenzie, *Principles of International Environmental Law* (4th edn, CUP 2018) 125, ftnote 144, 198

4 Owen McIntyre, 'Chapter 20: The Making of International Natural Resources Law' in Catherine Brölmann and Yannick Radi (eds), *Research Handbook on the Theory and Practice of International Lawmaking* (Edward Elgar 2016) 454

DOI: 10.4324/9780367823283-4

a definite judicial authority,[5] resulting in endless doctrinal discussions.[6] This is a "somewhat fruitless exercise, which in fact has very little practical significance" as "the importance which States attach to international obligations is not exclusively conditioned by the legal nature of these obligations."[7] Yet, it is one element on which States base their respect for the underlying obligations, entailing some practical relevance.

Principles "that are candidates for continuing application during armed conflict" are incorporated into treaties and are, or are soon to be, considered customary international law.[8] As the latter is universally applicable and opposable to the international community of States, it cannot be suspended or terminated during armed conflict, even though a treaty including the same customary obligation could be. In *Nicaragua v. the United States of America*, the ICJ had to rule on a preliminary objection of jurisdiction. The US had accepted the ICJ compulsory jurisdiction, with a reservation excluding disputes related to multilateral treaties, unless all parties affected joined the case. It argued that, since the applicability of multilateral treaties was barred, the ICJ could not examine US's obligations under customary international law, as identical norms included in the treaties had "subsumed and supervened" these. The ICJ held that even though rules contained in different sources of law could have an identical content, custom and treaties retained their separate existence and applicability.[9] Though the theory that a custom, even if codified, retains its separate existence is "controversial,"[10] it is based on the notion that there is no hierarchical order between the sources of international law[11] and the ICJ ruling "might still be supportable by a more fully reasoned analysis."[12]

In the *Armed Activities* case, the ICJ affirmed that rules, such as "the conduct of any organ of a State must be regarded as an act of that State"[13] and the principle of permanent sovereignty over natural resources,[14] were customary international law that applied to the case. Though this determination lacked examination of practice and *opinio juris*,[15] the judgement confirms that customary international law principles

5 Sands 198

6 Malgosia Fitzmaurice, 'Precautionary Principle' in *Contemporary Issues in International Environmental Law* (Edward Elgar 2009) 4. McIntyre 162

7 Fitzmaurice 7

8 ILC, *Special Rapporteur Marie G. Jacobsson, Preliminary Report on the Protection of the Environment in Relation to Armed Conflicts, A/CN.4/674* (2014) par.117, 121

9 *Military and Paramilitary Activities in and against Nicaragua (Nicaragua v. United States of America). Merits, Judgment.* ICJ Rep 1986, p. 14, par.177–178

10 Anthony Aust, 'Vienna Convention on the Law of Treaties (1969)' in *MPEPIL* (2006) par.19

11 Joost Pauwelyn, *Conflict of Norms in Public International Law, How WTO Law Relates to Other Rules of International Law* (CUP 2003) 94

12 Richard B. Bilder and others, 'Disentangling Treaty and Customary International Law' 81 ASIL Proceedings, 8–11 April (1987) 161

13 *Armed Activities on the Territory of the Congo (DRC v. Uganda), Judgment* ICJ Rep 2005, p. 168, ICJ par.213–214

14 Ibid, par.244

15 Tullio Treves, 'Customary International Law' MPEPIL, par.20

that are not part of the LOAC corpus remain applicable during armed conflict or at least that its potential application will be analysed by the courts.

Applicability of IEL principles outside purely environmental disputes has been examined by the WTO Appellate Body, in a case concerning disputed trade measures.[16] It held that language similar to the precautionary principle, which was not yet recognized as customary international law, had been included in an international trade treaty and as such there may be simultaneous application of trade law measures and IEL principle. The decision though does not support applicability, in the event of armed conflict, of IEL principles that are not yet considered customary law or general principles of international law. IEL principles relevant to the subject at hand and their status under international law should be determined.

2. *Sovereignty over natural resources*

A State's sovereign right over its natural resources is constrained by its responsibility to prevent environmental damage, when exercising its right. The two are analysed separately.

2.1 Origin of the principle

During the decolonization process, the UNGA debated on economic development and right to self-determination[17] adopting Resolution 1803 (1962) recognizing that "[t]he right of peoples and nations to permanent sovereignty over their natural wealth and resources must be exercised in the interest of their national development and of the wellbeing of the people of the State concerned,"[18] reaffirmed later.[19] Such right was recognized for peoples in international human rights covenants[20] and for States "to exploit their own resources pursuant to their own environmental" and "developmental policies," in Principles 21 and 2 of Stockholm and Rio Declarations respectively and IEL treaties.[21] A State's sovereignty over its own territory and waters and the need to safeguard a neighbouring State's interests were also raised in case law.[22]

16 *EC Measure Concerning Meat and Meat Products (Hormones Case), Report of the Appellate Body* WTO

17 UN Audiovisual Library of International Law, 'Permanent Sovereignty over Natural Resources General Assembly resolution 1803 (XVII), New York, 14 December 1962, Procedural History'

18 UNGA, *Permanent Sovereignty over Natural Resources, Res. 1803 (XVII)* (1962) par.1

19 UNGA, *Declaration on the Establishment of a New International Economic Order, A/RES/S-6/3201 (S.VI)* (1974); UNGA, *Programme of Action on the Establishment of a New International Economic Order, A/RES/S-6/3202 (S.VI)* (1974); UNGA, *Charter of Economic Rights and Duties of States, Res. 3281 (XXIX)* (1974)

20 Common article 1 par.2 of both Covenants: ICESCR (ICESCR); ICCPR (ICCPR)

21 Sands 203.

22 *Affaire du Lac Lanoux (Espagne, France), 16 November 1957* RIAA, Vol XII, pp. 281–317.

2.2 Status

Principle 21 reflected customary international law for States present at the Stockholm Conference.[23] Resolution 1803 was recognized to be customary law in international arbitrations[24] and by the ICJ,[25] though this affirmation was based on non-binding UNGA resolutions reiterating the principle.[26] Considered an established general principle of international law, sovereignty over natural resources was cited by national courts[27] and referred to by State practice, by Guatemala and the US. As part of the right of peoples to self-determination, the principle has become a jus cogens norm[28] accepted as such by a substantial number of States.[29] It is mentioned in several countries' constitution, such as the Bolivian constitution stipulating that hydrocarbon resources are the inalienable and imprescriptible property of the Bolivian people.[30]

2.3 Application in armed conflict

The ICJ found that UNGA resolutions do not suggest that the principle was "applicable to the specific situation of looting, pillage and exploitation of certain natural resources by members of the army of a State militarily intervening in another State."[31] It is uncertain whether it meant that the principle does not apply to armed conflicts[32] or that looting was not based on a governmental policy of natural

23 Alan Boyle and Catherine Redgwell, *Birnie, Boyle and Redgwell's International Law and the Environment* (4th edn, OUP 2021) 161

24 *Texaco Overseas Petroleum Co. and California Asiatic Oil Company v. the Government of the Libyan Arab Republic,* 17 ILM 1 (1978), par.87. *Kuwait v. American Independent Oil Co.,* 21 ILM 976 (1982), par.90(2) and 143

25 *Armed Activities (2005)* par.244

26 A. Mark Weisburd, 'The International Court of Justice and the Concept of State Practice' 31 U Pa J Int'l L 2 (2009) 330

27 *International Association of Machinists v. Organisation of Petroleum,* US District Court for the Central District of California – 477 F Supp 553 (CD Cal 1979), 18 September 1979, and United States Court of Appeals, Ninth Circuit (6 July 1981)

28 Mara Tignino, *L'eau dans le Processus de Paix au Proche-Orient: Eléments d'un Régime Juridique* (Genève: Institut Universitaire de Hautes Etudes Internationales 2004) 32

29 Blaine Sloan, *Study of the Implications, under International Law, of the UN Resolutions on Permanent Sovereignty over Natural Resources, on the Occupied Palestinian and other Arab Territories and on the Obligations of Israel Concerning its Conduct in these Territories, Report of the Secretary-General, Annex, UNGA A/38/50/Rev.1* (1983) par.13

30 Kim Talus, 'Chapter 12: Oil and Gas: International Petroleum Regulation' in Elisa Morgera and Kati Kulovesi (eds), *Research Handbook on International Law and Natural Resources* (Edward Elgar 2016)

31 *Armed Activities (2005) par.244*

32 ILC, *Special Rapporteur Marja Lehto, First Report on Protection of the Environment in Relation to Armed Conflicts, A/CN.4/720* (2018) par.34; Daniëlla Dam-de Jong, *International Law and Governance of Natural Resources in Conflict and Post-Conflict Situations, Doctoral Thesis* (Open Access edn, Meijers 2013) 194; Phoebe Okowa, 'Sovereignty Contests and the Protection of Natural Resources in Conflict Zones' 66 Curr Legal Probl (2013) 58

resources exploitation.[33] Under UNGA Resolutions[34] and according to Judge Koroma, interests and rights of peoples and nations under UNGA Resolution 1803 remain in effect during armed conflicts.[35] It is relevant to armed conflict[36] and applicable to occupation.[37] It would make no sense to put aside the application of the principle to temporary occupations, while sovereignty over natural resources is permanent.

The principle has legal implications. Permanent sovereignty over natural resources is an inalienable right to use, control and dispose of such resources freely.[38] Part of the right to self-determination,[39] it includes the right of peoples to regain effective control over their natural resources.[40] During occupation, control over land, water and other natural resources should be restored to the local population by allowing local authorities to assume responsibilities they exercised prior to occupation, until full restoration of control over occupied territories to States and peoples concerned.[41] It supports a restrictive interpretation of occupants' usufructuary powers.[42] In case the occupant violates its obligations thereunder, its responsibility is engaged, giving rise to a right to reparation,[43] including a right to restitution and full compensation.[44]

3. *Prevention of transboundary harm and environmental damage*

3.1 Customary law origin

States' obligation to prevent transboundary harm originated under customary international law. In the *Trail Smelter* case concerning damage caused to private

33 *Armed Activities (2005) par.234, 242*

34 UNGA Resolutions 3005 (XXVII) of 15 December 1972, par.4. Sloan par.9, UNGA Res. until 1982; UNGA, *Resolution 66/225 on Permanent Sovereignty of the Palestinian people in the Occupied Palestinian Territory, including East Jerusalem, and of the Arab Population in the Occupied Syrian Golan over their Natural Resources* (2011)

35 *Armed Activities (2005) Declaration of Judge Koroma, 284, par.11*

36 Daniëlla Dam-de Jong 194

37 Mara Tignino, *L'eau et la Guerre, Eléments pour un Regime Juridique* (Bruylant 2011) 203

38 ICESCR art.1(2); Sloan par.15(a), 50(a)

39 Sloan par.15(b). UNGA Res. 837 (IX), 1314 (XIII), 1803 (XVII) and 2692 (XXV) refer to "peoples and nations." ICESCR art.1

40 UNGA Res.3171 (XXVIII); Sloan par.15(d))

41 Sloan par.50(b)

42 Iain Scobbie, 'Natural Resources and Belligerent Occupation: Mutation through Permanent Sovereignty' in Stephen Bowen (ed), *Human Rights, Self-Determination and Political Change in the Occupied Palestinian Territories* (Martinus Nijhoff 1997) 281; Antonio Cassese, 'Powers and Duties of an Occupant in Relation to Land and Natural Resources' in Emma Playfair (ed), *InternationalLlaw and the Administration of Occupied Territories, Two Decades of Israeli Occupation of the West Bank and Gaza Strip* (OUP 1992) 426

43 Tignino, *L'eau dans le Processus de Paix* 34; Sloan 50(b)

44 Sloan par.15(e). UNGA Res. 3201 (S-VI), paragraph 4 (f). UNGA Res. 3281 (XXIX), art.16. UNGA Res. 3362 (S-VII), Lima Declaration endorsed by the General Assembly, par.33

timber and agricultural property in Washington from sulphur dioxide emissions by a smelter at Trail, British Columbia, Canada, the arbitral tribunal concluded that

> "under the principles of international law . . . no State has the right to use or permit the use of its territory in such a manner as to cause injury by fumes in or to the territory of another or the properties or persons therein, when the case is of serious consequence and the injury is established by clear and convincing evidence."[45]

In the *Corfu Channel* case about damage to two UK warships hitting mines in the Straits of Corfu in Albanian territorial waters, the ICJ ruled that Albania had obligations to notify the shipping industry generally of the existence of the minefield and to warn the approaching British ships of imminent danger, on the basis, among others, of "every State's obligation not to allow knowingly its territory to be used for acts contrary to the rights of other States."[46] "The grave omissions" by Albania "to prevent the disaster" involve its international responsibility for the explosions and resulting damage and loss of life.[47] In a dispute between France and Spain about proposed works to build a barrage in France to divert water from a river flowing from the Lake Lanoux in France to Spain to a hydroelectric power plant and to return the same amount to Spain, the arbitral tribunal concluded that Spain's rights under the treaties between the two countries were not infringed.[48]

3.2 Codification

Principles 21 and 2 of Stockholm and Rio Declarations enshrined States' "responsibility to ensure that activities within their jurisdiction or control do not cause damage to the environment of other States or of areas beyond the limits of national jurisdiction," repeated in UNGA resolutions[49] and IEL treaties.[50] The geographical scope of the customary obligation that was confined to transboundary harm has been extended. The so-called confusingly labelled "no-harm principle"[51] may be considered distinct from, or seen as reflecting, the IEL prevention principle that

45 *Trail Smelter Case (United States, Canada), 16 April 1938 and 11 March 1941,* RIAA, Vol III, 1905, 1905 1965

46 *Corfu Channel case, Judgment of April 9th, 1949, I.C.J. Reports,* 4, 22

47 Ibid, 23

48 *Lac Lanoux 301, par.3 a), 305*

49 UNGA, *Co-operation between States in the Field of the Environment, Res. 2995 (XXVII)* (1972) par.1; UNGA, *International Responsibility of States in regard to the Environment, A/RES/2996* (1972); UNGA, Charter of Economic Rights and Duties of States, Res. 3281 (XXIX) art.30

50 UNCLOS, 10 December 1982 art.194(2); Convention on Biological Diversity, Rio de Janeiro, 5 June 1992; UN Framework Convention on Climate Change, 1992 Preamble

51 Boyle and Redgwell 161

requires States to prevent damage to the environment generally, including their own potentially.[52] It is explicitly or indirectly referred to in IEL documents and a plethora of IEL treaties.[53]

3.3 Status

Principle 21/2 is established customary international law.[54] Regarded as such by States participating to the Stockholm Conference[55] and to the *Nuclear Weapons* proceedings,[56] it was considered part of the "corpus of international law relating to the environment" by the ICJ[57] and an arbitral tribunal[58] and even claimed to have evolved into "an *erga omnes* obligation of prevention of damage" in *Gabčikovo-Nagymaros.*[59] The duty to prevent or at least mitigate significant harm to the environment was considered "a principle of general international law" applicable to activities undertaken on their own or for the implementation of treaties between the Parties, according to an arbitral tribunal[60] and a customary rule originating from the due diligence required of States in their own territory by the ICJ.[61]

52 Sands 211, 212; Johan D. van der Vyver, 'The Environment: State Sovereignty, Human Rights, and Armed Conflict' 23 Emory Int'l L Rev 1 (2009) 91; Nicolas de Sadeleer, 'Chapter 9: The Principles of Prevention and Precaution in International Law: Two Heads of the Same Coin?' in Malgosia Fitzmaurice, David M. Ong and Panos Merkouris (eds), *Research Handbook on International Environmental Law* (Edward Elgar 2010) 182

53 Stockholm Declaration, Principles 6, 7, 15, 18 and 24; The 1982 World Charter for nature; UNEP, *Draft Principles of Conduct in the Field of the Environment for the Guidance of States in the Conservation and Harmonious Utilization of Natural Resources Shared by Two or More States* (1978) Principle 3; Sands 213, Table 214–215

54 Alan Boyle, 'Globalising Environmental Liability: the Interplay of National and International Law' 17 JEL 1 (2005) 3–4. Boyle and Redgwell 152–153; Sands 206; ILC, *Special Rapporteur, Pemmaraju Sreenivasa Rao, International Liability for Injurious Consequences Arising Out of Acts Not Prohibited by International Law (prevention of transboundary damage from hazardous activities), Agenda Item 3, A/CN.4/487 and Add.1, First report on prevention of transboundary damage from hazardous activities* (1998) par.10, 28

55 Boyle and Redgwell 161

56 *Legality of the Threat or Use of Nuclear Weapons, Advisory Opinion* ICJ Rep 1996, 226; Sands 210; *Letter dated 20 June 1995 from the Acting Legal Adviser to the Department of State, together with Written Statement of the Government of the United States of America* 39–40

57 *Nuclear Weapons* par.29 (n.59)

58 *The South China Sea Arbitration (The Republic of Philippines v. The People's Republic of China), Award of 12 July 2016* PCA par.941

59 *Gabčikovo-Nagymaros Project (Hungary/Slovakia), Judgment* ICJ Rep 1997, 7, 7 par.97

60 *In the Arbitration Regarding the Iron Rhine ("Ijzeren Rijn") Railway between the Kingdom of Belgium and the Kingdom of Netherlands, Award of Arbitral Tribunal, The Hague, 24 May 2005* PCA paras. 59, 222

61 *Pulp Mills on the River Uruguay (Argentina v. Uruguay), Judgment, ICJ Reports 2010, p. 14* par.101

3.4 *Requirements of due diligence obligation*

Under customary international law, it was unclear what measures due diligence requirements entailed.[62] They were clarified by case law since 1996 and by the 2001 ILC Prevention Articles that codified existing obligations.[63] An ILC study on civil liability for harmful consequences of lawful activities started in 1977 was divided in 1997 into two topics: the Prevention Articles and Principles on Loss Allocation.[64] Under the Prevention Articles, States have an obligation regarding activities under their jurisdiction or control that involve a high or low risk of causing significant or disastrous transboundary harm, respectively, to take appropriate measures to prevent such harm or minimize its risk.[65] These measures include:

- States' obligation of cooperation,[66] through notification, consultation and negotiation.[67] Cooperation is an IEL principle[68] referred to in *Lac Lanoux* and multiple conventions.[69] In *Gabcikovo*, a dispute on obligations under a treaty regarding building hydro-electric dams on the Danube, parties were required to establish a joint operational regime.[70] In *The South China Sea*, China breached the United Nations Convention on the Law of the Sea ("UNCLOS", 1982) provisions by failing to cooperate with other States and to communicate an environmental impact assessment (EIA) to the competent international organization,[71]
- Adoption of legislative and administrative implementation measures,[72]
- Vigilance for their enforcement and control, including continuous monitoring of environmental risks.[73] An obligation to "preserve the aquatic environment, and in particular to prevent pollution by prescribing appropriate rules and measures," under a treaty between the parties, was a due diligence obligation requiring taking of measures, their control and monitoring,[74] as was "responsibility to ensure" that a sponsored contractor's activities in the Area conform to the rules under UNCLOS,[75]

62 Sadeleer 183
63 ILC, *Draft Articles on Prevention of Transboundary Harm from Hazardous Activities, with commentaries, A/56/10* (ILC YB 2001, vol II (2)); Boyle and Redgwell
64 ILC, *Principles on the Allocation of Loss in the Case of Transboundary Harm arising out of Hazardous Activities, A/61/10* (ILC YB 2006, vol II (2)))
65 ILC Prevention Articles, art.1, 2(a), 3
66 Ibid, art.4
67 Boyle and Redgwell 300
68 Principles 24 and 27, Stockholm and Rio Declarations. ILC, Prevention Articles. ILC Commentary on Prevention Articles, Commentary on art.4 par.(1).
69 Sands 213
70 *Gabčikovo* par.77–78, 155(2)C
71 *South China Sea* par.984–986, 947–948, 989–991
72 ILC Prevention Articles, art.5
73 *Gabčikovo* par.112, 140; *Pulp Mills Judgement* par.197, 204
74 *Pulp Mills Judgement* par.197
75 *ITLOS, Responsibilities and Obligations of States Sponsoring Persons and Entities with Respect to Activities in the Area, Advisory Opinion, 2011* ITLOS Reports 2011, 10 par.103, 110

- State authorization prior to any activities,[76]
- Environmental impact assessment ("EIA").[77] It is a process by which the environmental impact of proposed activities is taken into account in decision-making.[78] EIA was deemed required in cases of risk of significant transboundary harm by major road construction works[79] or significant adverse impact by a proposed industrial activity that could affect the regime and quality of the waters of a shared resource.[80] The same may apply to activities affecting the environment beyond national jurisdiction and resources that are common heritage of mankind.[81] Inversely, dredging activities that do not raise risk of transboundary harm do not require an EIA.[82] Procedural obligations of EIA and notification, linked to substantive obligations of due diligence regarding harm prevention and cooperation,[83] were considered by dissenting judges to be "essential indicators" of breach of substantive obligations.[84] EIA is an international law requirement and a customary international law obligation, though its content is not specified under general international law.[85]

Other cases found that Principle 21/2 and the duty to prevent or mitigate environmental harm inform the obligation to protect and preserve the marine environment under UNCLOS articles 192 and 194, entailing a duty of due diligence which was breached by China's activities.[86] The failure to take precautionary measures to prevent aerial spraying of herbicides and control their harmful effects, resulting in significant harm to persons, property, health, natural resources, ecosystems and the environment in Ecuador, was alleged to be a violation by Columbia of its international law obligations in a case discontinued following agreement between the parties prior to the ICJ judgement.[87]

Due diligence obligations may not be determined precisely, as they evolve with time in accordance with law development incorporating scientific advancement and best environmental practices.[88] However, they may be prescribed in primary

76 ILC Prevention Articles, art.6
77 Ibid, art.7; Rio Declaration Principle 7
78 Sands 657
79 *Certain Activities Carried Out by Nicaragua in the Border Area (Costa Rica v. Nicaragua) and Construction of a Road in Costa Rica along the San Juan River (Nicaragua v. Costa Rica), Judgment* ICJ Rep 2015, p. 665, 665, par.156, 159 (Costa Rica v. Nicaragua)
80 *Pulp Mills Judgement* par.204
81 *ITLOS Activities in the Area* par.148
82 *Costa Rica v. Nicaragua* par.156, 159
83 *Pulp Mills Judgement* par.68–79, 204
84 Ibid, par.68–79, 204; Joint dissenting opinion Judges Al-Khasawneh and Simma, par.26–27
85 Ibid, par.204–205; *ITLOS Activities in the Area* par.145
86 *South China Sea* par.941, 944, 964; ILA Study Group on Due Diligence in International Law, *Second Report, July 2016* 19
87 *Case Concerning Aerial Herbicide Spraying Ecuador v. Columbia,* Memorial of Ecuador, Volume I, 28 April 2009, p. 277, par.8.9
88 *ITLOS Activities in the Area* par.117, 136–137

rules or be indispensable to avoid harm.[89] Measures to prevent harm or minimize damage are obligations of conduct. Liability is raised when the State does not exert its best efforts to fulfil its due diligence obligation.[90]

3.5 *Application in armed conflict*

As customary rule, the duty to prevent or mitigate transboundary harm is applicable during armed conflict. Though the ILC Prevention Articles were intended for transboundary harm prevention during peacetimes, their application in times of armed conflict cannot be excluded.[91] At issue is the scope of activities "under the control" of a State. The notion is used to attach legal consequences to situations where a State is exercising de facto jurisdiction not recognized under international law, such as unlawful intervention, illegal occupation and annexation.[92] Barboza suggested that it "aims to cover . . . also activities carried on by the State itself in any jurisdiction, its own or that of another State," such as State liability under the 1972 Convention on International Liability for Damage Caused by Space Objects, for a launching carried out in the jurisdiction of another State.[93] The ILC confirmed the principle's applicability during occupation and the ICJ underlined South Africa's obligations towards other States when physically controlling occupied territory.[94]

Nonetheless, it is not clear how the principle translates into practice. Imposing on belligerents an obligation to control military activities that may cause environmental damage to others during armed conflict seems illogical and contradicts the essence of warfare.[95] Not quite so. The LOAC precautions in attacks, requiring belligerents to consider the impact of their chosen warfare means to avoid or minimize environmental damage or cancel attacks that risk causing excessive damage,[96] bear similarities to States' obligation under IEL to take measures to prevent or mitigate transboundary harm or minimize its risk. They share an obligation to inform

89 ILA Study Group on Due Diligence in International Law 7–8

90 ILC, Prevention Articles commentary art.3, par.(7); *ITLOS Activities in the Area* par.110–111, 115–116; *Pulp Mills Judgement* par.187

91 ILC, Jacobsson Environment and Armed Conflict (2014) par.112

92 ILC Prevention Articles, commentary on art.1 par.12

93 ILC, *International Liability for Injurious Consequences Arising out of Acts not Prohibited by International Law, Special Rapporteur Julio Barboza Fourth Report, A/CN.4/423 and Corr.1 & 2* (ILC YB 1989, volII (1)) articles 1 and 3 proposed by Mr. Barboza in his fourth report (Yearbook . . . 1988, vol. II (Part One), p. 251, document A/CN.4/413) and fifth (Yearbook . . . 1989, vol. II (Part One), p. 131, document A/CN.4/423) reports.

94 *Legal Consequences for States of the Continued Presence of South Africa in Namibia notwithstanding Security Council Resolution 276 (1970), Advisory Opinion* ICJ Rep 1971, p. 16 par.118 (South Africa in Namibia, ICJ Advisory Opinion 1971); ILC, *Draft Principles on Protection of the Environment in Relation to Armed Conflicts, with commentaries, A/77/10* (ILC YB 2022, vol II, (2), 2022) Principle 21

95 Michael Schmitt, 'Green War: An Assessment of the Environmental Law of International Armed Conflict' 22 Yale J Int'l L (1997) 1, 46

96 Protocol I, art.57(2)(a) (ii) and (2)(a)(iii) and art.57(2)(b)

oneself before the attacks or the potentially harmful activities.[97] Excessive damage under the LOAC is determined in comparison with anticipated military advantage, while damage under IEL is qualified by a threshold. Based on a systemic interpretation of LOAC and IEL obligations, "excessive" damage from attacks under the LOAC should be reconciled with the threshold of damage from harmful activities under IEL, whether "significant" in relation to the customary IEL prevention principle or that found under IEL conventional primary rules or, absent such provision, "significant" or "disastrous" depending on its risk, as qualified in the ILC Prevention Articles.

4. The precautionary principle

4.1 Content

The precautionary principle emerged to bridge scientific uncertainty on the level of risk of environmental damage and the responsibility to prevent it.[98] Under the Rio Declaration, States shall use a "precautionary approach" to protect the environment, according to their capabilities. In case of threat of serious or irreversible damage, scientific uncertainty shall not be a reason to postpone cost-effective measures to prevent environmental degradation.[99] The principle lacks a common accepted understanding. It means generally "that states agree to act carefully and with foresight" regarding activities that may adversely affect the environment;[100] specifically, it represents "an obligation of diligent prevention and control of foreseeable risks."[101]

4.2 Status and application to armed conflict

It is not accepted in all areas of environmental law,[102] despite figuring in declarations, resolutions, guidelines and major IEL agreements.[103] International courts have been reluctant to endorse it, when pleaded before them.[104] Its influence is

97 Kimberley N. Trapp and Edmund Robinson, 'Extra-territorial "Fiducuary" Obligations and Ensuring Respect for International Humantarian Law' 63 McGill L J 3&4 (2018) 677, 691–692

98 Marco Martuzzi and Joel A. Tickner, 'Introduction – the Precautionary Principle: Protecting Public Health, the Environment and the Future of Our Children' in *The Precautionary Principle: Protecting Public Health, the Environment and the Future of Our Children* (WHO Regional Office for Europe 2004) 7

99 Rio Declaration, Principle 15

100 Sands 222

101 Boyle and Redgwell 170

102 Alexander Gillespie, 'The Precautionary Principle in the Twenty-First Century: A Case Study of Noise Pollution in the Ocean' 22 Int'l J Marine Coastal L 1 (2007) 61, 86

103 Arie Trouwborst, 'The Precautionary Principle in General International Law: Combating the Babylonian Confusion' 16 RECIEL 2, July (2007) 185, 187

104 UNESCO, World Commission on the Ethics of Scientific Knowledge and Technology (COMEST), *The Precautionary Principle* (UNESCO 2005) 23; Alan Boyle, 'The Environmental Jurisprudence

manifest in Australia,[105] in Europe,[106] appearing in EU treaties and laws,[107] in German legislation and the French Constitution,[108] while the US does not recognize it as a principle.[109]

The *Beef Hormone* case[110] illustrates opposed States' views. Canada and the United States challenged the banning, under EU directives, of import and introduction on the EU market of meat and meat products from animals to which hormones had been administered, alleging that the EU failed to undertake a risk assessment in conformity with the WTO's Agreement on Sanitary and Phytosanitary Measures (SPS Agreement). They argued that the precautionary "approach" was not a customary international law principle,[111] and was "an emerging principle of international law" that "has not yet become part of public international law."[112] For the European Communities, it was "a general customary rule of international law or at least a general principle of law" that should inform the relevant articles of the SPS Agreement.[113] The WTO Appellate Body ruled that it would be unnecessary and imprudent to take a position on the important but abstract question of the status – or not – of the principle as a general or customary international law.[114] It found that precautionary elements were included in articles of the SPS Agreement, but the precautionary principle did not override them.[115] Subsequent cases moved further away from the precautionary principle emphasizing the necessity of sufficient scientific evidence to take sanitary measures.[116]

The ITLOS, in the *Southern Bluefin Tuna*, relied on scientific uncertainty regarding tuna stocks' conservation, without mentioning the precautionary principle[117] and concluded in another case that the obligation to apply a precautionary

of the International Tribunal for the Law of the Sea' 22 Int'l J Marine Coastal L 3 (2007) 373; The principle has been pleaded in the PCA, *MOX Plant Case (Ireland v. United Kingdom)*; *Gabčikovo Pulp Mills on the River Uruguay (Provisional Measures)* ICJ

105 Scott LaFranchi, 'Surveying the Precautionary Principle's Ongoing Global Development: The Evolution of an Emergent Environmental Management Tool' 32 BC Envtl Aff L Rev 3 (2005) 689

106 Trouwborst 187

107 Boyle and Redgwell 173

108 Dominique Bourg and Kerry H. Whiteside, 'France's Charter for the Environment: Of Presidents, Principles and Environmental Protection' 15 Mod Contemp Fr 2 (2007)

109 LaFranchi 680

110 *WTO Appellate Body, EC Measures Concerning Meat and Meat Products (Hormones case), AB-1997–4, Report*

111 Ibid, par.43, US position

112 Ibid, par.60, Canada

113 Ibid, par.16

114 Ibid, par.123

115 Ibid, par.124–125

116 Makane Moïse Mbengue and Brian McGarry, 'Chapter 23: General Principles of International Environmental Law in the Case Law of International Courts and Tribunals' in Mads Andenas, Malgosia Fitzmaurice, Attila Tanzi, and Jan Wouters (eds), *General Principles and the Coherence of International Law*, vol 37 (Brill | Nijhoff 2019) 433–434

117 *Southern Bluefin Tuna Cases (Provisional Measures) ITLOS Reports 1999 par.77–79*

approach under regulations applicable to the Seabed Area also existed for sponsoring States under their due diligence obligation outside these regulations. Including this approach in treaties signalled the start of making it part of customary international law.[118] This is debatable as the normative character of rule of law seems to be missing.[119] The WTO found its status unsettled[120] and the ICJ simply noted that it may be relevant to interpret an environmental treaty.[121]

Doctrine has been divided on whether the principle has attained a "general international law" status,[122] was only emerging as customary international law[123] or, more recently, whether it has arguably sufficient broad support to reflect customary international law[124] or an uncertain status.[125] The principle could be viewed as "soft" customary law[126] or as general principle having a legal impact from the influence it "can exert on the interpretation, application and development of other rules of law," by redefining existing international rules of risk control and natural resource conservation,[127] with some finding even general principle qualification uncertain.[128] Regarding its practical effect, Bothe considers the principle a "fundamental rule of modern customary environmental law" which applies in armed conflict.[129] Regardless of its status, it mirrors precautions to be taken prior to attacks during armed conflict under the LOAC, in terms of evaluation and assessment of risks. Taken together, they may help to approach the prevention principle.[130] The ICRC specified that scientific uncertainty in the assessment of the risk of environmental damage from military operations should not prevent the belligerent from taking precautions in that regard.[131] It fused the precautionary principle with

118 *ITLOS Activities in the Area par.131, 135 (n.75)*
119 Boyle and Redgwell 179
120 *European Communities – Measures Affecting the Approval and Marketing of Biotech Products – Reports of the Panel WT/DS291/R, WT/DS292/R, WT/DS293/R* par.7.89
121 *Pulp Mills Judgement* par.164
122 Trouwborst 187
123 Minna Pyhälä, Anne Christine Brusendorff, and Hanna Paulomäki, 'Chapter 10: The Precautionary Principle' in Malgosia Fitzmaurice, David M. Ong, and Panos Merkouris (eds), *Research Handbook on International Environmental Law* (Edward Elgar 2010) 203
124 Sands 239
125 Frédéric Gilles Sourgens, 'The Precaution Presumption' 31 EJIL 4, November (2020) 1278; Boyle and Redgwell 179
126 Gillespie 86
127 Boyle, 'Jurisprudence of ITLOS' 375
128 Jan Klabbers, *International Law* (3rd edn, CUP 2021) 286
129 Michael Bothe, 'Protection of the Environment in Relation to Armed Conflicts' in Dieter Fleck (ed), *The Handbook of International Humanitarian Law* (4th edn, OUP 2021) 10.2 par.3
130 ILC, Lehto Environment and Armed Conflict (2018) 6, par.7
131 ICRC, *Customary International Humanitarian Law, Vol. I Rules* (Jean-Marie Henckaerts and Louise Doswald-Beck eds, 3rd edn, CUP 2009) Rule 44

belligerents' precautionary duties when assessing the effects of their chosen warfare methods or means on the environment.[132]

5. *Sustainable development and intergenerational equity*

The concept of sustainable development mentioned in Rio Declaration, Principle 3, expresses the necessity to reconcile economic development and human needs with protection of the environment and its resources.[133] In *Pulp Mills*, the ICJ noted that "the optimum and rational utilization of the River Uruguay" under a treaty between the parties "should allow for sustainable development," reconciling conservation of the river's environment and economic development rights of riparian States.[134] Sustainable development represents a policy objective, underlined by principles of sustainability and equity in the use of natural resources between States and among current and future generations (intragenerational and intergenerational) and integration of environment with the right to development.[135] As to its application during armed conflict, Das concluded that, given the difficulties to shield the environment in armed conflicts and allowing sustainable development, the importance of pre-conflict prevention of environmental harm and post-conflict reparations should be highlighted.[136] However, during occupation, the occupying power must administer natural resources of the occupied territory "in a way that ensures their sustainable use and minimizes harm to the environment."[137]

Intergenerational equity, referred to in IEL documents (Brundtland Report, Stockholm Declaration Principle 2), ENMOD Convention Preamble and other treaties,[138] posits that each generation should use, develop and transmit the planet's natural and cultural resources to the next generation in a state no worse than they were.[139] It is not recognized as general or customary international law principle, despite a dissenting opinion in the *Nuclear Weapons*[140] and being a feature in case

132 Mara Tignino, *Water during and After Armed Conflicts: What Protection under International Law?* (Brill 2016) 35–36

133 *Gabčikovo* 140; ILC, Jacobsson Environment and Armed Conflict (2014) par.125

134 *Pulp Mills Judgement* par.75; *Pulp Mills on the River Uruguay (Argentina v. Uruguay), Provisional Measures, Order of 13 July 2006,* ICJ Rep 2006, p. 133, par.80

135 Sands 218–219; Boyle and Redgwell 119–125

136 Onita Das, *Environmental Protection, Security and Armed Conflict, A Sustainable Development Perspective* (Edward Elgar 2013) 181

137 ILC, Environment Protection Principles Principle 20

138 London Ocean Dumping Convention (1979), Convention on International Trade in Endangered Species (1973), Convention Concerning the Protection of the World Cultural and Natural Heritage (1972) Ozone Convention (1985) Climate Change Convention (1992) CBD (1992)

139 Edith Brown Weiss, 'Our Rights and Obligations to Future Generations for the Environment' 84 AJIL 1, January (1990) 200; Boyle and Redgwell 121

140 Kirsten Stefanik, 'The Environment and Armed Conflict, Employing General Principles to Protect the Environment' in Carsten Stahn, Jens Iverson, and Jennifer S. Easterday (eds), *Environmental Protection and Transitions from Conflict to Peace* (OUP 2017) 106; *Nuclear Weapons, (n.59), Dissenting Opinion, Judge Weeramantry, 233*

law, including before the ICJ as an element of environmental protection.[141] Practical implementation of intergenerational rights and representation of future generations in international litigations is problematic. Having reviewed IEL principles, IEL treaty obligations should be examined.

II. IEL Treaties

1. Treaty applicability during armed conflict

The effect of armed conflict on international treaties needs to be assessed, as most treaties are silent on the question. The issue has long remained obscure.[142] Traditional doctrine held that eruption of war terminated ipso facto treaties concluded between belligerents, except those specially concluded for war, though there was no uniform State practice or commonly held doctrinal opinion.[143] For example, regarding applicability of IEL obligations during the first Gulf War, some contended that UNCLOS provisions conferring sovereignty over maritime areas were applicable during war, while its environmental protection provisions were unlikely to apply,[144] while others came to the opposite conclusion[145] or pointed to the obligation of States to protect and preserve the marine environment, their responsibility being engaged in case of violation under UNCLOS articles 192 and 235.[146]

Following the Institute of International Law 1985 resolution,[147] the ILC elaborated, during 11 years, Articles on the Effect of Armed Conflicts on Treaties[148] that were not transposed into a convention.[149] Under these Articles, an armed conflict outbreak does not ipso facto terminate or suspend a treaty between belligerents or between a belligerent and a third State.[150] The treaty may provide for its continuing operation during armed conflict.[151] If it is silent or inconclusive, it shall be inter-

141 Malgosia Fitzmaurice, 'Some Reflections on Legal and Philosophical Foundations of International Environmental Law' XXXII PYIL (2012) 89, 101–104

142 Mollard-Bannelier 227; James Crawford, *Brownlie's Principles of Public International Law* (9th edn, OUP 2019) 592; Wil D. Verwey, 'Protection of the Environment in Times of Armed Conflict: in Search of a New Legal Perspective' 8 Leiden J Int'l L 1 (1995) 7, 24

143 Silja Vöneky, *Armed Conflict, Effect on Treaties* (2011) par.1–2

144 Luan Low and David Hodgkinson, 'Compensation for Wartime Environmental Damage: Challenges to International Law after the Gulf War' 35 Va J Int'l L (1994–1995) 444, 445

145 Alice Louise Bunker, 'Protection of the Environment during Armed Conflict: One Gulf, Two Wars' 13 RECIEL 2 (2004) 201 202, 203

146 Christopher Joyner and James Kirhope, 'The Persian Gulf War Oil Spill: Reassessing the Law of Environmental Protection and the Law of Armed Conflict' 24 Case W Res J Int'l L 1, Winter (1992) 41, 42

147 IDI, *Effects of Armed Conflict on Treaties* (1985) art.4

148 ILC, *Articles on the Effects of Armed Conflicts on Treaties, with commentaries (A/66/10)* (2011), Summary ("ILC, Effects of Armed Conflicts")

149 UNGA A/Res/66/99 (2011), A/Res/69/125 (2104), A/Res/72/121 (2017)

150 ILC, Effects of Armed Conflicts art.3

151 Ibid, art.4

preted according to treaty interpretation rules, taking into account relevant external factors, depending on the treaty's nature and the armed conflict's characteristics.[152] A non-international armed conflict should not impact on a State's conventional obligations towards other non-belligerent States.[153]

The majority position has evolved towards recognizing applicability of certain types of treaties during armed conflict, depending on their subject matter.[154] Besides treaties compatible with the maintenance of war,[155] those relating to international protection of human rights or the environment or concerning international watercourses, aquifers and related installations and facilities are presumed to continue to operate wholly or partly during armed conflict;[156] those concerning protection of the environment of non-belligerent States or of areas beyond national jurisdiction limits remain applicable, unless they are inconsistent with the LOAC.[157] Given the number of IEL treaties and diversity of subject matters, their legal status during armed conflict should be evaluated case by case.[158]

2. *Suspension*

Though treaties could be considered suspended during armed conflict, the law is not clear.[159] Suspending obligations under multilateral treaties without affecting non belligerent and neutral parties to the conflict may constitute an obstacle to their suspension.[160] Examination of State practice is complicated by the absence of public recording for more than 50 years in countries such as the US and France.[161] An ILC survey reveals that few treaties were suspended during World War II.[162] In 1973, a Seychelles court held that an extradition treaty suspended during World War II had been revived by the conclusion of a peace treaty at the end of the war. A survey of 18 armed conflicts shows few related suspensions, terminations or withdrawals from treaties. Though the wars between Iran and Iraq and in Afghanistan must have affected treaties to which these countries are parties, the

152 Ibid, art.5, 6 and commentaries

153 Karine Mollard-Bannelier, *La Protection de l'Environnement en Temps de Conflit Armé* (Editions A. Pedone 2001) 233; ILC, Effects of Armed Conflicts, Commentary on art.1

154 L. Oppenheim, *Disputes, War and Neutrality*, vol II (H. Lauterpacht ed, 7th edn, Longmans 1955) 302; Vöneky par.1–3, 5

155 Vöneky par.7

156 ILC, Effects of Armed Conflicts art.7 and Annex

157 ICRC, Guidelines par.5; Vöneky par.10

158 Laurence Boisson de Chazournes, *La Protection Internationale de l'Environnement* (Ed. Pedone 2005); Schmitt 50; *Case C-162/96, A. Racke GmbH & Co. (c.) Hauptzollamt Mainz 1998* ECR I-3655, CJEU

159 Crawford 376

160 Mollard-Bannelier 266–269. Bunker 203

161 ILC, *The Effect of Armed Conflict on Treaties: an Examination of Practice and Doctrine, Memorandum by the Secretariat (A/CN.4/550)* (2005) 6

162 Ibid, par.80

effect is unclear.[163] Belligerent States engaged in armed conflicts have argued at the UNGA about environmental treaties' obligations, demonstrating that they did not consider treaties suspended.[164] During their 1980–1988 conflict, the UNSC called upon Iran and Iraq to refrain from any action that may endanger marine life in the Gulf region.[165] Neither of them was party to ENMOD or Additional Protocol I, but each accused the other of violations of its obligations under a regional convention for protection of the marine environment.[166] The Federal Republic of Yugoslavia (FRY), supported by Russia, denounced NATO bombardments during 1999 to the UN Secretary General, arguing that they violated the LOAC and IEL treaties and seized the ICJ for breach of obligation not to cause substantial damage to the environment.[167] Conversely, States disagreed in their written statements regarding the *Nuclear Weapons* case on whether environmental treaties remained in operation during armed conflict.[168] In its related advisory opinion issued before the ILC Articles were adopted, the ICJ found that the issue was not whether environmental protection treaties were applicable during an armed conflict but whether obligations covered thereunder supposed total restraint during military conflicts,[169] implicitly considering that such treaties were not suspended or terminated.

More recently, treaties were suspended following the eruption of armed conflict. In *Racke* the EU suspended unilaterally a trade agreement with Yugoslavia, when armed conflict started there, based on fundamental changed circumstances of threat to peace and stability, recognized applicable by the Court of Justice of the European Union ("CJEU").[170] However, their scope was too wide and the agreement did not allow for suspension but provided for denunciation upon six months' notice.[171] In response to Crimea annexation by the Russian Federation in 2014 and the Russia-Ukraine armed conflict, the EC suspended an agreement with the Russian Federation on issuance of visas, citing its article 15(5) allowing suspension for protection of national security.[172] In the same context, the Russian Federation suspended a 2013 Agreement on nuclear cooperation with the US, justifying it as a countermeasure to US sanctions against

163 Ibid, 48–68

164 Mollard-Bannelier 272

165 UNSC, *Resolution 540, 31 October 1983, S/Res. 540* (1983)

166 Kuwait Regional Convention for Co-operation on the Protection of the Marine Environment from Pollution; *Note verbale dated 20 April 1983 from the Permanent Representative of the Islamic Republic of Iran to the UN addressed to the Secretary-General (A/38/163-S/15723)* (22 April 1983) *Letter dated 5 May 1983 from the Permanent Representative of Iraq to the UN addressed to the Secretary-General (A/38/187-S/15752)* (9 May 1983)

167 Mollard-Bannelier 275-276; *Letter dated 4 June 1999 from the Chargé d'affaires a.i. of the Permanent Mission of the Federal Republic of Yugoslavia to the United Nations addressed to the Secretary-General, E/1999/71 (and S/1999/659) 7 June 1999*

168 *Nuclear Weapons* par.27–28; ILC, Effects of Armed Conflicts Commentary on Annex, par.55

169 *Nuclear Weapons* par.30

170 *Case C-162/96, A. Racke GmbH & Co. v. Hauptzollamt Mainz, 1998* ECR I-3655, CJEU

171 Klabbers 70–71ILC, *Articles on Responsibility of States for Internationally Wrongful Acts, with Commentary, A/56/10* (ILC YB 2001, vol II (2)) Commentary on art.54, par.(4)

172 *Council Decision (EU) 2022/333 of 25 February 2022* (Official Journal of the EU, L 54, Vol 65)

it, their constant renewal and the US suspension of nuclear cooperation, which some suggested violated US obligations under the WTO.[173] However, cooperation on transboundary watercourses has continued despite tensions and armed conflicts, such as management of the Indus River by Pakistan and India[174] or the committee of riparian States in charge of the Mekong river.[175] Ultimately, non-suspension is the rule, unless the treaty provides for suspension or derogation during armed conflict,[176] with notification to be given to the parties to the treaty.[177]

3. Termination

Grounds for treaty termination under the VCLT may affect its operation during armed conflict.[178] First, impossibility of performance is due to permanent destruction or disappearance of an object indispensable to the execution of a treaty; in case of temporary impossibility, only suspension of the treaty may be invoked.[179] State practice is scarce.[180] Examples are "the submergence of an island or the drying up of a river."[181] In *Gabčikovo*, the ICJ found that Hungary could not rely on its own breach of an existing treaty to justify impossibility of performance that it claimed resulted from permanent disappearance of "the essential object of the Treaty," an economic investment operated jointly by the parties.[182]

Second, fundamental change of circumstances, ("*rebus sic stantibus*" doctrine) must be unforeseen, affect radically the extent of the obligations still to be performed and concern circumstances existing at the time of conclusion of the treaty that were essential to the parties' consent to be bound by it.[183] Courts are reluctant to apply it, to avoid destabilizing pacta sunt servanda.[184] The ICJ did not recognise it in the *Fisheries* and *Gabcikovo* cases.[185] Arguably, armed conflict may constitute a fundamental change of circumstances, but as political statements on treaties' fate during armed conflicts are made when irrelevant, a clear conclusion is difficult

173 Alexandra Hofer, *Russia's Unilateral Suspension of the 2013 Agreement on Nuclear Cooperation with the United States* (EJIL: Talk! 2016)

174 James Kraska, 'Sustainable Development Is Security: The Role of Transboundary River Agreement as Confidence Building Measure in South Asia' 28 Yale J Int'l L (2003) 486; Helmut Kulz, 'Further Water Disputes between India and Pakistan' 18 Int'l Comp L Q (1969) 718

175 Tignino, *L'eau et la Guerre* 375–377

176 Boyle and Redgwell 216; Vöneky par.3; Oppenheim 302; Bunker 203; Contra: H. Wassgren, 'The UN Compensation Commission: Lessons of Legitimacy, State Responsibility and War Reparations' Leiden J Int'l L (1998) Wassgren favoured suspension, prior to the ILC Articles

177 ILC, Effects of Armed Conflicts art.9

178 Ibid, art.18 and commentary; Crawford 376

179 VCLT art.61.

180 ILC, Effects of Armed Conflicts: Practice and Doctrine 76–77

181 ILC, Effects of Armed Conflicts 257

182 *Gabčikovo* par.103; VCLT art.61.2

183 VCLT art.62.

184 Klabbers 70

185 *Gabčikovo* par.104 *Fisheries Jurisdiction (UK v. Iceland), Jurisdiction* ICJ Rep 1973, p. 3, par.40–43

to draw. The British government announced in 1983 that the 1790 Nootka Sound Convention was terminated in 1795, following war between Britain and Spain.[186] In 2000, a Greek court found that the 1913 Treaty of Athens had been abolished by the 1923 Treaty of Lausanne following exceptional change of circumstances in World War I. Fundamental change of circumstances was applied to three cases during war in the 1940s, with one igniting controversy.[187] In conclusion, IEL treaties are applicable during armed conflict. The issue is how different branches of international law can apply in parallel.[188]

4. Implementation of obligations belonging to different legal fields

The VCLT article 30 regulates application of successive treaties dealing with the same subject matter that may create incompatible obligations. Yet, classifying treaties according to their subject matter is subjective, such as maritime carriage of chemical substances being a shipping issue for insurers and an environmental concern for environmental organizations.[189] The LOAC treaties do not share the same subject matter as IEL or IHRL treaties. They "have different foci but overlapping issue areas," creating difficulties unaddressed in the VCLT.[190] Applying norms from different legal fields to the same issue, may result in one norm helping to interpret another or in a conflict of norms.[191] The latter arises if a State is bound by incompatible obligations, when "one norm constitutes, has led to, or may lead to, a breach of the other"[192] or in "conflicts between obligations and permissive norms," one norm setting obligations and another setting rights.[193] The ILC interprets norms conflict "as a situation where two rules or principles suggest different ways of dealing with a problem."[194]

4.1 Resolution of a conflict of norms

A few techniques are used to resolve norms conflict, previously mentioned.[195] The *lex posterior* maxim, giving priority to later rules, does not apply to conflict

186 ILC, Effects of Armed Conflicts: Practice and Doctrine par.5

187 Ibid, par.122–126

188 ILC, Jacobsson Environment and Armed Conflict (2014) par.6

189 ILC, *Fragmentation of International Law: Difficulties Arising from the Diversification and Expansion of International Law, Report of the Study Group of the ILC, (A/CN.4/L.682)* (2006) par.22 (ILC Fragmentation Report)

190 J. Christopher Borgen, 'Resolving Treaty Conflicts' 37 Geo Wash Int'l L Rev (2005) 573, 603

191 ILC, *Conclusions of the Work of the Study Group on Fragmentation of International Law: Difficulties Arising from the Diversification and Expansion of International Law, A/61/10* (ILC YB, vol II (2), 2006) par.25 (ILC Fragmentation Conclusions)

192 Joost Pauwelyn, *Conflict of Norms in Public International Law: How WTO Law Relate to Other Rules of International Law* (2003) 175

193 Marko Milanovic, 'Norm Conflict in International Law: Wither Human Rights?' 20 Duke J Int'l Comp L (2009) 72

194 ILC, Fragmentation Report par.25

195 Chapter 3, section IV

between IEL and LOAC norms. *Lex specialis* indicates that specific rules prevail over more general rules. Interpretation of norms related to two legal regimes will vary, depending on which special law is retained as framework for interpretation.[196] Two specific regimes may be found applicable to the same issue, as "specificity is in the eye of the beholder."[197] The ILC considers that "special regimes" constituted by a group of rules and principles concerned with a particular subject matter may be applicable as "*lex specialis*," deviating from general rules of State responsibility, leaving open the question of the extent to which general international law rules are affected.[198] The debate whether IEL is a special law branch that applies different interpretative rules or is a collection of treaty and customary rules dealing with the environment is too abstract to be relevant.[199] Regarding armed conflict, the LOAC is generally assumed to be *lex specialis* and IEL *lex generalis*. An obligation to protect the environment under IEL should then be interpreted according to the LOAC requirements.[200] However, whether the *lex specialis* should be decisive depends on other elements to be considered, including the will of the parties, the nature of the instruments, their object and purposes and a reasonable interpretation that would least disturb the operation of the legal system.[201]

"Systemic integration" requires interpreting obligations by reference to their normative environment ("system") and systemic objectives.[202] A general clause recognizing the potential for existing parallel and conflicting obligations under different IEL treaties is inserted in their preamble, calling for treaties to "mutually support" their objectives.[203] The normative environment covering any relevant international law rules applicable between the parties under VCLT article 31.3(c) must be taken into account widely.[204] A question is whether international law in force at the conclusion of the treaty reflecting the parties' intent should be considered or if their changing views with time on the meaning of a treaty, new circumstances and legal development should be taken into account.[205] If the terms of a treaty are evolutionary and obligations described generally, they should be interpreted according to the law at the time of its application.[206] Case law supports integration of IEL development into interpretation of treaties. The WTO Appellate Body interpreted "natural resources" and "exhaustible" terms in the WTO Agreement, according to international customary law and general principles, finding these terms

196 ILC, Fragmentation Report par.55
197 Borgen 612
198 ILC, Fragmentation Report par.128–129, 133, 152(5), 158, 173; ILC, Fragmentation Conclusions par.11–12; ILC, Jacobsson Environment and Armed Conflict (2014) par.118
199 ILC, Fragmentation Report 133
200 Bunker 204
201 ILC, Fragmentation Report par.410; VCLT art.31.1, 31.3(c)
202 Ibid, par.412, 413; VCLT art.31.3(c)
203 ILC, Fragmentation Report, par.272–282
204 Ibid, par.415, 426, 462, 470
205 Ibid, par.429–431, 475–476
206 Ibid, 478

"evolutionary" by reference to UNCLOS.[207] The ICJ judged in *Gabcikovo* in 1997 that "newly developed norms of environmental law are relevant for the implementation of the Treaty," signed in 1977, which the parties must take into consideration, in carrying out their obligations related to water quality in the Danube and nature protection, when constructing and operating a locks system on the Danube.[208] These obligations are "necessarily evolving" and current standards must be taken into consideration to evaluate environmental risks, developed in response to scientific insights.[209]

4.2 Practical application

These methods are "difficult to use when determining conflict between two normative orders *in abstracto*, [and are] more suited to determination of relation between two norms in concrete case."[210]

Incompatible obligations of belligerents would arise in cases where respect of LOAC obligations during armed conflict would breach IEL obligations. A case where implementation of IEL obligations would breach LOAC obligations is unlikely, while violation of a LOAC rule leading to breach of an IEL obligation is not a case of incompatible obligations, but of different obligations breached. Potential norms conflict may arise around the notion of environmental damage and liability standard under the LOAC Protocol I, articles 35.3 and 55 and an IEL treaty; obligations in preventing or minimizing harm under the LOAC precautions in attacks and IEL due diligence duty. Systemic interpretation requires interpreting the LOAC environmental damage threshold that is outdated, considering the development of IEL and scientific knowledge, by recourse to the IEL notion of environmental damage applicable to the natural resource concerned, as a general damage definition under IEL is not clear.

III. Shared natural resources: water under international law

Fundamental for survival, water is critical to ensure food security and health, essential for sustainable development and to fight poverty.[211] The human right to water and sanitation is covered under IHRL during occupation (Chapter 3). Rules regarding shared water resources under IWL and IEL may add to its protection during armed conflict.

207 Ibid, par.443; *WTO Appelate Body, United States – Import Prohibition of Certain Shrimp and Shrimp Products* WT/DS58/AB/R, DSR 1998:VII, 2793 par.126–134

208 *Gabčikovo* par.112

209 Ibid, par.140

210 Anja Lindroos, 'Addressing Norm Conflicts in a Fragmented Legal System: The Doctrine of Lex Specialis' 74 Nordic J Int'l L (2005) 44

211 UNGA 2nd Committee, *Agriculture development, food security and nutrition (A/C.2/78/L.31)* (2023) 6

IWL is constituted by international conventions, rules and customary law. The 1992 UNECE Water Convention, amended in 2003 to open it to global membership, covers the use of shared international watercourses,[212] supplemented in 2012 by non-binding guidance applicable to transboundary groundwaters.[213] The 1997 UN Watercourses Convention (Helsinki Convention) regulates non-navigational uses of international watercourses.[214] The ILA Helsinki rules (1966), revised in 2004 at the ILA Conference (Berlin rules), codify international rules on utilization and protection of international drainage basins, constituted by interconnected waters flowing into a common terminus, i.e. the sea or a lake.[215] The ILC adopted Draft Articles on Transboundary Aquifers (2009).[216] IEL customary principles and rules (Stockholm Principle 21/Rio principle 2, EIA and procedural requirements related to the duty to cooperate) are applicable to activities that may harm international watercourses.[217] Finally, technical rules, procedures and standards developed by organizations (such as International Hydropower Association and World Bank policy on international waterways) influence IWL's practice.[218] The 1997 Watercourses Convention representing the "modern development of international law"[219] and the ILA Berlin Rules (2004) incorporating IHRL and IEL developments since 1966 broadly reflect customary international law.[220] Under IWL, riparian States are required to comply with IHL obligations.[221] Different instruments affirm protection of water and water installations during armed conflicts, strengthening IHL rules.[222] Occupants must manage transboundary freshwater resources according to the LOAC and IWL rules.[223]

A few doctrines were advanced that underpin rights and obligations of States concerning transboundary watercourses on their territory. Absolute territorial

212 UNECE Convention on the Protection of Transboundary Watercourses and International Lakes, 1992, (entry into force 1996) amended by MoP Decision III/I, 'Amendment to Articles 25 and 26 of the Convention' (12 January 2004) UN Doc ECE/MP/WAT/14 (entry into force 2013)

213 UNECE Model Provisions on Transboundary Groundwaters, (UN Doc ECE/MP.WAT/40), 2012

214 Convention on the Law on Non-Navigational Uses of International Watercourses (1997) (entry into force 2014)

215 ILA Water Resources Committee, *Helsinki Rules on the Uses of the Waters of International Rivers (1966), updated by Berlin Rules on Water Resources (2004)* art.1

216 ILC, *Draft Articles on the Law of Transboundary Aquifers 2008, A/63/10* (2009)

217 Sands 339

218 Owen McIntyre, 'Chapter 15: Water' in Elisa Morgera and Kati Kulovesi (eds), *Research Handbook on International Law and Natural Resources* (Edward Elgar 2016) 316

219 *Gabčikovo par.85, 147*

220 ILA, *Berlin Rules on Water Resources, 2004* 3; Sands 337

221 The 1997 UN Watercourses Convention, art.29; ILC Draft Articles on Transboundary Rivers, art.18

222 ILA, *Resolution on the Protection of Water Resources and Water Installations in Times of Armed Conflict, Madrid, 1976, Report of the Fifty-Seventh Conference* (1976) ILA, Berlin Rules on Water Resources, 2004 Berlin Rules art.50–54 TigninoWater During and After Armed Conflicts: What protection under International Law? 46–47

223 Eyal Benvenisti, 'Water Conflicts during the Occupation of Iraq' 97 AJIL No. 4, October (2003) 860, 870

sovereignty favours upstream States through the first appropriation principle. It is "the so-called 'Harmon Doctrine' which embodies the claim that a State has the unqualified right to utilize and dispose of the waters of an international river flowing through its territory." Invoked in early transboundary waters disputes, it is rejected under IWL and by the majority of States.[224] Absolute territorial integrity confers a "right upon a lower basin State to demand the continuation of the full flow of waters of natural quality from an upper co-basin State" (downstream in the direction of river flows, towards the sea or end of the river). It has been consistently rejected by States and arbitration.[225] The prevailing doctrine is limited territorial sovereignty based on sovereign equality of States,[226] which "provides the theoretical basis for the principle of equitable and reasonable utilization" that entitles each co-basin State to use waters flowing through its territory.[227]

This principle is the "cardinal rule in the field" widely supported in treaty law, judicial and arbitral decisions, State practice, codification and publicists' work.[228] It requires an equitable balancing of co-basin States' needs and uses of water, factoring in geography, hydrology, social and economic needs of the State and population.[229] The obligation to use equitably and reasonably shared waters reflects in an optimal way "the concept of common utilization" of such a resource. Czechoslovakia was judged to have deprived Hungary of its right to a reasonable and equitable share of the Danube by assuming unilateral control over it and failed to respect proportionality required by international law.[230] At the heart of the regime, "the community of interest in an international river becomes the basis of a common legal right" characterized by "perfect equality of all riparian states," without preferential privilege for any in the use of the river,[231] including non-navigational uses.[232] The right applies to any shared natural resources, including lakes and underground water or fisheries, limits States' rights in the resource[233] and requires them to consider each other's rights and examine necessary measures for conservation, development and equitable exploitation.[234] Negotiations must be undertaken with a view to resolve equitably issues of pollution or excessive use affecting shared rivers.[235]

224 McIntyre, 'Water' 308–309; *Kasikili/Sedudu Island (Botswana/Namibia), Judgment of 13 December 1999* ICJ Rep 1999, 1045 Separate opinion of Judge Kooijmans; République Française, Assemblée Nationale, La Commission des Affaires Etrangères, *Rapport d'information, la géopolitique de l'eau* (2011) 212
225 McIntyre, 'Water' 309; *Lac Lanoux*
226 UN Charter art.2(1)
227 McIntyre, 'Water' 310
228 Ibid, 306, 310
229 Ibid, 310; Watercourses Convention art.6
230 *Gabčikovo* par.85, 147
231 *Territorial Jurisdiction of the International Commission of the River Oder,* Judgment No 16, 1929 PCIJ Series A, No 23, p. 27, PCIJ
232 *Gabčikovo* par.85; *Pulp Mills Judgement* par.281; *Botswana/Namibia par.37 (n.224)*; McIntyre, 'Water' p. 312
233 Sands 340, 512
234 *Fisheries Jurisdiction (UK v. Iceland), Merits, Judgment* ICJ Rep 1974, p. 3, par.72; *Fisheries Jurisdiction (Federal Republic of Germany v. Iceland), Merits, Judgment* ICJ Rep 1974, p. 175, par.64
235 Sands 341

The obligation of upstream States to take measures to prevent harm bears similarities to occupants' obligation, under occupation usufruct rules to use the fruit and protect the capital of water resources from overuse and prevent diminution of quality and quantity of water downstream. Benvenisti claims that the prevention obligation could be waived if the harm is within boundaries of reasonable and equitable water use by upstream State, though the obligation to consult with riparian States, to mitigate or eliminate harm and to agree on compensation remains,[236] according to a customary "obligation of negotiating an agreement."[237] The Watercourses Convention does not, however, absolve States from the obligation to take preventive measures but provides that harm may occur despite taking measures to prevent it, as "significant harm nevertheless is caused to another watercourse State."[238] The determination of the threshold of "significant" damage is the issue, as a State could claim that the damage it caused is not "significant."

The concept of equitable and reasonable water use is vague to allow flexibility leading to different views regarding its application.[239] Recourse to common management agreements is endorsed by the international community, whereby a whole basin is managed as one unit, with rights to use water resources vested collectively in the community or divided between co-riparian States under institutional supervision.[240] It incorporates key IEL duties to prevent significant transboundary harm, utilize equitably and reasonably and cooperate in the management of shared water resources that are established IWL rules.[241]

IV. IEL rules as a basis of State accountability

Responsibility refers to the primary obligation which breach results in a wrongful act and liability to the secondary obligation, namely the consequences of the breach of a primary obligation, according to the ILC distinction.[242]

1. *State responsibility*

Under general international law, State responsibility is considered objective when raised by breach of an obligation, or subjective when breach of standard of conduct is additionally necessary, depending on the requirements of the primary rules that contain the obligation.[243] Some previous doctrine supported subjective responsibility, suggesting that a State must have acted wilfully and maliciously in case of

236 Watercourses Convention art.7(2); Benvenisti 867, 870

237 Brunson MacChesney, 'Lake Lanoux Case (France-Spain)' 53 AJIL 1, January (1959) 163–164; *Lac Lanoux* 306

238 Watercourses Convention art.7(2)

239 McIntyre, 'Water' 310–311

240 Watercourses Convention, articles 5(2), 8(2), 9, 21, 24 and 33(2); UNECE Water Convention (art.9(2))

241 Watercourses Convention art.5, 7(1) and 8; McIntyre, 'Water' 306, 311

242 Katja Creutz, *State Responsibility in the International Legal Order, a Critical Appraisal* (CUP 2020) 31; *ITLOS Activities in the Area* par.66

243 ILC, States' Responsibility Articles Commentary art.2 par.(3), (4)

delicts or with culpable negligence for acts of omissions,[244] with few arbitral decisions supporting culpa as the basis of responsibility.[245] Yet a realistic approach to international relations is incompatible with analysis of a state of mind of specific natural persons representing, or not, the State, to determine negligence, malice or reckless intention.[246] The near impossibility of determining responsibility based on fault eventually led to a move away from it.[247] Wrongfulness of an act was adopted as an objective notion more suited to responsibility of legal persons, such as States.[248] Objective responsibility is raised when agency and causal connection between the international wrongful act and injury are established. It is generally adopted by States and jurisprudence, as better suited to maintain acceptable standards and uphold the reparations principle in international law. Culpa could be relevant as lack of due diligence, when required under a primary rule of law.[249]

Regarding IEL, a similar shift from subjective to objective responsibility can be discerned. State responsibility "remains the starting point in any enquiry as to how accountability in this field can be achieved."[250] Doctrinal analysis of older case law loosely connected to environmental issues is inconclusive on a standard of conduct for State responsibility, as interpretations contradict each other and theories vary.[251] In *Corfu Channel*, Albania's responsibility was based on its knowledge about laying of mines in her territorial waters, its notification obligations and failure to prevent damage, though there were one separate and five dissenting opinions, including one concluding that proof of Albania's knowledge and of evidence of culpable negligence was lacking.[252] *Trail Smelter* was decided ex aequo et bono, not under international law.[253] The damage being proven and Canada's responsibility accepted from the outset, the award was not concerned with determination of a responsibility standard and does not support strongly liability without fault.[254] *Lac Lanoux* focused on interpretation of obligations under treaties signed between

244 L. Oppenheim, *International Law, Vol. I Peace* (H. Lauterpacht ed, 7th edn, 1948) par.154

245 Crawford 540, n.106; *Corfu Channel case, Judgment of April 9th, 1949, I.C.J. Reports*, Dissenting opinion by Judge Krylov, 72

246 Crawford 539

247 Creutz 102

248 Jean Combacau and Serge Sur, *Droit International Public* (13th edn, LGDJ 2019) 586

249 Crawford, *Brownlie's Principles of Public International Law* 539–540

250 Phoebe Okowa, 'Chapter 15: Responsibility for environmental damage' in Malgosia Fitzmaurice, David M. Ong, and Panos Merkouris (eds), *Research Handbook on International Environmental Law* (Edward Elgar 2010) 303

251 Crawford 425; Jutta Brunnée, 'Sense and Sensibility: Reflections on International Liability Regimes as Tools for Environmental Protection' 53 ICLQ (2004) 351, 353; Sands 746; Creutz par.4.3.1.1

252 *Corfu Channel case, Judgment of April 9th, 1949, I.C.J. Reports, Dissenting Opinion by Judge Krylov, 72*

253 Karl Zemanek, 'Chapter 7: State Responsibility and Liability ' in Winfried Lang, Hanspeter Neuhold, and Karl Zemanek (eds), *Environmental Protection and International Law* (1st edn, Graham & Trotman/Martinus Nijhoff 1991) 194

254 Boyle and Redgwell 226

Spain and France rather than State responsibility. Apart from these precedents, judicial cases analysing liability for environmental damage are scarce.[255]

Boyle concludes that "fault" in the subjective sense "requiring intention, malice or recklessness on the part of the State or its agents (i.e. fault-based responsibility) . . . is almost never the basis of responsibility in environmental disputes," although the reckless or intentional infliction of environmental damage by Iraq on Kuwait in 1991 "could be said to involve subjective fault" and it is not a "necessary condition of responsibility."[256] State responsibility, in the objective sense of fault, (i.e. objective responsibility) arises from a breach of an obligation to act with due care or diligence, under customary law.[257] Fault-based responsibility is opposed to objective responsibility, with some advocating that absolute responsibility or strict liability, which disregard both fault and wrongful act, constitute the end of the spectrum.[258] As doctrine and modern case law[259] support objective responsibility based on breach of obligation of due diligence, it may be considered as an emerging required standard of conduct under customary international law.

1.1 Obligations of conduct and result and impact on wrongful act

The obligation not to cause transboundary damage is paramount for State responsibility purposes.[260] Though it was known as "the no-harm" principle, it is not an absolute prohibition on environmental damage (obligation of result) but rather concerns the activities leading to it and the means utilized to prevent it (obligation of conduct).[261] In its civil law sense, an obligation of result requires a specific result (seller's obligation to deliver the goods) while an obligation of conduct is an obligation to endeavour, to take measures which are reasonably expected, to attain a certain result (such as doctor's obligation).[262] Transposed unto the international order, the distinction applies to the wrongful act: it is constituted, for obligations of result, when the injured party suffers damage, whatever preventive actions the responsible State may have taken, whereas it occurs for obligations of conduct when the responsible State does not use all efforts expected to be used, breaching

255 Boyle, 'Jurisprudence of ITLOS' 370; Boyle and Redgwell 226

256 Boyle and Redgwell 224

257 Ibid, 225. Boyle, 'Globalising Environmental Liability' 3; Brunnée 354 Anne Daniel, 'Civil Liability Regimes as a Complement to Multilateral Environmental Agreements: Sound International Policy or False Comfort?' 12 RECIEL 3 (2003) 225, 238

258 Creutz par.2.3.2, n.108

259 *Pulp Mills Judgement* par.197; *ITLOS Activities in the Area* par.110; Gabcikovo, Pulp Mills, ITLOS Activities in the Area, South China

260 Sands 740

261 Boyle and Redgwell 124, 162, 226; Ilias Plakokefalos, 'Causation in the Law of State Responsibility and the Problem of Overdetermination: In Search of Clarity' 26 EJIL 2 (2015) 481; Contra: Tullio Scovazzi, 'State Responsibility for Environmental Harm' 12 YB Int'l Env L 1 (2001) 48–49

262 Pierre-Marie Dupuy, 'Reviewing the Difficulties of Codification: On Agos' Classification of Obligations of Means and Obligations of Result in Relation to State Responsibility' 10 EJIL 2 (1999) 371, 375; Combacau and Sur 592

"an obligation to behave (in a legally defined way)."[263] The injured State must prove that damage could have been prevented if measures that were not taken were implemented[264] (the "but-for test").[265] It is the essence of the due diligence obligation.[266] It is then an obligation of conduct.[267] Liability arises then from a failure to regulate and control the source of damage.[268] If Scovazzi considers the no-harm principle as an obligation of result prohibiting the harm itself, he admits that conduct of States will be judged according to a due diligence obligation.[269]

1.2 Standard of due diligence

The standard of due diligence does not exist as a uniform specific benchmark against which to weigh States' conduct across all circumstances. It should be measured against what is "appropriate and proportional to the level of risk of transboundary harm" in each case. Whether a standard of care or due diligence or appropriate procedure, standard or rule is considered reasonable may differ in time[270] when considering scientific and technological knowledge and risks involved.[271] Risk should be assessed objectively, as damage does not indicate that an activity was risky, and conversely risk may be underestimated.[272] However, in the face of difficulties of finding proof of lack of proper care, "the issue becomes one of causation."[273] The UNCC concluded that claims for compensable natural resource damages must show contamination by oil or by hazardous substances, that caused or was likely to cause physical or biological impairment, contamination on its own being insufficient, and the chain of causation must be unbroken.[274] The injured party seeking compensation must prove "the existence of a causal nexus between the internationally wrongful act and the injury suffered."[275]

263 Combacau and Sur 592
264 Dupuy 379
265 Plakokefalos 476
266 Combacau and Sur 592
267 Dupuy 375; ILC, *International Liability for Injurious Consequences Arising Out of Acts Not Prohibited by International Law. Report of the Working Group – A/CN.4/L.533 and Add.1* (ILC YB 1996, vol II (2), annex I) Commentary art.3 par. (12), in its work prior to subdividing the subject in two. ILC Prevention Articles, commentary on art.3 par.7; Boyle and Redgwell 226, 227
268 Boyle and Redgwell 226, 227
269 Scovazzi 48, 49
270 ILC Prevention Articles, commentary on art.3 par.11
271 *ITLOS Activities in the Area* par.117 (n.75)
272 ILC Prevention Articles, commentary on art.1, par.14
273 Crawford 541
274 Michael T. Hugienin and others, 'Chapter 3, Assessment and Valuation of Damage to the Environment' in Cymie R. Payne and Peter H. Sand (eds), *Gulf War Reparations and the UN Compensation Commission* (OUP 2011) 83; José R. Allen, 'Chapter 6, Points of Law' in Cymie R. Payne and Peter H. Sand (eds), *Gulf War Reparations and the UN Compensation Commission* (OUP 2011) 159–160
275 *Armed Activities on the Territory of the Congo (DRC v. Uganda), Reparations, Judgement* ICJ Rep 2022, p. 13, par.93

2. *State liability*

IEL has seen an explosion of multilateral environmental agreements covering issues of global concerns, such as deforestation, desertification, ozone layer depletion, climate change, introduction of toxic substances in food chain and extinction of species of fauna and flora.[276] State responsibility for breach of a standard under an IEL convention is a rare bird. Most treaties contain broad obligations, as they represent a compromise between diverse participants and do not include specific environmental standards, the breach of which would constitute a wrongful act.[277] A rare example of liability imposed on States concerns space activities. A launching State shall bear absolute liability for damage caused by its space object on the Earth's surface or an aircraft flight and fault-based liability for damage elsewhere to a space object or to persons or property on board a space object.[278] Liability is strict when it allows circumstances for exemption from liability and absolute when no exemption is allowed.[279] Following the break-up of a Soviet satellite over Canadian territory in 1979, Canada brought a successful claim against the USSR under this convention and general principles of international law for the clean-up of radioactive debris.[280]

Since State responsibility seemed inadequate to resolve issues of liability and compensation for environmental damage, civil liability treaties imposing liability on the operator have been concluded for damage compensation by sectors of activities.[281] Civil liability regimes currently in force for hazardous activities, mostly relevant as potentially applicable by analogy to armed conflicts, concern nuclear activities[282] and oil pollution at sea.[283] Their common underlying assumption is that

276 Scovazzi 51

277 Elli Louka, *International Environmental Law, Fairness, Effectiveness, and World Order* (CUP 2006) 468; Creutz 186–187

278 The Convention on International Liability for Damage Caused by Space Objects, 29 March 1972 (in force 1 September 1972), 961 UNTS 187. art.II, III, IV

279 Boyle and Redgwell 225; Sands Chap. 16

280 Canada, Claim against the USSR for damage caused by Cosmos 954, 23 January 1979, 18 ILM 899–908, 1979

281 Scovazzi 51; Sands

282 (i) The Convention on Third Party Liability in the Field of Nuclear Energy of 29 July 1960, (Paris Convention), negotiated under the aegis of the OECD, covering most Western countries, as amended by Additional Protocols of 28 January 1964 (in force 1 April 1968), of 16 November 1982 (in force 7 October 1988) and of 12 February 2004 (in force 1 January 2022) (ii) Vienna Convention on Civil Liability for Nuclear Damage, 21 May 1963 (in force 12 November 1977) negotiated under the auspices of the IAEA has a worldwide character (the Vienna Convention) and its Protocol of 29 May 1997 (in force 4 October 2003). Convention on Supplementary Compensation for Nuclear Damage (Vienna, 29 May 1997) (in force 15 April 2015), (CSC) (iii) The Joint Protocol Relating to the Application of the Vienna Convention and the Paris Convention of 21 September 1988, (in force 27 April 1992)

283 (i) International Convention on Civil Liability for Oil Pollution Damage, 29 November 1969, Brussels (in force 19 June 1975) and International Convention on the Establishment of an International Fund for Compensation for Oil Pollution Damage, Brussels, 18 December 1971 (in force 16 October 1978) both amended by Protocols of 27 November 1992, London (in force 30 May 1996),

accidents occur, causing transboundary harmful impact. Therefore, liability should be objective and proof of fault unnecessary.[284] "Liability results from the risk, irrespective of fault."[285] The oil pollution and nuclear regimes and the 2006 ILC Principles on Loss Allocation adopt a strict liability approach, respectively channelling liability to the ship owner, the nuclear installation operator – though there may be a direct right of action against its insurer or other financial guarantor under specific condition – or the operator in command or control of the hazardous activity causing transboundary damage.[286] A few exemptions from liability are provided, such as natural disaster under the oil pollution regime and war under both regimes.[287]

The issue is whether a liability standard may be inferred from IEL liability treaties and apply to States. As strict liability for ultrahazardous or dangerous activities is known in national legislations and IEL civil liability treaties, a liability standard could be derived by analogy from general principles of law or treaties.[288] International agreements for high-risk transboundary activities, such as the Basel Convention on movements and disposal of hazardous wastes[289] and Helsinki Convention on effects of industrial accidents, have entered into force – but not their liability protocols.[290] Other liability conventions regarding transport of dangerous goods by road, rail or inland navigation vessel[291] or of hazardous and noxious substances by sea[292] or the sole treaty instituting a general, as opposed to sectoral, regime on civil

---

(1992 CLC and 1992 Fund Convention). Protocol to the Fund Convention, London, 16 May 2003 (in force 3 March 2005) (the Supplementary Fund Protocol) (ii) International Convention on Civil Liability for Bunker Oil Pollution Damage, London, 23 March 2001, (in force 21 November 2008) (Bunker Convention)

284 Creutz 291

285 IAEA, *The 1997 Vienna Convention on Civil Liability for Nuclear Damage and the 1997 Convention on Supplementary Compensation for Nuclear Damage, Explanatory Texts* (Int'l L Series No 3, 2007) 1

286 1992 CLC, art. III and IV. Bunker Convention, art.3; Paris Convention, art.3, 6; Vienna Convention, art. II, IV; ILC, ILC Allocation Principles art.4.2

287 Ibid, art.9; Vienna Convention, Art. IV (2) and (3).

288 Lisa M. Kaplan, 'International Responsibility of an Occupying Power for Environmental Harm: The Case of Estonia' 12 Transnat L (1999) 153, 187; Sands 747

289 The Basel Convention on the Control of Transboundary Movements of Hazardous Waste and their Disposal, 22 March 1989 (into force 5 May 1992). Basel Protocol on Liability and Compensation for Damage Resulting from Transboundary Movements of Hazardous Wastes and their Disposal, 10 December 1999, not yet into force.

290 Protocol on Civil Liability and Compensation for Damage Caused by the Transboundary Effects of Industrial Accidents on Transboundary Waters to the 1992 Convention on the Protection and Use of Transboundary Watercourses and International Lakes and to the 1992 Convention on the Transboundary Effects of Industrial Accidents (Kiev, 21 May 2003) (Kiev Protocol on Civil Liability)

291 The Convention on Civil Liability for Damage Caused During Carriage of Dangerous Goods by Road, Rail and Inland Navigation Vessels, Geneva, 10 October 1989, ("CRTD Convention")

292 The International Convention on Liability and Compensation for Damage in Connection with the Carriage of Hazardous and Noxious Substances by Sea, 3 May 1996, ("HNS Convention") superseded by 2010 Protocol, 30 April 2010, not yet in force.

liability for environmental damage from dangerous activities,[293] have not entered into force, due to difficulty to obtain States' agreement on liability for hazardous activities. International liability for hazardous activities does not require breach of international obligation but damage caused by the activities,[294] though additional fault-based liability may be provided.[295]

Therefore, imposing strict liability could be construed as the imposition by courts of obligations not usually accepted by States, as liability is only accepted under specific regimes and even those treaties tend to channel liability to entities in charge of the activities that may cause transboundary harm.[296] Differences in scope of strict liability under common and civil law systems and between national legal systems render reliance on municipal liability systems unfeasible. *A fortiori* imposing strict or absolute liability is a non-starter. Consequently, Boyle considers objective responsibility for breach of obligation a firmer foundation for liability standard for environmental damage under international law.[297] Sands remains sceptical about the role that State responsibility principles can play concerning global issues such as climate change, where causation and attribution of liability are difficult.[298] However, this difficulty, based on the existence of multiple actors and factors impacting climate, does not apply to a breach by a state of specific due diligence obligations under an IEL treaty or customary law, engaging its responsibility. Moreover, during armed conflicts, environmental damage is expected from specific military operations for which a State is responsible, arising from breach of an IEL or LOAC obligation.

3. Environmental damage

Environmental damage is not specifically determined. It evolved with increased scientific understanding of the impact of human activities on the environment, covering different concerns over time.[299] It covers damage to natural resources of the environment (air, water, soil, flora, fauna and characteristic aspects of landscape). As cultural heritage is not included in any definition of the environment in a treaty currently in force, the issue is whether damage to cultural heritage resources is covered under environmental damage. The UNCC considered it was.[300] A rare example where such damage is covered is under the 1992 convention of transboundary effects of industrial accidents (article 1(c)(iv)) that entered into force, while the

293 Convention on Civil Liability for Damage resulting from Activities Dangerous to the Environment, Lugano, 21 June 1993
294 CRTD art.5, HNS art.7, Basel Protocol art.4
295 Basel Protocol art.5; Kiev Protocol on Civil Liability, art.5
296 Boyle and Redgwell 229–230; Creutz
297 Ibid, 229–230
298 Sands 803
299 Marie-Louise Larsson, 'Legal Definitions of the Environment and of Environmental Damage' 38 Scand Stud L (1999) 155, 1
300 Chapter 1 environment definition

Lugano Convention including cultural heritage in its environment definition is not yet in force. An EU directive defined environmental damage as damage to air, water and land with significant adverse effects on each resource or risks to human health.[301] Armed conflicts affect similarly the environment, impacting water systems, agriculture, mining and forests.[302] When processing conflict-related claims for environmental damage and natural resources depletion, the UNCC assessed damage to terrestrial environment, desert land and soil caused by oil contamination,[303] contamination in the areas of coastal oil deposit and mainland coastal oil trench, leading to disappearance of plant and animal life[304] and damage to terrestrial ecosystem from the disposal and destruction of ordnances.[305] A few treaties extend the obligation towards the environment to ecosystem.[306]

Civil liability regimes use notions of (i) pollution defined as detrimental alteration in the quantity or quality of international watercourses' waters[307] and (ii) adverse effects on biological diversity[308] or deleterious effects on air[309] or the marine environment.[310] Diverse approaches to pollution prevent using it "as a reasonably precise and generally accepted concept in international law."[311] The oil pollution liability regime that does not define environmental damage, referring to pollution as damage caused by oil contamination from a ship, has witnessed significant practice.

There is no agreed international threshold of damage required to entail liability under international law.[312] Jurisprudence mentioned "serious consequence" of polluting acts.[313] Treaties vary in their approach, with UNCLOS (article 194(2)) referring only to "damage" while no civil liability treaty requires a threshold of serious or significant damage.[314] The ILC settled on prevention of "significant" transboundary harm or at least minimizing its risk, which could be a high probability of causing significant transboundary harm or low probability of causing

301 Directive 2004/35/CE of 21 April 2004 on environmental liability with regard to the prevention and remedying of environmental damage art.2.1

302 UNEP, *Sierra Leone, Environment, Conflict and Peacebuilding Assessment* (February 2010)

303 UNCC, *Report and Recommendations Made by the Panel of Commissioners Concerning Part Two of the Fourth Installment of "F4" Claims, S/AC.26/2004/17* (2004) par.78–79

304 Ibid, *S/AC.26/2004/16* (2004) par.171

305 Ibid, *S/AC.26/2004/16 (2004)* par.227–228

306 Protocol on Environmental Protection to the Antartic Treaty, 1991 art.2; Watercourses Convention art.20

307 Watercourses Convention art.21.1

308 Nagoya – Kuala Lumpur Supplementary Protocol on Liability and Redress to the Cartagena Protocol on Biosafety, 15 October 2010 art.2.2(b)

309 Convention on Long-Range Transboundary Air Pollution, Geneva, 13 November 1979 art.1(a)

310 UNCLOS art.1(4)

311 Allen L. Springer, *The International Law of Pollution: Protecting the Global Environment in a World of Sovereign States* (Quorum Books 1983) Chap.3

312 Sands 743

313 *Trail Smelter*

314 Boyle and Redgwell 211 CRTD, art.1(10)(c)

disastrous transboundary harm.[315] The threshold of damage is not defined by regulatory standards in that case but is dependent on a variable, the probability of the event happening. The UNCC decided that the threshold of damage required for State responsibility for transboundary harm was not applicable to the claims it assessed to be compensable, as the UNSC did not impose such a threshold.[316] Most scholars, jurisprudence and State practice refer to "substantial" or "significant" damage.[317] The threshold should be assessed in each case. Since a single measure of environmental damage does not exist under IEL, one could look at the notion of environmental damage under a regime governing a particular resource. A scale of Environmental Impact Assessment could be developed in relation specifically to damage to the environment from armed conflict.

Environmental damage differs from compensable damage. Legal terms vary from environmental harm or impairment, to damage to natural resources or ecological damage; they have different meanings under European and US laws and differ from a scientific notion of damage.[318] The UNCC relied in its work on the only framework for natural resources damage assessment ("NDRA") existing in 1991 under the International Oil Pollution Compensation Funds ("IOPCF") and developing US practice, as what constituted compensable environmental damage was not clear.[319] According to the UNCC Governing Council, compensable damage included losses and expenses from abatement and prevention of environmental, damage, its monitoring and assessment, monitoring of public health to combat health risks from it, reasonable measures taken or to be taken to clean and restore the environment and depletion of or damage to natural resources.[320] A fundamental issue is whether compensation should include pure environmental damage[321] or there should be a connection to human beings in the sense that, if environmental pollution does not cause them harm, they should not be compensated for pollution.[322]

Regarding "natural resources that have no commercial value, i.e., resources that are not traded in the market," the UNCC agreed that there was "no justification for the contention that general international law precludes compensation for pure environmental damage."[323] The ICJ judged that "compensation is due for damage

315 ILC, *Articles on the Prevention of Transboundary Harm from Hazardous Activities* (2001) art.2, 3; ILC, ILC Allocation Principles Principle 2

316 Allen 156–157

317 Sands 743

318 Edward H.P. Brans, *Liability for Damage to Public Natural Resources: Standing, Damage and Damage Assessment* (Kluwer Law International 2001) 9

319 Hugienin and others 70

320 UNCC Governing Council decision 7 (S/AC.26/1991/7/Rev.1) par.35

321 Louise De la Fayette, 'The Concept of Environmental Damage in International Liability Regimes' in Michael Bowman and Alan Boyle (eds), *Environmental Damage in International and Comparative Law, Problems of Definition and Valuation* (OUP 2002) 150

322 Peter Cane, 'Are Environmental Harms Special?' 13 JEL 3 (2001) 3, 6

323 Reports and recommendations of the Governing Council, Fifth instalment of F4 claims, S/AC.26/2005/10, 30 June 2005, par.45–47

caused to the environment, in and of itself" and "damage to the environment, and the consequent impairment or loss of the ability of the environment to provide goods and services, is compensable under international law."[324]

V. Conclusion

State responsibility will be engaged by violation of its obligations under IEL and IWL treaties and under principles of permanent sovereignty over natural resources, prevention and obligations such as cooperation, negotiation and EIA that are customary international law applicable during armed conflicts. The precautionary principle does not share that status but could be used to interpret the LOAC obligation of precautions in attacks. Sustainability may inform the use of natural resources by an occupant, strengthening its obligation of reasonable exploitation. Objective responsibility based on due diligence standard of conduct seems the most appropriate responsibility basis. The applicability of IEL and IWL treaties in armed conflicts is established and they should be brought into interpretation of LOAC obligations by systemic interpretation. International jurisprudence and the UNCC have sufficiently developed and clarified obligations related to due diligence and notion of compensable environmental damage to allow future claims for armed conflict-related environmental damage to be brought on that basis. The case studies analyse whether IEL obligations are respected during armed conflict.

Bibliography

Treaties

Convention on Biological Diversity, Rio de Janeiro, 5 June 1992
Convention on Civil Liability for Damage resulting from Activities Dangerous to the Environment, Lugano, 21 June 1993
Convention on International Liability for Damage Caused by Space Objects, 29 March 1972 (in force 1 September 1972), 961 UNTS 187
Convention on Long-Range Transboundary Air Pollution, Geneva, 13 November 1979
Convention on the Law on Non-Navigational Uses of International Watercourses (1997)
ICCPR
ICESCR
Kuwait Regional Convention for Co-operation on the Protection of the Marine Environment from Pollution
Nagoya – Kuala Lumpur Supplementary Protocol on Liability and Redress to the Cartagena Protocol on Biosafety, 15 October 2010
Protocol on Environmental Protection to the Antarctic Treaty, 1991
UN Charter
UN Framework Convention on Climate Change, 1992
UNECE Convention on the Protection of Transboundary Watercourses and International Lakes, 1992
VCLT

324 *Certain Activities Carried Out by Nicaragua in the Border Area (Costa Rica v. Nicaragua), Compensation, Judgment* ICJ Reports 2018, p. 15, par.41, 42; *Armed Activities (2022)* par.348

International organizations documents

Council Decision (EU) 2022/333 of 25 February 2022 (Official Journal of the EU, L 54, vol 65)
Directive 2004/35/CE of 21 April 2004 on Environmental Liability with Regard to the Prevention and Remedying of Environmental Damage
IAEA, *The 1997 Vienna Convention on Civil Liability for Nuclear Damage and the 1997 Convention on Supplementary Compensation for Nuclear Damage, Explanatory Texts* (Int'l L Series No 3, 2007)
ICRC, *Customary International Humanitarian Law, Vol. I Rules* (Henckaerts J-M and Doswald-Beck L eds, 3rd edn, CUP 2009)
———, *Guidelines on the Protection of the Natural Environment in Armed Conflict* (2020)
IDI, *Effects of Armed Conflict on Treaties* (1985)
ILA, *Resolution on the Protection of Water Resources and Water Installations in Times of Armed Conflict, Madrid, 1976, Report of the Fifty-Seventh Conference* (1976)
ILA Study Group on Due Diligence in International Law, *Second Report* (July 2016)
ILA Water Resources Committee, *Helsinki Rules on the Uses of the Waters of International Rivers (1966), updated by Berlin Rules on Water Resources* (2004)
ILC, *Articles on Responsibility of States for Internationally Wrongful Acts, with Commentary, A/56/10* (ILC YB 2001, vol II (2))
———, *Articles on the Effects of Armed Conflicts on Treaties, with Commentaries, A/66/10* (2011)
———, *Articles on the Prevention of Transboundary Harm from Hazardous Activities* (2001)
———, *Conclusions of the Work of the Study Group on Fragmentation of International Law: Difficulties Arising from the Diversification and Expansion of International Law, A/61/10* (ILC YB, vol II (2), 2006)
———, *Draft Articles on Prevention of Transboundary Harm from Hazardous Activities, with Commentaries, A/56/10* (ILC YB 2001, vol II (2))
———, *Draft Articles on the Law of Transboundary Aquifers 2008, A/63/10* (2009)
———, *Draft Principles on Protection of the Environment in Relation to Armed Conflicts, with commentaries, A/77/10* (ILC YB 2022, vol II, (2), 2022)
———, *Fragmentation of International Law: Difficulties Arising from the Diversification and Expansion of International Law, Report of the Study Group of the ILC, (A/CN.4/L.682)* (2006)
———, *International Liability for Injurious Consequences Arising Out of Acts Not Prohibited by International Law, Special Rapporteur Julio Barboza Fourth Report, A/CN.4/423 and Corr.1 & 2* (ILC YB 1989, vol II (1))
———, *International Liability for Injurious Consequences Arising Out of Acts Not Prohibited by International Law, Report of the Working Group – A/CN.4/L.533 and Add.1* (ILC YB 1996, vol II (2), annex I)
———, *Principles on the Allocation of Loss in the Case of Transboundary Harm Arising Out of Hazardous Activities, A/61/10* (ILC YB 2006, vol II (2))
———, *Special Rapporteur Marie G. Jacobsson, Preliminary Report on the Protection of the Environment in Relation to Armed Conflicts, A/CN.4/674* (2014)
———, *Special Rapporteur Marja Lehto, First Report on Protection of the Environment in Relation to Armed Conflicts, A/CN.4/720* (2018)
———, *Special Rapporteur, Pemmaraju Sreenivasa Rao, International Liability for Injurious Consequences Arising Out of Acts Not Prohibited by International Law (prevention of transboundary damage from hazardous activities), Agenda Item 3, A/CN.4/487 and Add.1, First Report on Prevention of Transboundary Damage from Hazardous Activities* (1998)
———, *The Effect of Armed Conflict on Treaties: An Examination of Practice and Doctrine, Memorandum by the Secretariat (A/CN.4/550)* (2005)

UN Audiovisual Library of International Law, 'Permanent Sovereignty over Natural Resources General Assembly Resolution 1803 (XVII), New York, 14 December 1962, Procedural History'
UNCC, *Report and Recommendations Made by the Panel of Commissioners Concerning Part One of the Fourth Installment of "F4" Claims, S/AC.26/2004/16* (2004)
———, *Report and Recommendations Made by the Panel of Commissioners Concerning Part Two of the Fourth Installment of "F4" Claims, S/AC.26/2004/17* (2004)
UNCED, Rio de Janeiro, 3–14 June 1992, *Report, A/CONF.151/26/Rev.1 (Vol. I)*
UNCHE, Stockholm, 5–16 June 1972, *Report (A/CONF.48/14/Rev.1)*
UNCLOS, 10 December 1982
UNECE Model Provisions on Transboundary Groundwaters, (UN Doc ECE/MP.WAT/40), 2012
UNEP, *Draft Principles of Conduct in the Field of the Environment for the Guidance of States in the Conservation and Harmonious Utilization of Natural Resources Shared by Two or More States* (1978)
———, *Sierra Leone, Environment, Conflict and Peacebuilding Assessment* (February 2010)
UNESCO, World Commission on the Ethics of Scientific Knowledge and Technology (COMEST), *The Precautionary Principle* (UNESCO 2005)
UNGA, *Charter of Economic Rights and Duties of States, Res. 3281 (XXIX)* (1974)
———, *Co-operation between States in the Field of the Environment, Res. 2995 (XXVII)* (1972)
———, *Declaration on the Establishment of a New International Economic Order, A/RES/S-6/3201 (S.VI)* (1974)
———, *International Responsibility of States in Regard to the Environment, A/RES/2996* (1972)
———, *Permanent Sovereignty over Natural Resources, Res. 1803 (XVII)* (1962)
———, *Programme of Action on the Establishment of a New International Economic Order, A/RES/S-6/3202 (S.VI)* (1974)
———, *Resolution 66/225 on Permanent Sovereignty of the Palestinian people in the Occupied Palestinian Territory, including East Jerusalem, and of the Arab Population in the Occupied Syrian Golan over Their Natural Resources* (2011)
UNGA 2nd Committee, *Agriculture Development, Food Security and Nutrition (A/C.2/78/L.31)* (2023)
UNSC, *Resolution 540, 31 October 1983, S/Res. 540* (1983)

National legislation and documents

République Française, Assemblée Nationale, La Commission des Affaires Etrangères, *Rapport d'information, la géopolitique de l'eau* (2011)
Letter dated 5 May 1983 from the Permanent Representative of Iraq to the UN addressed to the Secretary-General (A/38/187-S/15752) (9 May 1983)
Letter dated 20 June 1995 from the Acting Legal Adviser to the Department of State, together with Written Statement of the Government of the United States of America
Note verbale dated 20 April 1983 from the Permanent Representative of the Islamic Republic of Iran to the UN addressed to the Secretary-General (A/38/163-S/15723) (22 April 1983)

International tribunals decisions and documents

Affaire du Lac Lanoux (Espagne, France), 16 November 1957 RIAA, vol XII, pp. 281–317
Armed Activities on the Territory of the Congo (DRC v. Uganda), Judgment ICJ Rep 2005, p. 168 (ICJ)

Armed Activities on the Territory of the Congo (DRC v. Uganda), Reparations, Judgement ICJ Rep 2022, p. 13
Case C-162/96, A. Racke GmbH & Co. v. Hauptzollamt Mainz, 1998 ECR I-3655, CJEU
Case Concerning Aerial Herbicide Spraying Ecuador v. Columbia, ICJ, Memorial of Ecuador, Volume I, 28 April 2009
Certain Activities Carried Out by Nicaragua in the Border Area (Costa Rica v. Nicaragua) and Construction of a Road in Costa Rica along the San Juan River (Nicaragua v. Costa Rica), Judgment ICJ Rep 2015, p. 665
Certain Activities Carried Out by Nicaragua in the Border Area (Costa Rica v. Nicaragua), Compensation, Judgment ICJ Rep 2018, p. 15
Corfu Channel case, Judgment of April 9th, 1949, ICJ. Rep.
EC Measure Concerning Meat and Meat Products (Hormones Case), Report of the Appellate Body (WTO)
European Communities – Measures Affecting the Approval and Marketing of Biotech Products – Reports of the Panel WT/DS291/R, WT/DS292/R, WT/DS293/R
Fisheries Jurisdiction (Federal Republic of Germany v. Iceland), Merits, Judgment ICJ Rep 1974, p. 175
Fisheries Jurisdiction (UK v. Iceland), Jurisdiction ICJ Rep 1973, p. 3
Fisheries Jurisdiction (UK v. Iceland), Merits, Judgment ICJ Rep 1974, p. 3
Gabčikovo-Nagymaros Project (Hungary/Slovakia), Judgment ICJ Rep 1997, p. 7
In the Arbitration Regarding the Iron Rhine ("Ijzeren Rijn") Railway between the Kingdom of Belgium and the Kingdom of Netherlands, Award of Arbitral Tribunal, The Hague, 24 May 2005 (PCA)
International Association of Machinists v. Organisation of Petroleum, US District Court for the Central District of California – 477 F Supp 553 (CD Cal 1979), 18 September 1979
ITLOS, Responsibilities and Obligations of States Sponsoring Persons and Entities with Respect to Activities in the Area, Advisory Opinion, 2011 ITLOS Reports 2011
Kasikili/Sedudu Island (Botswana/Namibia), Judgment of 13 December 1999 ICJ Rep 1999
Kuwait v. American Independent Oil Co., 21 ILM 976 (1982)
Legal Consequences for States of the Continued Presence of South Africa in Namibia notwithstanding Security Council Resolution 276 (1970), Advisory Opinion ICJ Rep 1971 p. 16
Legality of the Threat or Use of Nuclear Weapons, Advisory Opinion ICJ Rep 1996
Military and Paramilitary Activities in and against Nicaragua (Nicaragua v. United States of America). Merits, Judgment. ICJ Rep 1986, p. 14
Pulp Mills on the River Uruguay (Argentina v. Uruguay), Judgment, ICJ Rep 2010, p. 14
Pulp Mills on the River Uruguay (Argentina v. Uruguay), Provisional Measures, Order of 13 July 2006, ICJ Rep 2006, p. 133
Southern Bluefin Tuna Cases (Provisional Measures) ITLOS Reports 1999
Territorial Jurisdiction of the International Commission of the River Oder, Judgment No 16, 1929 PCIJ Series A, No 23, p. 27 (PCIJ)
Texaco Overseas Petroleum Co. and California Asiatic Oil Company v. the Government of the Libyan Arab Republic, 17 ILM 1 (1978)
The South China Sea Arbitration (The Republic of Philippines v. The People's Republic of China), Award of 12 July 2016 (PCA)
Trail Smelter Case (United States, Canada), 16 April 1938 and 11 March 1941, RIAA, vol III, 1905
WTO Appellate Body, EC Measures Concerning Meat and Meat Products (Hormones case), AB-1997–4, Report
——, *United States – Import Prohibition of Certain Shrimp and Shrimp Products* WT/DS58/AB/R, DSR 1998:VII

Journal articles

Benvenisti E, 'Water Conflicts during the Occupation of Iraq' 97 AJIL 4, October 2003 860

Bilder RB and others, 'Disentangling Treaty and Customary International Law' 81 ASIL Proceedings April 8–11 1987 157

Borgen JC, 'Resolving Treaty Conflicts' 37 Geo Wash Int'l L Rev 2005 573 573

Bourg D and Whiteside KH, 'France's Charter for the Environment: Of Presidents, Principles and Environmental Protection' 15 Mod Contemp Fr 2 2007 117

Boyle A, 'Globalising Environmental Liability: the Interplay of National and International Law' 17 JEL 1 2005 3 3

———, 'The Environmental Jurisprudence of the International Tribunal for the Law of the Sea' 22 Int'l J Mar Coast L 3 2007 369

Brunnée J, 'Sense and Sensibility: Reflections on International Liability Regimes as Tools for Environmental Protection' 53 ICLQ 2004 351

Bunker AL, 'Protection of the Environment during Armed Conflict: One Gulf, Two Wars' 13 RECIEL 2 2004 201

Cane P, 'Are Environmental Harms Special?' 13 JEL 3 2001 3

Daniel A, 'Civil Liability Regimes as a Complement to Multilateral Environmental Agreements: Sound International Policy or False Comfort?' 12 RECIEL 3 2003 225 225

Dupuy P-M, 'Reviewing the Difficulties of Codification: On Agos' Classification of Obligations of Means and Obligations of Result in Relation to State Responsibility' 10 EJIL 2 1999 371

Fitzmaurice M, 'Some Reflections on Legal and Philosophical Foundations of International Environmental Law' XXXII PYIL 2012 89

Gillespie A, 'The Precautionary Principle in the Twenty-First Century: A Case Study of Noise Pollution in the Ocean' 22 Int'l J Mar Coast L 1 2007 61 61

Joyner C and Kirhope J, 'The Persian Gulf War Oil Spill: Reassessing the Law of Environmental Protection and the Law of Armed Conflict' 24 Case W Res J Int'l L 1, Winter 1992 29

Kaplan LM, 'International Responsibility of an Occupying Power for Environmental Harm: The Case of Estonia' 12 Transnat L 1999 153 153

Kraska J, 'Sustainable Development Is Security: The Role of Transboundary River Agreement as Confidence Building Measure in South Asia' 28 Yale J Int'l L 2003 465

Kulz H, 'Further Water Disputes between India and Pakistan' 18 Int'l Comp L Q 1969 718

LaFranchi S, 'Surveying the Precautionary Principle's Ongoing Global Development: The Evolution of an Emergent Environmental Management Tool' 32 Boston Coll Environ Aff L Rev 3 2005 679

Larsson M-L, 'Legal Definitions of the Environment and of Environmental Damage' 38 Scand Stud L 1999 155 155

Lindroos A, 'Addressing Norm Conflicts in a Fragmented Legal System: The Doctrine of Lex Specialis' 74 Nordic J Int'l L 2005 27

Low L and Hodgkinson D, 'Compensation for Wartime Environmental Damage: Challenges to International Law after the Gulf War' 35 Va J Int'l L 1994–1995 405

MacChesney B, 'Lake Lanoux Case (France-Spain)' 53 AJIL 1, Jan. 1959 156

Milanovic M, 'Norm Conflict in International Law: Wither Human Rights?' 20 Duke J Int'l Comp L 2009 69

Okowa P, 'Sovereignty Contests and the Protection of Natural Resources in Conflict Zones' 66 Curr Leg Probl 2013 33

Plakokefalos I, 'Causation in the Law of State Responsibility and the Problem of Overdetermination: In Search of Clarity' 26 EJIL 2 2015

Schmitt M, 'Green War: An Assessment of the Environmental Law of International Armed Conflict' 22 Yale J Int'l L 1997 1

Scovazzi T, 'State Responsibility for Environmental Harm' 12 YB Int'l Env L 1 2001 43

Sourgens FG, 'The Precaution Presumption' 31 EJIL 4, November 2020 1277

Trapp KN and Robinson E, 'Extra-territorial "Fiducuary" Obligations and Ensuring Respect for International Humantarian Law' 63 McGill L J 3&4 2018 677
Trouwborst A, 'The Precautionary Principle in General International Law: Combating the Babylonian Confusion' 16 RECIEL 2, July 2007 185 185
van der Vyver JD, 'The Environment: State Sovereignty, Human Rights, and Armed Conflict' 23 Emory Int'l L Rev 1 2009 85
Verwey WD, 'Protection of the Environment in Times of Armed Conflict: in Search of a New Legal Perspective' 8 Leiden J Int'l L 1 1995 7
Weisburd AM, 'The International Court of Justice and the Concept of State Practice' 31 U Pa J Int'l L 2 2009 295
Weiss EB, 'Our Rights and Obligations to Future Generations for the Environment' 84 AJIL 1, January 1990 198

Electronic articles

Hofer A, *Russia's Unilateral Suspension of the 2013 Agreement on Nuclear Cooperation with the United States* (EJIL: Talk! 2016)
Treves T, 'Customary International Law' MPEPIL

Books and reports

Boisson de Chazournes L, *La Protection Internationale de l'Environnement* (Ed. Pedone 2005)
Boyle A and Redgwell C, *Birnie, Boyle and Redgwell's International Law and the Environment* (4th edn, OUP 2021)
Brans EHP, *Liability for Damage to Public Natural Resources: Standing, Damage and Damage Assessment* (Kluwer Law International 2001)
Combacau J and Sur S, *Droit International Public* (13th edn, LGDJ 2019)
Crawford J, *Brownlie's Principles of Public International Law* (9th edn, OUP 2019)
Creutz K, *State Responsibility in the International Legal Order, a Critical Appraisal* (CUP 2020)
Dam-de Jong DA, *International Law and Governance of Natural Resources in Conflict and Post-Conflict Situations, Doctoral Thesis* (Open Access edn, Leiden: Meijers 2013)
Das O, *Environmental Protection, Security and Armed Conflict, A Sustainable Development Perspective* (Edward Elgar 2013)
Klabbers J, *International Law* (3rd edn, CUP 2021)
Louka E, *International Environmental Law, Fairness, Effectiveness, and World Order* (CUP 2006)
Mollard-Bannelier K, *La Protection de l'Environnement en Temps de Conflit Armé* (Editions A. Pedone 2001)
Oppenheim L, *International Law, Vol. I Peace* (Lauterpacht H ed, 7th edn, 1948)
———, *Disputes, War and Neutrality*, vol II (Lauterpacht H ed, 7th edn, Longmans 1955)
Pauwelyn J, *Conflict of Norms in Public International Law, How WTO Law Relates to Other Rules of International Law* (CUP 2003)
Sands P and Peel J, Adriana Fabra, Ruth MacKenzie, *Principles of International Environmental Law* (4th edn, CUP 2018)
Sloan B, *Study of the Implications, under International Law, of the UN Resolutions on Permanent Sovereignty over Natural Resources, on the Occupied Palestinian and other Arab Territories and on the Obligations of Israel Concerning its Conduct in these Territories, Report of the Secretary-General, Annex, UNGA A/38/50/Rev.1* (1983)
Springer AL, *The International Law of Pollution: Protecting the Global Environment in a World of Sovereign States* (Quorum Books 1983)

Tignino M, *L'eau dans le Processus de Paix au Proche-Orient: Eléments d'un Régime Juridique* (Institut Universitaire de Hautes Etudes Internationales 2004)
———, *L'eau et la Guerre, Eléments pour un Regime Juridique* (Bruylant 2011)
———, *Water during and after Armed Conflicts: What Protection under International Law?* (Brill 2016)
Vöneky S, *Armed Conflict, Effect on Treaties* in *MPEPIL* (OUP 2011)

Book chapters

Allen JR, 'Chapter 6, Points of Law' in Payne CR and Sand PH (eds), *Gulf War Reparations and the UN Compensation Commission* (OUP 2011)
Aust A, 'Vienna Convention on the Law of Treaties (1969)' in *MPEPIL* (OUP 2006)
Bothe M, 'Protection of the Environment in Relation to Armed Conflicts' in Fleck D (ed), *The Handbook of International Humanitarian Law* (4th edn, OUP 2021)
Cassese A, 'Powers and Duties of an Occupant in Relation to Land and Natural Resources' in Playfair E (ed), *International Law and the Administration of Occupied Territories, Two Decades of Israeli Occupation of the West Bank and Gaza Strip* (OUP 1992)
De la Fayette L, 'The Concept of Environmental Damage in International Liability Regimes' in Bowman M and Boyle A (eds), *Environmental Damage in International and Comparative Law, Problems of Definition and Valuation* (OUP 2002)
Fitzmaurice M, 'Precautionary Principle' in *Contemporary Issues in International Environmental Law* (Edward Elgar 2009)
Hugienin MT and others, 'Chapter 3, Assessment and Valuation of Damage to the Environment' in Payne CR and Sand PH (eds), *Gulf War Reparations and the UN Compensation Commission* (OUP 2011)
Martuzzi M and Tickner JA, 'Introduction – the Precautionary Principle: Protecting Public Health, the Environment and the Future of Our Children' in *The Precautionary Principle: Protecting Public Health, the Environment and the Future of Our Children* (WHO Regional Office for Europe 2004)
Mbengue MM and Brian McGarry, 'Chapter 23: General Principles of International Environmental Law in the Case Law of International Courts and Tribunals' in Andenas M and others (eds), *General Principles and the Coherence of International Law*, vol 37 (Brill | Nijhoff 2019)
McIntyre O, 'Chapter 15: Water' in Morgera E and Kulovesi K (eds), *Research Handbook on International Law and Natural Resources* (Edward Elgar 2016)
McIntyre O, 'Chapter 20: The Making of International Natural Resources Law' in Catherine Brölmann and Radi Y (eds), *Research Handbook on the Theory and Practice of International Lawmaking* (Edward Elgar 2016)
Okowa P, 'Chapter 15: Responsibility for Environmental Damage' in Fitzmaurice M and others (eds), *Research Handbook on International Environmental Law* (Edward Elgar 2010)
Pyhälä M and others, 'Chapter 10: The Precautionary Principle' in Fitzmaurice M and others (eds), *Research Handbook on International Environmental Law* (Edward Elgar 2010)
Sadeleer Nd, 'Chapter 9: The Principles of Prevention and Precaution in International Law: Two Heads of the Same Coin?' in Fitzmaurice M and others (eds), *Research Handbook on International Environmental Law* (Edward Elgar 2010)
Scobbie I, 'Natural Resources and Belligerent Occupation: Mutation through Permanent Sovereignty' in Bowen S (ed), *Human Rights, Self-Determination and Political Change in the Occupied Palestinian Territories* (Martinus Nijhoff 1997)
Stefanik K, 'The Environment and Armed Conflict, Employing General Principles to Protect the Environment' in Stahn C and others (eds), *Environmental Protection and Transitions from Conflict to Peace* (OUP 2017)

Talus K, 'Chapter 12: Oil and Gas: International Petroleum Regulation' in Morgera E and Kulovesi K (eds), *Research Handbook on International Law and Natural Resources* (2016)

Zemanek K, 'Chapter 7: State Responsibility and Liability ' in Winfried L and others (eds), *Environmental Protection and International Law* (1st edn, Graham & Trotman/Martinus Nijhoff 1991)

5 Environment under war

Israel and Hezbollah, Lebanon, 2006

The chapter addresses the case of environmental damage arising out of the armed conflict fought between Israel and Hezbollah in Lebanon in 2006. The context of the conflict sets broadly the historical background of relations between Israel and Lebanon, including Hezbollah's role, and presents the legal framework, after determining the qualification of the conflict that affects the applicable laws. The chapter then analyses the environmental legacy of the conflict under the LOAC and IEL rules, focusing on damage to land, Mediterranean Sea and natural resources from the use of cluster munitions in the South and from an oil spill following an attack on a power plant. The main legal rules are discussed herein; reference should be made to Chapters 2 and 4 for detailed analysis. The chapter does not address the 2023–2024 war between Israel and Hezbollah.

I. Context of the armed conflict

1. Historical background

Explanations as to the chain of events differ. The conflict is generally assumed to have started when Israel crossed into Lebanon in pursuit of Hezbollah who had abducted two soldiers in a cross-border raid.[1] Others consider the kidnapping as a pretext for a conflict in the planning.[2] According to Hersh, the attack by Israel was planned well in advance of the kidnapping and shared with the US, in a prelude to a major attack on Iran by the US.[3] The only certainty is that the war was the result of a state of enmity between Israel and Lebanon since the Arab-Israeli war in 1948 to which Lebanon participated. A 1949 Armistice Agreement was never implemented.[4]

1 A. Harel, 'Hezbollah Kills 8 Soldiers, Kidnaps 2 in Offensive on Northern Border' Haaretz (2006)
2 Jurgen Cain Külbel, 'La longue route d'Israel vers la guerre de juillet 2006' Voltaire Édition Internationale
3 Seymour M. Hersh, 'Watching Lebanon, Wahington's Interests in Israel's War' The New Yorker (21 August 2006)
4 The Lebanese-Israeli General Armistice Agreement, March 23, 1949. The Taif Agreement, signed by Lebanese factions gathered in Saudi Arabia in 1989 after a war against Syria by Lebanese Army

DOI: 10.4324/9780367823283-5

In 1969, the secret Cairo Agreement between Lebanon and the Palestinian Liberation Organisation ("PLO") gave PLO fighters in the camps of Palestinian refugees who came to Lebanon after the 1948 war the right to arm themselves, which they used for their armed struggle against Israel from Lebanon's territory.[5] In retaliation for attacks on its territory, Israel breached Lebanon's territorial sovereignty with frequent aerial raids and repeated attacks on the country.[6] It invaded and occupied Southern Lebanon in 1978. The UNSC adopted Resolution 425 calling on Israel to cease its military actions and withdraw its forces from Lebanese territory[7] and Resolution 426 establishing the UN Interim Force in Lebanon ("UNIFIL") to confirm the withdrawal of Israeli forces, restore international peace and security and assist the government in ensuring the return of its effective authority in Southern Lebanon.[8] The UNSC Member States voted 12–0, with 2 abstentions; China did not participate in the vote. The mandate of UNIFIL has been regularly renewed thereafter.

Syrian forces had entered into Lebanon in 1976 as part of an Arab peacekeeping force and were later to become an occupation force until April 2005.[9] Syria established "rules" governing the relations between the government of Lebanon and Hezbollah and the role of the latter in the South. As such, the government did not send its army to the South.[10] In 1982, Israel launched a full-scale invasion that reached Beirut, during a three-month war. The PLO relocated to Tunis. Backed by Iran and Syria, Hezbollah started its armed resistance to the Israeli occupation of Southern Lebanon, around that time.[11] A US brokered peace agreement signed on 17 May 1983 was abrogated by President Gemayel in 1984, under pressure from Syria and its local allies, following the withdrawal from Lebanon of American forces participating in a multinational peacekeeping force, after an attack revendicated by Islamic Jihad, blamed later on Hezbollah, killed 241 US marines in Beirut.[12] Israeli operations continued unabated in the South, notably two military campaigns in 1993 and 1996, reinforcing local support for Hezbollah.[13] In 2000, Israel withdrew from South Lebanon, except from Shebaa Farms and the village of Ghajar. UNSC Resolution 1559 (2004) called for "disbanding and

General Aoun, mentioned the need to revive the 1949 Armistice Agreement with Israel, The Taif Agreement, September 1989 Third, B

5 Cairo Agreement between the Lebanese Authorities and the Palestinian Commando Organizations, November 3, 1969, repudiated by Parliament in 1987.

6 David Hirst, 'Beware of Small States: Lebanon, Battleground of the Middle East'(2008)

7 UNSC, *Resolution 425, Israel-Lebanon, 19 March 1978* (1978)

8 Ibid

9 Are Knudsen, *Precarious Peacebuilding: Post-war Lebanon, 1990–2005, CMI Working Paper 2005:12* (2005) 2

10 Judith Palmer Harik, *Hezbollah: The Changing Face of Terrorism* (I.B. Tauris 2005) 116, 190; Knudsen

11 Harik 27, 38–41, 172.

12 Harik 36; The Editors of Encyclopaedia Britannica, online ed., '1983 Beirut Barracks Bombings'; Bassel Salloukh, 'Syria and Lebanon: A Brotherhood Transformed' 236 Middle East Report Fall (2005), 14, 16

13 Harik 112

disarmament of all Lebanese and non-Lebanese militias," which presence prevented the government from exercising its sovereignty over all Lebanese territory, though the government objected to the term "militia" referring to Hezbollah as "national resistance group."[14] However, Hezbollah kept its arsenal.

By 2006 when the war erupted, Lebanon was amid political chaos. Under Syrian "suzerainty" of "unprecedented levels" in post-war Lebanon, the "Syrian intelligence grew to become a dominant force in Lebanon with power to veto all important political decisions."[15] The controversial extension of the term of President Lahoud in October 2004, under "pressures and threats from the Syrian and Lebanese security services,"[16] was followed by a two-year period of instability and a wave of politically motivated murders of politicians, intellectuals and journalists campaigning against Syria's role in Lebanon.[17] The assassination in February 2005 of Prime Minister Hariri in a car explosion in Beirut prompted huge demonstrations and precipitated the withdrawal of Syrian troops from Lebanon in April.[18] That did not put an end to Syria and Iran's support to Hezbollah,[19] Syrian security services' influence and the flow of arms through the Syrian-Lebanese border to different groups, including Hezbollah, continued.[20] Political institutions and processes proved inefficient in the face of strong internal divisions. Despite many rounds of negotiations among Lebanese politicians between March and June 2006, there was no agreement over Lebanon's defence strategy and especially the issue of Hezbollah's arms.[21] The National Dialogue was suspended at the end of 2006 over disagreements on that question, reinstated by President Michel Suleiman in 2008 and put on hold again in 2010.[22]

On July 12, 2006 Hezbollah attacked an Israel Defence Forces ("IDF") patrol in a cross-border raid, killing three soldiers and taking two hostages. The Hezbollah leader called for an exchange of prisoners through indirect negotiations. Later that day, four Israeli soldiers sent on a rescue mission, were killed inside Lebanon

14 *Report of the Secretary-General pursuant to Security Council resolution 1559 (2004), S/2004/777* (1 October 2004) par.19

15 Knudsen 11

16 *Third semi-annual report of the Secretary-General to the Security Council on the implementation of Security Council resolution 1559 (2004), S/2006/248* (Sec. Gen. Report S/2006/248) Letter from current and former members of Parliament to Speaker Berri (20 February 2006)

17 *UN Common Country Assessment Lebanon* (2007) 9; Detlev Mehlis, 'Chronology of Events Mid 2004- September 2005'; Robert Fisk, 'Despite Floods of Soldiers, Assassinations Still Continue. No One Is Safe in Lebanon' *The Independent* (13 December 2005); International Crisis Group, *Lebanon: Managing the Gathering Storm* (5 December 2005) 10, 11, 16; Robert Fisk, 'The Arab Awakening Began Not in Tunisia This Year, but in Lebanon in 2005' The Independent (Friday 15 April 2011), UN CCA Lebanon 9

18 Marwan George Rowayheb, 'Political Change and the Outbreak of Civil War: The Case of Lebanon' 13 Civil Wars 4 (2011) 414 419, 420

19 Rowayheb 419, 423

20 Sec. Gen. Report S/2006/248 par.64

21 UN CCA Lebanon 10–11; Rowayheb 419.

22 Rowayheb 419

when their tank hit a mine. In response, Israel launched its military operations.[23] The IDF entered into action and began heavy artillery, tank fire and air raids. Hezbollah responded by firing rockets into Northern Israel. On 13 July, Israel imposed a sea and air blockade on Lebanon and bombarded Beirut's international airport.[24] The conflict raged mainly in the South of Lebanon, in a neighbourhood in southern Beirut (Dahiye) and the Bekaa, although all the territory of the country came under attack. The war lasted 34 days and was officially terminated by UNSC Resolution 1701 adopted on 11 August 2006 calling for a full cessation of hostilities on 14 August.[25] It authorized an increase in UNIFIL troops, prorogated its mandate and determined its duties additional to its original 1978 mandate. There has been no peace agreement since then between Israel and Lebanon. Hezbollah opened a military support front for Hamas in its war against Israel since October 2023, imposing its move on Lebanon. The caretaker Lebanese government, running without a president of Lebanon, was shining by its absence in such a momentous decision engaging the fate of the country and its people in another war.

During the 2006 war, 153 Israelis were killed, of which 119 soldiers,[26] and about 2,000 people injured.[27] In Lebanon, 1191 Lebanese citizens were killed, 4,409 injured and 900,000 people displaced.[28] The number of Hezbollah fighters killed is contested (Israel claiming 600, Hezbollah 250, UN estimates 500).[29] Lebanon withstood tremendous casualties.[30] Its environment, economy, agriculture and social and physical infrastructure were damaged. Direct expenditures for early recovery and reconstruction were estimated to be US$2.8 billion, of which the government of Lebanon was to cover US$1.75 billion. The indirect costs of the conflict were approximately US$2.2 billion, and private sector losses – mainly in agriculture and tourism – were to be alleviated by up to US$950 million in government financial assistance.[31]

2. *Legal framework*

2.1 Qualification of the conflict

Applicability of the LOAC rules depends on the classification of the armed conflict as international or non-international, though it may seem a redundant question

23 Victor Kattan, 'The Use and Abuse of Self-Defence in International Law: The Israel-Hezbollah Conflict as a Case Study' 12 YIMEL (2005–2006) 36

24 Raphael Cohen-Almagor and Sharon Haleva-Amir, 'The Israel-Hezbollah War And The Winograd Committee' JPPL 2 (2008) 27–44, 27

25 UNSC, *Resolution 1701, 11 August 2006, S/RES/1701,* (2006)

26 Israel Ministry of Foreign Affairs, 'Israel-Hizbullah Conflict: Victims of Rocket Attacks and IDF Casualties' accessed 16 October 2014

27 Cohen-Almagor and Haleva-Amir 28

28 UN Commission of Inquiry, *Report on Lebanon pursuant to Human Rights Council Resolution S-2/1, A/HRC/3/2* (2006) (UN Inquiry Commission Report), par.11

29 Cohen-Almagor and Haleva-Amir 28

30 UN Commission of Inquiry par.11

31 Lebanese Republic, 'Recovery, Reconstruction and Reform, International Conference for Support to Lebanon, 2007'

following the Tadic jurisprudence and convergence of customary rules in international and non-international armed conflicts.[32] The 2006 conflict does not qualify as a NIAC that requires the use of regular military forces by the legal government against insurgents recognized as belligerents under GC common article 3[33] or as one taking place between the government's armed forces and "dissident armed forces or other organized armed groups," under Additional Protocol II (AP/II) article 1.1,[34] as it did not involve the armed forces of Lebanon fighting against Hezbollah or insurgents on Lebanon's territory.

The fighting occurred between the IDF and Hezbollah, while the Lebanese Armed Forces ("LAF") were not involved. As an international armed conflict is defined as an inter-State conflict under GC common article 2, the conflict does not seem to fit prima facie in that category either. Scholarly opinions, struggling in "the fog of uncertainty" to characterize the conflict,[35] varied between a minority opinion asserting the existence of a "transnational" hybrid conflict falling into a regulatory gap,[36] to "an international armed conflict between Israel and Lebanon and a parallel extraterritorial non-international armed conflict between Israel and Hezbollah."[37] The issues are whether Hezbollah's conduct may be attributed to the State of Lebanon under the ILC State Responsibility Articles, as an organ of the State, an entity exercising governmental authority or an entity whose conduct is directed or controlled by the State[38] or whether there are other elements to be accounted for in order to conclude that the conflict was international.

Hezbollah is a military organization that transformed itself into a political party in the wake of the 1992 elections, retaining its military branch.[39] The latter is not part of the LAF, does not answer to its chain of command, is not subject to executive control and operates outside the legality of the State's institutions. Having no status of State organ under Lebanese law as required for the ILC State Responsibility Articles, article 4, which is customary law,[40] it is not de jure an organ of the State. The fact that Hezbollah had two ministers in the government in 2006 is not enough to attribute responsibility of its actions to the government as a whole "in the

32 See chapter 1 on classification of conflict

33 *Commentary on Convention (III) relative to the Treatment of Prisoners of War, Geneva, 12 August 1949* (ICRC 1960) commentary on article 3

34 Protocol Additional to the Geneva Conventions of 12 August 1949, and relating to the Protection of Victims of Non-International Armed Conflicts (Protocol II) art.1.1

35 Andrew Yuile, 'At the Fault-Lines of Armed Conflict: The 2006 Israel-Hezbollah Conflict and the Framework of International Humanitarian Law' 16 Austl Int'l L J (2009) 112

36 Geoffrey S. Corn, 'Hamdan, Lebanon, and the Regulation of Hostilities: The Need to Recognize a Hybrid Category of Armed Conflict' 40 Vand J Transnat L (2007) 305, 331

37 Iain Scobbie, 'Lebanon 2006' in Elizabeth Wilmhurst (ed), *International Law and the Classification of Conflicts* (OUP 2012) 417

38 ILC, *Responsibility of States for Internationally Wrongful Acts* (ILC YB 2001, vol II (Part Two)) art.4, 5 and 8 respectively. See chapter 1

39 Harik 52, generally 43–52

40 *Application of the Convention on the Prevention and Punishment of the Crime of Genocide (Bosnia and Herzegovina v. Serbia and Montenegro), Judgment* ICJ Rep 2007, 43 p. 43, par.386

absence of collusion, authorization or ratification of that act by the government."[41] This double role of Hezbollah inside and outside the government has been recognized by the Israeli Supreme Court.[42] Furthermore, at the beginning of the conflict, in a public address and letters addressed to the UN Secretary-General and the president of the UNSC, Lebanese Prime Minister Siniora stated that the government had no prior knowledge of the operation carried out by Hezbollah, which led to the abduction of the Israeli soldiers, was not responsible for these events and did not endorse them.[43] Hezbollah cannot then be considered to have exercised governmental authority either de jure under article 5 of the ILC State Responsibility Articles, as that would require a domestic law[44] – which was not the case – or de facto under article 9 of the ILC State Responsibility Articles requiring necessity to act in the absence of governmental authority.[45]

Finally, given the strength of Syrian interference in the Lebanese political process and continuing Iranian and Syrian support for Hezbollah, the government of Lebanon was neither in a position to control Hezbollah nor direct it. Hezbollah was viewed as effectively controlling the Lebanese State since 2005, following the withdrawal of Syrian troops.[46] The government did not exercise fully its sovereignty over all Lebanese territory and had limited control in the South.[47] It could not disarm Hezbollah through a militarily confrontation; neither could it succeed in that task by political means.[48] The National Dialogue had broken up on that issue. Though the Lebanese wanted to see Hezbollah transformed into a regular political party, they "prefer this to be a political and negotiated process – not a confrontation. No one in Lebanon wants another civil war."[49] Hezbollah cannot be deemed to be de facto organ of the State or an entity under the control of the State, under the ILC State Responsibility Articles article 8, as such control was manifestly lacking,[50] as demonstrated. Therefore the conduct of Hezbollah cannot

41 Scobbie 403

42 Ibid, 403, n.87

43 *PM Address to the Lebanese People, 15 July 2006* A/60/938-S/2006/518, Identical letters dated 13 July 2006 from the Chargé d'affaires a.i. of the Permanent Mission of Lebanon to the United Nations addressed to the Secretary-General and the President of the Security Council, 13 July 2006.

44 ILC, *Articles on Responsibility of States for Internationally Wrongful Acts, with Commentary, A/56/10* (ILC YB 2001, vol II (2)) Commentary on art.5 par.(5)

45 Scobbie 406–407

46 MENA Research Centre, 'Les Politiques du Hezbollah au Liban: Des Crimes qui Dépassent l'Assassinat, November 26, 2021'

47 *First semi-annual report of the Secretary-General to the Security Council on the implementation of resolution 1559 (2004), S/2005/272, 26 April 2005*

48 Casey L. Addis, 'Analyst in Middle Eastern Affairs and Christopher M.Blanchard, Analyst in Middle Eastern Affairs' in *Hezbollah: Background and Issues for Congress* (CRS Report for Congress Prepared for Members and Committees of Congress, 8 October 2010) 1.

49 Address of Prime Minister Siniora to the US Congress, 'Lebanon Today Is Taking the First Steps in a New Phase of Its Modern History' The Daily Star (1 August 2005)

50 Scobbie 405. For a contrary opinion based on erroneous assumptions on the role and status of Hezbollah and its relations with the government of Lebanon, see Catherine Bloom, 'The Classification of Hezbollah in Both International and Non-International Armed Conflicts' 14 Ann Surv Int'l Comp L (2008) 80

be attributed to the government and the responsibility of the State of Lebanon be engaged for Hezbollah's military actions in 2006, under the ILC Articles on State responsibility. The conflict is not deemed international on that basis.

However, considering that:

- The State of Lebanon was party to the conflict, as a victim; the conflict was between two States. This was the official view of the government,[51]
- All its territory was subjected to attacks on its population and infrastructure and temporary occupation.[52] Territory and population being essential attributes of the State, the use of force against the territory of a foreign State in a conflict involving an armed group without the consent of the territorial State is an international conflict, which will trigger the application of the GC and at a minimum AP/I,[53]
- Israel imposed a maritime and aerial blockade on Lebanon from 13–14 July 2006, a belligerent act traditionally related to an IAC under the LOAC,[54]
- Israel targeted the Lebanese Armed Forces[55] and government and public facilities; The 2006 conflict was an international armed conflict.[56]

2.2 Applicable law

2.2.1 LAW OF ARMED CONFLICT

Both Lebanon and Israel are parties to the four 1949 GC since 1951. Lebanon has signed the two 1977 Additional Protocols, while Israel has not.[57] Therefore, only the provisions of AP/I that have attained customary status are applicable to the conflict.[58] Neither Lebanon nor Israel has signed the ENMOD Convention.[59] It is not relevant to the present case. Israel has signed the 1980 Convention on Conventional Weapons ("CCW") and its Protocols I, II and IV. However, Lebanon had not joined the 1980 CCW or any Protocol in 2006. Therefore, the CCW and its

51 UN Commission of Inquiry par.59

52 Ibid, par.58

53 See chapter 1

54 UN Commission of Inquiry on Lebanon, *Report of the UN Commission of Inquiry on Lebanon pursuant to Human Rights Council Resolution S-2/1* (2006) par.58 Scobbie 407

55 Scobbie 408

56 Andreas Paulus and Mindia Vashakmadze, 'Asymmetrical War and the Notion of Armed Conflict – a Tentative Conceptualization' 91 IRRC 873 (2009) 95, 123–124

57 ICRC, 'States Party to the Following International Humanitarian Law and Other Related Treaties, as of 3rd September 2024'

58 Jean-Marie Henckaerts and Louise Doswald-Beck, *Customary International Humanitarian Law, Vol. I Rules* (3rd edn, ICRC and CUP 2009); ICRC, 'States Party to the Following International Humanitarian Law and Other Related Treaties, as of 3rd September 2024'

59 See Chapter 1 on ENMOD

Protocols were not applicable during the 2006 conflict, by application of the CCW art. 7.2 requiring reciprocity of obligations thereunder.

The question raised by doctrine as to whether Israel's actions may qualify as self-defence and proportionality should be judged in that perspective, or as an act of aggression, are not delved upon as it relates to *jus ad bellum* rules and not to rules applicable to the conduct of hostilities.[60] Scholars considered that as the conflict reached a large-scale war, LOAC rules, such as proportionality, must be assessed by reference to *jus in bello*,[61] which is our main concern.

2.2.2 INTERNATIONAL ENVIRONMENTAL LAW

IEL treaties are not suspended during armed conflict. The following are relevant. UNCLOS is ratified by 168 parties. Lebanon signed it on 7 December 1984 and ratified it on 5 January 1995.[62] UNCLOS is not applicable between Lebanon and Israel or opposable to Israel, as it did not sign it, except for its provisions that have attained customary international law status. UNCLOS Part XII on protection and preservation of the marine environment constitutes customary international law, as evidenced widely by State practice in accordance with national and international treaties' rules.[63] These clauses are then opposable to Israel.

Both Lebanon and Israel are parties to the 1976 Barcelona Convention for the Protection of the Mediterranean Sea against Pollution, a framework convention with seven protocols, modified in 1995 and renamed the Barcelona Convention for Protection of the Marine Environment and Coastal Region of the Mediterranean (Barcelona Convention). The amendments to the Barcelona Convention were not in force between the two countries in July 2006, as Lebanon accepted them on

60 Kattan; David Kretzmer, 'The Inherent Right to Self-Defence and Proportionality in *Jus ad Bellum*' 24 EJIL 1 (2013) 281; Enzo Cannizzaro, 'Contextualizing Proportionality: *Jus ad Bellum* and *Jus in Bello* in the Lebanese War' 88 IRRC 864

61 Kretzmer 278, n.208; Andreas Zimmermann, 'The Second Lebanon War: Jus ad bellum, jus in bello and the Issue of Proportionality' UNYB (2007) 99; Yaël Ronen, 'Israel Hezbollah and the 2nd Lebanon War' 9 YB Int'l Humanit L (2006)

62 UN Division of Ocean Affairs and the Law of the Sea, *UNCLOS, Consolidated table of ratifications/ accessions* A list established by the Ministry of Environment, Lebanon, states that Lebanon ratified UNCLOS on 22 February 1994 by Law N. 295 in Lebanese Republic Ministry of Environment, *International Environmental Agreements, Treaties and Protocols signed or ratified by the Government of Lebanon* (list in Arabic obtained by the author from the Ministry of Environment).

63 Philippe Sands, Jacqueline Peel, Adriana Fabra, Ruth MacKenzie, *Principles of International Environmental Law* (4th edn, CUP 2018) 462; UNCED, Rio 3–4 June 1992, *Agenda 21, the UN Programme of Action from Rio* par.17.1, 17.22

22 April 2009 while Israel accepted them on 29 September 2005.[64] The following protocols are relevant to the present case:

- The Emergency Protocol of 16 February 1976 and ratified on 8 November 1977 and 3 March 1978 respectively. Israel only signed the New Emergency Protocol on 22 January 2003 but has not ratified it,[65]
- The Specially Protected Areas (SPA) Protocol (1982) to which Lebanon acceded on 27 December 1994 and signed by Israel on 3 April 1982 and ratified on 28 October 1987. The 1995 amended SPA and Biodiversity Protocol was not in force for, or applicable between, the two countries in 2006, as Israel only had signed it on 10 June 1995, without ratifying it.[66]

Other relevant conventions include the 1971 Ramsar Convention on Wetlands[67] that entered into force for Lebanon on 16 August 1999 and for Israel on 12 March 1997. Only Israel accepted the 1987 amendments that entered into force in 1994. The 1972 World Heritage Convention[68] was ratified by Lebanon on 3 February 1983 and Israel acceded to it on 6 October 1999. The Hague Convention for the Protection of Cultural Property in the Event of Armed Conflict, 14 May 1954 and its 1954 Protocol have been ratified by Lebanon on 1 June 1960 and Israel on 3 October 1957 and 1 April 1958 respectively. None of them ratified the second Protocol to the Hague Convention of 26 March 1999.

II. Use of cluster bombs and damage to land, forests and agriculture

Israel launched four million cluster bombs over Southern Lebanon, 90 percent of them in the last 72 hours of the conflict, after the UNSC had voted on Resolution 1701 calling for a cease-fire.[69] Latest estimates have reassessed the number

64 UNEP, 'Mediterranean Action Plan, Status of Signatures and Ratifications of the Barcelona Convention and its Protocols' 1976 Barcelona Convention: Lebanon accession 8.11.1977, Israel signing 16.02.1976, ratification 3.03.1978

65 The Protocol Concerning Co-operation in Combating Pollution of the Mediterranean Sea by Oil and other Harmful Substances in Case of Emergency, (the Emergency Protocol), 16 February 1976, Barcelona; to be replaced between parties to both instruments by the Protocol concerning Co-operation in Preventing Pollution from Ships and, in cases of Emergency Combating Pollution of the Mediterranean Sea (the Prevention and Emergency Protocol), 25 January 2002, Malta

66 The Protocol Concerning Mediterranean Specially Protected Areas, 3 April 1982, Geneva, (the SPA Protocol), to be replaced between parties to both instruments by the Protocol concerning Specially Protected Areas and Biodiversity in the Mediterranean, (the SPA and Biodiversity Protocol), 10 June 1995, Barcelona

67 The Convention on Wetlands of International Importance especially as Waterfowl Habitat, Ramsar, 2.2.1971 as amended by the Protocol of 3.12.1982 and the Amendments of 28.5.1987

68 UNESCO Convention for the Protection of the World Cultural and Natural Heritage, 23 November 1972

69 Landmine Action, *Foreseeable Harm, the Use and Impact of Cluster Munitions in Lebanon: 2006* (2006) 5 HRW, *Flooding South Lebanon: Israel's Use of Cluster Munitions in Lebanon in July and August 2006* (2008) 439

of unexploded sub-munitions at 40 percent, i.e., 1,600,000,[70] up from 1 million previously. The land in Southern Lebanon bore the brunt of the 2006 conflict. It is essentially a rural agricultural area constituted of small villages and towns, among the poorest regions in Lebanon.[71] Agriculture is the main economic activity; it is the only source of income for half of the working population and provides approximately 70 percent of total household incomes in the region.[72] Agricultural practice encompasses apiculture, pine nut collection, wood collection and charcoal production, cultivation of olives, citrus, fruit orchards and medicinal and aromatic plants. Olive groves account for approximately 39 percent of Lebanon's olive groves.[73] Olive, citrus and tobacco crops are important sources of livelihood.[74]

Clearance of unexploded cluster remnants was projected to end in 2007,[75] then in 2012.[76] Operations were delayed, due to financing difficulties, reassessments of previous estimates of unexploded sub-munitions that were too low and Israel's refusal to hand over the technical strike data and related maps of the cluster munitions used, until 14 May 2009.[77] Lebanon has committed to an obligation to clear cluster munitions remnants within ten years of joining the 2008 Convention on Cluster Munitions ("CCM")[78] as a State party, under its article 4. It has requested an extension of the deadline for its obligations, to 1 May 2026, though an additional year may be needed for financial reasons.[79]

1. General presentation of cluster munitions

Under the CCM, cluster munition "means a conventional munition that is designed to disperse or release explosive sub-munitions each weighing less than 20 kilograms, and includes those explosive sub-munitions."[80] As the CCM was non-existent in 2006, there was no commonly accepted definition of cluster munitions but a general understanding that they are weapons containing sub-munitions

70 MAG (Mines Advisory Group) website, 'Lebanon, Why We Work in Lebanon'

71 FAO, *Lebanon: Damage and Early Recovery Needs: Assessment of Agriculture, Fisheries and Forestry* (2006) 7; Consultation and Research Institute, *The Post-Conflict Social and Livelihoods Assessment in Lebanon* (2007) (CRI) 10, prepared for the Ministry of Social Affairs with World Bank funding

72 FAO 7 HRW 78

73 Association for Forests Development and Conservation, *War impact on forest resources and olive groves in South Lebanon* (2007) 34

74 HRW 78

75 UNDP, *Lebanon Rapid Environmental Assessment for Greening Recovery, Reconstruction and Reform (prepared by ELARD)* (2007) xvi; UNDP, *CBU Contamination by Land Use* (2006)

76 UNDP, *Support to the National Demining Office* (2008)

77 Landmine monitor, *Landmine monitor report* (2009) 992

78 Convention on Cluster Munitions (CCM), Dublin, 30 may 2008, Oslo 3–4 December 2008, entry into force 1 August 2010.

79 Mine Action Review, *Lebanon, Clearing Cluster Munitions Remnants 2020* 1; Landmine and Cluster Munitions Monitor, 'Lebanon, Impact, 15 September 2023'

80 Convention on Cluster Munitions (CCM), Dublin, 30 may 2008, Oslo 3–4 December 2008, entry into force 1 August 2010 art.2.2

with explosives.[81] Once fired, cluster munitions open in the air and release the sub-munitions (or "bomblets") over a wide area. These are small fragmentation bombs, consisting of a casing, an explosive fill and a fuse (arming and safety mechanism); the casing is built to break up, upon impact, into numerous pieces of shrapnel flying at high velocities to kill or injure troops (anti-personnel effect) or to penetrate armour (anti-armour effect).[82] The sub-munitions have a known failure (or dud) rate, which is the percentage that does not explode on impact, usually between 5 and 20 percent when tested by manufacturers, but it has proven to be higher when cluster munitions are used in armed conflicts.[83] Cluster sub-munitions can blow up any time after their landing upon pressure of someone stepping on them; they are frequently mistaken for toys by children in conflict zones because of their size, appearance and colour.[84]

2. *Specifications of cluster munitions used in 2006*

Israel used five main types of sub-munitions: M42, M46, M77, M85 (with and without self-destruct devices) and BLU-63 cluster munitions, delivered by artillery projectiles, ground rockets and aircrafts. All of them except BLU-63 are Dual Purpose Improved Conventional Munitions (DPICMs) whose purpose is to injure persons and pierce armour.[85] The M42 and M46 are delivered by artillery projectiles, each projectile carrying 88 M42 and M46. The M77 are delivered by M26 Multiple Launch Rocket Systems ("MLRS") that can fire up to 12 rockets at once, each rocket containing 644 M77 sub-munitions. A typical volley of six rockets delivers 3,864 sub-munitions over an area with a one-kilometre radius. M85 are fired by artillery projectiles, each projectile holding 49 or 63 M85 sub-munitions. Finally, the CBU-58B cluster bombs, each containing 650 BLU-63 bomblets, are delivered aerially.[86]

About 1.8 million sub-munitions were delivered by rockets: 1,800 rockets were fired by a reserve MLRS battalion delivering about 1.2 million munitions and 1,000 rockets fired by an active-duty battalion delivering 644,000 sub-munitions.[87] The high dynamics range ("HDR") or failure rate of MLRS-delivered cluster sub-munitions ranges between 5 and 23 percent.[88] Approximately 16,000 to 32,000 artillery cluster

81 Alexander Breitegger, 'Preventing Human Suffering during and after Conflict? The Complementary Case for a Specific Convention on Cluster Munitions' 10 Austrian Rev Int'l Eur L (2005) 3, 6

82 Thomas Michael McDonnell, 'Cluster bombs over Kosovo: a violation of international law?' 44 Ariz LRev (2002) 31, 43

83 HRW 19; Karen Hulme, 'Of Questionable Legality: The Military Use of Cluster Bombs in Iraq in 2003' 42 Can YB Int'l L (2004) 143, 148

84 McDonnell 80

85 HRW 29

86 Ibid, 32; Landmine Action 8

87 Eitan Barak, 'None to Be Trusted: Isreal's Use of Cluster Munitions in the Second Lebanon War and the Case for the Convention on Cluster Munitions' 25 Am U Int'l L Rev (2009–2010) 423, 438; HRW 38 cites 1,159,200 M77 sub-munitions delivered by 1,800 MLRS

88 Barak 438

shells containing a total of 1.4 to 2.8 million sub-munitions were fired. The Lebanese Mine Action Centre ("LMAC")[89] based this calculation on estimating that about 10 to 20 percent of the 160,000 artillery shells fired contained sub-munitions.[90] The official failure rate of artillery delivered cluster sub-munitions ranges from 3 to 14 percent.[91] Finally, an unknown number of Vietnam-era CBU-58B cluster bombs, each containing 650 BLU-63 sub-munitions, were aerially delivered.[92]

According to LMAC, the total number of sub-munitions delivered by aerial bombing, ground-based artillery and rocket fire was between 2.6 and 4 million sub-munitions,[93] while Human Rights Watch ("HRW") estimated, based on additional information it obtained from IDF soldiers, that between 3.2 to 4.6 million sub-munitions were used.[94]

3. *Legal analysis of the use of cluster munitions*

The analysis of the legality of the use of cluster munitions involves an analysis of their legality per se and the legality of their use in the 2006 conflict, in accordance with the LOAC rules and API provisions deemed to have attained customary status.

3.1 Discrimination principle

The principle requires a distinction be made between military objectives that are legitimate targets of attacks and civilians and civilian objects which should be spared. Indiscriminate attacks are prohibited, including the use of war means or methods indiscriminately and of weapons that are indiscriminate by their nature.

3.1.1 CLUSTER MUNITIONS AS INHERENTLY INDISCRIMINATE WEAPONS

Cluster munitions have three main characteristics. First, cluster munitions and sub-munitions are unguided weapons, with very few exceptions.[95] They are "blind" or "dumb" weapons relying on the wind for direction, with no guidance system. Even if fitted with a targeting mechanism to guide the canister containing the sub-munitions – such as the CBU-103 that includes a "Wind Corrected Munitions Dispenser" (not used in Lebanon) – the sub-munitions cannot be guided.[96] In Lebanon all cluster bombs used were unguided.[97] Second, cluster munitions are

89 The UN Mine Action Coordination Centre South Lebanon (UN MACC SL) was renamed the Lebanese Mine Action Centre.

90 HRW 38 Barak gives a number of 173,293 artillery projectiles fired in Lebanon, at Barak 447

91 Barak 447

92 HRW 38 Barak 438

93 Landmine monitor note 9

94 HRW 38–39. HRW's estimate, according to its own calculations.

95 HRW 19

96 Breitegger 7

97 HRW 19

a weapon of choice to target a wide area with explosives within a short period of time,[98] as they can destroy broad targets such as airfields.[99] Their "footprint" is the area covered by munitions and sub-munitions when they hit the ground; it is much smaller though than the area within which injuries can occur, which can amount to several football fields, due to flying fragments from sub-munitions.[100] Third, the cluster munitions' high failure rate, causing essentially civilian casualties after the end of the conflict, transforms them into "ultra-sensitive anti-personnel mines"[101] or "unmarked and unmapped mine without modem self-destruct mechanisms."[102] They are in effect unexploded ordnances because of a known manufacturing defect.[103] In Lebanon the failure rate was high as old munitions were used and estimated to be around 30 percent, as communicated to the UK House of Commons' Foreign Affairs Committee by Chris Clark, Programme Manager for the mine action programme in South Lebanon and the UN Mine Action Coordination Centre South Lebanon ("UN MACC SL" today "LMAC").[104] The failure rate was later reassessed at 40 percent.[105]

Consequently, the cluster munitions used by Israel are inherently indiscriminate, due to (i) their inaccuracy, as they do not have a target detection capability and (ii) their wide dispersal pattern, both leading to the result that these weapons cannot be directed at specific military objectives, in contravention of AP/I art. 51.4(b)[106] and (iii) their high dud rates, the result of which being that their effects cannot be limited, violating AP/I article 51.4(c); all three characteristics breaching the principle of distinction. As an "intransgressible" international customary law principle,[107] it is opposable to, and has been violated by, Israel.

3.1.2 USE OF CLUSTER BOMBS THROUGH INDISCRIMINATE ATTACKS

Cluster munitions strikes were spread over an area of about 1,400 km^2 north and south of the Litani river, equivalent to about 13 percent of Lebanon's territory (10,452 km^2),[108]

98 Breitegger 9
99 HRW 19–20
100 Virgil Wiebe, 'Footprints of Death: Cluster Bombs as Indiscriminate Weapons under International Humanitarian Law' 22 Mich J Int'l L (2000–2001) 85, 109
101 Hulme 147
102 McDonnell 80
103 Karen Hulme, *War Torn Environment: Interpreting the Legal Threshold* (Martinus Nijhoff 2004) 264
104 Foreign Affairs Committee House of Commons, *Global security: the middle east* (2007): Appointed in 2003, Chris Clark was responsible for management and co-ordination of landmines' clearance following Israeli withdrawal in May 2000 and unexploded cluster bombs' clearance, following the 2006 Lebanon War.
105 MAG website
106 Hulme, 'Of Questionable Legality: The Military Use of Cluster Bombs in Iraq in 2003' 174. Barak 470
107 *Legality of the Threat or Use of Nuclear Weapons, Advisory Opinion* ICJ Rep 1996, 226 par.79; ICRC, *Customary International Humanitarian Law, Vol. I Rules* (Jean-Marie Henckaerts and Louise Doswald-Beck eds, 3rd edn, CUP 2009) Rules1, 7
108 Lebanon, Ministry of Tourism

an area slightly bigger than the US state of Rhode Island (1,214 km^2).[109] Civilian lives in the whole 1,400 km^2 were affected, while the aggregate area directly contaminated by sub-munitions was 38.7km^2, including 4.3 km^2 of urban areas, 20 km^2 of agricultural land and 4 km^2 of woodland.[110] In its September 2011 report, LMAC revised its estimate of contaminated land to approximately 54.9km^2 resulting from strikes on 1,277 locations.[111] At the end of 2022, an area of 5.23 km^2 was still contaminated by cluster munitions.[112]

Cluster munitions were launched over population centres and agricultural areas. Towns and villages were "littered with bomblets" and agricultural fields "blanketed" by unexploded sub-munitions "transforming olive and citrus groves and tobacco fields into de facto minefields."[113] In September 2006, the UN MACC-SL recorded at least 90 towns and villages hit by cluster strikes. Some 60 percent of all recorded strikes fell within 500 metres of a populated area, whereas in some areas, such as the Tyre pocket (the area south and east of Tyre), the proportion climbs to 70 percent.[114] Testimonies from the former political adviser to the wartime Israeli Minister of Defence[115] and Israeli members of the armed forces confirm that a "decision was taken to blanket an area occupied by large numbers of civilians with small and volatile explosives."[116] Orders were given to "flood" areas with cluster weapons, covering "entire towns in cluster bombs," according to an MLRS launching unit commanding officer[117] and for each team in a battalion to "flood" its allotted part of the village, as the entire village was the target.[118]

The IDF acknowledged that cluster munitions were used against populated areas but claimed that this occurred against military targets identified as rocket launchers and after warning the population of the targeted area.[119] Incidental damage to civilians and civilian infrastructure from attacks targeting Hezbollah positions was claimed to result from Hezbollah using the civilian population as "human shields,"[120] as evidenced by few photographs of rocket launchers positioned near civilian buildings in an Israeli report.[121] Responding to rockets launched by

109 HRW 3, 36

110 Ibid, 3, 36; UNDP, "CBU Contamination by Land Use." The FAO estimates that 26 per cent of agricultural land is contaminated in FAO 10

111 Lebanon Mine Action Centre, *Lebanon Mine Action Strategy 2011–2020* (September 2011) 5

112 Landmine and Cluster Munitions Monitor

113 UN Commission of Inquiry on Lebanon par.253; HRW 57

114 Landmine Action 13

115 Barak 463

116 UNHRC, *Mission to Lebanon and Israel, Implementation of General Assembly Resolution 60/251 of 15 March 2006, UN Doc. A/HRC/2/7* (2 October 2006) 13

117 HRW 45 UN Commission of Inquiry on Lebanon par.251

118 Meron Rapoport, 'What Lies Beneath' Haaretz (7 September 2006)

119 HRW 42, 44

120 Amnesty International, *Israel/Lebanon: Deliberate Destruction or "Collateral Damage"? Israeli Attacks on Civilian Infrastructure* (2006) 3

121 Amichai Cohen, *The Lebanon War and the Application of the Proportionality Principle* (International Law Forum of the Hebrew University of Jerusalem, Law Faculty 2007) 7 citing: Intelligence and Terrorism Information Center at the Center for Special Studies, *Hezbollah's Use of Lebanese Civilians as Human Shields* (2006) Pictures pp. 41, 42, map p. 134.

Hezbollah, the IDF would strike back with six rockets at the launch site within a minute and a half.[122] It is possible that Hezbollah has fired rocket launchers from among civilians, though doubtful that it was most of the cases; most were pre-prepared positions outside villages.[123] Assuming Hezbollah was using civilians as shields from attacks in villages and towns, in violation of AP/I article 51.7, this does not release Israel from its obligations to protect civilians under the LOAC and observe precautionary measures (AP/I article 51.8). Israel's own *Inquiry Commission into the Second Lebanon War* ("Winograd Report"), which reviewed the legality of Israel's use of cluster munitions, found that allowing cluster munitions in populated areas was "unacceptable" "even after their residents have been temporarily evacuated" and should be subject to stringent and individual reviews.[124] None of the few inhabitants left in the villages could identify a military target, such as the presence of Hezbollah forces, rocket launchers or munitions in the village attacked; neither could HRW find evidence of any military objective, except in one village from more than 40 visited, where there was clear evidence of Hezbollah forces' presence.[125] HRW field research corroborates an assessment based on the extent of the damage, by UN MACC SL programme manager in charge of clearance operations, that cluster weapons were deliberately directed to villages and towns.[126]

The pattern and scope of attacks, number of civilian casualties and amount of damage sustained, whether to civilian homes and industry or extensive destruction of public works and power systems, are strong evidence that damage was deliberate and integral to the military strategy, rather than "collateral damage."[127] Attacks by cluster munitions did not distinguish between separate military objectives and civilians or civilian objects within a town or a village. They constituted direct attacks on civilian population centres, in violation of the discrimination principle and AP/I articles 48, 51.2, 51.6 and 52.1. A land area may be considered a military objective, subject to being restricted to a specific area with a distinctive feature.[128] However, the cluster munitions strikes were so widespread that they cannot pass that standard and be justified thereunder. Further, as these attacks treated distinct and separate military objectives within the whole southern area of Lebanon as one military objective, they are indeterminate attacks under AP/I article 51.5.(a) breaching the prohibition thereunder of such attacks and the principle of discrimination.

122 HRW 40
123 Ibid, 40
124 Barak 468
125 HRW 8, 105
126 Ibid, 8, 105
127 Amnesty International 3
128 ICRC, *Commentary on the Protocol Additional to the Geneva Conventions of 12 August 1949, and relating to the Protection of Victims of International Armed Conflicts (Protocol I), 8 June 1977* (Yves Sandoz, Christophe Swinarski and Bruno Zimmermann eds, Martinus Nijhoff 1987) p. 621

3.2 Military necessity and proportionality

Under the military necessity principle, the right of belligerents to choose warfare weapons is not unlimited, codified in AP/I article 35.1. The choice of cluster munitions to hit a rocket launcher within civilian areas or agricultural fields breaches that rule as they are not precision guided weapons. Military necessity requires that the weapons used are limited to what is absolutely militarily necessary to achieve the military objectives. The principle is battered by the "magnitude of cluster munitions use against the relatively populated area of South Lebanon."[129] The number of munitions fired during the 2006 conflict was "unprecedented."[130] It was "the most extensive use of the weapon anywhere in the world since the 1991 Gulf War and was concentrated in a relatively small geographical area."[131] The number and density of cluster munitions used in Lebanon (4 million) vastly exceeded the number used by NATO in Kosovo (1,765 cluster bombs with about 295,000 sub-munitions), the Coalition Forces in Iraq (about 13,000 cluster munitions and about 1.9 million sub-munitions) and the US Air Forces in Afghanistan (1,228 cluster bombs with about 248,000 sub-munitions).[132] As South Lebanon covers an area of approximately 2,020 km^2, equivalent to less than a fifth of the size of Kosovo, the numbers are staggering.[133] Even the use of aerial munitions was unprecedented given an average of 350 sorties that the IDF conducted per day.[134] The spread of cluster munitions over a vast portion of Lebanon's territory and enormity of their numbers was well beyond what was militarily necessary.

Proportionality prohibits attacks expected to cause excessive civilian losses and damage in relation to the concrete and direct anticipated military advantage (AP/ article 51.5(b)). Though there is some debate over whether proportionality should be assessed on the whole campaign or for each operation, the "overall operation" frame of reference does not mean the whole bombing campaign but should be understood as finite event.[135] Assessing proportionality of each cluster munitions attack over South Lebanon requires considering that each strike contaminates an area equal to seven football fields and releases 88 M42 or M46 if delivered by artillery, 6 to 12 rockets containing each 644 M77 sub-munitions if delivered by MRLS and CBU-58B cluster bombs, each containing 650 BLU-63 bomblets if delivered aerially, and even if villages were empty, when inhabitants return to their land, foreseeable civilian losses and damage are excessive compared to the anticipated military damage resulting from allegedly targeting a Hezbollah rocket launcher in the middle of a village or field.

129 Barak 456
130 Ibid, 469
131 HRW 38
132 Ibid, 38
133 Landmine monitor note 9
134 Barak 461
135 Chapter 2

Assessing proportionality based on the whole campaign leads to the same conclusion, in particular comparing 4,000 missiles that Hezbollah launched in total[136] with Israel's 4 million cluster bombs. Israel's justification that the military campaign was based on the threat from Hezbollah's missiles relates to *jus ad bellum* arguments.[137] The numbers – and extent of dissemination – of cluster munitions in the region, density of the strikes, number of casualties, displacement of huge number of civilians and damage to land and impact on livelihood of the population are overwhelming evidence that civilian losses and damage were excessive compared to the concrete and direct anticipated military advantage resulting from alleged targeting and destruction of rocket launchers. The determination of the anticipated military advantage is not even clear. As the "overwhelming" "saturation cluster bombing" was launched during the last 72 hours of the armed conflict,[138] even considering that Hezbollah increased its rocket launches during that period,[139] it is highly improbable that all the strikes were directed at Hezbollah rocket launchers or that these still constituted military objectives which destruction would bring a military advantage at that point in time. The motivation behind the strikes was most probably to empty the South from its inhabitants by delaying or deterring their return.

Consequently, Israel breached the customary international law proportionality principle, AP/I articles 51.5(b) and 57.2. An indeterminate attack leading to "clearly" excessive losses compared to the military advantage is a war crime under the ICC Statute article 8.2.(b)(iv). Military necessity does not allow one to derogate from proportionality and distinction principles. Precautions in attacks require those planning an attack to minimize civilian losses and damage (AP/I article 57), which is considered customary international rule. It has clearly been violated.

3.3 AP/I livelihood objects

The agriculture sector was targeted, resulting in damage to Lebanon's forestry, freshwater and marine fisheries, agriculture warehouses and animal husbandry farms.[140] Its economic performance declined by an average of 43 percent in the year following the war, resulting in a significant part of a vulnerable population losing its only source of income,[141] with the tobacco production estimated to have been hit at about 60 to 70 percent.[142] About half the area contaminated by sub-munitions were agricultural lands[143] though other "very conservative" figures differ.[144] Raging

136 Cohen 6. HRW 108
137 HRW 108–109
138 Ibid, 6
139 Ibid, 41
140 UNDP, Lebanon Environmental AssessmentRapid Environemntal Assessment, xiii
141 Consultation and Research Institute 27
142 Landmine Action 29
143 UNDP, CBU Contamination by Land Use
144 HRW 78. Estimate of the FAO of 26 percent.

fires added to damage to land and forests and could not be extinguished rapidly, as civil defence personnel, including fire-fighters, were already stretched by helping a fleeing population.[145] The irrigation infrastructure was destroyed, and the loss of animals, crops, fisheries and forests amounted to approximately US$280 million.[146]

Clearance of unexploded ordnances started immediately at the end of the conflict. Prioritizing safe return of internally displaced persons to their homes meant that clearance focused first on public roads, then on paths to houses and schools and last on agricultural fields.[147] Farmers lost their crops, as they were unable to access their fields for the harvest and could not prepare them for the following season.[148] Some chose to work their land, nonetheless, taking the risk to step on unexploded ordnances,[149] and others used "artisanal" methods instead of waiting for professional cluster bombs' clearance.[150] Concern was raised about the "unknown effects of bomb-induced soil contamination on crop production and human health."[151] The local population noticed disappearance or reduced production of fruit and vegetables, due to declining fertility of soil and trees, that may be attributed to the intensity of bombardments, the size or type of bombs, and the extreme heat. In August 2009, it was reported that since 2006 olive crops had decreased below the usual minimum yield in Tebnine, a village east of Tyre, and olive trees had not borne any fruit in Sarba, a village east of Saida.[152]

Water resources were contaminated by cluster munitions. "The banks and streambeds of 173 streams and rivers in South Lebanon are littered with unexploded cluster bombs putting shepherds and farmers irrigating their fields at risk."[153] Water services, including pipes beneath roads extensively damaged, water wells, mains, storage tanks, pumping stations and water treatment works, were destroyed throughout South Lebanon.[154] Israel bombed irrigation canals supplying Litani River water to more than 10,000 acres of farmland and 23 villages in Southern Lebanon and the Bekaa, affecting negatively the banana crops and citrus groves that were left dry.[155] Water infrastructure and natural resources such as the

145 Association for Forests Development and Conservation 26
146 FAO 20
147 UNDP, *UNDP's Participation in Lebanon's Recovery in the Aftermath of the July 2006 War* (2007) 26
148 Consultation and Research Institute
149 HRW 79 Patrick Cockburn, 'Deadly Harvest, Lebanese Villagers Must Risk Death in Fields "Flooded" with More Than a Million Israeli Cluster Bombs – or Leave Crops to Rot' The Independent (18 September 2006)
150 FAO 10
151 Ibid, 7
152 *Interview by the author of Pr Farran from the American University of Beirut, advisor to the Ministry of Agriculture during the post-conflict phase (2006)* (August 2009)
153 Landmine Action 26
154 Amnesty International 4, 9
155 Kim Murphy, 'Old Feud Over Lebanese River Takes New Turn' Los Angeles Times (10 August 2006)

transboundary Litani river and Wazzani springs came under attack. The Litani river, Litani dam and several irrigation canal and water pipes were targeted.[156]

Objects indispensable to survival and livelihood of the population (foodstuffs, agricultural areas, crops, drinking water installations and supplies and irrigation works) were destroyed or rendered unusable by cluster sub-munitions, with the purpose of denying civilians who came back as soon as the conflict stopped their livelihood means, in breach of AP/I customary law article 54.2 prohibiting their destruction.

3.4 AP/I environmental protection

Though AP/I articles 35.3 and 55 are considered international customary rules by the ICRC, their status is still uncertain, but the prohibition to use means and methods of war intended or expected to cause widespread, long-term and severe damage to the environment is widely accepted. Previous analysis of the threshold of environmental damage, under these articles, has shown that the traditional understanding of duration may not be applicable anymore, given the evolution of the concept of environment since the adoption of AP/I and increased damaging capacity of weapons. Assuming nonetheless that "long-term" is still measured in decades, it has been reached, as it will take at least about 20 years for Lebanon to clear its land of the unexploded sub-munitions, with the end of clearance operations projected to end by 2026. The characteristics of the damage were sufficiently demonstrated earlier to conclude that it was widespread, severe and long-term under AP/I. It constitutes a war crime under the Statute of the ICC, though Lebanon and Israel are not party to it.

Military necessity cannot be used to derogate from the environmental protection clauses under the LOAC. Consequently, Israel has breached the prohibition under both articles AP/I 35.3 and 55.

III. Attack on Jiyeh power station

On 13 and 15 July 2006, the IDF hit two fuel storage tanks at the Jiyeh power plant which is located on the coast about 30 km south of Beirut, containing respectively 10,000 m^3 and 15,000 m^3 of fuel. They were damaged and caught fire, which spread to the remaining tanks. Approximately 60,000 m^3 burned during 12 days. About 15,000 tonnes of heavy fuel oil spilled into the Eastern Mediterranean shores of Lebanon and stretched to about 150 km of coastline (out of Lebanon's total coastline of 220 km).[157] The oil spill affected the Mediterranean Sea, archaeological sites at Anfeh and Byblos, a World Heritage Site[158] and the Palm Islands Nature

156 Strategic Foresight Group, *Water and Violence: Attacks on Water Infrastructure* (Blue Peace Bulletin, Vol 10, October 2019) 8; Murphy

157 UNDP, Lebanon Environmental Assessment xv, par.7.2

158 UNEP, *Lebanon: Post-conflict Environmental Assessment* (2007) 134

Reserve, an area protected under two treaties. It had "repercussions for livelihoods, human health, economic development, ecosystems, fisheries, tourism and rare and endangered wildlife."[159]

1. Application of LOAC rules

Rules on military objectives, works releasing dangerous forces and precautions in attack must be examined. Military objectives are objects that make an effective contribution to military action and which destruction offers a definite military advantage (AP/I article 52.2). Power stations may be considered military objectives as they can have dual military and civilian use. Attacks on power stations are, however, controversial. As Israel is not a party to AP/I, article 52.2 may not be opposable to it, unless deemed customary law, which the ICRC considers it is.[160] Israel may have relied on the US doctrine enlarging the scope of military objectives, whereas the target of military operations is the political command and control system and its resources basis. The concept is rightly criticized as voiding the distinction between military and civilian objectives of any sense.[161]

Jiyeh power station was not used by Hezbollah as a means of generating electricity for their military purposes. Its location at about 40 kilometres south of Beirut, far from South Lebanon which was the theatre of combat between the IDF and Hezbollah, makes the hypothesis implausible. Given the notorious electricity shortages in Lebanon and the electricity deficit from the State supply capacity, most inhabitants, offices and industries in Lebanon rely on private electricity generators, as assessed in 2008.[162] It is absurd to consider that a military group would rely on such inadequate electricity supply source to wage combat against enemy forces. In these conditions, Jiyeh power station could not constitute a military objective, the destruction of which would confer a definite military advantage. Attacks on electricity generating facilities have been justified in the Iraq war, as corresponding to a military goal of incapacitating the regime.[163] The State of Lebanon was already in a weak position, following two years of instability and assassinations, so this could not have been a war objective. As to weakening Hezbollah, the destruction of Jiyeh power plant did not affect the group capacity to wage war. Israel breached AP/I article 52 and the customary understanding of military objective.

159 Steiner Achim, UNEP Executive Director, IMO-UNEP meeting in Athens, Greece, 17 August 2006 to agree an action plan to assist the authorities in Lebanon. See UNEP, News Centre, *Clean Up Strategy for Oiled Lebanese Coast Given Green Light, IMO and UNEP Meeting Backs Euro 50 Million Anti-Pollution Action Plan* (2006)

160 ICRC, Customary IHL Rules Rule 8, 29–32

161 Stefan Oeter, 'Methods of Combat' in Dieter Fleck (ed), *The Handbook of International Humanitarian Law* (4th edn, OUP 2021) 7.03, par.8

162 World Bank, Sustainable Development Department, MENA Region, *Report No. 41421-LB, Republic of Lebanon Electricity Sector Public Expenditure Review* (2008) 5

163 Judith Gail Gardam, *Necessity, Proportionality and the Use of Force by States* (CUP 2004) 21. See proportionality discussion in Chapter 2

The question may be raised whether the attack on Jiyeh power station comes under the scope of prohibited attacks against civilian or military objectives that are "works or installations containing dangerous forces" that "may cause the release of dangerous forces and consequent severe losses among the civilian population" (AP/I art.56). The provision is restricted to dams, dykes and nuclear electrical generating stations,[164] though the spirit of the rule has not been respected. Under a customary and conventional rule, precautions in attacks must be taken to avoid or minimize incidental environmental damage through the choice of means and methods of attack and of military objectives. Attacks expected to cause excessive environmental damage, compared to the anticipated military advantage, must be cancelled or suspended. The environmental damage resulting from the oil spill analysed later, which covered two-thirds of Lebanon coastline, was excessive compared to the military advantage gained from the destruction of a power station not used by Hezbollah in its combat, breaching AP/I article 57. Israel failed to take precautionary measures violating its obligation of protection of the natural environment and endangering inhabitants' health.[165]

2. *Analysis under IEL*

2.1 Obligations under IEL principles, UNCLOS and Barcelona Convention

Both Israel and Lebanon were bound by the Barcelona Convention (1976) in force between them in 2006 and by customary international environmental law duties to prevent environmental damage and transboundary harm expressed, regarding the marine environment, in UNCLOS Part XII articles 192 and 194, for which substantive and procedural obligations were developed by case law and the ILC Prevention Articles.

The Barcelona Convention 1976 and its protocols target specific cases of pollution caused by dumping from ships and aircrafts (article 5) or from ships (article 6), from exploration of the continental shelf and seabed (article 7) or from land-based sources (article 8), unapplicable for our purposes. However, its article 4 contains a general obligation that is arguably interpreted as pollution unrelated to these cases.

Israel and Lebanon have a general obligation to protect and preserve the marine environment (UNCLOS art.192) and to protect and enhance it in the Mediterranean Sea Area (Barcelona 1976, art. 4.1). They have obligations to take all measures:

(i) To prevent, abate and combat pollution of the marine environment and of the Mediterranean Sea Area under Barcelona 1976 art. 4.1 and the prevention principle, from any source, using the best practicable means at their disposal and according to their capabilities (UNCLOS article 194(1)),

164 ICRC Commentary on AP/I, art.56 par.2147, 2149–2150
165 UN Commission of Inquiry par.23

(ii) To ensure that activities under their jurisdiction or control do not cause damage by pollution to other States and their environment and that pollution arising from incidents or activities under their jurisdiction or control does not spread beyond the areas where they exercise sovereign rights, (UNCLOS article 194 (2) and "no-harm" principle),

(iii) To protect and preserve rare or fragile ecosystems and habitat of depleted, threatened or endangered species and marine life (UNCLOS art.194(5)).

UNCLOS article 1(4) and the Barcelona Convention 1995 article 2(a) define "pollution" as:

> the introduction by man, directly or indirectly, of substances or energy into the marine environment, including estuaries, which results or is likely to result in such deleterious effects as harm to living resources and marine life, hazards to human health, hindrance to marine activities, including fishing and other legitimate uses of the sea, impairment of quality for use of sea water and reduction of amenities.

As Israel signed the 1995 Barcelona Convention and Lebanon UNCLOS, both agreed to be bound by the same "pollution" definition; arguably it may be opposable to both, in addition to being considered customary law definition, as relating to UNCLOS Part XII. The Barcelona Convention 1976 article 2(a) omits "including estuaries," "marine life" and probable harm ("is likely to result"), mentioning instead "resulting." The issue is whether the impact of the oil spill is within the scope of pollution defined herein, to be determined by environmental impact assessments.

2.2 *Environmental impact assessments*

Environmental impact assessments ("EIA") were prepared by UN agencies and an independent expert jointly commissioned by the IUCN and Lebanon's Ministry of Environment.[166] Although the extent of the environmental impact was speculative due to uncertainty of the damage baseline prior to the war, the damage from 15,000 tons of a highly toxic fluid spilled into a coastal or marine environment would be expected to be "extensive."[167] It is interesting to see if a link can be made between scientific evaluation of war-related environmental impact and its legal definition under the LOAC.[168] The EIA methodology used in Lebanon for UNDP was adapted from that used by the oil industry in the Gulf States for over a decade

166 UNDP, Lebanon Environmental Assessment; UNEP, Lebanon: Post-conflict Environmental Assessment. Richard Steiner, *Lebanon Oil Spill Rapid Assessment and Response Mission: Final Report* (2006)

167 Steiner 10

168 See HulmeWar Torn Environment for development of a scientific base from EIA related to the LOAC environmental damage threshold

and expert judgement applied for impact effect estimation.[169] This raises the issue of the weight of expert judgment versus any objective scientific standard in determining environmental impacts and if that could lead to different EIA outcomes done by different experts on the same environmental damage. It is a difficult question to answer, especially when most of the impacts are assessed qualitatively. For some impacts, like air quality impacts, scientific models can be used to determine the extent of the impact and its magnitude, therefore introducing less subjectivity. Nevertheless, the scale is detailed enough to avoid substantial differences in assessments obtained from different EIA assessors. It would, however, be useful to develop a scale that could be more tailored to impacts from armed conflicts.[170]

Five environmental impacts from the oil spill were assessed, according to their effect, duration and severity (or significance). The impact or effect could be insignificant, limited, serious, considerable or catastrophic. Momentary duration was less than a week, short term under a year, medium term one to ten years and long term ten to 50 years. Severity could be negligible, marginal, critical non-significant, critical significant, serious or severe.[171] These terms should not be interpreted as defining environmental impacts under international conventions, as assessments were done to prioritize them to plan the post-conflict reconstruction phase;[172] though they should be taken into consideration as experts' assessments. Chemical and physical properties of the oil spilled determine its impact on the environment.[173] It was a heavy fuel oil, IFP 150 (n.6 fuel), difficult to combat due to its high viscous nature resulting in low mobility, low volatility, high specific gravity and tendency to break up into tar balls and sink to the seabed, leading to prolonged persistence in the marine environment and effect on the marine ecosystem.[174]

Impacts assessed were:

(i) Catastrophic, medium-term and severe on littoral pollution.[175] Large portions of the oil emulsified and solidified along the shores and tarry residues were left on the beaches.[176] Littoral invertebrates were coated with oil. Significant mortality most probably occurred among these organisms during July and August, yet they were thought likely to recover within one to a few years because

169 UNDP, Lebanon Environmental Assessment par.1.3.6

170 Ricardo Khoury, personal communication with the author. Khoury was Team Leader at Earth Link and Advanced Resources Development (ELARD) in charge of the environmental assessment prepared for UNDP.

171 UNDP, Lebanon Environmental Assessment xx–xxii, Table 1

172 Ibid, 7

173 UNEP, Lebanon: Post-conflict Environmental Assessment 140

174 Alia Hussein Sabra, *Oil Spill Contaminants in Selected Vertebrates and Invertebrates of the Eastern Mediterranean Sea, Master's Thesis* (American University of Beirut 2007) 2; UNEP, Lebanon: Post-conflict Environmental Assessment 134; IMO Marine Environment Protection Committee (MEPC), *Guidance on Managing Seafood Safety during and after Oil Spills, 46th session* (2001)

175 UNDP, Lebanon Environmental Assessment, xviii Table 1, par.10.1.3.1.3

176 Ibid, par.7.2.3

of their relatively rapid reproduction cycle.[177] The shoreline's pollution was more than could be handled by local institutions. International assistance, equipment and expertise had to be mobilized to carry out specialized clean-up activities under the leadership of the Ministry of Environment.[178] A Lebanese NGO constituted of fishermen participated in the clean-up as their livelihood was affected by the oil spill.[179] The disposal of the contaminated oil and oily waste collected was a major issue as the country has neither hazardous waste management facilities or landfills nor industrial incinerators.[180] By the end of December 2006, the total waste contaminated volume amounted to 5,800 m^3 and more than 30 km of sandy beaches had not yet been cleaned up. The amount of waste was underestimated by approximately 4,000 tons,[181]

(ii) Serious, long-term and severe effects on marine biodiversity, especially for species that use water surface (birds, seal and dolphins). Monk seals on the endangered list are present in the Palm Islands Nature Reserve area. Four known species of turtles, including the endangered loggerhead turtles and the critically endangered green turtles, reproduce on Lebanon's beaches. The soiling of the beaches coincided with the egg hatching period of the turtles, the eggs being laid from May to August, and the hatching occurring one to two months later; the effect of the oil spill was regarded as severely interfering with the hatching.[182] One year after the spill, turtles feeding on toxic algae were seen dead at the Palm Islands Nature Reserve.[183] Ninety-two oiled birds were observed between October 2006 and April 2007 on the Palm Islands Nature reserve.[184]

Research was conducted on "the level of selected organic chemical contaminants and heavy metals in two fish species . . . predominant in the artisanal fishing activity of Lebanon and in oysters,"[185] the latter being "particularly good indicators of Petroleum hydrocarbons (PHC) contamination."[186] The major chemical contaminants included polyaromatic aromatic hydrocarbons (PAH), polychlorinated biphenyls (PCB), Lead (Pb), Nickel (Ni) and Vanadium (V). They are known to cause serious harm to the marine ecology and to human health, as they move through the food chain to negatively affect human

177 UNEP, Lebanon: Post-conflict Environmental Assessment 140–143
178 Ibid, 140–143
179 Bahr Loubnan, interview with the author.
180 UNDP, Lebanon Environmental Assessment par.7.2.4.2
181 Ibid, par.7.2.1
182 Ibid, xviii Table 1, par.7.2.3; World Bank, 'Chapter 6, Oil Spill and Waste Due to Conflict: The Case of Lebanon (WB198-TCED.CH06)' in (Oil-spill-info) 93
183 Steiner. Sabra 33
184 World Bank 93
185 Alia Hussein Sabra, 'Oil spill contaminants in selected vertebrates and invertebrates of the eastern Mediterranean Sea' (American University of Beirut 2007) vi
186 UNEP, Lebanon: Post-conflict Environmental Assessment 141

consumers.[187] Fishermen's livelihood was affected. Commercial fisheries in Lebanon are artisanal, amounting to about 6,000 tons per year. Fishermen use small boats near the shore, mostly at night using lamplights. The industry supports roughly 30,000 fishermen and their dependents and was assessed to need at least a couple of years to recover.[188]

Previous incidents of oil spills around the world, including Exxon Valdez in Alaska in 1989, Apex Barge in Galveston Bay in 1990 and Erika in the Atlantic coast of France in 1999, have resulted in serious contaminations of marine life.[189] They are predicted to need decades for self-purification processes.[190] In the Exon Valdez case, the fish population collapsed only three years after the initial spill.[191] This uncertainty as to the duration of the effect of the oil spill reveals a clear inadequacy with the legal terminology used in the LOAC. Further, there is no single pollution index worldwide on contaminants of fish.[192] Guidelines used to assess permissible limits to organic and nonorganic contaminants (PAH, PHC and metals) in fish suitable for consumption vary depending on the region in the world and national or international agencies setting standards.[193] As there is no single scientific agreed upon measure of pollution in fish, the complexity of defining precisely the legal terminology "long-term, severe and widespread" under AP/I increases,

(iii) Impact of the marine sediment from sunken oil was severe and irreversible on the benthic ecosystem close to Jiyeh – as the baseline conditions there before the war will most probably not recover[194] – and of limited impact, medium-term and critically significant elsewhere, the oil having dissolved on reaching the

187 Ibid, 140–143; Sabra 3. For more details, see reports cited: Agency for Toxic Substances & Disease Registry (ATSDR), U.S. Department of Health and Human Services, Public Health Service, *Nickel, Toxicological Profile for Nickel* (2006), *PCB: Potential for Human Exposure. Toxicological profile for Polyaromatic Hydrocarbons* (2000), *Lead, Toxicological Profile for Lead (1999), Fuel oils, Toxicological profile for fuel oils.* (1995), *PAH: Potential for Human Exposure. Toxicological profile for Polyaromatic Hydrocarbons* (1995), *Vanadium Toxicological Profile for Vanadium* (1993)

188 Steiner 6 UNDP, Lebanon Environmental Assessment par.6.1.2.8

189 Sabra 16; State of Alaska Epidemiology Bulletin (SAEB), 'Are Alaskan Seafoods and Other Subsistence Foods Safe for Human Consumption?' *Bulletin No. 16, Oil Spill Public Health Advice* – Report No. 3 (1989). H. Budzinki, O. Mazéas, J. Tronczynski, Y. Désaunay, G. Bocquené, and G. Claireaux, 'Link between Exposure of Fish (Solea solea) to PAHs and Metabolites: Application to the "Erika" Oil Spill' 17 Aquatic Living Resources (2004) 329–334.

190 Mazéas and others 329–334; E.K. Barbour, R.J. Codsi, and R.A. Zurayk, 'Reproducibility of Bacterial and Copepod Density Assessment in Bathing and Artisanal Fishing Water of the Eastern Mediterranean'14 Int'l J Environ Health (2004) 315–321. National Oceanic and Atmospheric Administration (NOAA), *Managing Seafood Safety after an Oil Spill* (National Ocean Service, Office of Response and Restoration 2002).

191 Steiner 7

192 Interview with the author of Professor Barbour, American University of Beirut, Lebanon.

193 Sabra 35

194 UNDP, Lebanon Environmental Assessment xv

coastline.[195] The concentrations of PAH in seabed sediment and in molluscs (oysters) and levels of PHC in oyster tissue and fish tissue were found to be acceptable for a coastal area close to an urban zone,[196]

(iv) Impact was considerable and short-term on seawater quality[197] and coastal aquifers,[198]

(v) As to clean-up and waste issues, the type of fuel oil leaked generates a high quantity of waste in a very short time, though predictions of the quantity and quality of waste are difficult to make. In extreme cases, the waste produced may amount to 30 times the volume of oil originally spilled.[199]

3. *Application of the legal rules*

Israel has introduced into the Mediterranean Sea, indirectly through its attack on Jiyeh power plant that caused the oil spill, substances that resulted in damage to the marine environment, harming living resources, putting human health at risk, impairing marine activities, including fishing, affecting livelihood of fishermen and reducing the use of the beaches, corresponding to pollution (Barcelona Convention 1976, art. 2(a), UNCLOS art. 1(4)), breaching its conventional obligations to prevent, abate and combat pollution of the Mediterranean Sea Area, under Barcelona 1976 article 4.1. Israel also violated its customary law duty to prevent environmental damage and transboundary harm under IEL that informs UNCLOS articles 192 and 194 and failed to ensure that activities under its control – the bombing of Jiyeh power plant – do not cause damage by pollution to Lebanon, neighbouring States and their environment and that pollution arising therefrom does not spread beyond its area of sovereignty.

State parties to the 1976 Barcelona Convention "shall cooperate in taking the necessary measures in dealing with any pollution emergencies . . . whatever the causes of such emergencies" (article 9) and "in case of grave and imminent danger to the marine environment . . . due to the massive presence of oil . . . resulting from accidental causes . . . which are polluting or threatening to pollute" the Mediterranean Sea Area, under the Emergency Protocol, article 1. Israel breached its obligation under both provisions by imposing a naval blockade on Lebanon, prohibiting it from, and refusing to cooperate in, taking any necessary measures to deal with the oil pollution and blocking any international help from reaching the country. Cooperation is an IEL principle and an obligation codified under the ILC Prevention Articles (2001)[200] that was violated by Israel. Further, the 1995 amendments to the Barcelona Convention introduced the precautionary principle, according to

195 Ibid, par.10.1.3.1.3

196 Sabra UNEP, Lebanon: Post-conflict Environmental Assessment

197 UNDP, Lebanon Environmental Assessment par.9.1.3.1.3

198 Ibid, par.9.1.7, Table 9.1 Impact 5

199 Ibid, par.7.2.1

200 ILC, *Draft Articles on Prevention of Transboundary Harm from Hazardous Activities, with commentaries, A/56/10* (ILC YB 2001, vol II (2)) art.4; Alan Boyle and Catherine Redgwell, *Birnie,*

which Parties to the Convention "shall apply . . . the precautionary principle by virtue of which where there are threats of serious or irreversible damage, lack of full scientific certainty shall not be used as a reason for postponing cost-effective measures to prevent environmental degradation."[201] Israel, having signed but not ratified the amended Convention in 2005, has signified its intention to accept these amendments, even though it is not under a legal duty. Though the customary status of the precautionary principle is uncertain, the ICJ recognized its relevance in interpreting an environment treaty,[202] the Barcelona Convention and the Emergency Protocol in that case. Arguably, Israel should have allowed Lebanon in this emergency to take measures early on, to prevent further environmental degradation caused by the oil spill.

The Palm Islands Nature Reserve could not be accessed from the start of the war until the lifting of the naval blockade.[203] It is a Mediterranean SPA under the 1982 SPA Protocol. States have thereunder

> (i) a general obligation to "take all appropriate measures with a view to protect those marine areas which are important for the safeguard of natural resources and natural sites of the Mediterranean Sea Area, as well as for the safeguard of the cultural heritage in the region" (article 1);
>
> (ii) a specific obligation to establish an SPA to safeguard sites of biological and ecological value, genetic diversity of species and habitats, representative types of ecosystems and ecological processes and sites of particular scientific, educational or cultural importance (article 3), in their territorial waters, within the Mediterranean Sea Area (article 2). As clause (i) mentions the Mediterranean Sea Area and the region and not States' territorial waters, it does not necessarily refer to the obligation to establish an SPA provided under article 3 but to an obligation to protect those SPAs in the Mediterranean Sea Area. Israel has breached its obligation under 1982 SPA Protocol article 1 by harming the natural resources, including endangered species of turtles and monks, of the Palm Islands Nature Reserve. Further, Israel having signed the 1995 amended SPA Protocol showed its intention to abide by it, even prior to ratification and should respect its obligation not to authorize or undertake any activity that may be contrary to the objectives for which the SPAs (renamed SPA of Mediterranean Importance, SPAMI) were established (article 8.3(b)).

Boyle and Redgwell's International Law and the Environment (4th edn, OUP 2021) 300; Sands 213–217

201 The 1995 Barcelona Convention, art.4.3

202 *Pulp Mills on the River Uruguay (Argentina v. Uruguay), Judgment, ICJ Reports 2010, p. 14* par.164

203 World Bank, Sustainable Development Department, MENA Region, *Report No. 39787-LB, Republic of Lebanon: Economic Assessment of Environmental Degradation due to July 2006 Hostilities, Sector Note* (2007) 28

The Palm Islands Nature Reserve is also listed under the Ramsar Convention. Its parties have obligations to take measures to protect wetlands on their territory (article 3), by designating them as Ramsar Sites and conserving and managing them sustainably under the "wise use" concept (article 2.6).[204] A party can request listing its wetlands on the Montreux Record in case of adverse ecological change, allowing it to receive priority expert advice on how to respond to the threat, from the Ramsar Advisory Mechanism; such listing is practically non-existent in relation to armed conflict.[205] Any party may delete or restrict the boundaries of its listed wetlands, because of "urgent national interests" (article 2.5), using this provision to avoid its conservation obligations during armed conflict.[206] Apart from these provisions that could be used during armed conflicts, the Ramsar convention does not provide protection from damage during conflicts. Palm Islands Nature Reserve is also a designated Important Bird Area.

Byblos, a World Heritage Site, was affected by the oil spill that damaged the foundations of a citadel from the Venetian period and a medieval tower from the Crusades next to the small harbour.[207] A UNESCO mission identified "the urgent need to clean manually the stones at the base of the port's two medieval towers and other seashore archaeological remains," for an estimated cost of $100,000.[208] Under the World heritage Convention, article 6(3), "[e]ach State party undertakes not to take any deliberate measurers which might damage directly or indirectly the cultural and natural heritage referred to in articles 1 and 2 situated on the territory of other State Parties to this Convention." Included in cultural heritage are "structural works of archaeological nature . . . of outstanding universal value" (article 1) and in natural heritage "habitats of threatened species of plants and animals of outstanding universal value" (i.e. dolphins, endangered sea turtles, birds), "biological formations" (i.e. coral reefs) and other natural sites of beauty (i.e. Palm Islands Nature Reserve), (article 2). Israel has breached its obligations under such provisions by deliberately bombing the fuel tank that caused spilling of oil into the Mediterranean that has indirectly damaged the cultural and natural heritage of Lebanon.

AP/I article 53 prohibits the commission of "any acts of hostility directed against the historic monuments, works of art . . . which constitute the cultural or spiritual heritage of peoples" similarly to the 1954 Hague Convention for the Protection of Cultural Property in the Event of Armed Conflict, articles 4.1 and 4.2 imposing an obligation for belligerents to refrain from any act of hostilities

204 Ramsar, the Convention on Wetlands website, *Ramsar Handbooks 4th ed., Handbook 1 Wise Use of Wetlands* (2010) 16

205 Meng Wang, 'The Unprecedented Ramsar Resolution: Ukrainian Wetlands Protection in Armed Confict' 70 NILR 329–330, 333–334

206 Wang 333

207 Steiner 11

208 UNESCO, *Report by the Director General on the Implementation Programme adopted by the General Conference, Information Document on UNESCO Assistance to Post-Crisis Recovery and Reconstruction in Lebanon, (175 EX/INF.14), 27 September 2006* par.35

directed against cultural property. Those clauses do not seem applicable as the attacks did not target directly Byblos. Other cultural and historical property sites were affected independently of the oil spill. Chamaa, a cultural site in South Lebanon dating from the twelfth century, listed as a World Heritage Site, was "badly damaged by the bombardments" needing emergency rehabilitation and most old houses dating from the eighteenth century destroyed needing reconstruction.[209]

IV. Destruction of infrastructure and related effects on air pollution

The country's infrastructure suffered severe destruction. The Israeli Air Force launched more than 7,000 air attacks on about 7,000 targets in Lebanon, while the Navy conducted an additional 2,500 bombardments.[210] The UNDP assessed that: "the collective damages incurred across the country consisted of the destruction of approximately 445,000 m2 of road network, 92 bridges and overpasses, as well as the destruction or damage of an estimated total of 130,000 dwelling units in addition to water supply and wastewater infrastructure. . . . In the energy sector, key infrastructure damaged during the war includes the Jiyeh power plant fuel storage tanks, the kerosene fuel storage tanks of the Beirut Rafic Hariri International Airport, transmission and distribution networks, and petrol stations."[211]

This massive destruction of building and infrastructure led authorities to prioritize the removal of rubble after the war. Waste estimates ranged from 2.5 to 3 million cubic metres (m^3)[212] although the actual volume of waste removed reached 5.75 million m^3, including 3.32 million m^3 from the South.[213] UNDP financed approximately US$800,000 of rubble removal in 101 villages and towns in the South, each of which received up to US$25,000.[214] The implementation was left to municipalities that contracted private sector haulers with disastrous results. In Beirut, demolition waste was dumped in four sites.[215] In the South, municipalities with relatively little waste used it to fill depressions in roads or in construction. Where the amount of rubble was extensive, it was dumped, after removing most

209 Ibid, par.19; Sharp Roy, 'Impact of Israeli Bombs Shatters Lebanon's Priceless Roman Legacy' The Observer, 17 September (2006)

210 Amnesty International 2

211 UNDP, Lebanon Rapid Environmental Assessment, 12

212 Ibid, 12

213 World Bank, Report No. 39787-LB, Republic of Lebanon: Economic Assessment of Environmental Degradation due to July 2006 Hostilities, Sector Note 44

214 UNDP, UNDP's participation in Lebanon's recovery in the aftermath of the July 2006 warParticipation in Lebanon's Recovery, 15

215 World Bank, Report No. 39787-LB, Republic of Lebanon: Economic Assessment of Environmental Degradation due to July 2006 Hostilities, Sector Note 45

hazardous domestic material, on nearby land and in ecologically sensitive valleys, ponds and riparian areas.[216]

The removal of rubble and the reconstruction activities in Beirut led to an increase in pollution in the air. A study on particulate matter (PM) over Beirut between 2003 and 2007 was conducted to find the sources of pollutants that could originate from Lebanon or from long range transported pollutants. The average was found to be higher than that recommended by the World Health Organisation, due to low precipitations, dust storms in the fall and spring, sea and land breezes and increased traffic activities especially in the touristic summer season. A comparison between pre and post-war sites in Beirut found an increase in aged dust and much higher percentage of nitrates and sulphates in PM resulting from construction debris and heavy duty trucks transporting the debris from the damaged buildings to the dump sites.[217]

As to the estimated 60,000 m^3 of fuel that burned at Jiyeh, they are deemed to have caused extensive atmospheric contamination in a plume reaching about 60 km, resulting in short-term respiratory problems in the population exposed and releasing pollutants that do not break down, persisting in the environment for many years and accumulating in the soil, water, plants and animals.[218] Articles 35.3 and 55.1 of AP/I prohibit the use of warfare means resulting or expecting to result in widespread, severe and long-term environmental damage that affect the health of the population. Air is covered as part of the environment. An area of 60 km is sufficiently large compared to Lebanon's shoreline to be considered widespread. Severe and long-term are more difficult to assess and do not seem to have reached the threshold required. There is no international conventional obligation that could have been breached regarding air pollution.

V. Conclusion

Israel breached the LOAC rules providing protection to civilians and natural resources in 2006. The use of cluster munitions in the last 72 hours of the conflict breached the principles of proportionality, distinction, military necessity and humanity and the corresponding rules codified in the Regulations and AP/I. Environmental damage covered a widespread area, given the geographical size of Lebanon, and was severe and long-term, reaching the threshold of AP/I, endangering the population health and livelihood and constituting a war crime. The attack on Jiyeh power station breached the distinction principle and obligation to take precautions in attacks, as Jiyeh could not be considered a military object under the dual object doctrine. Simultaneously, Israel breached its obligations under IEL

216 World Bank, Report No. 39787-LB, Republic of Lebanon: Economic Assessment of Environmental Degradation due to July 2006 Hostilities, Sector Note 45

217 Najat Saliba, F. El Jam, G. El Tayar, w. Obeid, and M. Roumie, 'Origin and Variability of Particulate Matter (PM10 and PM2.5) Mass Concentrations over an Eastern Mediterranean City' Atmospheric Research (2010) 1

218 UNDP, Lebanon Environmental Assessment par.4.1.2.1.5

principles of prevention and due diligence, IEL treaties (Barcelona Convention and Protocols), UNCLOS articles representing customary international law and World Heritage Convention.

The right of Israel to defend itself is not a licence to conduct war in violation of the LOAC. Having benefited from impunity for its past violations of the LOAC, because there is no supranational authority policing State actions in armed conflicts, added to the unwillingness or inability of the international community to restrain or sanction it, Israel would ignore the LOAC rules in subsequent wars. Following its invasion of Lebanon in 1982, the MacBride Commission constituted by eminent international law scholars and a Nobel Peace Prize had found "indiscriminate character of attacks on civilians . . . use of dubious weapons such as cluster bombs and phosphorous bombs" against civilians[219] and the "enormous scale of death, destructions, dislocation and suffering . . . egregiously disproportionate" to the harm perpetrated on Israel.[220] In 2006, Israel established "a new doctrine of "disproportionality" breaching equally the distinction principle that would be applicable in its future wars.[221] The "Dahiye Doctrine" (from the name of the Beirut neighbourhood Israel flattened) commands to "use disproportionate force" to "cause immense damage and destruction" considering every village from where shots are fired as military bases, not civilian villages,[222] with the aim to inflict damage and punishment demanding an expensive and long reconstruction process.[223] It seems therefore surrealistic to analyse rationally the application of the LOAC, in the face of such State doctrine stamping on its fundamental principles.

Under general rules of State responsibility and the LOAC, Israel is liable to make full reparation for the damage caused, under the form of restitution, compensation or satisfaction.[224] Compensation must cover losses or expenses resulting from monitoring and assessment of environmental damage caused to the land in Southern Lebanon and the marine environment, abatement and prevention of environmental damage, reasonable measures taken or to be taken to clean and restore the environment, monitoring of public health to combat health risks from environmental damage and finally depletion or damage to natural resources, as assessed by

219 Eugene V. Rostow, Richard A. Falk, Francis A. Boyle, W. Michael Reisman, Frits Kalshoven, and Robbie Sabel, 'Problems of the Law of Armed Conflict in Lebanon' 77 ASIL Proceedings of the Annual Meeting, April 14–16, 1983 214, 217

220 Rostow and others 225

221 The Public Committee Against Torture in Israel (PCATI), Graeme Goodman, Dr. Ishai Menuchin, Dr. Assaf Oron, *Special Report: November 2009, No Second Thoughts, The Changes in the Israeli Defense Forces' Combat Doctrine in Light of "Operation Cast Lead*" 21

222 The Public Committee Against Torture in Israel (PCATI), 20; Mark Zeitoun, Karim Eid-Sabbagh and Jeremy Loveless, 'The Analytical Framework of Water and Armed Conflict: a Focus on the 2006 Summer War between Israel and Lebanon' 38 Disasters 1 (2014) 22, 23

223 The Public Committee Against Torture in Israel (PCATI) 21

224 The Hague Regulations art.3; Protocol Additional to the Geneva Conventions of 12 August 1949, and relating to the Protection of Victims of International Armed Conflicts (Protocol I), 8 June 1977 art.91; ILC, Responsibility of States for Internationally Wrongful Acts art.31, art.34

the UNCC.[225] UNGA Resolutions on "the oil slick on Lebanese shores" have been voted annually from 2006 to the latest to date in 2022.[226] Noting the "environmental disaster" that resulted from the attack on Jiyeh power plant, the Resolutions called for Israel "to assume responsibility for prompt and adequate compensation to the Government of Lebanon . . . for the costs of repairing the environmental damage caused by the destruction, including the restoration of the marine environment."[227] This resolution was considered "an important step forward in enhancing environmental protection in times of armed conflicts," providing for compensation for the costs of repairing environmental damage caused by an intentional attack during an armed conflict.[228]

There is, however, no international law mechanism to enforce liability and payment of compensation. The Barcelona Convention 1976, article 22 provides settlement of disputes through negotiation or any other peaceful means or arbitration by common agreement. A claim for reparation brought by Lebanon before the ICJ would have to be referred to the Court by special agreement (ICJ Statute article 36(1)) between both countries, to which Israel will not agree or fall under the ICJ compulsory jurisdiction (article 36(2)) that neither Lebanon nor Israel has accepted.

As of January 2025, Israel and Lebanon are in a fragile 60 day ceasefire agreed on 27 November 2024 extended to 18 February 2025, to halt the armed conflict between Israel and Hezbollah that started in October 2023.[229] The agreement calls for full implementation of UNSC Resolution 1701 adopted in 2006, deployment of the LAF to southern Lebanon following withdrawal of Israeli forces, dismantling Hezbollah infrastructure and confiscating its weapons. Having recently elected a president and appointed a prime minister, Lebanon needs to form a new government. Daily violations of the cease-fire and Resolution 1701 are recorded.[230]

The ceasefire should be a springboard for permanent arrangement of relations between Israel and Lebanon. Accountability is key to future peace and security between Israel and Lebanon. The LAF must control Lebanese territory, guaranteeing that no armed group shall attack Israel.

Israel must compensate Lebanon for damage to the environment and natural resources caused by the 2006 war and damage caused by its use of unlawful white phosphorous bombs in 2024.[231] Compensation claims could be settled by direct negotiations between Lebanon and Israel within the general framework of a peace treaty or by appointing by common agreement an institution similar to the UNCC for damage

225 UNCC Governing Council decision 7 (S/AC.26/1991/7/Rev.1) par.35

226 UNGA, *Oil Slick on Lebanese Shores, A/RES/61/194, 20 December 2006* UNGA, *Oil Slick on Lebanese Shores, A/RES/77/157, 27 December 2022*

227 Ibid, A/RES/77/157, 27 December 2022 par.5

228 Mara Tignino, *Water during and after Armed Conflicts: What Protection under International Law?* (Brill 2016) 33

229 Announcement of a Cessation of Hostilities and Related Commitments on Enhanced Security Arrangements and Towards the Implementation of UNSCR 1701, in Josephine Deeb, 'Full Text of the Ceasefire Agreement between Israel and Lebanon' Middle East Eye online 27 November (2024)

230 UN News website, 'UN officials Call for Ceasefire Compliance after 15 People Killed in Lebanon, 26 January 2025'

231 HRW, *Lebanon: Israel's White Phosphorous Use Risks Civilian Harm, June 5* (2024)

claims settlement. Lebanon has endured a 22-year occupation, several invasions and wars from Israel. It is time for diplomacy. It is the only route to emerge from this recurring cycle of violence. It is hoped that reason and humanity will prevail.

Bibliography

Treaties

Cairo Agreement between the Lebanese Authorities and the Palestinian Commando Organizations, 3 November 1969

Convention on Cluster Munitions (CCM), Dublin, 30 may 2008, Oslo 3–4 December 2008, entry into force 1 August 2010

Protocol Additional to the Geneva Conventions of 12 August 1949, and relating to the Protection of Victims of International Armed Conflicts (Protocol I), 8 June 1977

Protocol Additional to the Geneva Conventions of 12 August 1949, and relating to the Protection of Victims of Non-International Armed Conflicts (Protocol II)

Protocol Concerning Mediterranean Specially Protected Areas, 1982

The Convention on Wetlands of International Importance especially as Waterfowl Habitat, Ramsar, 2.2.1971 as amended by the Protocol of 3.12.1982 and the Amendments of 28.5.1987

The Hague Regulations

The Lebanese-Israeli General Armistice Agreement, 23 March 1949

The Taif Agreement, September 1989

UNESCO Convention for the Protection of the World Cultural and Natural Heritage, 23 November 1972

International organizations documents

Amnesty International, *Israel/Lebanon: Deliberate Destruction or "Collateral Damage"? Israeli Attacks on Civilian Infrastructure* (2006)

FAO, *Lebanon: Damage and Early Recovery Needs: Assessment of Agriculture, Fisheries and Forestry* (2006)

First Semi-annual Report of the Secretary-General to the Security Council on the Implementation of Resolution 1559 (2004), S/2005/272 (26 April 2005)

HRW, *Flooding South Lebanon: Israel's Use of Cluster Munitions in Lebanon in July and August 2006* (2008)

ICRC *Commentary on Convention (III) Relative to the Treatment of Prisoners of War, Geneva, 12 August 1949* (1960)

———, *Commentary on the Protocol Additional to the Geneva Conventions of 12 August 1949, and relating to the Protection of Victims of International Armed Conflicts (Protocol I), 8 June 1977* (Sandoz Y, Swinarski C and Zimmermann B eds, Martinus Nijhoff 1987)

———, *Customary International Humanitarian Law, Vol. I Rules* (Henckaerts J-M and Doswald-Beck L eds, 3rd edn, CUP 2009)

ILC, *Articles on Responsibility of States for Internationally Wrongful Acts, with Commentary, A/56/10* (ILC YB 2001, vol II (2))

———, *Draft Articles on Prevention of Transboundary Harm from Hazardous Activities, with commentaries, A/56/10* (ILC YB 2001, vol II (2))

———, *Responsibility of States for Internationally Wrongful Acts* (ILC YB 2001, vol II (Part Two))

IMO Marine Environment Protection Committee (MEPC), *Guidance on Managing Seafood Safety during and after Oil Spills, 46th session* (2001)

International Crisis Group, *Lebanon: Managing the Gathering Storm* (5 December 2005)

Landmine Action, *Foreseeable Harm, the Use and Impact of Cluster Munitions in Lebanon: 2006* (2006)
Landmine and Cluster Munitions Monitor, *Lebanon, Impact* (15 September 2023)
Landmine Monitor, *Landmine Monitor Report* (2009)
Lebanon Mine Action Centre, *Lebanon Mine Action Strategy 2011–2020* (September 2011)
MAG International website, 'Lebanon, Why We Work in Lebanon'
Mine Action Review website, *Lebanon, Clearing Cluster Munitions Remnants* (2020)
Ramsar. The Convention on Wetlands website, Ramsar Handbooks 4th ed., Handbook 1 Wise Use of Wetlands (2010)
Report of the Secretary-General pursuant to Security Council resolution 1559 (2004), S/2004/777 (1 October, 2004)
Third Semi-annual Report of the Secretary-General to the Security Council on the implementation of Security Council Resolution 1559 (2004), S/2006/248
UN Commission of Inquiry, *Report on Lebanon Pursuant to Human Rights Council resolution S-2/1, A/HRC/3/2* (2006)
UN Commission of Inquiry on Lebanon, *Report of the UN Commission of Inquiry on Lebanon pursuant to Human Rights Council Resolution S-2/1* (2006)
UN *Common Country Assessment Lebanon* (2007)
UN Division of Ocean Affairs and the Law of the Sea, *UNCLOS, Consolidated Table of Ratifications/accessions*
UNCED, *Agenda 21, the UN Programme of Action from Rio* (3–4 June 1992)
UNDP, *CBU Contamination by Land Use* (2006)
———, *Lebanon Rapid Environmental Assessment for Greening Recovery, Reconstruction and Reform (prepared by ELARD)* (2007)
———, *UNDP's Participation in Lebanon's Recovery in the Aftermath of the July 2006 War* (2007)
———, *Support to the National Demining Office* (2008)
UNEP, *Lebanon: Post-conflict Environmental Assessment* (2007)
——— 'Mediterranean Action Plan, Status of Signatures and Ratifications of the Barcelona Convention and its Protocols'
———, News Centre, *Clean Up Strategy for Oiled Lebanese Coast Given Green Light, IMO and UNEP Meeting Backs Euro 50 Million Anti-Pollution Action Plan* (2006)
UNESCO, *Report by the Director General on the Implementation Programme adopted by the General Conference, Information Document on UNESCO Assistance to Post-Crisis Recovery and Reconstruction in Lebanon, (175 EX/INF.14)* (27 September 2006)
UNGA, *Oil Slick on Lebanese Shores, A/RES/61/194* (20 December 2006)
———, *Oil Slick on Lebanese Shores, A/RES/77/157* (27 December 2022)
UNHRC, *Mission to Lebanon and Israel, Implementation of General Assembly Resolution 60/251 of 15 March 2006, UN Doc. A/HRC/2/7* (2 October 2006)
United Nations Environmental Programme (UNEP), *Lebanon: Post-conflict Environmental Assessment* (2007)
UNSC, *Resolution 425, Israel-Lebanon, 19 March 1978* (1978)
———, *Resolution 426, Israel-Lebanon, 19 March 1978* (1978)
———, *Resolution 1701, 11 August 2006, S/RES/1701* (2006)
World Bank, Sustainable Development Department, MENA Region, *Report No. 39787-LB, Republic of Lebanon: Economic Assessment of Environmental Degradation Due to July 2006 Hostilities, Sector Note* (2007)
World Bank, Sustainable Development Department, MENA Region, *Report No. 41421-LB, Republic of Lebanon Electricity Sector Public Expenditure Review* (2008)

National legislation and national institutions documents

Address of Prime Minister Siniora to the US Congress, 'Lebanon Today Is Taking the First Steps in a New Phase of Its Modern History' The Daily Star, 1 August 2005

Agency for Toxic Substances & Disease Registry (ATSDR), U.S. Department of Health and Human Services, Public Health Service, *Nickel, Toxicological Profile for Nickel* (2006)
Consultation and Research Institute, *The Post-Conflict Social and Livelihoods Assessment in Lebanon* (2007)
House of Commons FAC, *Global Security: The Middle East* (2007)
Israel Ministry of Foreign Affairs, 'Israel-Hizbullah Conflict: Victims of Rocket Attacks and IDF Casualties' accessed 16 October 2014
Lebanese Republic, *Recovery, Reconstruction and Reform, International Conference for Support to Lebanon* (2007)
Lebanese Republic Ministry of Environment, *International Environmental Agreements, Treaties and Protocols Signed or Ratified by the Government of Lebanon*
PM Address to the Lebanese People, 15 July 2006

International tribunal decisions

Application of the Convention on the Prevention and Punishment of the Crime of Genocide (Bosnia and Herzegovina v. Serbia and Montenegro), Judgment ICJ Rep 2007
Legality of the Threat or Use of Nuclear Weapons, Advisory Opinion ICJ Rep 1996
Pulp Mills on the River Uruguay (Argentina v. Uruguay), Judgment, ICJ Rep 2010, p. 14

Journal articles

Addis CL and Blanchard CM, 'Analyst in Middle Eastern Affairs' *Hezbollah: Background and Issues for Congress* (CRS Report for Congress Prepared for Members and Committees of Congress, 8 October 2010)
Barak E, 'None to Be Trusted: Isreal's Use of Cluster Munitions in the Second Lebanon War and the Case for the Convention on Cluster Munitions' 25 Am U Int'l L Rev 2009–2010 423 423
Bloom C, 'The Classification of Hezbollah in Both International and Non-International Armed Conflicts' 14 Ann Surv Int'l Comp L 2008 61
Breitegger A, 'Preventing Human Suffering during and after Conflict? The Complementary Case for a Specific Convention on Cluster Munitions' 10 Austrian Rev Int'l Eur L 2005 3 3
Cannizzaro E, 'Contextualizing Proportionality: *Jus ad Bellum* and *Jus in Bello* in the Lebanese War' 88 IRRC 864 779
Cockburn P, 'Deadly Harvest, Lebanese Villagers Must Risk Death in Fields "Flooded" with More Than a Million Israeli Cluster Bombs – Or Leave Crops to Rot' The Independent, 18 September 2006
Cohen-Almagor R and Haleva-Amir S, 'The Israel-Hezbollah War and the Winograd Committee' JPPL 2 2008 27–44 27
Corn GS, 'Hamdan, Lebanon, and the Regulation of Hostilities: The Need to Recognize a Hybrid Category of Armed Conflict' 40 Vand J Transnat L 2007 305
Falk R and others, 'Problems of the Law of Armed Conflict in Lebanon' 77 ASIL Proceedings of the Annual Meeting, April 14–16, 1983 214
Fisk R, 'Despite Floods of Soldiers, Assassinations Still Continue. No One Is Safe in Lebanon' The Independent, 13 December 2005
———, 'The Arab Awakening Began Not in Tunisia This Year, but in Lebanon in 2005' The Independent, Friday 15 April 2011
Harel A, 'Hezbollah Kills 8 Soldiers, Kidnaps 2 in Offensive on Northern Border' Haaretz (2006)
Hersh SM, 'Watching Lebanon, Wahington's Interests in Israel's War' The New Yorker, 21 August 2006
Hirst D, '*Beware of Small States: Lebanon, Battleground of the Middle East*' (Faber and Faber (GB), Nation Books (US), 2010)
Hulme K, 'Of Questionable Legality: The Military Use of Cluster Bombs in Iraq in 2003' 42 Can YB Int'l L 2004 143 143

Kattan V, 'The Use and Abuse of Self-Defence in International Law: The Israel-Hezbollah Conflict as a Case Study' 12 YIMEL 2005–2006 31

Kretzmer D, 'The Inherent Right to Self-Defence and Proportionality in *Jus ad Bellum*' 24 EJIL No.1 2013

McDonnell TM, 'Cluster Bombs over Kosovo: A Violation of International Law?' 44 Ariz L Rev 2002 31 31

Murphy K, 'Old Feud Over Lebanese River Takes New Turn' Los Angeles Times (10 August 2006)

Paulus A and Vashakmadze M, 'Asymmetrical War and the Notion of Armed Conflict – a Tentative Conceptualization' 91 IRRC 873 2009 95

Rapoport M, 'What Lies Beneath' Haaretz (7 September 2006)

Ronen Y, 'Israel Hezbollah and the 2nd Lebanon War' 9 YB Int'l Humanit L 2006

Rowayheb MG, 'Political Change and the Outbreak of Civil War: The Case of Lebanon' 13 Civil Wars 4 2011 414

Roy S, 'Impact of Israeli Bombs Shatters Lebanon's Priceless Roman Legacy' The Observer, 17 September 2006

Saliba N and others, 'Origin and Variability of Particulate Matter (PM10 and PM2.5) Mass Concentrations over an Eastern Mediterranean City' 97 Atmospheric Research, Issues 1–2, July 2010, 106

Salloukh B, 'Syria and Lebanon: A Brotherhood Transformed' 236 Middle East Report, Fall (2005), 14

Wang M, 'The Unprecedented Ramsar Resolution: Ukrainian Wetlands Protection in Armed Confict' 70 NILR 323

Wiebe V, 'Footprints of Death: Cluster Bombs as Indiscriminate Weapons under International Humanitarian Law' 22 Mich J Int'l L 2000–2001 85 85

Yuile A, 'At the Fault-Lines of Armed Conflict: The 2006 Israel-Hezbollah Conflict and the Framework of International Humanitarian Law' 16 Austl Int'l L J 2009 189

Zeitoun M, Eid-Sabbagh K, and Loveless J, 'The Analytical Framework of Water and Armed Conflict: A Focus on the 2006 Summer War between Israel and Lebanon' 38 Disasters 1 2014 22

Zimmermann A, 'The Second Lebanon War: Jus ad bellum, jus in bello and the Issue of Proportionality' 11 Max Planck YB UN L. 2007 99

Electronic articles

Deeb J, 'Full Text of the Ceasefire Agreement between Israel and Lebanon' Middle East Eye online 27 November 2024

Encyclopaedia Britannica, 'Israel, War in Lebanon' accessed 5 January 2021

ICRC, 'States Party to the Following International Humanitarian Law and Other Related Treaties, as of 3rd September 2024'

Külbel JC, 'La longue route d'Israel vers la guerre de juillet 2006' Voltaire Édition Internationale

Mehlis D, 'Chronology of Events Mid 2004- September 2005'

MENA Research Centre, 'Les Politiques du Hezbollah au Liban: Des Crimes qui Dépassent l'Assassinat, November 26, 2021'

UN News website, 'UN officials Call for Ceasefire Compliance after 15 People Killed in Lebanon, 26 January 2025'

Books – reports

Association for Forests Development and Conservation, *War Impact on Forest Resources and Olive Groves in South Lebanon* (2007)

Boyle A and Redgwell C, *Birnie, Boyle and Redgwell's International Law and the Environment* (4th edn, OUP 2021)

Cohen A, *The Lebanon War and the Application of the Proportionality Principle* (International Law Forum of the Hebrew University of Jerusalem, Law Faculty 2007)
Gardam JG, *Necessity, Proportionality and the Use of Force by States* (CUP 2004)
Harik JP, *Hezbollah: The Changing Face of Terrorism* (I.B. Tauris 2005)
Henckaerts J-M and Doswald-Beck L, *Customary International Humanitarian Law, Vol. I Rules* (3rd edn, ICRC and CUP 2009)
HRW, *Lebanon: Israel's White Phosphorous Use Risks Civilian Harm, June 5* (2024)
Hulme K, *War Torn Environment: Interpreting the Legal Threshold* (Martinus Nijhoff 2004)
Knudsen A, *Precarious Peacebuilding: Post-war Lebanon, 1990–2005, CMI Working Paper 2005:12* (2005)
Sabra AH, *Oil Spill Contaminants in Selected Vertebrates and Invertebrates of the Eastern Mediterranean Sea, Master's Thesis* (American University of Beirut 2007)
Sands P and others, *Principles of International Environmental Law* (4th edn, CUP 2018)
Steiner R, *Lebanon Oil Spill Rapid Assessment and Response Mission: Final Report* (2006)
Strategic Foresight Group, *Water and Violence: Attacks on Water Infrastructure* (Blue Peace Bulletin, vol 10, October 2019)
Studies IaTICatCfS, *Hezbollah's Use of Lebanese Civilians as Human Shields* (2006)
Tamer-Chammas A, *Interview by the author of Pr Farran from the American University of Beirut, Advisor to the Ministry of Agriculture during the Post-conflict Phase (2006)* (August 2009)
The Public Committee Against Torture in Israel (PCATI), Graeme Goodman, Dr. Ishai Menuchin, Dr. Assaf Oron, *Special Report: November 2009, No Second Thoughts, The Changes in the Israeli Defense Forces' Combat Doctrine in Light of "Operation Cast Lead"*
Tignino M, *Water during and after Armed Conflicts: What Protection under International Law?* (Brill 2016)

Book chapters

Oeter S, 'Methods of Combat' in Fleck D (ed), *The Handbook of International Humanitarian Law* (4th edn, OUP 2021)
Scobbie I, 'Lebanon 2006' in Wilmhurst E (ed), *International Law and the Classification of Conflicts* (OUP 2012)
World Bank, 'Chapter 6, Oil Spill and Waste Due to Conflict: The Case of Lebanon (WB198-TCED.CH06)' in (Oil-spill-info)

6 Environment under occupation

Occupied Palestinian Territory

This chapter analyses the legal regime regulating natural resources that are part of the environment, mainly land and water, in the Occupied Palestinian Territory ("OPT"), in view of Israel's obligations as its occupant under the LOAC, IEL and IHRL. The general background is presented, from its historical political setting to the legal framework applicable to the OPT. The land and water legal regimes are then studied separately. Rules are recalled herein but reference should be made to Chapter 3 for detailed analysis of occupation and IHRL rules and Chapter 4 for IEL and IWL rules. This chapter written before the 2023–2024 war in Gaza between Israel and Hamas started, does not cover it or other wars in the OPT since 1967. The focus is on natural resources under occupation.

I. General background

1. Historical political setting

Part of the Ottoman Empire until 1918, Palestine did not gain independence despite Britain's promise of support and recognition of the independence of Arabs in Palestine and other countries, against their assistance in fighting the Turks in World War I,[1] repeated in the Sykes-Picot agreement[2] and Palestine's recognition as nation and State by treaty and arbitration. Palestine was among Ottoman "territories" to be disposed into "new States within their frontiers," under the Versailles Treaty[3] and whose former "communities" were sufficiently developed (Iraq, Palestine and Syria) that their "existence as independent nations" was provisionally recognized, subject to Mandatory assistance[4] and confirmed, except for Palestine, at the 1920 San Remo Conference granting mandate over these nations to Britain and France.[5]

1 Victor Kattan, *From Coexistence to Conquest, International Law and the Origins of the Arab-Israeli Conflict, 1891–1949* (Pluto Press 2009) 40, and Chapter 4 The Hussein-MacMahon Correspondence, 98–116 for a detailed analysis

2 The Sykes Picot Agreement, 16 May 1916 art.1

3 Treaty of Peace with Germany (Treaty of Versailles) of 28 June 1919 art.434

4 Covenant of the League of Nations, Part I of the Treaty of Versailles, June 28 1919 (entry into force 10 January 1920) art.22

5 San Remo Conference (UK, France, Italy, Japan), Resolution of 25 April 1920

DOI: 10.4324/9780367823283-6

The Ottoman public debt arbitration referred to newly created States (Iraq, Palestine, Transjordan, Syria and Lebanon), required to pay annuities on the debt under the Lausanne Peace Treaty,[6] in its decision.[7] Britain was responsible for implementing the declaration made by Balfour, British Secretary for Foreign Affairs, in 1917 to Lord Rothschild that the government viewed favourably "the establishment in Palestine of a national home for the Jewish people."[8] It administered Palestine and Transjordan under two separate legal regimes,[9] transferring authority to Transjordan in 1928[10] and independence in 1946.[11]

In 1947, the UNGA voted on the partition of Palestine, comprising about 1.25 million Arab Palestinians and 650,000 Jewish inhabitants into independent Arab and Jewish States, with Jerusalem under international Trusteeship[12] giving 56 percent of Mandate Palestine to the Jewish population who owned less than 7 percent of the land.[13] Scholars discussed whether the UNGA had legal competence to dispose of a territory and if its resolution was legally binding at the time.[14] The UN Partition Resolution was never implemented.[15] Armed conflict erupted between Palestinians and Jews, Arab countries joining later. Israel declared its establishment on 14 May 1948. At the end of the war, it controlled about three-fourths (78 percent) of Mandate Palestine,[16] including West Jerusalem which was supposed to be internationalized.[17]

6 British Empire, France, Italy, Japan, Greece, & C. and Turkey, Treaty of Peace (Lausanne, 24 July 1923) art.47, 60, Protocol XII art.9

7 *Affaire de la Dette publique ottomane (Bulgarie, Irak, Palestine, Transjordanie, Grèce, Italie et Turquie) 18 avril 1925, 1 UNRIIA pp. 529–614* 529 609

8 Mandate for Palestine, League of Nations, 12 August 1922 Preamble, art.2, art.4; Kattan 42; Declaration of November 2, 1917 'Palestine for the Jews: Official Sympathy' The Times, 9 November 1917, 7

9 Iain Scobbie, with Sarah Hibbin, *The Israel-Palestine Conflict in International Law: Territorial Issues* (The U.S./Middle East Project 2009) 5

10 20 February 1928 Agreement between the United Kingdom and Transjordan respecting the Administration of the Latter. See 128 British and Foreign State Papers 273; and United Kingdom Treaty Series No7 (1930). Scobbie 5–6

11 22 March 1946 Treaty, (Treaty Series Vol. 6, No.74, p. 143), replaced by 15 March 1948 Treaty of Alliance between the United Kingdom and Transjordan, (77 United Nations Treaty Series No. 994, p. 1)

12 UNGA, *Resolution 181 adopted on the Report of the Ad Hoc Committee on the Palestinian Question, 29 November 1947* Part I, A, par.3; Instead of the old denominations "Arabs of Palestine," "Arab Palestinians" or "Arabs" reference is made to Palestinians.

13 Benny Morris, *The Birth of the Palestinian Refugee Problem Revisited* (Online publication date: June 2012, 2nd edn, CUP 2004) 7, 360; UN Ad Hoc Committee on the Palestinian Question, *Report of Sub-Committee 2, A/AC.14/32* (1947) par.67–68, Appendix 4, 5. Rachad Antonius, 'Palestine-Israel: Moments structurants et droit international (1917–2015)' Guerres mondiales et conflits contemporains, No. 262, Moyen-Orient et conflits au XXe siècle (Avril–Juin 2016) 116; John Quigley, *Palestine and Israel, A Challenge to Justice* (DUP 1990) 36

14 Quigley Chap.6, Whose Land to Give, the UN Power over Palestine

15 Ernst C. Dawn, 'The Arab-Israeli Confrontation: A Historian's Analysis' 5 Denver J Int'l L Policy (1975) 373, 373 For a legal analysis of the events preceding the creation of Israel, see Kattan

16 Alexandre (Sandy) Kedar, 'The Legal Transformation of Ethnic Geography: Israeli Law and the Palestinian Landholder 1948–1967' 33 NYU J Int'l L Policy (2000–2001) 923 945–946

17 UN Committee on the Exercise of the Inalienable Rights of the Palestinian People, *The Status of Jerusalem* (1977) 6

The borders of the 1949 Armistice Agreements between Israel and its neighbours were never formally recognized by Israel or the international community yet became de facto annexation of this 22 percent of Palestine territory.[18] From about 800,000 to 900,000 Palestinians who lived before 1948 in the territory incorporated into Israel, 160,000 remained by the end of 1949,[19] (half of them Bedouins in the Negev),[20] with about 750,000 Palestinian refugees in 1950.[21] The West Bank (20 percent of Mandate Palestine) was merged with Transjordan into the Hashemite Kingdom of Jordan in 1950, in an annexation illegal under international law and not recognized internationally.[22] The Gaza strip (3 percent of Mandate Palestine) was under Egyptian military rule, although never annexed.

During the 1967 six-day war, Israeli forces occupied East Jerusalem, Gaza and the West Bank. UNSC Resolution 242 (1967) called for Israeli withdrawal from occupied territories and peace negotiations.[23] The 1987 popular uprising (*intifada)* in the OPT, followed by severance of links between the West Bank and Jordan[24] and a declaration of the State of Palestine by the Palestine National Council,[25] led to an Israeli-Palestinian Declaration of Principles in 1993 ("Oslo I")[26] and a temporary Interim Agreement on the West Bank and Gaza Strip in 1995 ("Oslo II").[27] Israel recognized the Palestinian Liberation Organisation ("PLO") as the representative of the Palestinian people and the PLO recognized the right of the State of Israel to live in peace and security.[28] Hamas, an armed group established in 1987 opposed to the peace process, designated as terrorist by multiple countries, ruled Gaza since winning elections for the Palestinian Legislative Council in 2006, except for a period of government between 2014 until 2018 by the Palestinian Authority ("PA") when it cut its funding, as it was unable to govern Gaza.[29] Negotiations on a permanent settlement have stalled, leading to multiple violent clashes, *intifada*, military

18 Antonius 117

19 Kedar 943–944; George E. Bisharat, 'Land, Law, and Legitimacy in Israel and the Occupied Palestinian Territories' 43 Am Uni L Rev (1993–1994) 467, 503 Bisharat notes that between December 1947 and November 1948 about 770,000 to 780,000 Palestinians left the territory of Palestine that would become included in Israel.

20 Quigley 86, citing 900,000 Palestinians in 1947 and 120,000 remaining

21 UNRWA, 'Where We Work'; Morris Appendix 1 the Number of Palestinian Refugees, 602–604

22 Eyal Benvenisti and Eyal Zamir, 'Private Claims to Property Rights in the Future Israeli-Palestinian Settlement' 89 AJIL No. 2, April (1995) 301–302 and ftnote 34.

23 UNSC, *Resolution 242, 22 November 1967, S/RES/242* (1967)

24 'Statement Concerning Disengagement from the West Bank and Palestinian Self-Determination, Address by His Majesty King Hussein I to the Nation, 31 July 1988' 27 ILM 6, November (1988) 1637

25 Palestine National Council, *Letter dated 18 November 1988 from the Permanent Representative of Jordan to the United Nations addressed to the Secretary-General, A/43/827, S/20278* (1988)

26 Israeli-Palestinian Declaration of Principles on Interim Self-Government Arrangements (13 September 1993) art.1

27 Israeli-Palestinian Interim Agreement on the West Bank and the Gaza Strip (28 September 1995) (Oslo II), Preamble, art. XXXI

28 Yitzhak Rabin, Prime Minister of Israel, *Letter to Yasser Arafat, September 9, 1993*; Yasser Arafat, PLO Chairman, *Letter to Yitzhak Rabin, Prime Minister of Israel, 9 September 1993*

29 The Editors of Encyclopaedia Britannica and Adam Zeidan, 'Hamas (2023)'

confrontations, Israeli invasion and blockade of Gaza since 2007 and full scale wars, the latest one between Israel and Hamas in Gaza starting in 2023.

As of June 2024, 146 States have recognized the State of Palestine.[30] The ICJ and ICC drew similar conclusions.[31] A UNGA resolution granted to Palestine the status of non-member observer State.[32] A UNSC vote on admitting Palestine as a UN full member State was vetoed by the US, with the UK and Switzerland abstaining.[33]

2. *Population*

The West Bank is a territory of 5,660 km^2 (5.660 million dunums), excluding the East Jerusalem area and Gaza, a coastal strip of 365 km^2.[34] Palestinians were estimated at 5.6 million in the OPT (3.3 million in the West Bank, including East Jerusalem and 2.2 million in Gaza) as of mid-2024.[35] More than 70 percent of Gaza's population are descendants from historic Palestine refugees from the 1948 war, the majority living in eight camps established in 1952 by the United Nations Relief and Works Agency for Palestine Refugees in the Near East ("UNRWA"). More than 871,000 registered refugees live in the West Bank.[36] As of 2021, 280 Israeli settlements (138 officially recognized), including 150 outposts not officially recognized and 40 agricultural farms, were established in the West Bank.[37] Between Oslo I Declaration of Principles in 1993 and the 2020 breakdown of negotiations on permanent status at camp David, settlers' population increased by 50 percent in the OPT[38] and, between 2016 and 2022, by 12 percent in the West Bank and East Jerusalem.[39] By 2023, settlers numbered about 465,000 in the West Bank and 230,000 in East Jerusalem.[40]

3. *Legal framework of administration of Occupied Palestinian Territory*

3.1 Applicable laws

The Hague Regulations (the "Regulations") are customary international law applicable to the OPT, as recognized by the Israeli High Court of Justice ("HCJ"). Israel's

30 UN, *UN Experts Urge all States to Recognise State of Palestine, 3 June 2024*

31 *Legal Consequences of the Construction of a Wall in the Occupied Palestinian Territory, Advisory Opinion* ICJ Rep 2004, 136 par.162; Hugh Lovatt, European Council on Foreign Relations, *Occupation and Sovereignty: Renewing EU Policy in Israel-Palestine* (2017) 10

32 U.N. Doc. A/RES/67/19 (29 November 2012)

33 UNSC, *S/PV.9609, 18 April 2024* (2024)

34 PCBS, 'Area, Population, and Population Density in Palestine by Governorate, 2021'; 1 dunum = 1,000 m^2. 10 dunums = 1 hectare. Referred to also as dunams

35 PCBS, 'Estimated Population in Palestine Mid-Year by Governorate,1997–2026'

36 UNRWA Gaza Strip, West Bank; Basem Shomar, 'Water Scenarios in the Gaza Strip, Palestine: Thirst, Hunger and Disease' 68 Int'l J Env Stud 4 (2011) 477, 479

37 B'Tselem, *This Is Ours – And This, Too, Israel's Settlement Policy in the West Bank* (2021) 9

38 David Kretzmer and Yaël Ronen, *The Occupation of Justice, The Supreme Court of Israel and the Occupied Territories* (2nd edn, OUP 2021) 181

39 UN, *Report of the Committee on the Exercise of the Inalienable Rights of the Palestinian People, A/77/35* (2022) par.12–13, 94

40 UNHCHR, *Israeli settlements in the Occupied Palestinian Territory, including East Jerusalem, and in the occupied Syrian Golan, A/HRC/55/72, 1st February* (2024) par.9

previous claim that GC IV was unapplicable, because the OPT were not part of the territory of a High Contracting Party under GC IV article 2[41] or under a legitimate sovereign authority, as claimed by the Levy report,[42] is "universally rejected"[43] by the international community[44] and invalid under international law.[45] According to Kretzmer, the Levy Committee was "established to find a way, if possible, to 'legalize' settlements established in the Territories without government approval."[46] The OPT and East Jerusalem "are incontrovertibly subject to" GC IV.[47] Israel declared that it would act according to its "humanitarian" provisions.[48] The provisions of AP/I, not signed or ratified by Israel, are applicable to the extent they are customary international law.[49] International environmental law, water law and human rights law are applicable during occupation, the LOAC being considered *lex specialis* applicable to armed conflicts.

3.2 Oslo process and Israeli withdrawal from Gaza

A debated question is whether occupation of Palestinian Territory ended, following the Oslo Accords and 2005 Israeli withdrawal from Gaza. Under Oslo II, West Bank and Gaza are divided into three administrative areas:[50] "A" and "B" under Palestinian police control[51] and "C" (60 percent of the West Bank) under Israeli control.[52] In Area B, police movement is subject to Israeli agreement[53] and Israel is responsible for public order, internal, external and overall security, despite

41 Orna Ben-Naftali, Aeyal M. Gross, and Keren Michaeli, 'Illegal occupation: framing the Occupied Palestinian Territory' 23 Berkeley J Int'l L 3 (2005) 551 567

42 Yehuda Z. Blum, 'The Missing Reversioner: Reflections on the Status of Judea and Samaria' 3 Israel L Rev (1968) 279. The Levy Commission, 'Report on the Legal Status of Building in Judea and Samaria, Conclusions and Recommendations, Jerusalem' 42 J Palestine Stud 1 (9 July 2012) 179–182.

43 Kretzmer, 'Bombshell for the Settlement Enterprise in Levy Report' Haaretz, July 10 (2012)

44 Richard Falk and Burns H. Weston, 'The Relevance of International Law to Israeli and Palestinian Rights in the West Bank and Gaza' in Emma Playfair (ed), *International Law and the Administration of the Occupied Territories* (OUP 1992) 132; Adam Roberts, 'What Is Military Occupation' 50 Brit YB Int'l L (1984) 249 281–282; Iain Scobbie, 'H2O after Oslo: Legal Aspects of Water in the Occupied Territories' 8 PYBIL (1994–1995) 79, 82; Ben-Naftali 569

45 Knut Dörmann and Sylvain Vité, 'Occupation' in Dieter Fleck (ed), *The Handbook of International Humanitarian Law* (4th edn, OUP 2021) 9.2 par.5

46 Kretzmer

47 Ardi Imseis, 'On the Fourth Geneva Convention and the Occupied Palestinian Territory' 44 Harvard Int'l L J 1, 97; *Resolution 5, Implementation of the Memorandum of Understanding and Agreement on Operational Arrangements, dated 28 November 2005, between the Palestine Red Crescent Society and the Magen David Adom in Israel* (ICRC 2011) par.1; *The Wall* par.101

48 Mazen Qupty, 'The Application of International Law in the Occupied Territories as Reflected in the Judgements of the High Court of Justice in Israel' in Emma Playfair (ed), *International Law and the Administration of the Occupied Territories* (OUP 1992) 88; Eyal Benvenisti, *The International Law of Occupation* (2nd edn, OUP 2012) 217

49 Ben Clarke, 'Military Occupation and the Rule of Law: the Legal Obligations of Occupying Forces in Iraq' 10 Int'l Trade Bus L Rev (2006) 133, 143

50 Oslo II, art. XI

51 Ibid, art. XI.2, art.XIII.1 (Area A), Oslo II, art. XI.2, XIII.2.b.(4)-(7) (Area B)

52 Ibid, art. XI.2, Annex III art. IV

53 Ibid, art. XI.2, XIII.2.b.(4)-(7)

military forces' redeployment obligation.[54] In Area C, transfer of powers to the PA's administration is limited.[55] Therefore, Israel maintains its controls over the West Bank which is still under occupation.[56]

In 2005, Israeli military troops withdrew from Gaza. Whether it remained occupied rests on determination of facts and the notion of effective control under international law.[57] The HCJ considered that the occupation ended and that Israel no longer has effective control over Gaza and no obligation to ensure public order, given that occupants' exercise of administrative powers requires forces on the ground.[58] However, arguing that Gaza occupation terminated with Israeli troops' withdrawal and the PA's assumption of authority[59] ignores the fact that the latter is incomplete. Israeli forces have maintained a blockade, a warfare means,[60] since 2007, controlling borders and space above the territory and the right to re-enter the area for security purposes,[61] as demonstrated by the conflict that started on October 2023. The ICJ judged that, after withdrawing its troops, Israel retains its capacity to exercise key elements of authority, border control, tax collection, restrictions of movements and military control over the buffer zone, exercising effective control over Gaza which remains under occupation.[62] Gross proposes a "functional" approach, as the conceptual approach as to whether an occupation exists amounts to "transcendental nonsense."[63]

54 Ibid, art. X, X.4, XX.1, XIII.2.a

55 Ibid, art. XI.2, Annex III art. IV

56 Kretzmer and Ronen 11 Scobbie 84–85; *The Wall* par.77; Benvenisti 211

57 Ben-Naftali 551

58 HCJ 102/82 *Tzemel v. Minister of Defence*. HCJ 201/09 Physicians for Human Rights v. Prime Minister, par.14

59 Leslie C. Green, *The Contemporary Law of Armed Conflict* (3rd edn, MUP 2008) 105 Elizabeth Samson, 'Is Gaza Occupied: Redefining the Status of Gaza under International Law' 25 Amsterdam Uni Int'l L Rev (2010) 915, 917 Avi Bell, and Dov Shefia, 'The Mythical Post-2005 Israeli Occupation of the Gaza Strip' 16 Israel Affairs 2 (2010) 268 Yaffa Zilbershats, 'Apartheid, International Law, and the Occupied Palestinian Territory: A Reply to John Dugard and John Reynolds' 24 EJIL 3 (2013) 915, 918

60 L. Oppenheim, *International Law, Vol. II Disputes, War and Neutrality* (H. Lauterpacht ed, 7th edn, Longmans, Green and Co. 1952) 768, par.368

61 Raja Shehadeh, 'The Gaza Occupation: Beginnings and Endings' 14 Palestine YB Int'l L (2006–2007) 13, 25; HRW, 'Israel/Egypt: Choking Gaza Harms Civilians' News release; John Dugard, *Report of the Special Rapporteur on the Situation of Human Rights in Palestinian Territories Occupied Since 1967* (2007)

62 *Legal Consequences arising from the Policies and Practices of Israel in the Occupied Palestinian Territory, including East Jerusalem, ICJ Advisory Opinion, 19 July 2024* ICJ par.90–94; See Shehadeh 25; HRW; Dugard; Yoram Dinstein, *The International Law of Belligerent Occupation* (2nd edn, CUP 2019) par.845–862

63 Aeyal Gross, *The Writing on the Wall, Rethinking the International Law of Occupation* (CUP 2017) 131

3.3 Military administration

Since 1948, Israel has been in an emergency state.[64] Britain's emergency regulations enacted between 1937 and 1945, comprehensive in scope, unlimited in time and excessive, including the 1945 Emergency (Defence) Regulations, were incorporated into Israeli legislation by the first act of its Provisional Council of State.[65] Administrative emergency orders, enacted for three months since 1948, are indefinitely renewable and remain applicable.[66] Israel has ruled the OPT through wide-ranging Military Orders ("MO") and secondary legislation, while applying Israeli law to settlers in the OPT.[67] Israel's Supreme Court, sitting as a first-instance High Court of Justice, has supervisory power over the military government in the OPT, through judicial review of its acts.[68] Since the 1960s, it has not interfered in decisions taken for military necessity by military authorities. Appeal of such decisions does not lead to results, arbitrariness of decisions remaining mostly unchallenged[69] with some changes from 2002. In 1981 Israeli military authorities established the Israeli Civil Administration ("ICA"), the military agency responsible for civil life in the West Bank, Area C, transferring its powers to the Palestinian Authority ("PA") under Oslo II.[70]

II. Land legal regime

1. Ottoman Empire

Early Ottoman codes integrated Islamic law with ordinances and decrees from the Sultan and local practices and customs.[71] The 1858 Ottoman Land Code remained the backbone of Palestine's land law system of Palestine, then Israel, until the 1964 Israeli land law.[72] Following legal reforms between 1870 and 1876, a Civil Code

64 The Knesset, 'Lexicon of Terms, Declaring a State of Emergency' The State of Israel, the Knesset website

65 Yoav Mehozay, 'The Fluid Jurisprudence of Israel's Emergency Powers: Legal Patchwork as a Governing Norm' 46 L Soc Rev March (2012) 137, 143; Law and Administration Ordinance No. 1 of 5708–1948, Laws of the State of Israel, Vol. I, Ordinances, 5708–1948, 7 par.11

66 Mehozay

67 Norwegian Refugee Council, *A Guide to Housing, Land and Property Law in Area C of the West Bank* (2012) 14, 15

68 Dinstein par.79; Basic Law: Judicature, 38 LSI 101, 104 (1983–4); Benvenisti 319

69 Geoffrey Aronson, 'Israel's Policy of Military Occupation' 7 J Palestine Stud 4, Summer (1978) 90–91

70 Norwegian Refugee Council 13

71 Ibid, 13; Melanne Andromecca Civic, 'A Comparative Analysis of the Israelis and Arab Water Law Traditions and Insights for Modern Water Sharing Agreements' 26 Denver J Int'l L Policy 3 (1997–1998) 437, 444

72 Raja Shehadeh, 'The Land Law of Palestine: An Analysis of the Definition of State Lands' 11 J Palestine Stud 2 (Winter 1982) 84; Kedar 932; Ahmad Amara, 'Civilizational Exceptions: Ottoman Law and Governance in Late Ottoman Palestine' 36 L Hist Rev 4 (November 2018) 915, 929

("Mejelle"), still residually applied in Jordan and Palestine, adapted and secularized previous law while retaining Islamic law principles on water and land.[73]

The Land Code classified land as:

(i) Endowment entrusted to charitable institutions[74] (*waqf*),
(ii) Publicly owned land administered for the population's benefit: *Miri*, *matrouk* and *mawat*.[75] Though the ultimate ownership (*rakaba*) lies with the sovereign, they were not State land but similar to land owned by the Crown and held directly or indirectly from it by tenants, under English law,[76]
(iii) Privately owned land (*mulk*), including land in built-up areas within a town suitable for dwellings or adjacent to *miri* land that was turned into *mulk* within the town boundaries as they were in 1858.[77]

Miri lands were arable fields, meadows, pasturing grounds and woodland close to villages, owned by the Sultan.[78] Public lands held in usufructuary,[79] usufruct (use of the land, *tasaruf*), was granted to a community member.[80] Use of *miri* land determined its ownership. Anyone who cultivated it during ten years at least without contest could acquire the land title and register it in his name (acquisition by adverse possession)[81] whereas he would lose his rights to land uncultivated during three years.[82] Most agricultural lands in the Ottoman Empire were *miri*.[83] *Matrouk* was land "left" to be used for public purposes, such as public highways or common pasture between several villages.[84] *Mawat* ("dead") land was "uncultivated wasteland remote from populated places,"[85] vacant, unpossessed by title-deed, where no

73 Civic 443; Abouali 445–446
74 Ilias Bantekas, 'Land Rights in Nineteenth Century Ottoman State Succession Treaties' 26 EJIL 2 (2015) 375, 380
75 Shehadeh, 'Land Law of Palestine' 86; Salman Abu Sitta, *The Denied Inheritance: Palestinian Land Ownership in Beer Sheba* (2009) 4
76 Shehadeh, 'Land Law of Palestine' 90, 93
77 Ibid, 86. Norwegian Refugee Council 23–24
78 Ibid, 84, 87; Ottoman Land Code, art.3
79 A. Cohen, 'Miri' Encyclopaedia of Islam. E. Attila Aytekin, 'Agrarian Relations, Property and Law: An Analysis of the Land Code of 1858 in the Ottoman Empire' 45 Middle E Stud 6, November (2009) 935, 937.
80 Abu Sitta 4. Shehadeh, 'Land Law of Palestine' 90–91
81 The Ottoman Land Code 1858 art.78; Kedar 935; Mogannam E. Mogannam, 'Palestine Legislation under the British' 64 Ann Am Acad Pol Soc Sci (November 1932) 51; Mark LeVine, 'Conquest Through Town Planning: The Case of Tel Aviv, 1921–48' 27 J Palestine Stud 4, Summer (1998) 37
82 Shehadeh, 'Land Law of Palestine' 83–84. Dr Gatteschi, 'Des Lois sur la Propriété Foncière dans l'Empire Ottoman et particulièrement en Egypte' 13 Rev Hist Dr F Etran (1855–1869), Editions Dalloz, (1867) 436, 450
83 Ibid, Abu Sitta Abu Sitta posits that 90 per cent of state land was *miri* land in Ottoman times.
84 Ottoman Land Code, art.5 Shehadeh, 'Land Law of Palestine' 87; LeVine 37.
85 Geremy Forman and Alexandre Kedar, 'Colonialism, Colonization, and Land Law in Mandate Palestine: The Zor al-Zarqa and Barrat Qisarya Land Disputes in Historical Perspective' 4 Theoretical Inq L (2003) 491, 502

human voice could be heard from it.[86] The person who revived the land by cultivating it with authorization acquired right to usufructuary title (*miri*)[87] and without authorization would be granted title deed against payment.[88]

2. *British mandate*

Ottoman land law was still in force in Mandate Palestine.[89] The Transfer of Land Ordinance (1920–1921) made it compulsory to record all land dispositions.[90] The 1928 Land (Settlement of Titles) Ordinance implemented a lengthy process of settlement of titles (not to be confused with settlements in later Israel) for disputed lands, through judicial investigation, surveys, determination of plots' boundaries and registration of titles. It remains, mostly unchanged, the legal basis for land in Palestine. By the end of the Mandate, settlement of about 20 percent only of land was done.[91] Under Ottoman law, title deed (*kushan*) was proof that the individual was given the right to use (*tasaruf*) but not actual ownership (*rakaba*) of the land. With more accurate land registration under British Mandate, the *kushan* came to recognize full ownership, though for historical reasons they were rare in the West Bank and most Palestinians relied on land cultivation and possession during ten years to acquire land title.[92] The British Mandate Supreme Court held that possession of *miri* land was acquired, even if left uncultivated during a ten-year cultivation period and not registered at the Land Registry.[93] Courts developed a "reasonable cultivation" doctrine, taking into consideration the nature of the land and suitability of crops.[94]

The 1921 *Mawat* Land Ordinance prohibited unauthorized future use of *mawat* land and required registration of title within two months from its date.[95] Cultivation of land without authorization could not lead to obtention of title deed.[96] Though *mawat* land understanding changed,[97] British authorities continued to recognize *mawat* rights acquired before the Ordinance, regardless of registration.[98] In the Negev, land matters were subject to tribal customary law and State law.[99] A "public

86 Islamic encyclopaedia; Gatteschi 442; The Ottoman Land Code, art.103 (Stanley Fisher trans., 1919).

87 Forman and Kedar 514 A.-M Delcambre, *Mawāt* (Brill Online 2012)

88 The Ottoman Land Code 1858 art.103

89 Cohen Gatteschi 441 Adam S. Hofri-Winograd, 'Zionist Settlers and the English Private Trust in Mandate Palestine' 30 L Hist Rev 3, August (2012) 813 826–827

90 Dov Gavish and Ruth Kark, 'The Cadastral Mapping of Palestine, 1858–1928' 159 Geogr J 1, March (1993) 70, 78

91 Kedar 938–939. Michael R. Fischbach, 'The United Nations and Palestinian Refugee Property Compensation' 31 J Palestine Stud No. 2 (2002), 41 Norwegian Refugee Council 34

92 Norwegian Refugee Council 25–26

93 B'Tselem, *By Hook and by Crook, Israeli Settlements Policy in the West Bank* (2010) 26

94 Norwegian Refugee Council 26–27

95 Forman and Kedar 514

96 Mogannam 51 Abu Sitta 19

97 LeVine 37

98 Forman and Kedar 515 Abu Sitta 19

99 Ahmad Amara, 'The Negev Land Question: Between Denial and Recognition' 42 J Palestine Stud Summer (2013) 27, 34

lands" category was introduced, comprising lands subject to the control of the Government of Palestine under treaty or succession and lands used or acquired for public service,[100] with rights in public lands, mines and minerals under concessions, vested in the High Commissioner, in trust for the Government of Palestine.[101] Lands over which the sovereign does not exercise control (*miri*, *mawat*, *matrouk*) are excluded.[102] Recognizing the need to avoid creating a "considerable landless Arab population,"[103] the 1940 Land Transfer Regulations prohibited land transfers in two zones in Palestine, except to Palestinians, subject to cases decided differently by the High Commissioner and a smaller one free of restrictions.[104]

3. West Bank under Jordanian rule

A 1952 law enacted to settle disputes regarding private rights and claims to land and water existing under applicable Ottoman law, created a centralized titles registry ("Land Registry").[105] Under Jordanian legislation, the State had ultimate ownership of *miri* land but no right of possession and permanent occupancy; it was not State land. Title to ownership of *miri* land could be proven by a sales contract with active land possession during ten years, even absent a settlement, amending previous law requiring registration at the Land Registry.[106] Jordanian law changed the category of lands from *miri* to *mulk* within municipal boundaries only.[107]

4. Israel 1948–1967

At the end of the 1948 war, areas controlled by Israel that were not part of the territory granted to it under the UN Partition Resolution were technically occupied territory under international law, though the issue has not been discussed much by doctrine. It may be considered that occupation law should have applied immediately after the war, particularly to Palestinian land and property in those areas, if Israel intended to observe the UN Resolution on the Partition Plan and withdraw from them. This section discusses how such properties were appropriated, mentioning relevant provisions under occupation law, though they would not be applicable to the territory assigned to Israel under the Resolution. Palestinian refugees' private claims to their property rights, including the right to regain possession of properties left behind or receive compensation for them, were postponed until

100 The Palestine Order-in-Council, 1922 art.2
101 Ibid, art.12
102 Shehadeh, 'Land Law of Palestine' 94
103 *British White Paper of 1939* Section III Land. Abu Sitta 19
104 The Land Transfers Regulations, 1940 par.3 and 4
105 The Law for Settlement of Titles to Land and Water, Law No. 40, 1952, at Official Gazette (Jordan) no. 1113, 16 June 1952, 279 art.17(1)
106 *The Concept of State Land in the Occupied Territories, Affidavit of Aziz Shehadeh* Palestine YB Int'l L 1985, 163; Jordanian Law No 51/58
107 Changing Miri Land to Mulk Land Law (No. 41), 1953; Norwegian Refugee Council 24

negotiations on a permanent status that were supposed to start in 1996 after Oslo II.[108] They are shelved at present.

4.1 Closed areas

Originally enacted by the British to protect military and police locations from terrorist activities, Regulation 125 allows the Military Commander to order an area closed and prohibit any movement in or out of it without written permission.[109] Three areas inhabited by about 85 percent of the Palestinians inside the armistice lines were "closed areas" until 1966 or later for some villages, subject to martial law under Regulation 125: a northern area including Galilee, central area and Beersheeba in the Negev desert, the largest sub-district of Palestine (about 62 percent of Israel today).[110] Prior to 1948, 103,820 Palestinians and 1,020 Jews lived in Beersheeba, while in Galilee Palestinians were 86,200 and the Jews 28,750.[111] The 11,000 Palestinian Beduins remaining in Beersheba, the others having fled during the war or been expelled, were transferred to a "closed area" of about 8 percent of the Negev.[112]

4.2 Abandoned and absentee private property

4.2.1 LEGISLATION

At the end of the war, a Ministerial Committee for Abandoned Property granted jurisdiction over abandoned villages to counter a policy of "destruction of villages, settlement of abandoned sites and prevention of Arab cultivation of fields"[113] was unable to control the situation.[114] Jewish agricultural settlements seized abandoned agricultural lands, requesting government's authorization to cultivate. The Agriculture Ministry, working with settlement councils and the Jewish federation of labour, allocated lands and provided subsidies.[115] Emergency Regulations on uncultivated lands (1948, 1949) empowered the Agriculture Minister to ratify past

108 Benvenisti and Zamir 295
109 Defense (Emergency) Regulations (1945), Regulation 125 Closed Areas
110 Quigley 106
111 UN Ad Hoc Committee on the Palestinian Question par.65–66, Appendix 2 Estimated population of proposed Jewish State as of 31 December 1946
112 Abu Sitta 21 Quigley 85, 106, 109; Amara, 'The Negev Land Question: Between Denial and Recognition' 35
113 Morris 349: The Transfer Committee proposal, "Retroactive transfer, a scheme for the solution of the Arab question in the State of Israel," May–June 1948; Quigley 57–58
114 Morris 172, 353–356. Geremy Forman and Alexandre (Sandy) Kedar, 'From Arab Land to 'Israel Lands': The Legal Dispossession of the Palestinians Displaced by Israel in the Wake of 1948' 22 Environ Plan D (2004) 809, 813
115 Morris 361, 362, 365. Forman and Kedar 813

and future seizure of lands by settlers and validate their exploitation and cultivation.[116] He could assume control of lands left uncultivated by landowners and of water resources and installations insufficiently utilized, employ workers or hand the land to others for cultivation.[117] Declaring an area closed would prevent Palestinian cultivators from reaching their land, which would be declared "fallow" (or "waste") and transferred to Jewish possession.[118] Ten million dunums were considered wasteland and transferred to the State of Israel.[119]

The 1948 Emergency Regulations Concerning Absentee Property allowed temporary possession only and prohibited sale or lease of absentee property for more than five years. However, "absentee" property was treated as State property, and one million dunums sold to the Jewish National Fund ("JNF"), a month after the regulations' promulgation.[120] The 1950 Absentees Property Law replaced them to provide permanent ownership. Absentees' immovable and movable property, proceeds and rights were vested in the Custodian Council for Absentee Property.[121] The "absentee" was (i) legal owner of property or property right in Israel, between 29 November 1947 and the day on which the state of emergency will cease, (ii) a Palestinian who left his residence in Palestine before 1 September 1948 for another State or area of Palestine held by Arab League forces at war with Israel or (iii) a national of – or in one of – these countries.[122] Palestinians who returned after leaving the land, even for a few days, were considered "present-absentees" or "non-absentees" even though they became Israeli residents or citizens.[123] The Custodian Council for Absentee Property was prohibited from selling or transferring ownership right of immovable property or leasing it for more than six years, except to the Development Authority ("DA") if it was established.[124] Established simultaneously, the DA was empowered to sell property to the State of Israel or the JNF.[125]

As the Custodian Council for Absentee Property had no title to property that he could sell, the 1953 Land Acquisition Law addressed the issue.[126] Property that was not in its owners' possession on 1 April 1952, and "was used or assigned for purposes of essential development, settlement or security" from 14 May 1948 to 1 April 1952 and still required for these purposes was vested in the DA to be

116 The Emergency Regulations (Cultivation of Waste Lands), (Extension of Validity) Ordinance No. 36 of 5709–1949 art.24; Also referred to as the Emergency Regulations regarding the Cultivation of Fallow Lands and Unexploited Water Sources, October 1948 (State of Israel, 1948b, pages 3–8), Forman and Kedar 814

117 Ibid, art.7, 17

118 Forman and Kedar 814

119 Amnesty International, *Israel's Apartheid against Palestinians* (2022) 126

120 Forman and Kedar 815

121 Absentees' Property Law, 5710–1950 art.1(a). 4(a) and (b)

122 Ibid, art.1(b)

123 Quigley 107; Forman and Kedar 815; Benvenisti and Zamir 300–301

124 Absentees' Property Law, 5710–1950 art.19(a)

125 Development Authority (Transfer of Property) Law, 5710–1950 art.2(a) and (b), art.3(a)

126 Norwegian Refugee Council, *The Absentee Property Law and its Implementation in East Jerusalem, a Legal Guide and Analysis* (2013) 10; Forman and Kedar 817

registered in its name in the Land Registry.[127] The law legalized retroactively past seizure of land, giving immunity to the State and the DA for any act done to the property before it became "acquired."[128] Though mentioned in the law, absentee owners received no compensation.[129] Under a Compensation Law promulgated in 1973,[130] after the illegal annexation of East Jerusalem rendered absentees residing there residents of Israel, compensation was inadequate and limited.[131] A 1965 law confiscated absentee *waqf* land.[132]

4.2.2. APPLICATION OF THE LAWS

Land confiscations were carried out based primarily on these laws. In Galilee, northern Israel, the Palestinians retained most of the land.[133] Israel created a land transfer fund. It accelerated settlement of titles that would freeze time for purposes of adverse possession, to prevent Palestinians from acquiring titles to lands possessed before 1948. It lengthened the period for which cultivators were required to prove unchallenged land possession to establish their titles to 15 years for unregistered lands and 25 years for registered lands.[134] Between 1948 and 1953, 350 settlements were established on "absentee" land.[135] The first year following the 1953 law, 1.2 million dunums were expropriated.[136] Within ten years between 3,200 km^2 and 4,600 km^2 of Palestinian lands were transferred to Jewish ownership.[137]

In the Negev, 85 percent of land was confiscated.[138] Before the war, Jews possessed less than 1 percent of the district's land, Palestinians 14 percent (i.e. *mulk*) and the remaining were "waste lands and lands under public ownership, consisting mainly of grazing lands attached to villages," (i.e. *mawat* and *miri* lands), according to the British government Survey of Palestine.[139] Lands of Palestinians transferred to a "closed area," considered "present-absentees," were confiscated under the Absentee Property Law and those located at the Armistice Line sold to the JNF.[140] Individual claims submitted by dispossessed landowners or entire villages, for return of their properties were unsuccessful. Return orders issued by the Supreme Court, if any, were ignored and villages destroyed, for example

127 Land Acquisition (Validation of Acts and Compensation) Law, 5713–1953 art.1, art.2(a), (b), (c)
128 Ibid, art.19
129 Ibid, art.3–8
130 The Absentee Property (Compensation) Law 5733–1973
131 Benvenisti and Zamir 301; Norwegian Refugee Council, Absentee Property Law 32
132 Quigley 108
133 UN Ad Hoc Committee on the Palestinian Question par.67
134 Bisharat 520; Kedar 949–953; Amnesty International 125; Prescription Law 5718–1958 art.22
135 Quigley 108
136 Forman and Kedar 821
137 Martin Gilbert, *Israel, a History* (Doubleday 1998) 256
138 Quigley 108
139 UN Ad Hoc Committee on the Palestinian Question par.67
140 Abu Sitta 21 Quigley 85, 106, 109; Amara, 'The Negev Land Question: Between Denial and Recognition' 27

Ikrit (1951) and Bikram (1953),[141] after being declared closed military zones, with court proceedings continuing for over 50 years in some cases.[142] Israel established "townships" for the Beduins, underfunded and lacking basic adequate services, water, healthcare and education. While they are 37 percent of the population, recognized Beduin villages constitute 1 percent of the Negev area, with about 90,000 living in 34 "unrecognized" villages, under constant threat of forced displacement and house demolition.[143]

4.2.3 ANALYSIS

The Regulations article 23(g) allowing seizure of property for military necessity during war, was arguably applicable to lands seized under the Emergency Regulations on uncultivated lands (1948) during transition between war and occupation, though not to lands seized under the amended 1950 Regulations, as hostilities had ended. There was no military necessity justifying seizure of lands belonging to Palestinians who had left; empty villages did not pose a military threat. Objectives of land seizures and confiscations were the need to develop Israel's economy and exploit the land[144] and prevent Palestinians from returning to their lands, as "the political decision to bar a return [of Palestinian refugees] . . . had become official policy" of Israel. "Jewish agriculture had to have the abandoned lands. Jewish settlements . . . needed more land. And the immigrants . . . required land and houses."[145]

Both Absentee Property (1950) and Land Acquisition (1953) laws legalized sale of Palestinian "Absentees" properties by the Custodian Council of Absentee Property and vested their ownership into the DA.[146] By selling property to the State or the JNF, the DA would give land title to the government,[147] acting as a "land-laundering" intermediary.[148] The UN partition resolution prohibited expropriation except for public purposes and subject to prior compensation.[149] Israel's failure to return properties to "absentees" owners returning to their land was not expropriation under the 1953 Law for public purposes, as no compensation was granted.[150] Legislators were seemingly aware of the illegality of transferring property in this way, as the 1953 law included provisions legalizing past and future land seizures, giving immunity to the government and the DA for their actions. Seizures

141 Forman and Kedar 819; Quigley 106

142 *International Law and the Israeli-Palestinian Conflict, a Rights-Based Approach to Middle East Peace* (Susan M. Akram and others eds, Routledge 2011) Chap.3 Refugees restitution and compensation, by Terry Rempel and Paul Pretittore, 85

143 Adalah, *Forced Displacement, Position Paper, May 2023*; US Department of State, *2022 Country Reports on Human Rights Practices: Israel, West Bank and Gaza* 76

144 Norwegian Refugee Council, Absentee Property Law 10, 12

145 Morris 334

146 Land Acquisition (Validation of Acts and Compensation) Law, 5713–1953 art.1, art.2(a),(b),(c)

147 Quigley 108; Development Authority (Transfer of Property) Law, 5710–1950 art.2(a),(b), art.3(a)

148 Norwegian Refugee Council, Absentee Property Law 11; Forman and Kedar 817

149 UNGA Resolution 181, Chap.2 par.8e

150 Benvenisti and Zamir 301

and confiscations violated the Regulations articles 23(g), 46, 47 and GC IV article 33 prohibiting confiscation and pillage of private property.

4.3 Requisitions

The 1949 Emergency Land Requisition (Regulation) Law authorized requisition of land which included any building, tree, portion of the sea, seashore or river and right in and over land or water "for the defence of the State, public security, the maintenance of essential supplies or essential public services, the absorption of immigrants or the rehabilitation of ex-soldiers or war invalids."[151] Requisitions of movable private property (foodstuffs) are only authorized for army maintenance needs and of immovable property restricted to quartering the army (Regulations art.52). Requisitions' purposes of "rehabilitation of ex-soldiers or war invalids" corresponds to accommodation needs and "maintenance of essential supplies" could arguably fall thereunder. However, "absorption of immigrants" and "defence of the State" do not, as army maintenance needs do not encompass security.[152] Requisitions for such purposes were confiscations of private property without compensation violating the Regulations articles 46 and 52 and violated the Regulations article 55 on administration under usufruct of public property, in addition to GC IV article 49 prohibiting settlements on occupied territory.

4.4 Public property

All public movable and immovable property of the Palestine authorities situated in Israel, mines and minerals wherever situated, and rights held by the British Mandate Government of Palestine (1 million dunums) and any ownerless property from 15 May 1948 or the day on which it becomes ownerless, if later, was declared to be property of the State of Israel from 15 May 1948,[153] violating the Regulations article 55 obligation to administer public immovable property as usufructuary, the UN Partition Resolution prohibiting expropriation without compensation and the principle of permanent sovereignty of Palestinians over their natural resources.

4.5 Land transfers

The Land Transfer Regulations were repealed in 1948 by an ordinance providing that "no judgement given on the basis of these Regulations shall be a bar to the lodging of a new claim in the same matter," with retroactive effect from 18 May 1939.[154]

151 The Emergency Land Requisition (Regulation) Law, 5710–1949, Laws of the State of Israel, Vol. 4, 5710–1949/50, 3 art.1, art.3(b)

152 Dörmann and Vité 9.33 par.3

153 State Property Law (5711–1951), Laws of the State of Israel: Authorized Translation from the Hebrew, Volume V, Laws, 5711–1950/51, 45, No. 19 art.1–3; Kedar 948

154 Law and Administration Ordinance 1, 1948 p. 9, par.13(b)

5. *OPT after 1967*

5.1 Suspension of land settlement procedures

MO 291 (1968) suspended the effectiveness of settlement orders and measures taken under the 1952 Jordanian Law for Settlement of Titles to Land and Water – allowing courts to reconsider claims already settled – and froze land registrations at the Land Registry.[155] Seventy percent of land was left unregistered. It would arguably facilitate reclassification of unregistered land of undetermined status and its declaration as State land in the 1980s and 1990s, allowing Israel to claim ownership over land and water that could be considered public property, in line with the 1959 Water Law, as it was on public land.[156] "A major tool of land dispossession" in the Negev,[157] it adversely affected Palestinian land rights, as the majority did not have title but relied on possession.[158] Disputes around land ownership and title were decided by administrative military tribunals with no appeal possible, as the HCJ refused to intervene in these matters.[159]

5.2 Abandoned private and public property

MO 58 (1967) vested in the Custodian of Abandoned Property the right to every abandoned private property, empowering him to act as property owner of property to which he had no title.[160] Lands were then allocated to settlements.[161] MO 59 (1967) authorized the Custodian of Government Property to take possession of properties belonging to an "enemy state" and take any measures he deemed necessary.[162] The definition of "Government Property" thereunder was widened retroactively in 1984 to allow Palestinian property left uncultivated after 1967 to be declared State land even if had been cultivated for ten years prior to 1967.[163] Lands registered in the name of the Jordanian government and Turkish and British-owned

155 IDF, *Order No. 291 Concerning the Settlement of Titles and the Regulation of Water (West Bank/ Judea and Samaria), 1968* (V Palestine YB Int'l L 1989, 355) art.3(a) and (b)

156 B'Tselem, By Hook and by Crook, Israeli Settlements Policy in the West Bank 25 Kretzmer and Ronen 206–207; Norwegian Refugee Council, Law Guide 34; Jeffrey D. Dillman, 'Le pillage de l'eau dans les territoires occupés' 35 Revue d'études Palestiniennes, 1990 Printemps (1990) 37 44, 52; Harold Dichter, 'The Legal Status of Israel's Water Policies in the Occupied Territories' 35 Harv Int'l L J 2, Spring (1994) 565 579–581 UN Committee on the Exercise of the Inalienable Rights of the Palestinian People, *Water Resources of the Occupied Palestinian Territory* (1992)

157 Amara, 'The Negev Land Question: Between Denial and Recognition' 36

158 Norwegian Refugee Council, Law Guide 25–26

159 Ian Lustick, 'Israel and the West Bank after Elon Moreh: The Mechanics of De Facto Annexation' 35 Middle E J 4, Autumn (1981) 557, 568

160 IDF, *Order No. 58, Order on Abandoned Properties (Private Property), 23 July 1967* art.4(a), (b)

161 Norwegian Refugee Council, Law Guide 40

162 *Order Regarding Government Property (Judea and Samaria) (No. 59), 5727–1967*

163 B'Tselem, By Hook and by Crook, Israeli Settlements Policy in the West Bank 26

properties, with numbers varying between 13 percent[164] and 40 percent of the West Bank,[165] were declared State land under MO 59 and allocated to settlements. Until 2021, authorities confiscated more than a third of the West Bank land (about 2 million dunums), 65 to 75 percent of land owned by Palestinians before 1948 in Israel and 40 to 60 percent of land owned by those who remained after 1948 and became Israeli citizens (at least 4.5 million dunums).[166]

Though the Custodian of Abandoned Property should safeguard absentee property owners' interests, abandoned lands were allocated for settlements during the 1970s and 1980s and their owners "blacklisted" to prevent them from returning to their properties.[167] No compensation seems to have been paid to absentee owners; land transfers from absentee owners to settlements, through the Custodian's intermediary, were not expropriation. They were confiscations or requisitions of agricultural land and wells, including for the Wall construction, violating the Regulations article 46 and 52 and GC IV article 53.[168] Declaration of government owned property as State land violated the Regulations article 55 and the customary law principle of permanent sovereignty over natural resources, recognized in ICESCR to which both Israel and the State of Palestine are parties. In East Jerusalem, the Absentee Property Law (1950) is applied to Palestinians unable to get to their properties since the Wall's construction, rendering them "absentees" even when living in the West Bank and facilitating transfer of their homes to organizations settling Jews in East Jerusalem,[169] violating the Regulations articles 46 and 47.

5.3 Requisitions for military and security needs

From 1967, the Israeli military requisitioned private Palestinian lands for "military needs" in East Jerusalem and its annexed environs and the West Bank.[170] In 1979, in the *Beit El* case, the HCJ concluded that no distinction can be made in a belligerency situation between the needs of the occupation army and State security; consequently, a civilian settlement fulfilling a security function can be regarded

164 B'Tselem, *Land Grab, Israel's Settlement Policy in the West Bank* (2002) 52–53

165 James Crawford SC, *Opinion, Third Party Obligations with respect to Israeli Settlements in the Occupied Palestinian Territories* (2012) par.9; Pliya Albeck, former head of the Civil Department in the Israeli State Attorney's Office. Lands in Judea and Samaria (in Hebrew) (lecture at Bet Hapraklit on 28 May 1985, Israel Bar Association), 5 cited at B'tselem 51

166 HRW, *A Threshold Crossed* (2021) 11, 12; *Report of the Independent International Commission of Inquiry on the Occupied Palestinian Territory, including East Jerusalem, and Israel (A/77/328)* (2022) par.39

167 Norwegian Refugee Council, Law Guide 40 citing State Comptroller, *State Comptroller's Annual Report 56a, 2005* 220–221; Akiva Eldar, 'Ministry Admits 'Blacklist' of Palestinians Who Left W. Bank, 5 July 2006' Ha'aretz (2006)

168 *The Wall par.132, 133*

169 Ilene Prusher, 'Israel's Absentee Property Law Exposes an Absence of Morality in Jerusalem' Haaretz, June 7, 2013 (2013); The "Wall" is called the "fence" or the "barrier." The "wall" is used herein as it was the term used by the ICJ

170 B'Tselem, By Hook and by Crook, Israeli Settlements Policy in the West Bank 23

as fulfilling army needs and private land requisitioned under article 52.[171] The HCJ judged in the *Elon Moreh* case that "any requisitioning of private land in the occupied territories for the establishment of settlements not required for security reasons was contrary to article 52 of the Hague Regulations."[172] "What may have swayed the court's opinion . . . was the open espousal of the settlers that the settlement was not for security reasons but linked to a divine right to settle the 'Land of Israel.'"[173] Scholars agree: "claims that the occupied lands belong to Israel because they were part of the Biblical Israel cannot be seriously accepted as a matter of international law."[174] Building settlements on private lands continued.[175] The HCJ held in Beit Sourik that land requisitions to build the barrier (or Wall) were based on the regulations articles 23(g) and 52, citing military needs.[176] Requisitions are strictly for army maintenance needs and do not extend to security needs under regulations article 52 which Israel violated.

5.4 State lands

5.4.1 STATE PRACTICE

After *Elon Moreh*, Israeli authorities resorted to reclassifying land as State land, allocating it almost exclusively for settlements,[177] for example, declaring 1,000 acres near Bethlehem as State land[178] and for Israeli military infrastructure and installations.[179] The renamed Custodian of Government and Abandoned Property (the "Custodian") would make a declaration of State land, without conducting any

171 HCJ 606/78, Ayoub v Minister of Defense, 33(2) PD 113, 391–392; David Kretzmer, 'The Advisory Opinion: The Light Treatment of International Humanitarian Law' 99 AJIL (2005) 88, 98

172 Blaine Sloan, *Study of the Implications, under International Law, of the UN Resolutions on Permanent Sovereignty over Natural Resources, on the Occupied Palestinian and other Arab Territories and on the Obligations of Israel Concerning its Conduct in these Territories, Report of the Secretary-General, Annex, UNGA A/38/50/Rev.1* (1983) par.27.

Elon Moreh Settlement, unofficial English translation in International Legal Materials, vol. 19 (1980), p. 148.

173 Carl Dundas, 'In the Absence of Law: Legal Aspects of the Palestinian-Israeli Conflict' XIV Middle East Policy 1, Spring (2007) 42, 45; HC 390/79 Mustafa Dweikat et al. v. The State of Israel et al.

174 Suzanne Weaver and others, 'Territories Occupied by Israel: Settlements and Exploration of Oil Resources' 72 ASIL Proceedings April (1978) 122; Kedar 941–942 Biblical sources and Zionist movement

175 Gross 157

176 Kretzmer, 'The Advisory Opinion: The Light Treatment of International Humanitarian Law' 98; *Beit Sourik Village Council v. Israel (30 June 2004)* HCJ 2056/04, 43 ILM 1099 (2004), par.32

177 ARIJ, 'Report on the Israeli Colonization Activities in the West Bank & the Gaza Strip, 2012'; Dundas 45; Yesh Din, *Ill-Gotten Gains, Theft of Palestinian Land – Declaring "State Land" Where Settlement of Title Was Halted When Israel Occupied the West Bank* (2021) 21

178 Marco Longobardo, 'The Palestinian Right to Exploit the Dead Sea Coastline for Tourism' 58 German YB Int'l L (2015) 317 320–321; Yesh Din, *The Legal Status of Israeli occupation, Legal opinion* (2023) par.19; Kretzmer and Ronen 212–213; Sophia Jones, 'Here's What The World Thinks of Israel's Controversial Land Grab' The Huffington Post (2014)

179 Kretzmer and Ronen 274

land settlement procedure or registration at the Land registry.[180] Since 1967, the Custodian has allocated about 60 percent of State land in the OPT to the Settlement Division of the World Zionist Organisation ("WZO"), which the latter manages without any supervision, 40 percent to public authorities and between 0.25 percent and 1.27 percent for Palestinian purposes.[181] About 90 percent of settlements in the OPT including Jewish neighbourhoods in East Jerusalem are established on State land.[182] In 2015 more than half of the areas ratified as State land were in "closed areas" inaccessible to Palestinians.[183] No organization had standing to sue for illegal seizure of State lands, while individuals could challenge private land expropriations before the HCJ.[184]

A 1969 law declared that all *Mawat* land is State land and that long-time possession does not confer ownership rights.[185] The Israeli Supreme Court did not recognize the customary long-term possession of cultivated *mawat* land leading to *miri*; it imposed heavy evidentiary requirements on possessors, prohibiting them from registering land in their names and required registration of *mawat* rights before the 1921 Ordinance, contrary to the British authorities' practice.[186] This would allow Israel to incorporate *mawat* land as State land.[187]

5.4.2 ANALYSIS

After *Elon Moreh*, private lands were declared State lands rising between 1979 and 1992, from 530,000 dunums in 1967 to 1.4 million dunums, constituting about 25 percent of the West Bank.[188] The detailed survey of land ownership in Palestine, submitted during the 1947 UNGA debate on the partition of Palestine, concluded that only 8 percent of the land was "public" land and 88 percent privately owned,[189] a proportion that could not have changed prior to 1967. An Israeli 1980 survey found that private ownership claims existed for a "decisive majority" of the West Bank.[190] The surge of State lands that were previously private is dubious and unfounded.

180 Norwegian Refugee Council, Law Guide-44
181 Peace Now, *Unraveling the Mechanism behind Illegal Outposts* (2017) par.1 mentions 1.27 percent; Yesh Din, Ill-Gotten Gains 21 cites 0.25 percent
182 Crawford SC par.9; B'Tselem, *Land Grab, Israel's Settlement Policy in the West Bank* 51–52; Pliya Albeck, former head of the Civil Department in the Israeli State Attorney's Office. Lands in Judea and Samaria (in Hebrew) (lecture at Bet Hapraklit on 28 May 1985, Israel Bar Association), 5 cited at B'tselem 51 and Crawford SC par.9
183 UNOCHA, 'Sharp Increase in Ratification of Declarations of "State Land"' The Monthly Humanitarian Bulletin (June 2016)
184 Lustick 568
185 Land Law, 5729–1969 Chap.10 Miscellaneous, Art.1 Abolition of categories of immovable property, par.155 Abu Sitta 25
186 Kedar 953, 956, 969 and for detailed analysis 953–969
187 Kedar 939–940
188 Norwegian Refugee Council, Law Guide-44
189 Lustick 569; UN Ad Hoc Committee on the Palestinian Question par.67, Appendix V
190 Lustick 569

First, Benvenisti wrongly advances that, under local laws, unregistered lands that are uncultivated are considered State lands.[191] Under customary and codified Ottoman law applied during the British Mandate and Jordanian rule, possession of *miri* land was acquired after ten years of cultivation, even if leaving the land afterwards uncultivated and unregistered. Contrary to the "reasonable cultivation" doctrine established by courts during the Mandate and under Jordanian rule that recognized rights to *miri* land cultivated sporadically given the nature of the land and crops, Israeli authorities considered that such land can be declared "State land" based on their own interpretation of "cultivation," adding a criterion that it should cover more than 50 percent of the land.[192]

The HCJ judged that Israeli settlers do not own State land on which settlements are built, as the military authorities cannot pass title to property they do not own, rendering the settlements "impermanent."[193] Given the duration of the occupation and Israel's proposed plans to extend settlements, the ICJ dismissed Israel's claim that the Wall was temporary. It considered that Israel presented as "fait accompli" the land taking, including settlements that could become permanent and a de facto annexation.[194] Confiscations of private and public lands by declaring them State lands to establish settlements breached the Regulations articles 46, 52 and 55.[195]

Second, extensive changes were made to customary law and legislation related to land ownership rights. Lands, whether *miri*, *mawat*, owned privately, by Mandate Palestine authorities or by foreign governments, were reclassified as State lands by law and by declaration of the Custodian; settlement of titles was ended; Land Transfer Regulations (1940) repealed, judgements and claims thereunder retroactively annulled; criteria for long-term *miri* and *mawat* land possession modified. Civil laws on private property are immune to legal change. Modifications to property must not have a permanent effect and be undertaken to the detriment of the displaced government or local population.[196] Any legislative change must be taken in the interest of the Palestinian population, a necessary requirement recognized by the HCJ,[197] which was ignored by Israel. It violated its obligation to respect, unless absolutely prevented, existing laws in the OPT (Regulations articles 43, GC IV 64).

Assuming State lands in the OPT were to be administered by military authorities under the Regulations article 55, they must be exploited for the benefit of Palestinian civilians, using lands for roads, public facilities and parks for them[198] – and not for settlements in breach of the said article. Finally, the IEL principle of permanent

191 Benvenisti and Zamir 315, note 106

192 B'Tselem, By Hook and by Crook, Israeli Settlements Policy in the West Bank 25–26; Amnesty International 125–127; Norwegian Refugee Council, Law Guide 26–27

193 Dinstein par.759–761

194 *The Wall* par.121

195 *OPT Policies and Practices 120, 122*

196 Antonio Cassese, 'Powers and Duties of an Occupant in Relation to Land and Natural Resources' in Emma Playfair (ed), *International Law and the Administration of Occupied Territories, Two Decades of Israeli Occupation of the West Bank and Gaza Strip* (OUP 1992) 422–423

197 Scobbie 277 citing the *Christian Society* case.

198 Yesh Din, Ill-Gotten Gains 21

sovereignty of the Palestinian people over their natural resources was ignored and violated.

5.5 Settlements

Israel Land Administration ("ILA"), composed of JNF and the Agriculture Ministry's representatives, supervises land acquisition and use in the OPT and functions in the West Bank and East Jerusalem through the Office of the Custodian of Government and Abandoned Property. Under Oslo II, its powers in the West Bank and Gaza should be transferred to the Palestinians, while in Area C it will be gradual.[199] The Settlement Division coordinates development of settlements in the West Bank.[200] JNF, ILA and WZO serve exclusively the Jewish community.[201] Settlements are established under government-coordinated schemes, while outposts are set up by individuals without official support, often against government policy,[202] though they receive tacit support from ministries and settlers' organizations.[203] Objectives of the settlement plans drawn up in 1978, later revised, were to build "blocs" in the West Bank around and among Palestinian towns "to reduce to the minimum the possibility for the development of another Arab state" and create obstacles for Palestinians "to form a territorial continuity and political unity when it is fragmented by Jewish settlement."[204]

Since 1967, Israeli authorities have designated about 35 percent of East Jerusalem for Israeli neighbourhoods and settlements, 35 percent as green space and national parks, on land that previously was mostly Palestinian private land and about 15 percent for residential development by Palestinians.[205] In the West Bank, settlements occupy 59 percent of the land.[206] In its Area C, less than 1 percent is designated for exclusive Palestinian use, the rest off-limits to them with 68 percent reserved for settlements and the remaining closed areas and nature reserves.[207]

MO 59 is used to legalize settlements built on State lands.[208] Dinstein notes that illegal settlements encouraged by the government should be distinguished from voluntary outposts, because anyone could purchase land lawfully in occupied territory.[209] The ICJ was not impressed by the distinction, noting that outposts

199 Oslo II Annex III, Appendix 1, art.16(1) and (2)
200 Lustick 566–567 previously Jewish Agency Settlement Department; Peace Now par.1; Kretzmer and Ronen 180
201 HRW, A Threshold Crossed 54
202 Dinstein par.744
203 Kretzmer and Ronen 182
204 Ibid, 180; Matityahu Drobles, *Settlement in Judea and Samaria: Strategy, Policy and Planning (WZO Settlement Division)* (1980) 3; B'Tselem, This Is Ours – And This, Too, Israel's Settlement Policy in the West Bank 6–7
205 US Department of State 79
206 Gross 154
207 World Bank, *West Bank and Gaza, Area C and the Future of the Palestinian Economy, Report No. AUS2922* (2013) par.9, 10
208 B'Tselem, By Hook and by Crook, Israeli Settlements Policy in the West Bank 26
209 Dinstein par.741–746

are regularly regularized by Israel.[210] The HCJ judged the 2017 Law Regularising Settlement in Judea and Samaria unconstitutional and declared it void, as it violated Palestinian property and equality rights in the West Bank. The law required the military authority to take private land where illegal settlers' construction was built and declare it government property. The government defended the use of private lands for settlements under MO 59 on the basis of settlers' "good faith," as advocated by the Attorney General.[211] Following a judgement in August 2020 by the HCJ that overturned a lower court decision that legalized an outpost built on Palestinian private land and ordered evacuation within 36 months, Israel's Prime Minister declared that the government would find alternatives to maintain settlers in place.[212] The government legalized outposts in October 2020, by declaring them "neighbourhoods" of settlements although they were not contiguous.[213]

Settlements in occupied territory violate GC IV Article 49(6) providing that the occupant "shall not deport or transfer parts of its own civilian population into the territory it occupies." It is a grave breach under AP/I article 85(4)(a). Israel military authorities consider that once a settlement is built settlers become part of the protected population,[214] in contradiction to occupation rules. The HCJ held that protecting widely the occupant's military and security interests and protecting the settlers is a legitimate military need, based on the military powers and obligations under the Regulations article 43.[215] It interpreted restrictions on legislative power of the military authority as meaning that the need to change the law is judged by the duty to ensure public order and civil life, rendering restrictions on legislative changes meaningless.[216] It is an erroneous interpretation of the rule, as the settlement project contradicts Israel's obligation to ensure public life and order under article 43, cannot be considered military necessity and does not derive from any authority under the Regulations.[217] The HCJ would not examine the legality of settlements under GC IV art.49(6) but would examine the legality of private properties' requisitions for security.[218] Such requisitions breach the Regulations article 52, as requisitions are strictly for army maintenance needs that do not extend to security issues.

The ICC concluded that "there is a reasonable basis to believe that, in the context of Israel's occupation of the West Bank, including East Jerusalem, members

210 *OPT Policies and Practices par.112, 116*

211 Kretzmer and Ronen 184–185; UNHCHR, *Israeli Settlements in the Occupied Palestinian Territory, Including East Jerusalem, and in the Occupied Syrian Golan, A/HRC/46/65* (2021) par.16

212 UNHCHR, Israeli Settlements in the Occupied Palestinian Territory, including East Jerusalem, and in the Occupied Syrian Golan, A/HRC/46/65 par.17

213 Ibid, par.17

214 Norwegian Refugee Council, Law Guide 172

215 Kretzmer and Ronen 136–137

216 Ibid, 140, 143

217 Benvenisti 241

218 Kretzmer and Ronen 34

of the Israeli authorities have committed war crimes under article 8(2)(b)(viii) in relation, inter alia, to the transfer of Israeli civilians into the West Bank since 13 June 2014."[219]

The ICJ concluded that Israel's settlement policy was in breach of GC IV article 49(6).[220] UNSC Resolution 2334 declared settlements illegal and urged Israel to stop expanding them in breach of international law.[221] Israel breached its obligations to comply with the UNSC binding decision under the UN Charter article 25, pursuant to which it agreed "to accept and carry out the decisions of the Security Council."

5.6 Restrictions on access to land

5.6.1 PHYSICAL OBSTACLES

The entire West Bank was declared a closed area on 8 July 1967 (MO. 34).[222] Since 1970, a military commander may declare an area closed and prohibit Palestinians from entering, staying in or leaving the area, with possible exemptions, under military legislation,[223] later renewed.[224] The West Bank is divided into 227 disconnected territories lacking an integrated infrastructure, by over 600 military checkpoints, settlements, gates and roads exclusive to Israeli settlers and the Wall. Area C, the only contiguous part, which has the most valuable natural resources, encompassing most of agricultural land of Palestinian villages, remains under Israeli control and inaccessible to Palestinians.[225] Due to ICA restrictions, the area where Palestinians can build amounts to 0.5 percent of the West Bank.[226] "Closed military areas" of about 1,765 million dunums cover about a third of the West Bank (over half of Area C).[227] East Jerusalem is severed from the West Bank.[228] In Gaza, 35 percent of

219 ICC, *Situation in Palestine, Summary of Preliminary Examination Findings* par.4
220 *The Wall* par.120; *OPT Policies and Practices* par.119
221 UNSC, *Resolution 2334, 23 December 2016, S/RES/2334*; UNSC, *Resolution 446, Territories Occupied by Israel, 22 March 1979*
222 Kerem Navot, *A locked garden, Declaration of closed areas in the West Bank* (2015) 8
223 Norwegian Refugee Council, Law Guide 40; IDF, *Order No.378 Concerning Security Provisions (Judea and Samaria), 1970* art.90
224 IDF, *Order No.1651 Regarding Security Directives, [Consolidated Version] (Judea and Samaria), 2009* art.318
225 UNCTAD, *Report on UNCTAD assistance to the Palestinian people: Developments in the economy of the Occupied Palestinian Territory, TD/B/67/5* (2020) par.16; UNOCHA, *Occupied Palestinian Territory, Humanitarian Facts and Figures* (2017) 10; Kretzmer and Ronen 274
226 Kretzmer and Ronen 275
227 Navot 8; UNOCHA, 'Sharp Increase in Ratification of Declarations of "State Land"' Mentions 18 percent
228 Gross 154

farmland is within a "buffer zone" where farmers are exposed to threat and use of force should they wish to exploit their arable lands.[229]

5.6.2 THE WALL

The Wall[230] was built at a distance from the internationally recognized border (the Green Line, 1967), including the greatest possible number of settlements, incorporating Palestinian territories and "cantonizing" them.[231] This area appropriated for "security needs" between the Green Line and the Wall represents more than 10 percent of the West Bank, home to 237,000 Palestinians. It enclosed settlements of about 320,000 Israeli settlers that would encircle another 176,000 Palestinians.[232] It was declared "closed" and its resources and infrastructure destroyed[233] resulting in (i) confiscation of about 10,000 hectares of the West Bank's most fertile agricultural land and important wells;[234] (ii) cutting off farmers from their lands, especially in highly productive rainfed areas around Bethlehem, Jenin, Nablus, Qalqilya, Ramallah and Tulkarem governorates and[235] (iii) isolating 2,700 establishments, disrupting 219 Palestinian localities, damaging 5,300 establishments and undermining the livelihood of 35,000 households.[236]

Al-Walaja, a village of about 2,000 inhabitants, had agricultural land seized for the Wall construction, following land confiscation in 1948 and annexation in 1967, to build Gilo and Har-Gilo settlements.[237] The Wall cut off al-Walaja from its neighbouring villages, its main freshwater source and an ancestral cemetery and blocked farmers' access to their land, except through one tunnel crossing at

229 UNHRC, *Human Rights Situation in the Occupied Palestinian Territory, including East Jerusalem, with a Focus on Access to Water and Environmental Degradation, A/HRC/40/73* (2019) (UNHRC, OPT HR, Water and Environmental Degradation)

230 The Wall is used by the ICJ. Also called fence or barrier

231 *The Wall* par.121, 132, 133; Uri Ben-Eliezer and Yuval Feinstein, '"The Battle Over Our Homes": Reconstructing/Deconstructing Sovereign Practices Around Israel's Separation Barrier on the West Bank' 12 Israel Studies 1 171, 178; UNCTAD par.39

232 Numbers vary. 9.4 percent at Mélanie Jacques, 'Case Study: Israeli Settlements, the Separation Wall and Displacement of Civilians in the Occupied Palestinian Territory' in *Armed Conflict and Displacement, the Protection of Refugees and Displaced Persons under International Humanitarian Law* (CUP 2012) 100–101; 16.6 percent at *The Wall* par.84, 85, 122; *Report of the Secretary-General prepared pursuant to General Assembly resolution ES-10/13 (A/ES-10/248)* (2003) par.8; Ben-Eliezer and Feinstein 178

233 Bornstein 122

234 *The Wall par.132, 133*

235 UNDP, *Human Development Report, Beyond scarcity: power, poverty and the global water crisis* (2006) 217

236 UNCTAD par.39

237 Tanya Abdallah and Swaileh Khaled, 'Effects of the Israeli Segregation Wall on Biodiversity and Environmental Sustainable Development in the West Bank, Palestine' 68 Int'l J Env Stud 4 (2011) 543, 547; B'Tselem, *Human Rights in the Occupied Territories, Annual Report* (2011) 50; Steffi Unsleber, '"This Village Is a Microcosm of Palestine," al-Walaja Fights the Separation Wall (2011)' The Palestine Monitor

Har-Gilo, subject to Israeli authorities' permit. A park inaugurated in 2018 for Jerusalem residents was built on 1,000 dunums of al-Walaja village lands, incorporating its water source, to which its inhabitants have no access. In 2011, the HCJ Court rejected a petition by al-Walaja residents for a change to the wall route, to prevent destruction of traditional terrace farming dating back to the first millennium.[238]

5.7 *Expropriation orders*

Three hundred thirteen expropriation orders for "public purposes" have been issued between 1967 and 2022 by the West Bank military authorities, covering 74,000 dunams, of which a little less than half is used exclusively by settlers, a similar area used by both Palestinians and settlers and 2 percent (1,532 dunams) used exclusively by Palestinians.[239]

5.8 *Natural resources destruction*

Natural resources destruction is part of a wider context of built structures' destruction. In 2021, 17,755 trees, 2,930 dunums of crops and 15,722 m^3 of water storage capacity in tanks and cisterns were destroyed and over 1 million trees destroyed since 2000.[240] Olive trees, livelihood for 80,000 to 100,000 farmers and a symbol of Palestinian identity, are uprooted by bulldozers by the IDF[241] or destroyed by settlers.[242] The rate of incidents between 2017 and 2019 increased by more than 100 percent, affecting 2,700 trees and 160 tons of produce during the 2019 olive season (September–November).[243] This occurs in a general context of violence against Palestinians by settlers[244] and instances of soldiers denying farmers access to their lands.[245]

Israeli armed forces justify destruction of olive or fruit trees for national security reasons, to increase visibility, install checkpoints, add roads and fences around

238 B'Tselem, 'The Village of al-Walajah: Dispossession and Home Demolitions, 2022' Palestinian Centre for Human Rights, 'IDF continue bulldozing works to construct the Annexation Wall and isolate al-Walaja Village, Northwest of Bethlehem' UNRWA West Bank Field Office, 'Mini Profile: Al Walaja'

239 Kerem Navot, *For the Common Good, Military Expropriation Orders in the West Bank, 1967–2022* (2022) 3, 4

240 UNCTAD par.37–38

241 Atyah Alwazir, 'Uprooting Olive Trees in the West Bank, ICE Case Number: 110' Inventory of Conflict and Environment (ICE)

242 UNHRC par.26; Jeremy Sharon, 'Palestinians Say Settlers Destroy Dozens of Olive Trees, Harass Farmers' The Times of Israel (2022); Irus Braverman, 'Uprooting Identities: The Regulation of Olive Trees in the Occupied West Bank' 32 PoLAR 2 (2009) 237, 247 Yesh Din, *Police Investigation of Candalization of Palestinian Trees in the West Bank, Yesh Din Monitoring, 2005–2011* (2011) 1; Land Research Centre (LRC), *Palestinian Olive Agony* 2018

243 UNCTAD par.37–38

244 US Department of State 75–80; *OPT Policies and Practices* par.148–154

245 Yesh Din, *Summary of the 2022 harvest season* (2023)

settlements, prevent stone throwers or gunmen hiding in trees or to make way for construction of settlements, infrastructure, or the Wall.[246] These actions benefiting exclusively settlers cannot be justified by military necessity (Regulations art.23(g)), or operations (GC IV art.53), violating these articles. Military operations taken "with a view to fighting" are acts distinct from security.[247] Repeated destruction patterns through the widespread use of bulldozers requires Israel to prove necessity;[248] for example, the HCJ allowed pruning of trees situated next to the home of an Israeli Minister of Defence to increase visibility but prohibited their cutting.[249] Prevention and punishment of stone throwing and gunmen hiding come under ensuring public order and criminal law and do not require destroying olive trees on the scale it is happening. Israel also violated AP/I article 54 prohibiting destruction of objects indispensable for civilians' survival, including foodstuffs, agricultural areas and crops.

Considering a wider context, the ICJ judged acts of violence against Palestinians as contrary to the Regulations article 46 protecting the right to life, GC IV article 27 and ICCPR articles 6(1) and 7.[250] Israel did not take adequate measures to prevent harm to the protected population under its duty to ensure public order and life under the Regulations article 43, violating its obligations under this article, which include a duty of vigilance to prevent looting and destruction by private citizens in occupied territory, as judged by the ICJ in the *Armed Activities* case.[251] Extensive and wanton destruction is a grave breach of the regulations (art.147) and a war crime (ICC Statute art.8(2)(b)(xiii). Israel also violated the IEL principle of environmental harm prevention.

5.9 Quarries exploitation

Land is expropriated for purposes of Israeli quarry exploitation.[252] Since the 1970s, occupation authorities have granted concessions permits to Israeli companies for mining and quarrying new mines in the West Bank that were inexistent pre-occupation. They extract approximately 17 million tons of stone annually, almost all of which (94 percent of substances quarried) are destined for the Israeli market, the remaining being used by the army and settlers.[253] Quarries located in

246 Braverman 247 B'Tselem, 'End the Uprooting of Trees (2001)'
247 Kretzmer and Ronen 381–382; ICRC Commentary on GC IV art.30, 49(2), 62, 64, 78
248 Dinstein par.606
249 Ibid, par.605
250 *OPT Policies and Practices*
251 *Armed Activities on the Territory of the Congo (DRC v. Uganda), Reparations, Judgement* ICJ Rep 2022, p. 13, par.79, 275
252 ARIJ and Land Research Center (LRC), 'Wadi Al Teen Quarry and the Systematic Expropriation of Palestinian Natural Resources, 1997'
253 UNHRC par.26; Yesh Din, *The Great Drain, Israeli Quarries in the West Bank: High Court Sanctioned Institutionalized Theft* (2017) 7; Guy Harpaz, Yuval Shany, Eyal Benvenisti, Amichai

areas controlled by the PA are largely exhausted, while major quarrying reserves in Area C are inaccessible to Palestinian firms,[254] as transfer of jurisdiction over them to the PA was never completed. Under tight Israeli control, Palestinian-owned quarries in the West Bank had no new or renewed permit issued since 1994, expensive equipment confiscated and some quarries closed.[255]

The HCJ dismissed a petition by a human rights organization challenging the legality of mining and quarrying by Israeli companies in the West Bank,[256] judging that reasonable operation of new quarries by private concessionaire, even if their products are sold outside occupied territory, is required to adjust reality on the ground to long-term occupation, concurring with the government[257] and refusing to consider "political-security-national" arguments. According to the petitioner, such interpretation "creates a legal basis for irreparable economic exploitation" and "a license for pillage" of occupied territory by the Occupying Power. The payment of royalties to the ICA and creation of a few jobs for Palestinians cannot be considered to benefit the civilian population but "enables the robbery of [their] collective wealth."[258] A new petition (2012) by Yesh Din was rejected.[259] Israeli scholars found the HCJ's interpretation of occupation law inaccurate and irreconcilable with its principles and HCJ case law and the judgment erroneous.[260] Granting quarrying licenses other than for benefit of the protected population violated the Regulations article 43 including Israel's obligation to preserve safety and order, the article 55 obligation to use the fruits and preserve the capital – as finite quarries' resources will be exhausted in 38 years in Area C according to the Interior Ministry –[261] and to respect the prohibition from opening new quarries. The decision ignored the irreversible environmental damage and damage to landscape.[262] Israel is bound by IEL principles of sustainable development, "polluter pays" principle and prohibition on transboundary damage.[263] The obligation of due diligence under the latter was violated.

Cohen, Yael Ronen, Barak Medina, and Orna Ben-Naftali, *Expert Legal Opinion, HCJ 2164/09 Yesh Din – Volunteers for Human Rights v. Commander of IDF Forces in West Bank et. al. (26 December 2011)* par.5, 160

254 UNCTAD par.18

255 Allegra Pacheco, Esq., 'The Israeli Supreme Court Case on Israeli Quarrying Licenses in the West Bank: Why a Second ICJ Advisory Opinion on Palestine Is Needed' Palestine YB Int'l L (2014) 60

256 *Yesh Din – Volunteers for Human Rights v. Commander of the IDF Forces in the West Bank et. al.* HCJ 2164/09

257 Dinstein par.664

258 Yesh Din, 'Yesh Din's Response to the HCJ Ruling in the Organization's Petition Challenging the Legality of Israeli Quarrying Activities in the Occupied West Bank (HCJ 164/09)'

259 Yesh Din website, Petition to halt all Israeli quarry and mining activities in the West Bank

260 Harpaz par.1, 3, 17, 88, 161

261 Ibid, par.131

262 Ibid, par.48, 104–105, 91, 160

263 Ibid, par.48; Dinstein par.660; HCJ 1661/05 Gaza v. Knesset

5.10 Jerusalem

"The territorial claim of Palestine over Jerusalem has never been refuted"; East Jerusalem is part of the OPT, as reaffirmed in UNGA, UNSC and UN HRC resolutions and the ICJ.[264] After occupying East Jerusalem in 1967, Israel illegally annexed de facto about 70,000 dunums of West Bank land to Jerusalem that was 6,000 dunums under Jordanian rule, applying Israeli law there.[265] In 1980 it enacted legislation formally annexing East Jerusalem and proclaiming the united city its capital. It is an illegal annexation rejected by the international community that considers Israel's actions invalid and those actions purporting to change East Jerusalem's status or demography to be null and void and devoid of legal effect under international law.[266] The ICJ judged that Israeli "policies and practices amount to annexation of large part of the OPT," breaching "Israel's obligation to respect the right to self-determination of the Palestinian people."[267]

III. Water legal regime

The Jordan River and the Mountain Aquifer underlying the West Bank are its two main water sources. The Mountain Aquifer consists of Eastern, Western and North Eastern Aquifers.[268] The West Bank contains 95 percent of the Mountain Aquifer feeding basin, 80 percent of its stocking basin[269] and 70 percent of its surface water and the quasi-totality of the Eastern Basin.[270] The Jordan River has its sources in the river Hasbani in Lebanon, Dan in Israel and Banias in Syria, all joining in the Hulley Valley, then flowing into Lake Tiberias[271] in Northern Israel. The Upper Jordan River meets its main tributary, the Yarmouk river, in Syria. The Lower Jordan River is the border between Israel and the West Bank.[272]

In Gaza, several streams (*wadi*) that supplied water prior to the early 1970s, including Wadi Gaza, one of the longest rivers in Palestine before 1948, dried

264 Professor Richard Falk, *Situation in the State of Palestine, Amicus Curiae Submissions Pursuant to Rule 103, ICC-01/18, 16 March 2020* par.24 for resolutions references; *The Wall par.119–120*

265 B'Tselem, 'East Jerusalem (2017 updated 2019)'

266 Professor Richard Falk par.24, 27, 28; UN Committee on the Exercise of the Inalienable Rights of the Palestinian People 24; UNGA, *Resolutions 2253 and 2254 (ES-V), 4 and 14 July 1967*; UNSC, *S/RES/252, 21 May 1968* par.2; UNSC, *S/RES/267, 3 July 1969* par.4; UNGA, *A/RES/ES-10/19, 22 December 2017* par.1

267 *OPT Policies and Practices par.173, 243*

268 UNEP, *Desk Study on the Environment in the Occupied Palestinian Territories* (2003) 16 UNEP refers to the North Eastern Aquifer as the Northern Aquifer.

269 UNEP, *State of Environment and Outlook Report for the occupied Palestinian territory* (2020) 65–66

270 République Française, Assemblée Nationale, La Commission des Affaires Etrangères, *Rapport d'information, la géopolitique de l'eau* (2011) 117

271 Lake Tiberias for all riparian and Kinneret for Israelis, Stephen C. McCaffrey, 'Water Scarcity and Security Issues in the Middle East' 108 ASIL Proceedings (2014), 298 or Sea of Galilee, Ori Tal-Spiro, The Knesset, The Research and Information Center, *Israeli-Palestinian Cooperation on Water Issues, Presented to the Internal Affairs and Environment Committee* (2011) 3

272 UNEP 2003, 16

following the construction of dams on the Israeli side that cut the upstream water supply.[273] The only water source is the Gaza Aquifer flowing underground along the coasts of Israel and Gaza. Highly susceptible to contamination by sewage and seawater infiltration, due to its sand and gravel surface, it is a shallow salty aquifer that depends on precipitation for recharge.[274]

1. Water ownership and use rights

1.1 Ottoman Empire

Islamic law principles and customary law applicable to water resources in the Middle East were codified in the Mejelle.[275] It distinguishes communal water, private water and water on public domain owned by the State.[276] Uncaptured water, whether underground in aquifers or surface waters of streams, rivers, springs and other natural bodies, was property of the community, not vested in the Sultan or State and free for public consumption (*mubah*). The communal right to use (*musha'*) and capture it may be exercised by anyone, subject not to harm others (the reasonable use concept), while the primary right to drink supersedes private property rights.[277] Water becomes private property (*mulk*) when captured intentionally in a man-made container, in irrigation channels or by pumping it.[278] Water follows the land, and water ownership is linked to land ownership.[279] Therefore, the right to water from a well or spring being attached to the land of its location is the landowner's private property.[280]

1.2 British mandate

During the British mandate, local customs, Mejelle provisions and Ottoman legislation remained applicable, with no distinctive change to water regulation.[281] A 1940 Amendment Order that vested in the High Commissioner, in trust for the Government of Palestine, all surface waters and granted him regulatory powers over control

273 Shomar 477

274 Amnesty International, *The Occupation of Water* (2017)

275 UNEP 20 Gamal Abouali, 'Natural Resources under Occupation: The Status of Palestinian Waters under International Law' 10 Pace Int'l L Rev (1998) 411 444–445 Mejelle articles 1234–1326 Civic 443

276 Françoise Métral, 'Le droit de l'eau dans le Code civil ottoman de 1869 et la notion de domaine public' in *L'Homme et l'eau en Méditerranée et au Proche Orient* (Travaux de la Maison de l'Orient 1982) 128–129

277 Abouali 445, 471 Civic 443–444 Chibli Mallat, 'The Quest for Water Use Principles: Reflections of Shari'a and Customs in the Middle East' in J.A. Allan and Chibli Mallat (eds), *Water in the Middle East: Legal, Political and Cultural Implications* (I.B. Tauris Publishers 1995) 129, 131

278 Abouali 445; Mejelle art.1248, 1250; Mallat 129

279 Métral 130; Mejelle art.1238–1239

280 Abouali 452

281 Abraham Hirsch, 'Water Legislation in the Middle East' 8 Am J Comp L (1959) 168, 178 Civic 446

and exploitation of surface and underground water sources in Palestine,[282] was not "gazetted" or implemented until formally given effect by Israel on 26 April 1950.[283] Different Franco-British agreements endorsed water sharing and recognized water use rights of riparian States. A Convention of 23 December 1920 protected water interests of downstream areas, with surplus water from the Upper Jordan, Yarmouk and tributaries to be used by Palestine.[284] The rights of Lebanon, Syria and Palestine's inhabitants over the Jordan river, Lakes Huleh and Tiberias, including fishing and navigation, were maintained under the 3 February 1922 agreement delineating their boundary[285] and their water and cultivation rights on one side or the other of the frontier and water use rights under local laws, customs and village rights over communal properties, maintained under another agreement.[286] For the chief of the UN Truce Supervision organization, the treaty provisions represented the patterns of rights to the Jordan's waters, while Israel refused to accept the Mandate treaties' obligations.[287]

1.3 Israeli legislation after 1948

Israeli legislation declared surface[288] and ground water resources[289] publicly owned and entrusted with the State. The 1959 Water Law declared all water resources in Israel, above or underground, public property under the State's control and destined for the requirements of the inhabitants and development of the country.[290] It dissociated water rights from land rights.[291]

1.4 West Bank under Jordanian rule and Gaza 1948–1967

Under the 1952 law for titles settlement, private rights to water, including water exploitation installations, are attached to land and cannot be transferred separately, consistent with customary law codified by the Mejelle.[292] A law regulating natural

282 The Palestine Order-in-Council, 1922 art.16E (1), (2) and (3) introduced by the Palestine (Amendment) Order in Council, December 4, 1940; text in Great Britain, Government of Palestine, A Survey of Palestine: Prepared in December 1945 and January 1946 for the information of the Anglo-American Committee of Inquiry, vol. 1, pp. 391–92.

283 Hirsch 178

284 Abraham Hirsch, 'Utilization of International Rivers in the Middle East, a Study of Conventional International Law' 59 AJIL (1956) 87–88; 22 League of Nation Treaty Series (LNTS) 355, 361 art.8

285 22 LNTS 365, 372. It was ratified on 7 March 1923; Hirsch 86, 91

286 Agreement of Good Neighbourly Relations, 2 February 1926, 56 LNTS 81, art. III; Hirsch 91

287 Ibid, n.3, n.40

288 The General Agriculture Ordinance (1950). Samer Alatout, 'Water Multiples in Israeli Politics, Paper Prepared for Environmental Politics Workshop, Berkeley, October 2010' 14, Table 1: water regulation 1950–1959

289 Alatout 14, Table 1: water regulation 1950–1959. The Water Drilling Control Law (1955)

290 The Water Law 1959 par.1, 2

291 Ibid, par.4

292 The Law for Settlement of Titles to Land and Water, Law No. 40, 1952, at Official Gazette (Jordan) no. 1113, 16 June 1952, 279 art.17(2), art.2, art.8(5); Abouali 453, 470; Civic 448–449

resources declared all natural resources and minerals State property, leaving water ownership untouched.[293] A law regulating underground water maintained its private ownership.[294] Therefore, under local laws before occupation, water from wells, springs or rivers located on private and municipal property was private (*mulk*).[295] Public water meant water flowing on – or pumped from – land owned by Jordan (about 13 percent) in the West Bank and by Egypt in Gaza, though their water ownership was smaller, as local authorities owned rights to the main water sources.[296] Natural bodies of water and uncaptured water to which no private right has been claimed or registered (*mubah*) (Mountain Aquifer and Jordan river) were subject to communal property rights,[297] as were water springs used for irrigation or wells, unless on private property.[298] All ground or surface waters resources were declared State property in 1983 in Jordan.[299]

1.5 Palestinian territory under occupation

In Gaza, MO 498 transferred water resources to the military authority.[300] Overexploitation of the Gaza Aquifer groundwater due to high extraction rates on the Israeli side, exceeding recharge rates, barely leaves water reaching the Gaza Strip, leading to salinization and pollution by nitrates and chlorides, causing irreparable damage to the aquifer and destruction of agriculture.[301] Increased drilling of private

293 Provisional Law on the Regulation of Natural Resources, Law No. 37 of 1966, Official Gazette (Jordan) No. 1931, 16 June 1966, at 1113 art.3, 14(a), 30. Gamal Abouali, 'Continued Control: Israel, Palestinian Water and the Interim Agreement' IX Palestine YB Int'l L (1996–1997) 73–74

294 Law concerning the Supervision of Underground Water, Law No.88, 1966, at Official Gazette (Jordan) no. 1943, 16 August 1966, 1592.'Special Report, Sovereignty over Water Resources in the West Bank and Gaza Strip' V Palestine YB Int'l L 349, n.1

295 Abouali, 'Natural Resources under Occupation: The Status of Palestinian Waters under International Law' 455, 470–472; Dillman 44; Mara Tignino, 'Water, International Peace, and Security' 92 IRRC 879, September (2010) 647, 663; UNGA ESC, *Permanent Sovereignty over Natural Resources in the Occupied Palestinian and Other Arab Territories: Report of the Secretary-General* (1984) par.14

296 Abouali, 'Continued Control: Israel, Palestinian Water and the Interim Agreement' 84

297 Civic 448; Abouali, 'Natural Resources under Occupation: The Status of Palestinian Waters under International Law' 470–471

298 Julie Trottier, 'Le Rapport à l'Eau et à la Terre dans la Construction de Territoires Multisitués: le Cas Palestinien' Espace Géographique, 2015 7–8; Jeanne Perrier, *Les lois palestiniennes de l'eau: entre centralisation, décentralisation et mise en invisibilité* (Papiers de Recherche, Agence Francaise de Développement (AFD), n 2019–118, Décembre, 2019) 22

299 Water Authority Law, Law No. 34 of 1983, Official Gazette (Jordan) No. 3194, 15 December 1983. 'Special Report, Sovereignty over Water Resources in the West Bank and Gaza Strip' 349, n.1

300 IDF, *Order No. 498 of 4 November 1974* (V Palestine YB Int'l L 1989, 359)

301 Shomar 477–478; La Commission des Affaires Etrangères 49, 118, 121; UNDP 216; Iain Scobbie, 'Natural Resources and Belligerent Occupation: Mutation through Permanent Sovereignty' in Stephen Bowen (ed), *Human Rights, Self-Determination and Political Change in the Occupied Palestinian Territories* (Martinus Nijhoff 1997) 280–281

World Bank, *Toward Water Security for Palestinians, West Bank and Gaza Water Supply, Sanitation, and Hygiene Poverty Diagnostic* (WASH Poverty Diagnostic, 2018) 16, 37; UNDP 209

wells largely unregulated by the PA aggravates the issue.[302] Exploitation by Gaza's inhabitants of their territorial waters' resources, subject to blockade, was restricted to fishing within three miles, extended to 12 miles in 2019 – less than 20 miles under Oslo art. XIV – hampering livelihood of fishermen, 95 percent of whom live below the poverty line, exposed to intimidation and use of force.[303]

In the West Bank, in 1967, only about a third of land and water were claimed and registered,[304] as registration of water rights was required for their acquisition.[305] MO. 291 (1968) suspended land settlement procedures and froze registration of titles to land and water, allowing the military authority to cancel existing agreements and permits; it declared all water resources State property.[306] Israel imposed restrictions on water use:

- It is the only user of Lake Tiberias,[307]
- Curtailing Palestinian access to springs;[308] from 154.2 million cubic metres (mcm) supplied annually, Palestinians consume 63.8 mcm and Israelis 88.3 mcm,[309]
- Imposing limits to quantity of water allocated to Palestinians, to quantity and depth of wells restricted to 300 metres, under regulations unapplicable to settlers, while settlers' wells can be 1,500 metres deep.[310] A Jordanian law prohibiting drilling of new wells in the West Bank was repealed,[311]
- Ending Palestinian access to the Jordan River; its basin in Palestinian territory (1,564 km^2) was closed as military zone in 1967 or is in Area C under Israel's control since Oslo II.[312] Israel withdraws annually between 580 and 640 mcm[313] and diverts about 60 percent, from the Jordan River annual flow of 1.3 billion

302 World Bank, *Securing Water for Development in West Bank and Gaza* (2018) 3; Julie Trottier and Jeanne Perrier, 'Water-driven Palestinian Agricultural Frontiers: The Global Ramifications of Transforming Local Irrigation' 25 J Polit Ecol (2018) 300

303 UNCTAD par.22; UNHRC par.11

304 Abouali, 'Natural Resources under Occupation: The Status of Palestinian Waters under International Law' 453

305 Civic 448

306 Military order 291 (1968) art.3(a) and (b); McCaffrey 299; La Commission des Affaires Etrangères 120–121

307 Eliahu Rosenthal and Robbie Sabel, 'Water and Diplomacy in the Jordan River Basin' III Israel Journal of Foreign Affairs 2 (2009) 95 106 (400mcm annually from Kinneret/Tiberias); UN-ESCWA and BGR 171, 198

308 Julie Trottier and Perrier 298

309 Mark Zeitoun, *Power and Water in the Middle East, the Hidden Politics of the Palestinian-Israeli Water Conflict* (I.B. Tauris 2012) 51–52, 54 Table 3.2, 56

310 UNDP 210, 215; La Commission des Affaires Etrangères 117, 121, 124; UNHRC, *Allocation of Water Resources in the Occupied Palestinian Territory, including East Jerusalem, A/HRC/48/43* (2021) par.27 (UNHRC OPT Water Allocation)

311 Scobbie, 'H2O after Oslo' 101

312 UN-ESCWA and BGR, 202; UNHRC, OPT HR, Water and Environmental degradation par.44

313 UN-ECSWA 171

cubic meters, to the Negev desert, Jerusalem and Dan region,[314] causing the lower Jordan river to dry up, reducing it to an annual flow between 20 and 200 mcm into the Dead Sea, which is a small sewage stream, as Israel pumps into it saline springs and untreated wastewater.[315] Previously Jordanian law prohibited transfer of water between basins or required an authorization to transfer water between areas within the same basin. Under Israeli law, all water is part of a national network and may be transferred from one basin to another within the West Bank or from the West Bank to another basin within Israel or the Negev.[316]

1.6 Oslo agreement

Under Oslo II, Israel commits to supply 5 mcm of water to Gaza annually; it is the only provision regarding supply of water to Gaza.[317] Regarding the West Bank, Oslo II allocated 71 percent of the "estimated potential" of water of the Mountain Aquifer's three aquifers to Israel and 20 percent to Palestinians, as follows (actual water use in parentheses):

Israel: Western Aquifer (WA) 340 (411), North Eastern (NEA) 103 (103), Eastern (EA) 40 (150),

Palestinian Authority: WA 22 (38.7), NEA 42 (21.7), EA 54 (33).[318]

The Mountain Aquifer basins produce about 679 mcm annually.[319] As the WA and NEA were at the time totally used by Israel, negotiations could only concern the EA remaining unused waters.[320] In addition to their existing water use of 118 mcm at the time,[321] Palestinians' future water needs were estimated at 70–80 mcm/year,[322] based on assumptions of population numbers during a 5-year interim period, while the population had already doubled in 2011.[323] In the interim period, 28.6 mcm annually were to be made available for Palestinians' immediate needs, Israel committing to supply 4.5 mcm to the West Bank annually,[324] with the remainder to be developed by Palestinians from the EA and additional sources.[325] New Palestinian

314 UN-ESCWA and BGR 198, 200; La Commission des Affaires Etrangères 117
315 McCaffrey 298-299; Rosenthal and Sabel 106; Zeitoun 46; UN ESCWA 170-171
316 Dillman 45; Crawford SC par.86
317 Oslo II, Annex III, Appendix 1, art.40.7(a)(6), art.40.7(b)(3)
318 Ibid, Art.40.3(a), art.40.15 Schedule 8, par.1 and Schedule 10; World Bank, Securing Water for Development in West Bank and Gaza 4: Israel water uses in 2011 and PA in 2016. There are no data for Israeli uses after 2011
319 Oslo II UNEP 2020, 65–66 mentions 675mcm
320 La Commission des Affaires Etrangères 117
321 World Bank, Securing Water for Development in West Bank and Gaza 4
322 Oslo II, Annex III, Appendix 1 art.40.6.
323 La Commission des Affaires Etrangères 117; World Bank, Securing Water for Development in West Bank and Gaza 3
324 Oslo II, Annex III, Appendix 1, art.40.7(a)
325 Ibid, art.40.7(b)

wells drilled after Oslo II until 2013 were providing only 13 mcm/year.[326] Settlers hold 13 percent of the West Bank wells, accounting for about 53 percent of groundwater extracted, with unused water from the OPT flowing under Israeli territory and extracted from Israeli wells.[327] The bulk of water from wells managed by Mekorot goes to Israeli settlements and military bases (48.1 mcm) with little Palestinian consumption (6.9 mcm).[328] Eighty-seven percent of Mountain Aquifer waters were estimated to be used by Israelis and 13 percent by Palestinians, in 2014,[329] with Israel receiving more than half of its water from outside its borders.[330]

1.7 Analysis

Israel has extensively changed the legal regime of water ownership and use rights:

(i) Dissociating private ownership water rights from land rights,
(ii) Nationalization of water resources in Israel by the Water Law (1959) and declaration of State lands allowing appropriation of water rights on public land,
(iii) Suppression in the OPT of Palestinians' communal rights to water, access to springs and to the Jordan River, existing under pre-occupation law, similar to a common legal right in use of rivers' waters, under IWL,
(iv) Non-recognition of Palestinians' usage rights to water under Franco-British agreements,
(v) Confiscation of wells and springs on private and municipal property.

Legislative changes were not introduced for the benefit of the Palestinian population, breaching the prohibition to change laws under the Regulations article 43. The ICJ judged that Israel has applied its domestic law comprehensively to East Jerusalem and extended it to settlers in the West Bank, where it substituted military law for local laws, with "far-reaching changes to applicable law," in violation of the Regulations article 43 and GC IV article 64.[331] Appropriation and transfer to the State of Israel of Palestinian private rights to water and of publicly owned water violated the Regulations articles 46, 47 and 55.[332] They were not (i) requisition for army needs under the Regulations article 52, or (ii) seizure under its article 53 since water is not war munition, violating these two articles or (iii) expropriation under

326 World Bank
327 La Commission des Affaires Etrangères 121; Abouali, 'Continued Control: Israel, Palestinian Water and the Interim Agreement' 78
328 UNHRC, OPT Water Allocation par.18; Amnesty International; Zeitoun 51–52, 54 Table 3.2, 56
329 Ibid, par.27; La Commission des Affaires Etrangères 121
330 UNDP 210
331 *OPT Policies and Practices par.134–141*
332 Abouali, 'Natural Resources under Occupation: The Status of Palestinian Waters under International Law' 470; Tignino 663

pre-occupation existing law, if any.[333] Restrictions on water use by Palestinians breach GC IV article 46, providing that restrictive measures must be cancelled at the end of hostilities.

Israel is responsible for fulfilling existing cross-border treaties on water supply and cannot divert water to its territory as that would be ultra vires regarding occupation law.[334]

Israel does not observe limited territorial sovereignty that supports the prevailing doctrine of equitable and reasonable use of international shared watercourses. It applies the first appropriation principle rejected by the international community.[335] By prohibiting Palestinians' access to the Jordan River and diverting it, cutting streams' supply of water to Gaza, overexploiting the Gaza Aquifer, increasing salinization and causing irreparable damage, Israel breached its obligations:

(i) To respect Palestinians' permanent sovereignty over their natural resources, reaffirmed in numerous UNGA Resolutions.[336] This IEL principle entitles the Palestinian population to use freely its resources without interference from the military administration under control of local bodies and supports a restrictive interpretation of Israel's usufructuary powers, all of which were ignored,
(ii) To safeguard the capital of water resources and exploit them reasonably, not excessively, under the Regulations article 55 and sustainably in accordance with contemporary IEL developments. The UNSC requested a commission to investigate the "serious depletion of natural resources, particularly the water resources" in the OPT in 1980.[337] Exploitation for the benefit of the protected population requires ensuring a supply of clean water for drinking and irrigation and allowing functioning and maintenance of water installations.[338] Israel implemented none of these obligations,
(iii) To prevent environmental damage and transboundary harm,
(iv) To use shared international watercourses equitably and reasonably,
(v) To cooperate and negotiate to reach an equitable solution for problems resulting from excessive use or pollution, under a customary and conventional law obligation to negotiate.[339] The last three duties, included in the Helsinki Rules,

333 Dillman 55–56; Dichter 579–580; *The Wall par.132, 133*

334 A.P.V. Rogers, *Law on the Battlefield* (3rd edn, MUP 2012) 265; Scobbie, 'Natural Resources and Belligerent Occupation: Mutation through Permanent Sovereignty' 246–253

335 La Commission des Affaires Etrangères 212; Owen McIntyre, 'Chapter 15: Water' in Elisa Morgera and Kati Kulovesi (eds), *Research Handbook on International Law and Natural Resources* (Edward Elgar 2016) 310; Civic 438, n.5

336 UNGA resolutions too numerous to cite. Ex. Permanent sovereignty over natural resources in the Occupied Arab territories, Resolution 3336 (XXIX) of 17 December 1974; A/RES/65/179 UNGA Permanent sovereignty of the Palestinian people in the Occupied Palestinian Territory, including East Jerusalem, and of the Arab population in the occupied Syrian Golan over their natural resources, 20 December 2010.

337 UNSC, *Resolution 465, Territories Occupied by Israel, 1st March 1980* par.8

338 Eyal Benvenisti, 'Water Conflicts during the Occupation of Iraq' 97 AJIL 4, October (2003) 860, 864

339 Brunson MacChesney, 'Lake Lanoux Case (France-Spain)' 53 AJIL 1, January (1959) 163–164; Convention on the Law on Non-Navigational Uses of International Watercourses (1997) art.7(1)

are customary IEL and IWL obligations binding on Israel, even though it is not party to the 1977 Watercourses Convention codifying them. Oslo II provisions allocating 20 percent of the Mountain Aquifer to Palestinians and 80 percent to Israel according to existing Israeli uses of WA and NEA waters, resulting in water shortages in the OPT, affecting agricultural development and livelihoods, are unequitable and unreasonable.

2. *Institutional control and management of water resources*

Under Israeli laws between 1948 and 1967, the water commissioner was empowered to manage water resources: (i) monitoring water abstracts and controlling uses of underground water[340] and every water source;[341] (ii) delivering drilling permits and establishing water tariffs;[342] (iii) controlling winter floods and wastewater.[343] His powers were consolidated in the 1959 Water Law.

In the West Bank under Jordanian rule, management of water resources was decentralized; persons irrigating the land had obligation to redistribute surplus water.[344] Irrigation projects required prior administrative authorizations that were regularly granted, unless harmful to lands or other plans.[345] Wells operated as common property regime.[346] Palestinians used springs and accessed the Jordan river for domestic purposes and agriculture in the Jordan Valley.[347] In Gaza, the customary law right to use water was granted to landowners and to anyone necessitating basic drinking and irrigation needs.[348]

By 1967, Israel was using almost all its renewable water resources.[349] After occupation, it asserted its control over the OPT water resources and related infrastructure, transferring them to the military authority (MO 92, 498, 158).[350] An "Officer in Charge" of "water establishments" in the West Bank (MO. 92), including wells and irrigation installations[351] and a "Competent Authority" in Gaza (MO. 498) were vested with legislative and regulatory powers regarding water

340 Alatout Table 1 Water Regulation 1950–1959, Water Drilling Control Law (1955)

341 Ibid, Table 1 Water Regulation 1950–1959, Water Metering Law (1955)

342 Ibid, Table 1 Water Regulation 1950–1959, Water Drilling Control Law and Water Metering Law respectively (1955)

343 Drainage and Flood Control Law (1957),

344 Abouali, 'Natural Resources under Occupation: The Status of Palestinian Waters under International Law' 453 Mallat 130

345 Dillman 44 Jordanian law No.31, 1953

346 Julie Trottier and Perrier 299

347 Ibid, UNESCWA and BGR, *Inventory of Shared Water Resources in Western Asia, Chap.6 Jordan River Basin* (2013) 202

348 Dillman 45 UNGA ESC Annex, par.17

349 Basheer K Nijim, 'Water Resources in the History of the Palestine-Israel Conflict' 21 GeoJournal, Some Geographical Aspects of the Israeli-Palestinian Conflict 4 (August 1990) 317, 319; Jeffrey D. Dillman, 'Water Rights in the Occupied Territories' 19 J Palestine Stud 1, Autumn (1989) 47

350 McCaffrey 298–299; Zeitoun 68; Perrier 21. Eyal Benvenisti and Haim Gvirtzman, 'Harnessing International Law to Determine Israeli-Palestinian Water Rights: The Mountain Aquifer' 33 Nat Resources J (1993) 543, 545; Scobbie, 'H2O after Oslo' 91

351 Order No.158 of 30 October 1967. Art.2, art.4 (addition to article 5)

use and exploitation.[352] They deliver mandatory operating permits conditionally or may refuse them discretionarily without possible appeal.[353] The operating permit is nearly impossible to obtain for Palestinians, prohibiting them from drilling new wells, expanding existing ones, or installing pumps. Extremely few were granted by authorities in charge since 1967 or the Joint Water Committee (JWC).[354] It is responsible under Oslo II, of water and sewage issues in the West Bank during the interim period, subject to ICA approval,[355] though Israel must transfer to Palestinians power and responsibility regarding those.[356] The JWC, benefiting from an asymmetric power, uses its veto to restrict or block Palestinian development of water and sewage resources and stall desalination plants, irrigation and wastewater systems, approvals of deep-drilling wells and rain harvesting cisterns.[357] The situation is aggravated by Israeli restrictions on international and local investors[358] blocking development projects in the OPT while Israeli settlers are helped by international financial donors.[359] Existing arrangements in Gaza concerning water resources and sewage systems remain unchanged under Oslo II.[360]

Israel, the Jewish Agency and JNF own the institutions planning (Tahal), managing and developing (Mekorot) water resources in the OPT.[361] Mekorot owns all West Bank water supply systems and manages wells inside the West Bank.[362] The Palestinian Water Authority ("PWA") has little control over water produced or consumed inside the West Bank, while Israeli institutions control a quarter of water consumed by Palestinians inside the West Bank.[363] The West Bank Water Department ("WBWD") operates wells that serve settlers and Palestinians, under the PWA's jurisdiction, though its decisions are taken by the ICA. Despite international funding for several projects, half of the water from WBWD wells goes to Israeli settlements.[364]

352 IDF, *Order No. 92 of 15 August 1967* (V Palestine Y Int'l L 1989, 346) art.1, 2, 5; IDF, *Order No. 498 of 4 November 1974* par.1, 4

353 IDF, *Order No.158 of 30 October 1967* (V Palestine YB Int'l L 1989, 351) art.4 (addition 5A(e) – (g), addition 5A(ja)) for the Officer in charge; IDF, *Order No. 498 of 4 November 1974 par.3,16, 17, 24, 35* for the Competent Authority

354 Amnesty International 2017; International Inquiry Commission A/77/328 (2022) par.35; Abouali, 'Continued Control: Israel, Palestinian Water and the Interim Agreement' 78

355 Oslo II, Annex III Appendix 1 Art.40.11–12, art.40.14

356 Ibid, Art.40.4

357 Zeitoun 102; Perrier 24; World Bank, Toward Water Security for Palestinians, West Bank and Gaza Water Supply, Sanitation, and Hygiene Poverty Diagnostic 101; UNHRC, OPT Water Allocation par.28–29; Abouali, 'Continued Control: Israel, Palestinian Water and the Interim Agreement' 102; Elena Lazarou, *Water in the Israeli-Palestinian conflict* (European Parliamentary Research Service, Briefing January, 2016) 7

358 Lazarou 7

359 Dillman, 'Water Rights in the Occupied Territories' 55

360 Oslo II, Annex III Appendix 1 Art.40.25, Schedule 11

361 Dillman, 'Water Rights in the Occupied Territories' 54 citing JNF Memorandum of Association Article 3 (a)

362 UNHRC, OPT Water Allocation par.18; Amnesty International; Zeitoun 51–52, 54 Table 3.2, 56

363 Zeitoun 55

364 Ibid, 51–52, 54 Table 3.2, 56

Israel changed comprehensively customary and codified laws on management and control of water resources, for its and settlers' benefit, breaching the Regulations article 43. Existing water management was replaced by an extensive control of abstract and water uses, imposition of permits and conditions of use, allocated limits and metering. Israel justifies water regulations in the OPT by the necessity to adopt conservation measures adopted in Israel; the argument does not hold in view of the discriminatory treatment between settlers and Palestinians.[365]

3. *Water consumption, sanitation and human rights*

Numbers on water consumption vary and are difficult to get for recent years in Israel. The Israeli population, almost twice the size of the Palestinian population, uses a total of water about seven and a half times higher. Put another way, the Palestinian population, half the size of Israel's, consumes only 10–15 percent as much water.[366] In 2005, annual per capita consumption was about 620 m^3 for settlers, less than 100 m^3 for Palestinians in the West Bank and above 300 m^3 in Israel while it was 1,000 m^3 for settlers in Gaza before their evacuation.[367] West Bank settlers (excluding those who receive their water from Jerusalem water supply) consume about 27 percent of the total water consumed from sources inside the West Bank.[368] Available water for agriculture, industrial use and drinking was 646 l/p/d for Israelis and 133 l/p/d for Palestinians in 2011.[369] While the average water supply to agricultural land in Israel was 5,000 m^3/ha in 2000,[370] only 6.8 percent of the cultivated land in the West Bank is irrigated, due to the low quantities of water available to Palestinian farmers.[371]

In the West Bank, about 600,000 Palestinians have limited access to safely managed water sources.[372] In Area C, some communities survive on as little as 20 l/c/d,[373] while between 350,000 to 420,000 Palestinians receive fewer than 50 litres per person per day.[374] Between 170,000 and 200,000 in rural areas have no access to a water network – equivalent to 70 percent of communities in Area C, according to the UN Office for the Coordination of Humanitarian Affairs ("UNOCHA"), while McCaffrey cites well over 1,000 villages in the West Bank without water

365 Scobbie, 'H2O after Oslo' 91; UNGA ESC par.15

366 UNDP 215–216

367 Ibid, 20, 215–216

368 Zeitoun 54–55

369 McCaffrey 299

370 World Bank, Philippe Marin, Shimon Tal, Joshua Yeres, Klas Ringskog, *Water Management in Israel, Key Innovations and Lessons Learned for Water-Scarce Countries* (2017) 29

371 Lazarou 5

372 UNHRC, OPT Water Allocation par.26; West Bank Protection Consortium, *Palestinian Access to Water and Attacks on WASH Structures in Area C* (2021)

373 Lazarou 5.

374 350,000 at WHO, *Health conditions in the occupied Palestinian territory, including east Jerusalem, and in the occupied Syrian Golan, A74/22* (2021) par.34. 420,000 at UNHRC, OPT Water Allocation par.26

connections – relying on rain harvesting and water tanks to meet their basic needs,[375] with tanked water costing six times more than piped water.[376] In Gaza, between 93 percent and 96 percent of Gazan households are connected to the water network, though only 30 percent receive water daily.[377] Only 4 percent of the 180 mcm of water extracted annually from the Coastal Aquifer is considered safe drinking water[378] from 98.3 percent in 2000, increasing reliance on water tanks, containers and bottled waters to 89.6 percent.[379]

Infrastructure for bulk water supply is fragmented, linked piecemeal to the Mekorot network and constrained in its development by limitations on infrastructure crossing Area C.[380] Water and sanitation infrastructure requires electricity to operate, in short supply in Gaza. In addition to shortages of wastewater infrastructure – (about 25 mcm of sewage are released into the environment annually in the West Bank) – water infrastructure is confiscated and destroyed by Israel.[381] At least 50 settlements are discharging about 35 mcm of wastewater onto Palestinian lands, contaminating sources and crops and negatively affecting livestock and human health.[382]

Israel and the State of Palestine are parties to the ICESCR and other international agreements that recognize the right to water and sanitation.[383] Israel must respect, protect and fulfil the realization of this right by taking necessary measures to ensure access to the WHO minimum benchmark of 100 litres/capita/day (lcd) of water that is sufficient, safe and regular and access to water facilities and services on a non-discriminatory basis, free from physical threats and equitably distributed.[384] The amount of water supplied to Palestinians living under occupation is below the minimum required for some areas of the West Bank, insufficient, unsafe (only 4 percent of the Gaza Aquifer is drinkable) and irregular. Since institutions that manage and own the water infrastructure of the OPT are under Israel's control,

375 Amnesty International 2017. Lazarou 5 mentions 200,000 people UNOCHA, Occupied Palestinian Territory, Humanitarian Facts and Figures 12 WHO par.34 mentions 170,000 people UNHRC, OPT HR, Water and Environmental degradation par.52 mentions 180 communities UNHRC, OPT Water Allocation mentions 14,000 people base on a 2012 report McCaffrey 299

376 WHO par.34 based on a document from 2014 Lazarou mentions 400 percent more for every litre than those connected to the water network, Lazarou 5.

377 93 percent at UNEP 2020, 68 and 96 percent at WHO, par.34 WASH Cluster, *State of Palestine, Critical Access to Water during COVID-19 Endangered by a Rise in Demolitions in the West Bank: The Case of Masafer Yatta* (2021) 1

378 WHO par.34

379 UNEP 68; World Bank, Securing Water for Development in West Bank and Gaza 3; Julie Trottier and Perrier 300

380 World Bank, Toward Water Security for Palestinians, West Bank and Gaza Water Supply, Sanitation, and Hygiene Poverty Diagnostic 16

381 UNHRC, OPT Water Allocation par.22–24

382 WHO par.34

383 ICESCR article 11 Convention on the Elimination of All Forms of Discrimination against Women, article 14.2(h). Convention on the Rights of Persons with Disabilities, article 28.2(a) 15

384 UNCESCR, *General Comment No. 15: The Right to Water (Arts. 11 and 12 of the Covenant), E/C.12/2002/11* (2002) par.12; UNGA, *The Human Rights to Safe Drinking Water and Sanitation, A/Res.70/169* (2015); UNHRC, *The Human Rights to Safe Drinking Water and Sanitation, A/HRC/RES/39/8* (2018); WHO, *Domestic Water Quantity, Service Level and Health* (2020)

the PA has nominal power to ensure access to water to its people. Israel cannot deny or limit equal access to adequate water, non-discrimination and equality being key elements of the human right to water.[385] Discrimination between Palestinians and settlers characterizes water access, supply and distribution. Israel breached its obligations under IHRL and ICESCR article 11 and its obligation to ensure public health and hygiene under GC IV article 56. Destruction of water and sewage infrastructure during renewed hostilities breaches AP/I article 54 prohibiting destruction of objects indispensable to livelihood.

IV. Conclusion

It is a fiction to consider that Israel applies occupation law to the OPT. The analysis demonstrated that Israel has violated occupation law widely, ignoring the Regulations, GC IV and AP/I customary provisions applicable to occupation. It has covered its illegal manoeuvres and activities to appropriate Palestinian land, water, quarries and property and exploit its natural resources for the benefit of Israel and settlements that are an illegal enterprise in themselves, under a "pseudo legal web"[386] of military orders and legislation. Expanding the military necessity concept and making it the rule rather than the exception has eroded the principle of protection of the population.[387] Dispossession of Palestinians cannot be supported by arguments of fight against terrorism and self-defence that Israel uses to justify its military operations in Gaza. The West Bank is nominally under the PA authority which has signed the Oslo Accords, 60 percent of it under Israeli control (Area C) and the rest under Israeli internal, external and overall security (Area B). Israel's obligations under IEL, IHRL and IWL do not fare better and have been systematically put aside. Israel breached its obligations under principles of permanent sovereignty over natural resources, harm prevention and equitable and reasonable use of transboundary watercourses and ignored basics human rights to water and sanitation.

Israel acted with impunity in the OPT, rarely facing accountability, whether from its own HCJ or the international community of States. The HCJ has given a veneer of acceptability to military authorities' decisions in the OPT, deferring to its considerations of security, at least until 2002 when the ICC Statute entered into force, leading the HCJ to start limiting security punitive measures.[388] Sanctions could be applied but have been rarely taken against Israel, save a few against settlers,[389] while Trump removed those sanctions imposed by the Biden administration against settlers.[390] Foreign governments' "deep concerns" over approval of new constructions

385 Mara Tignino, *Water During and After Armed Conflicts: What protection under International Law?* (Brill 2016) 87

386 Abu Sitta 3

387 Gross 46

388 Benvenisti, *The International Law of Occupation* 218–220

389 Louis Imbert, 'A System of Sanctions against Israeli Settlers is in the Making' Le Monde (21 July 2024)

390 Jonathan Landay and Humeyra Pamuk, 'Trump Cancels Sanctions on Israeli Settlers in West Bank, 21 January 2025' Reuters online

in settlements cannot stop their expansion.[391] ICJ advisory opinions, such as the Wall opinion, are not enforceable. UNSC resolutions requesting Israel to withdraw from occupied territories or on illegality of its settlements and UNGA resolutions on permanent sovereignty over natural resources or right of self-determination of the Palestinian people are declarations without practical effect. Oslo II is a "paper commitment" easily ignored[392] resulting from an asymmetrical bargaining process that was weighted heavily in favour of Israel.[393] The conflict "remains a zone of legal exceptionalism."[394]

Scholars suggested solutions to specific issues, such as restoration of Palestinian private water rights existing pre-1967 in the OPT,[395] compensation for Palestinian claims to private properties confiscated including those properties left in 1948[396] and joint management of the West Bank Mountain Aquifer[397] and proposed comprehensive solutions to the Palestinian-Israeli conflict,[398] including overhauling the legal framework for Palestine applying precedent models used in similar cases such as Kosovo, Bosnia and South Africa.[399]

The ICJ concluded that Israel's continued presence in the OPT is a wrongful act entailing its responsibility, for which it has to make full reparations, by obligation of restitution to return land and immovable property seized since 1967 and evacuate settlements and, if impossible, by compensation.[400] All States are under an obligation not to recognize as legal the situation created by the illegal occupation and not to help maintain it.[401] The precise modalities to end the occupation should be decided by the UNGA and the UNSC.[402] The UNGA adopted a resolution demanding Israel comply with its obligations under the ICJ opinion, calling on all States to respect their obligations thereunder including the realization of Palestinian self-determination – which is an obligation *erga onmes* – and recognizing the need to establish an international mechanism for reparation of damage.[403]

391 Commonwealth & Development Office Foreign, Press Release, *Joint International Statement Following Recent Events in Israel and the West Bank*, 30 June 2023
392 Scobbie, 'Natural Resources and Belligerent Occupation: Mutation through Permanent Sovereignty' 285
393 Richard Falk, 'No Peace Without Rights: Why International Law Matters' 21 Transnat L Contemp Probs (2012) 31, 32
394 *International Law and the Israeli-Palestinian Conflict, a Rights-Based Approach to Middle East Peace* (Susan M. Akram and others eds, Routledge 2011) 4
395 Dichter 580
396 Benvenisti and Zamir
397 J.A. Allan and Chibli Mallat, 'Introduction' in J.A. Allan and Chibli Mallat (eds), *Water in the Middle East: Legal, Political and Commercial Implications* (I.B. Tauris Publishers 1995) 16
398 International Law and the Israeli-Palestinian Conflict, a Rights-Based Approach to Middle East Peace
399 Salman H. Abu Sitta, 'Chapter 11, The Geographic and Demographic Imperatives of the Palestinian Refugees' Return' in Hani Faris (ed), *The Failure of the Two-State Solution, the Prospect of One State in the Israel Palestine Conflict* (I.B. Tauris 2013) 14
400 OPT *Policies and Practices*, par.173, 243
401 Ibid, par.276–279
402 *OPT Policies and Practices par.279, 281*
403 UNGA, *A/ES-10/L.31, 11 September 2024*

The occupation of the Palestinian Territory is the longest unresolved conflict since 1948, involving the dispossession of the Palestinian people of its land on an unprecedented scale, a testament to the incapacity of international law and institutions to resolve military conflicts and a failure of international diplomacy. Yet, there will not be sustainable peace between Israelis and Palestinians without recognition of their respective rights within the framework of international law.[404]

Bibliography

Treaties

British Empire, France, Italy, Japan, Greece, & C. and Turkey, Treaty of Peace (Lausanne, 24 July 1923)
Convention on the Law on Non-Navigational Uses of International Watercourses (1997)
Israeli- Palestinian Declaration of Principles on Interim Self-Government Arrangements (13 September 1993)
Israeli-Palestinian Interim Agreement on the West Bank and the Gaza Strip (28 September 1995)
San Remo Conference (UK, France, Italy, Japan), Resolution of 25 April 1920
Hague Regulations The Sykes Picot Agreement, 16 May 1916
Treaty of Peace with Germany (Treaty of Versailles) of 28 June 1919

International organizations documents

Amnesty International, *The Occupation of Water* (2017)
Cluster Wash, *State of Palestine, Critical Access to Water during COVID-19 Endangered by a Rise in Demolitions in the West Bank: The Case of Masafer Yatta* (2021)
Covenant of the League of Nations, Part I of the Treaty of Versailles, June 28 1919 (entry into force 10 January 1920)
Dugard J, *Report of the Special Rapporteur on the Situation of Human Rights in Palestinian Territories Occupied Since 1967* (2007)
HRW, 'Israel/Egypt: Choking Gaza Harms Civilians' News release
———, *A Threshold Crossed* (2021)
ICC, *Situation in Palestine, Summary of Preliminary Examination Findings*
ILC, *Responsibility of States for Internationally Wrongful Acts* (ILC YB 2001, vol II (Part Two))
ICRC Resolution 5, Implementation of the Memorandum of Understanding and Agreement on Operational Arrangements, dated 28 November 2005, between the Palestine Red Crescent Society and the Magen David Adom in Israel (ICRC 2011)
League of Nations, Mandate for Palestine, 12 August 1922
Palestine National Council, *Letter dated 18 November 1988 from the Permanent Representative of Jordan to the United Nations addressed to the Secretary-General, A/43/827, S/20278* (1988)
Sloan B, *Study of the Implications, under International Law, of the UN Resolutions on Permanent Sovereignty over Natural Resources, on the Occupied Palestinian and other Arab Territories and on the Obligations of Israel Concerning its Conduct in these Territories, Report of the Secretary-General, Annex, UNGA A/38/50/Rev.1* (1983)
'Special Report, Sovereignty over Water Resources in the West Bank and Gaza Strip' V Palestine YB Int'l L 346

404 Falk 32, 40

UN Ad Hoc Committee on the Palestinian Question, *Report of Sub-Committee 2, A/AC.14/32* (1947)
UN Committee on the Exercise of the Inalienable Rights of the Palestinian People, *The Status of Jerusalem* (1977)
UN Doc. A/RES/67/19 (Nov. 29, 2012)
UN, *UN Experts Urge all States to Recognise State of Palestine* (3 June 2024)
———, *Water Resources of the Occupied Palestinian Territory*, Prepared for, and under the Guidance of, the Committee on the Exercise of the Inalienable Rights of the Palestinian People, (1992)
UNCESCR, *General Comment No. 15: The Right to Water (Arts. 11 and 12 of the Covenant), E/C.12/2002/11* (2002)
UNCTAD, *Report on UNCTAD assistance to the Palestinian People: Developments in the Economy of the Occupied Palestinian Territory, TD/B/67/5* (2020)
UNDP, *Human Development Report, beyond Scarcity: Power, Poverty and the Global Water Crisis* (2006)
UNEP, *Desk Study on the Environment in the Occupied Palestinian Territories* (2003)
———, *State of Environment and Outlook Report for the Occupied Palestinian Territory* (2020)
UNGA, *A/ES-10/L.31, 11 September 2024*
———, *A/RES/ES-10/19, 22 December 2017*
———, *Report of the Committee on the Exercise of the Inalienable Rights of the Palestinian People, A/77/35* (2022)
———, *Report of the Independent International Commission of Inquiry on the Occupied Palestinian Territory, including East Jerusalem, and Israel (A/77/328)* (2022)
———, *Resolution 181 adopted on the Report of the Ad Hoc Committee on the Palestinian Question, 29 November 1947*
———, *Resolutions 2253 and 2254 (ES-V), 4 and 14 July 1967*
———, *The Human Rights to Safe Drinking Water and Sanitation, A/Res.70/169* (2015)
UNGA ESC, *Permanent Sovereignty over Natural Resources in the Occupied Palestinian and Other Arab Territories: Report of the Secretary-General* (1984)
UNHCHR, *Israeli Settlements in the Occupied Palestinian Territory, including East Jerusalem, and in the Occupied Syrian Golan, A/HRC/46/65* (2021)
———, *Israeli Settlements in the Occupied Palestinian Territory, including East Jerusalem, and in the Occupied Syrian Golan, A/HRC/55/72, 1st February* (2024)
UNHRC, *Allocation of Water Resources in the Occupied Palestinian Territory, including East Jerusalem, A/HRC/48/43* (2021)
———, *Human Rights Situation in the Occupied Palestinian Territory, including East Jerusalem, with a Focus on Access to Water and Environmental Degradation, A/HRC/40/73* (2019)
———, *The Human Rights to Safe Drinking Water and Sanitation, A/HRC/RES/39/8* (2018)
UNOCHA, *Occupied Palestinian Territory, Humanitarian Facts and Figures* (2017)
———, 'Sharp Increase in Ratification of Declarations of "State Land"' The Monthly Humanitarian Bulletin (June 2016)
UNRWA and BGR, *Inventory of Shared Water Resources in Western Asia, Chap.6 Jordan River Basin* (2013)
UNRWA West Bank Field Office, 'Mini Profile: Al Walaja'
———, 'Where We Work'
UNSC, *Resolution 242, 22 November 1967, S/RES/242* (1967)
———, *Resolution 446, Territories Occupied by Israel, 22 March 1979*
———, *Resolution 465, Territories Occupied by Israel, 1st March 1980*
———, *Resolution 2334, 23 December 2016, S/RES/2334*
———, *S/PV.9609, 18 April 2024* (2024)
———, *S/RES/252, 21 May 1968*

———, *S/RES/267, 3 July 1969*

UN Secretary-General, *Report of the Secretary-General prepared pursuant to General Assembly resolution ES-10/13 (A/ES-10/248)* (2003)

West Bank Protection Consortium WBP, *Palestinian Access to Water and Attacks on WASH Structures in Area C* (2021)

WHO, *Domestic Water Quantity, Service Level and Health* (2020)

———, *Health Conditions in the Occupied Palestinian Territory, including East Jerusalem, and in the Occupied Syrian Golan, A74/22* (2021)

World Bank, *Securing Water for Development in West Bank and Gaza* (2018)

———, *Toward Water Security for Palestinians, West Bank and Gaza Water Supply, Sanitation, and Hygiene Poverty Diagnostic* (WASH Poverty Diagnostic, 2018)

———, *West Bank and Gaza, Area C and the Future of the Palestinian Economy, Report No. AUS2922* (2013)

World Bank, Philippe Marin, Shimon Tal, Joshua Yeres, Klas Ringskog, *Water Management in Israel, Key Innovations and Lessons Learned for Water-Scarce Countries* (2017)

Israel legislation and military orders and foreign governments documents

Absentees' Property Law, 5710–1950

British White Paper of 1939

Changing Miri Land to Mulk Land Law (No. 41), 1953

Defense (Emergency) Regulations (1945), Regulation 125 Closed Areas

Development Authority (Transfer of Property) Law, 5710–1950

UK Foreign, Commonwealth and Development Office, *Joint International Statement Following Recent Events in Israel and the West Bank*

IDF, *Order No. 58, Order on Abandoned Properties (Private Property), 23 July 1967*

———, *Order No.378 Concerning Security Provisions (Judea and Samaria), 1970*

———, *Order No. 92 of 15 August 1967* (V Palestine YB Int'l L 1989, 346)

———, *Order No.158 of 30 October 1967* (V Palestine YB Int'l L 1989, 351)

———, *Order No. 291 Concerning the Settlement of Titles and the Regulation of Water (West Bank/Judea and Samaria), 1968* (V Palestine YB Int'l L1989, 355)

———, *Order No. 498 of 4 November 1974* (V Palestine YB Int'l L 1989, 359)

———, *Order No.1651 Regarding Security Directives, [Consolidated Version] (Judea and Samaria), 2009*

République Française, Assemblée Nationale, La Commission des Affaires Etrangères, *Rapport d'information, la géopolitique de l'eau* (2011)

Land Acquisition (Validation of Acts and Compensation) Law, 5713–1953

Land Law, 5729–1969

Law and Administration Ordinance No. 1 of 5708–1948, Laws of the State of Israel, Vol. I, Ordinances, 5708–1948, 7

Prescription Law 5718–1958

Provisional Law on the Regulation of Natural Resources, Law No. 37 of 1966, Official Gazette (Jordan) No. 1931, 16 June 1966, at 1113

State Property Law (5711–1951), Laws of the State of Israel: Authorized Translation from the Hebrew, Volume V, Laws, 5711–1950/51, 45, No. 19

Tal-Spiro O, The Knesset, The Research and Information Center, *Israeli-Palestinian Cooperation on Water Issues, Presented to the Internal Affairs and Environment Committee* (2011)

The Absentee Property (Compensation) Law 5733–1973

The Emergency Land Requisition (Regulation) Law, 5710–1949, Laws of the State of Israel, Vol. 4, 5710–1949/50, 3

The Emergency Regulations (Cultivation of Waste Lands), (Extension of Validity) Ordinance No. 36 of 5709–1949

The Land Transfers Regulations, 1940

The Law for Settlement of Titles to Land and Water, Law No. 40, 1952, at Official Gazette (Jordan) no. 1113, 16 June 1952, 279
The Ottoman Land Code 1858
The Palestine Order-in-Council, 1922
The Water Law 1959
Water Authority Law, Law No. 34 of 1983, Official Gazette (Jordan) No. 3194, 15 December 1983
Yasser Arafat, PLO Chairman, *Letter to Yitzhak Rabin, Prime Minister of Israel, 9 September 1993*
Yitzhak Rabin, Prime Minister of Israel, *Letter to Yasser Arafat, 9 September 1993*

International tribunals decisions

Affaire de la Dette publique ottomane (Bulgarie, Irak, Palestine, Transjordanie, Grèce, Italie et Turquie) 18 avril 1925, 1 UNRIIA pp. 529–614
Application of the Convention on the Prevention and Punishment of the Crime of Genocide in the Gaza Strip (South Africa v. Israel) ICJ
Armed Activities on the Territory of the Congo (DRC v. Uganda), Reparations, Judgement ICJ Rep 2022, p. 13
Beit Sourik Village Council v. Israel (30 June 2004) HCJ 2056/04, 43 ILM 1099 (2004)
Crawford SC J, *Opinion, Third Party Obligations with Respect to Israeli Settlements in the Occupied Palestinian Territories* (2012)
Harpaz G and others, *Expert Legal Opinion, HCJ 2164/09 Yesh Din – Volunteers for Human Rights v. Commander of IDF Forces in West Bank et. al. (26 December 2011)*
HCJ 606/78, Ayoub v Minister of Defense, 33(2) PD 113
Legal Consequences Arising from the Policies and Practices of Israel in the Occupied Palestinian Territory, including East Jerusalem, ICJ Advisory Opinion, 19 July 2024 (ICJ)
Legal Consequences of the Construction of a Wall in the Occupied Palestinian Territory, Advisory Opinion ICJ Rep 2004
Statement of ICC Prosecutor Karim A.A. Khan KC: Applications for Arrest Warrants in the Situation in the State of Palestine, 20 May 2024
The Concept of State Land in the Occupied Territories, Affidavit of Aziz Shehadeh Palestine YB Int'l Law 1985
Yesh Din – Volunteers for Human Rights v. Commander of the IDF Forces in the West Bank et. al. (HCJ 2164/09)

Journal articles

Abdallah T and Khaled S, 'Effects of the Israeli Segregation Wall on Biodiversity and Environmental Sustainable Development in the West Bank, Palestine' 68 Int'l J Env Stud 4 2011 543 543
Abouali G, 'Continued Control: Israel, Palestinian Water and the Interim Agreement' IX Palestine YB Int'l Law 1996–1997 63
———, 'Natural Resources under Occupation: The Status of Palestinian Waters under International Law' 10 Pace Int'l L Rev 1998 411 411
Alatout S, 'Water Multiples in Israeli Politics, Paper prepared for Environmental Politics Workshop, Berkeley, October 2010'
Alwazir A, 'Uprooting Olive Trees in the West Bank, ICE Case Number: 110' Inventory of Conflict and Environment (ICE), American University, the School of International Service, Washington
Amara A, 'The Negev Land Question: Between Denial and Recognition' 42, Summer 2013 J Palestine Stud 2013 27 27

———, 'Civilizational Exceptions: Ottoman Law and Governance in Late Ottoman Palestine' 36 L Hist Rev 4, November 2018 915 915
Antonius R, 'Palestine-Israel: Moments structurants et droit international (1917–2015)' Guerres mondiales et conflits contemporains, No 262, Moyen-Orient et conflits au XXe siècle, Avril–Juin 2016 107
Aronson G, 'Israel's Policy of Military Occupation' 7 J Palestine Stud 4, Summer 1978 79
Aytekin EA, 'Agrarian Relations, Property and Law: An Analysis of the Land Code of 1858 in the Ottoman Empire' 45 Middle E Stud No. 6, November 2009 935
Bantekas I, 'Land Rights in Nineteenth Century Ottoman State Succession Treaties' 26 EJIL 2 2015 375 375
Bell A and Shefia D, 'The Mythical Post-2005 Israeli Occupation of the Gaza Strip' 16 Isr Aff 2 2010 268 268
Ben-Eliezer U and Feinstein Y, '"The Battle over Our Homes": Reconstructing/Deconstructing Sovereign Practices around Israel's Separation Barrier on the West Bank' 12 Isr Stud 1 171 171
Ben-Naftali O and others, 'Illegal Occupation: Framing the Occupied Palestinian Territory' 23 Berkeley J Int'l L 3 2005 551 551
Benvenisti E, 'Water Conflicts during the Occupation of Iraq' 97 AJIL No. 4, October 2003 860
Benvenisti E and Gvirtzman H, 'Harnessing International Law to Determine Israeli-Palestinian Water Rights: The Mountain Aquifer' 33 Nat Resources J 1993 543
Benvenisti E and Zamir E, 'Private Claims to Property Rights in the Future Israeli-Palestinian Settlement' 89 AJIL 2, April 1995 295
Bisharat GE, 'Land, Law, and Legitimacy in Israel and the Occupied Palestinian Territories' 43 Am Uni L Rev 1993–1994 467 467
Blum YZ, 'The Missing Reversioner: Reflections on the Status of Judea and Samaria' 3 Israel L Rev 1968 279
Bornstein A, 'Military Occupation as Carceral Society, Prisons, Checkpoints, and Walls in the Israeli-Palestinian Struggle' 52 Social Analysis 2 Summer 2008 106 106
Braverman I, 'Uprooting Identities: The Regulation of Olive Trees in the Occupied West Bank' 32 PoLAR 2 2009 237 237
Civic MA, 'A Comparative Analysis of the Israelis and Arab Water Law Traditions and Insights for Modern Water Sharing Agreements' 26 Denver J Int'l L Policy 3 1997–1998 437 437
Clarke B, 'Military Occupation and the Rule of Law: the Legal Obligations of Occupying Forces in Iraq' 10 Int'l Trade Bus L Rev 2006 133 133
Dawn EC, 'The Arab-Israeli Confrontation: A Historian's Analysis' 5 Denver J Int'l L Policy 1975 373 373
Dichter H, 'The Legal Status of Israel's Water Policies in the Occupied Territories' 35 Harv Int'l L J 2, Spring 1994 565
Dillman JD, 'Water Rights in the Occupied Territories' 19 J Palestine Stud 1, Autumn 1989 46
———, 'Le pillage de l'eau dans les territoires occupés' 35 Revue d'études Palestiniennes, 1990 Printemps 1990 37
Dundas C, 'In the Absence of Law: Legal Aspects of the Palestinian-Israeli Conflict' XIV Middle East Policy 1, Spring 2007 42 42
Eldar A, 'Ministry Admits 'Blacklist' of Palestinians Who Left W. Bank, 5 July 2006' Ha'aretz 2006
Falk R, 'No Peace Without Rights: Why International Law Matters' 21 Transnat L Contemp Probs 2012 31
Fischbach MR, 'The United Nations and Palestinian Refugee Property Compensation' 31 J Palestine Stud 2 2002 34

Forman G and Kedar AS, 'Colonialism, Colonization, and Land Law in Mandate Palestine: The Zor al-Zarqa and Barrat Qisarya Land Disputes in Historical Perspective' 4 Theoretical Inq L 2003 491 491
———, 'From Arab Land to "Israel Lands": The Legal Dispossession of the Palestinians Displaced by Israel in the Wake of 1948' 22 Environ Plan D 2004 809 809
Gatteschi D, 'Des Lois sur la Propriété Foncière dans l'Empire Ottoman et particulièrement en Egypte' 13 Rev Hist Dr F Etran (1855–1869), Editions Dalloz, 1867 436
Gavish D and Kark R, 'The Cadastral Mapping of Palestine, 1858–1928' 159 Geogr J 1, March 1993 70
Hirsch A, 'Utilization of International Rivers in the Middle East, a Study of Conventional International Law' 59 AJIL 1956 81
———, 'Water Legislation in the Middle East' 8 Am J Comp L 1959 168 168
Hofri-Winograd AS, 'Zionist Settlers and the English Private Trust in Mandate Palestine' 30 L Hist Rev 3, August 2012 813
Imbert L, 'A System of Sanctions against Israeli Settlers Is in the Making' Le Monde (21 July 2024)
Imseis A, 'On the Fourth Geneva Convention and the Occupied Palestinian Territory' 44 Harvard Int'l L J 1 2003 65
Kedar AS, 'The Legal Transformation of Ethnic Geography: Israeli Law and the Palestinian Landholder 1948–1967' 33 NYU J Int'l L Policy 2000–2001 923 923
Kretzmer D, 'Bombshell for the Settlement Enterprise in Levy Report' Haaretz
Kretzmer D, 'The Advisory Opinion: the Light Treatment of International Humanitarian Law' 99 AJIL 2005 88
LeVine M, 'Conquest Through Town Planning: The Case of Tel Aviv, 1921–48' 27 J Palestine Stud 4, Summer 1998 36
Longobardo M, 'The Palestinian Right to Exploit the Dead Sea Coastline for Tourism' 58 German YB Int'l L 2015 317 317
Lovatt H, 'European Council on Foreign Relations' Occupation and Sovereignty: Renewing EU Policy in Israel-Palestine (2017)
Lustick I, 'Israel and the West Bank after Elon Moreh: The Mechanics of De Facto Annexation' 35 Middle E J 4, Autumn 1981 557 557
MacChesney B, 'Lake Lanoux Case (France-Spain)' 53 AJIL 1, January 1959 156
McCaffrey SC, 'Water Scarcity and Security Issues in the Middle East' 108 ASIL Proceedings 2014 297
Mehozay Y, 'The Fluid Jurisprudence of Israel's Emergency Powers: Legal Patchwork as a Governing Norm' 46 L Soc Rev March 2012 137
Mogannam ME, 'Palestine Legislation under the British' 64 Ann Am Acad Pol Soc Sci November 47
Nijim BK, 'Water Resources in the History of the Palestine-Israel Conflict' 21 GeoJournal, Some Geographical Aspects of the Israeli-Palestinian Conflict 4, August 1990 317 317
Pacheco A, Esq., 'The Israeli Supreme Court Case on Israeli Quarrying Licenses in the West Bank: Why a Second ICJ Advisory Opinion on Palestine Is Needed' PYBIL online, 2014, p. 57
'Palestine for the Jews: Official Sympathy' The Times, 9 November 1917, 7
Prusher I, 'Israel's Absentee Property Law Exposes an Absence of Morality in Jerusalem' Haaretz, 7 June 2013
Roberts A, 'What Is Military Occupation' 50 Brit YB Int'l L 1984 249
Rosenthal E and Sabel R, 'Water and Diplomacy in the Jordan River Basin' III Isr J Foreign Aff 2 2009 95
Samson E, 'Is Gaza Occupied: Redefining the Status of Gaza under International Law' 25 Amsterdam Uni Int'l L Rev 2010 915 915

Scobbie I, 'H2O after Oslo: Legal Aspects of Water in the Occupied Territories' 8 PYBIL 1994–1995 79
Sharon J, 'Palestinians Say Settlers Destroy Dozens of Olive Trees, Harass Farmers' The Times of Israel 2022
Shehadeh R, 'The Gaza Occupation: Beginnings and Endings' 14 PYBIL 2006–2007 13
———, 'The Land Law of Palestine: An Analysis of the Definition of State Lands' 11 J Palestine Stud 2 Winter, 1982 82
Shomar B, 'Water Scenarios in the Gaza Strip, Palestine: Thirst, Hunger and Disease' 68 Int'l J Env Stud 4 2011 477 477
Sophia Jones, 'Here's What the World Thinks of Israel's Controversial Land Grab' The Huffington Post 2014
King Hussein I (King of Jordan), 'Statement Concerning Disengagement from the West Bank and Palestinian Self-Determination, Address by His Majesty King Hussein I to the Nation, 31 July 1988' 27 ILM 6, November 1988 1637
The Levy Commission, 'Report on the Legal Status of Building in Judea and Samaria, Conclusions and Recommendations, Jerusalem' 42 J Palestine Stud 1, 9 July 2012 179–182
Tignino M, 'Water, International Peace, and Security' 92 IRRC 879, September 2010 647
Trottier J, 'Le Rapport à l'Eau et à la Terre dans la Construction de Territoires Multisitués: le Cas Palestinien' Espace Géographique 2015
Trottier J and Perrier J, 'Water-driven Palestinian Agricultural Frontiers: The Global Ramifications of Transforming Local Irrigation' 25 JPE 2018 291
Weaver S and others, 'Territories Occupied by Israel: Settlements and Exploration of Oil Resources' 72 ASIL Proceedings April 1978 118
Zilbershats Y, 'Apartheid, International Law, and the Occupied Palestinian Territory: A Reply to John Dugard and John Reynolds' 24 EJIL 3 2013 915

Electronic articles

Abu Sitta S, *The Denied Inheritance: Palestinian Land Ownership in Beer Sheba* (2009)
ARIJ, 'Report on the Israeli Colonization Activities in the West Bank & the Gaza Strip, 2012'
ARIJ and Land Research Center (LRC), 'Wadi Al Teen Quarry and the Systematic Expropriation of Palestinian Natural Resources, 1997'
B'Tselem, 'East Jerusalem (2017 updated 2019)'
———, 'End the Uprooting of Trees (2001)'
———, *Human Rights in the Occupied Territories, Annual Report* (2011)
———, *Land Grab, Israel's Settlement Policy in the West Bank* (2002)
———, *This Is Ours – And This, Too, Israel's Settlement Policy in the West Bank* (2021)
———, 'The Village of al-Walajah: Dispossession and Home Demolitions, 2022'
Cohen A, 'Miri' Encyclopaedia of Islam
Delcambre A-M, *Mawāt* (Brill Online 2012)
Drobles M, *Settlement in Judea and Samaria: Strategy, Policy and Planning (WZO Settlement Division)* (1980)
Land Research Centre (LRC), *Palestinian Olive Agony*
Landay J. and Pamuk H, 'Trump Cancels Sanctions on Israeli Settlers in West Bank, 21 January 2025' Reuters online
Lazarou E, *Water in the Israeli-Palestinian conflict* (European Parliamentary Research Service, Briefing January, 2016)
Norwegian Refugee Council, *The Absentee Property Law and its Implementation in East Jerusalem, a Legal Guide and Analysis* (2013)
Palestinian Centre for Human Rights, 'IDF continue bulldozing works to construct the Annexation Wall and isolate al-Walaja Village, Northwest of Bethlehem'
PCBS, 'Area, Population, and Population Density in Palestine by Governorate, 2021'
———, 'Estimated Population in Palestine Mid-Year by Governorate,1997–2026'

Peace Now, *Unraveling the Mechanism behind Illegal Outposts* (2017)
Perrier J, *Les lois palestiniennes de l'eau: entre centralisation, décentralisation et mise en invisibilité* (Papiers de Recherche, Agence Francaise de Développement (AFD), n 2019–118, Décembre, 2019)
State Comptroller, *State Comptroller's Annual Report 56a* (2005)
The Editors of Encyclopaedia Britannica and Zeidan A, 'Hamas (2023)'
The Knesset, 'Lexicon of Terms, Declaring a State of Emergency' The State of Israel, the Knesset website
Unsleber S, '"This Village is a Microcosm of Palestine," al-Walaja Fights the Separation Wall (2011)' The Palestine Monitor

Books – reports

Adalah, *Forced Displacement, Position Paper* (May 2023)
Amnesty International, *Israel's Apartheid against Palestinians* (2022)
B'Tselem, *By Hook and by Crook, Israeli Settlements Policy in the West Bank* (2010)
Benvenisti E, *The International Law of Occupation* (2nd edn, OUP 2012)
Dinstein Y, *The International Law of Belligerent Occupation* (2nd edn, CUP 2019)
Falk R, *Situation in the State of Palestine, Amicus Curiae Submissions Pursuant to Rule 103, ICC-01/18* (16 March 2020)
Gilbert M, *Israel, a History* (Doubleday 1998)
Green LC, *The Contemporary Law of Armed Conflict* (3rd edn, MUP 2008)
Gross A, *The Writing on the Wall, Rethinking the International Law of Occupation* (CUP 2017)
International Law and the Israeli-Palestinian Conflict, a Rights-Based Approach to Middle East Peace (Susan M. Akram and others eds, Routledge 2011)
Kattan V, *From Coexistence to Conquest, International Law and the Origins of the Arab-Israeli Conflict, 1891–1949* (Pluto Press 2009)
Kretzmer D and Ronen Y, *The Occupation of Justice, The Supreme Court of Israel and the Occupied Territories* (2nd edn, OUP 2021)
Morris B, *The Birth of the Palestinian Refugee Problem Revisited* (Online publication date: June 2012, 2nd edn, CUP 2004)
Navot Kerem, *A Locked Garden, Declaration of Closed Areas in the West Bank* (2015)
———, *For the Common Good, Military Expropriation Orders in the West Bank, 1967–2022* (2022)
Norwegian Refugee Council, *A Guide to Housing, Land and Property Law in Area C of the West Bank* (2012)
Oppenheim L, *International Law, Vol. II Disputes, War and Neutrality* (Lauterpacht H ed, 7th edn, Longmans, Green and Co. 1952)
Quigley J, *Palestine and Israel, A Challenge to Justice* (DUP 1990)
Rogers APV, *Law on the Battlefield* (3rd edn, MUP 2012)
Scobbie I, with Hibbin S, *The Israel-Palestine Conflict in International Law: Territorial Issues* (The U.S./Middle East Project 2009)
Tignino M, *Water during and after Armed Conflicts: What Protection under International Law?* (Brill 2016)
US Department of State, *2022 Country Reports on Human Rights Practices: Israel, West Bank and Gaza* (2022)
Yesh Din, *Ill-Gotten Gains, Theft of Palestinian land – Declaring "State Land" Where Settlement of Title Was Halted When Israel Occupied the West Bank* (2021)
———, *Police Investigation of Vandalization of Palestinian Trees in the West Bank, Yesh Din Monitoring, 2005–2011* (2011)
———, *The Great Drain, Israeli Quarries in the West Bank: High Court Sanctioned Institutionalized Theft* (2017)
———, *The Legal Status of Israeli Occupation, Legal Opinion* (2023)

———, *Summary of the 2022 Harvest Season* (2023)
———, 'Yesh Din's Response to the HCJ Ruling in the Organization's Petition Challenging the Legality of Israeli Quarrying Activities in the Occupied West Bank (HCJ 164/09)'
Zeitoun M, *Power and Water in the Middle East, the Hidden Politics of the Palestinian-Israeli Water Conflict* (I.B. Tauris 2012)

Book chapters

Abu Sitta SH, 'Chapter 11, The Geographic and Demographic Imperatives of the Palestinian Refugees' Return' in Faris H (ed), *The Failure of the Two-State Solution, the Prospect of One State in the Israel Palestine Conflict* (I.B. Tauris 2013)
Allan JA and Mallat C, 'Introduction' in Allan JA and Mallat C (eds), *Water in the Middle East: Legal, Political and Commercial Implications* (I.B. Tauris Publishers 1995)
Cassese A, 'Powers and Duties of an Occupant in Relation to Land and Natural Resources' in Playfair E (ed), *International Law and the Administration of Occupied Territories, Two Decades of Israeli Occupation of the West Bank and Gaza Strip* (OUP 1992)
Dörmann K and Vité S, 'Occupation' in Fleck D (ed), *The Handbook of International Humanitarian Law* (4th edn, OUP 2021)
Falk R and Weston BH, 'The Relevance of International Law to Israeli and Palestinian Rights in the West Bank and Gaza' in Playfair E (ed), *International Law and the Administration of the Occupied Territories* (OUP 1992)
Jacques M, 'Case Study: Israeli Settlements, the Separation Wall and Displacement of Civilians in the Occupied Palestinian Territory' in *Armed Conflict and Displacement, the Protection of Refugees and Displaced Persons under International Humanitarian Law* (CUP 2012)
Mallat C, 'The Quest for Water Use Principles: Reflections of Shari'a and Customs in the Middle East' in Allan JA and Mallat C (eds), *Water in the Middle East: Legal, Political and Cultural Implications* (I.B. Tauris Publishers 1995)
McIntyre O, 'Chapter 15: Water' in Morgera E and Kulovesi K (eds), *Research Handbook on International Law and Natural Resources* (Edward Elgar 2016)
Métral F, 'Le droit de l'eau dans le Code civil ottoman de 1869 et la notion de domaine public' in *L'Homme et l'eau en Méditerranée et au Proche Orient* (Travaux de la Maison de l'Orient 1982)
Qupty M, 'The Application of International Law in the Occupied Territories as Reflected in the Judgements of the High Court of Justice in Israel' in Playfair E (ed), *International Law and the Administration of the Occupied Territories* (OUP 1992)
Scobbie I, 'Natural Resources and Belligerent Occupation: Mutation through Permanent Sovereignty' in Bowen S (ed), *Human Rights, Self-Determination and Political Change in the Occupied Palestinian Territories* (Martinus Nijhoff 1997)

7 In the aftermath of international armed conflicts

The book has drawn a panorama of relevant States' obligations towards the environment and natural resources constituting it under the LOAC and those under IEL, IWL and IHRL that are applicable during international armed conflict for which States should be held accountable in case of breach. The strength of LOAC customary principles of proportionality, discrimination, military necessity and humanity in creating meaningful legal obligations towards the environment during war may be questioned. Relevant issues concern the subjectivity surrounding proportionality and expansiveness of notions of military necessity and of dual-use objects when applying distinction, which belligerent States can stretch to accommodate their military conduct, preventing a robust protection of civilian and civilian objects, including environment. Those principles, incorporated in AP/I almost universally adhered to, remain nonetheless legal norms constraining military operations. States' conventional obligations during war under the LOAC applicable to natural resources protect them from destruction that is unnecessary militarily – or as objects indispensable to livelihood such as agricultural lands and water installations – and from attacks that could release dangerous forces, among others. Two AP/I provisions prohibit the use of warfare means potentially resulting in environmental damage reaching a threshold that is considered outdated today, as it was set almost half a century ago, at a time of infancy of IEL and given our increased knowledge about environmental issues and growing destructive power of warfare means. The threshold would benefit from a new interpretation, as was proposed.

Under occupation law, natural resources remain under the permanent sovereignty of the protected population and are protected from pillage, confiscation and requisitions that are strictly for army maintenance needs when privately owned and must be administered sustainably for the benefit of the people under occupation, if publicly owned. Rules and regulations relating to the conduct of occupiers towards natural resources in occupied territory sit on antiquated notions of enemy property, distinction of movable and immoveable oddly applied to natural resources and the inappropriate usufructuary concept covering exploitation of natural resources. Occupation law would require replacement or amendments by a new treaty, though it is not a palatable endeavour for the international community.

However, the LOAC treaties must be interpreted by considering international law development since their signature under IEL, IWL and IHRL, adapting them

DOI: 10.4324/9780367823283-7

to contemporary concerns. This has been the focus of the ICRC in its 2020 guidelines on the protection of natural environment in armed conflict and has figured in its study on IHL customary rules. The ILC also came up with its own principles on the subject. The occurrence of an armed conflict has been found not to affect applicability, during conflict, of treaties that are outside the LOAC field, such as IEL, IWL and IHRL, unless treaties provide for their suspension during armed conflict. Obligations under different law fields may clash with LOAC obligations or mutually support each other. Interpretation techniques to resolve contradictions between legal norms from various law branches were highlighted and *lex specialis* and systemic interpretation found suitable, depending on the issue.

IEL principles of permanent sovereignty over natural resources and prevention of environmental damage and transboundary harm, being customary law, remain applicable during armed conflict. The due diligence duty is implemented in practice through obligations of cooperation, negotiation and EIA, among others, recognized as applicable by jurisprudence. IEL principles that are not yet deemed customary law are not necessarily applicable during armed conflict, though their influence looms over interpretation of norms, such as sustainable use of natural resources replacing the LOAC usufruct concept in the ILC principles and precautionary principle reinforcing the LOAC precautions in attacks. IEL treaties may impose obligations linked to specific natural resources, adding to their protection in armed conflicts. IWL reinforces the protection granted to freshwater resources during armed conflict and imposes on occupants an obligation to share reasonably and equitably transboundary watercourses. Finally, when IHRL obligations converge with LOAC obligations on protection of civilian and civilian objects, including natural resources, they may strengthen each other, such as basic human rights to water, food and health enhanced by natural resource protection during occupation.

The question raised at the outset of this book was whether it is possible, under the current international legal regime, to attribute liability to a belligerent State for environmental damage based on obligations breached during an IAC under the LOAC and applicable IEL, IHRL or IWL. The analysis demonstrated that there exists a wide range of obligations imposed on States during war and occupation related to environment and natural resources that are sufficiently clear despite the imprecision of some of the norms, to entail State responsibility in case of breach. The issue is that LOAC obligations can be and are often ignored and breached during IAC, without much consequential State responsibility imposed in practice on belligerents.

Benvenisti, reviewing multiple occupation, concluded that occupation law is generally ignored. If there was some illusion that the LOAC provides at least, in accordance with its aims, a minimum of protection to civilian populations caught in armed conflicts and their environment, it has been shattered by recent wars. The two cases examined in this book illuminate the impressive dichotomy between rules and application. ICRC research concluded that implementation of humanitarian law and reparation for victims of violations and environmental protection figured among four main areas of IHL necessitating legal development.[1] Implementation of the LOAC is afflicted by the weakness of international law, the absence of a supranational authority policing State actions in armed conflicts or sanctioning body in a world of sovereign equals or one assumed as such. "International law and its institutions function in an inescapably political context."[2] The LOAC is no exception, being subject to the vagaries of State powers and rivalries of opposed political blocs. This may reflect a realist view of international relations positing that politics and power reign supreme relegating international law and State responsibility to a secondary obscure place.[3] The situation is aggravated by the complicity of major powers in supporting international law violations of their allies, such as recognizing illegal annexations, breaching their own obligation not to recognize any annexation as lawful or to aid and assist in maintaining the situation, as the prohibition of use of force to acquire territory is an obligation *erga omnes*, from which no derogation is permitted.[4] Similar analysis applies to the refusal to acknowledge LOAC violations or to the continuing supply by various countries, to belligerents in armed conflicts breaching the LOAC or subject to proceedings at the ICC for war crimes or crimes against humanity or at the ICC for genocide, at the risk for these countries to breach their obligations under State responsibility law.

International law cannot be applied selectively, lest we want to spread anarchy and chaos. We should push back against dismissing responsibility of a State for its actions in armed conflicts. Arguments in favour of imposing liability on States for their destructive environmental actions during conflicts are many. "Rules must conform to reasonable expectations of behaviour if their authority is not to be eroded."[5] Should States continue to violate the LOAC rules with impunity, their propensity to breach the rules will increase to the point where rules will be emptied of their substance. The right of self-defence of a State does not equate to a licence to throw out the LOAC rules. Imposing State liability on all belligerents could act as deterrent against breach in future conflicts and help restore a minimum of respect for LOAC obligations. Further, post-conflict remediation of the

1 Jacob Kellenberger, 'Strengthening legal protection for victims of armed conflict, the ICRC Study on the current state of international humanitarian law, Address by Dr Jakob Kellenberger, President of the International Committee of the Red Cross,' 92 IRRC 879, 21 September 2010 799 801–802

2 Tim Stephens, *International Courts and Environmental Protection* (CUP 2009) 307

3 Lauri Malksoo, 'State Responsibility and the Challenge of the Realist Paragdim: The Demand of Baltic Victims of Soviet Mass Repression for Compensation from Russia' 3 Baltic YB Int'l L (2003) 57, 70

4 ILC, *Draft Conclusions on Identification and Legal Consequences of Peremptory Norms of General International Law (jus cogens) 2022* Conclusion 3, 17, 19; ILC, *Responsibility of States for Internationally Wrongful Acts* (ILC YB 2001, vol II (Part Two)) art.40, 41

5 Allan Gerson, 'Off-Shore Oil Exploration by a Belligerent Occupant: The Gulf of Suez Dispute' 71 AJIL 4, October (1977) 725, 730

environment and infrastructure services are essential to peacebuilding and security in countries emerging from war or occupation. The international community will have to provide financial and technical support for environmental restoration to the affected State, if it lacks such capabilities, in addition to considerable costs that the injured State will have to bear, as the experience of cleaning the oil spill and cluster bombs after the 2006 war in Lebanon proved. Imposing on a belligerent State an obligation to pay compensation for the financial burden of environmental restoration will reestablish a balance between its military power and responsibilities. It will also help alleviate a sense of injustice festering in post-conflict situations when issues of impunity are left unresolved, potentially leading to reemergence of armed hostilities.

Different paths for accountability should be mentioned, even though the book focus is on State responsibility. It should be mentioned equally that accountability must extend to members of armed groups that should be bound to respect the LOAC. The LOAC mechanisms for its implementation (designation of Protecting Powers,[6] formal enquiry procedure[7] or inquiry by the International Fact-Finding Commission)[8] lack significance and have not been used much in the past. IEL treaties generally geared towards prevention and cooperation refer to settlements of disputes though conciliation or mediation and do not necessarily include provisions for imposition of liability and sanctions, except for civil liability treaties. Multiple human rights institutions exist as well as investigative commissions set up by the UNHR Council, the UNSC and the UNGA, among others. Usually mandated to examine IHRL violations, some have been reporting on LOAC violations, and they are increasingly being used to report on violations of both legal regimes.[9]

Criminal liability attaches to violations of rules on conduct of hostilities and occupation under the LOAC and each party to the GC must enact legislation providing applicable penal sanctions.[10] Under a rarely used GC IV provision also applicable to AP/I, each party to GC IV must search for persons who committed or ordered grave breaches to GC IV and shall try them before their own court or hand them to another party for trial (universal jurisdiction principle).[11] No party to GC IV and AP/I can be absolved from breaches of its obligations thereunder.[12] Individual criminal liability may be imposed by the ICC for environment-related war crimes, including (i) extensive environmental destruction, unjustified by military necessity

6 GC common Art.8/8/8/9, AP/I art.5

7 Ibid, Art.52/53/132/149

8 AP/I art.90

9 UN HR, Office of the High Commissioner, *Commissions of Inquiry and Fact-finding Missions on International Human Rights and Humanitarian Law: Guidance and Practice* (2015) 2

10 Geneva Convention IV Relative to the Protection of Civilian Persons in Time of War, 12 August 1949 art.146, 147 (GC IV); AP/I art.85

11 GC IV, art.146; AP/I art.85.1

12 Ibid, art.148

carried out unlawfully and wantonly;[13] (ii) intentionally launching an attack, with the knowledge that it will cause widespread, long-term and severe damage to the natural environment which would be clearly excessive in relation to the concrete and direct overall military advantage anticipated;[14] and (iii) destruction or seizure of natural resources, unless imperatively demanded by war necessities.[15] Violation of the LOAC rules during past IAC led the ICC to open investigations into these situations and issue arrest warrants for leaders of armed groups and States involved, bringing them to trial, with recent decisions concerning current armed conflicts in Ukraine and Israel questioned as neither Russia nor Israel are party to the ICC Statute. Proceedings were instituted at the ICJ for application of the Genocide Convention in different conflicts. Individual criminal liability may lead to more calculated military operations in the future, though it leaves the question of State accountability and environmental damage reparation not fully resolved.

Economic or trade sanctions may be imposed on belligerents, such as the embargo on Russian gas to European countries during the Russia-Ukraine war following Ukraine invasion.[16] Sanctions are political as much as legal tools. As Russia was condemned and sanctioned for its occupation of Ukraine, while other States acting as occupants were never sanctioned, accusations of Western hypocrisy in the face of double standards flourished.[17]

Under State responsibility law regarding consequences of breach of its obligations in IAC causing damage, the State responsible has an obligation to make full reparation for damage, through restitution, compensation and satisfaction. Compensation of environmental damage should cover losses and expenses from its abatement and prevention, monitoring and assessment, monitoring of public health to combat health risks from it, reasonable measures taken or to be taken to clean and restore the environment, and depletion or damage to natural resources, as assessed by the UNCC. In case of natural resources confiscated or exploited during occupation, reparation entails an obligation to return land and immovable property confiscated and, if impossible, compensation.

Claims for reparation for damage to the environment and natural resources arising from war or occupation could be brought before the ICJ, assuming belligerents had previously accepted – or made a declaration to accept – its compulsory

13 ICC Statute art.8.2 (a)(iv)

14 Ibid, (b)(iv)

15 Ibid, (b)(xiii)

16 Henry Foy, David Sheppard and Alice Hancock, 'G7 and EU to Heap Pressure on Russia with Ban on Reopening of Gas Pipelines' FT (2023) 1

17 Martin Wolf, 'The West Must Recognise Its Hypocrisy' FT (11 July 2023); Patrick Wintour, 'Why US Double Standards on Israel and Russia Play into a Dangerous Game' The Guardian (26 December 2023); Oliver Stuenkel, 'Why the Global South Is Accusing America of Hypocrisy' FP (2 November 2023)

jurisdiction (ICJ Statute article 36(2)) or consent by agreement to its jurisdiction. It seems doubtful that enemies getting out of a conflict will submit to the ICJ jurisdiction, though the Corfu case between Albania and the UK and Bosnia-Herzegovina proceeding against Serbia and Montenegro were brought before the ICJ between parties that were opposed belligerents during armed conflict. Negotiations for a permanent peace treaty may cover compensation for environmental damage. Belligerents may agree to submit settlement of claims to an arbitral tribunal or claims commission – which decisions are binding, such as the UNCC or Eritrea-Ethiopia Claims Commission – or choose to appoint an independent neutral mediator. Alternatively, a UNSC resolution on a cease-fire, imposing settlements of claims by an institution to be established on the model of the UNCC, has the merit to be binding, in principle, on belligerents. In the case of Ukraine, a different solution was adopted. Following a UNGA resolution of November 2022, the Council of Europe established, in May 2023, a register of claims for damage and injuries, including critical infrastructure, cultural property and environmental damage, occurring after the invasion of Ukraine in February 2022 that are the consequences of Russia's unlawful act.[18] Adjudication of claims and funds for compensation were left to future decisions. This model could be replicated elsewhere. In the Middle East, regional institutions could intervene to push for implementation of different UNSC and UNGA resolutions and international courts' judgments.

Enforcement on responsible States of their obligation of reparation for armed conflict-related environmental damage has been limited to the sole case of Iraq for damage caused from its invasion and occupation of Kuwait, under a UNSC resolution. Legal means to enforce directly State responsibility for breach of its obligations are few. States party to GC IV and AP/I must respect and ensure respect for the Convention or Protocol, in case of breach of its obligation thereunder by a State, "by doing everything in their power to ensure that the humanitarian principles underlying the Conventions are applied universally."[19] It is an obligation of due diligence, the contours of which are not clear. It is interpreted as an obligation of States supporting one party to the conflict, to use its influence to encourage respect for the LOAC or cease its support in case of risk of breach.[20] Encouraging breaches of IHL is prohibited.[21]

18 UNGA, *Furtherance of Remedy and Reparation for Aggression against Ukraine, 14 November 2022, A/RES/ES-11/5*; Council of Europe, *Resolution CM/Res (2023)3 establishing the Enlarged Partial Agreement on the Register of Damage Caused by the Aggression of the Russian Federation against Ukraine, 12 May 2023*

19 GC IV art.1; ICRC, *Commentary on the Fourth Geneva Convention* (1958) art.1; AP/I art.1

20 Kimberley N. Trapp and Edmund Robinson, 'Extra-territorial "Fiducuary" Obligations and Ensuring Respect for International Humantarian Law' 63 McGill L J 3&4 (2018) 677 687–689

21 *Military and Paramilitary Activities in and against Nicaragua (Nicaragua v. United States of America). Merits, Judgment.* ICJ Rep 1986, p. 14, par.220, 255

Ultimately, failure by belligerents to abide by the LOAC constraints represents also failure of governments to take the law of war seriously.[22] International institutions have stepped up to the challenges lately. The ICC and ICJ adopted decisions related to contemporary conflicts that cannot be pushed aside as an inconvenience and the UNGA adopted resolutions on that basis. States are responsible for taking actions for their implementation. Civil society got involved through professional and human rights organizations bringing claims before national courts to force their governments to change course, demanding enforcement of the LOAC in Israel-Hamas war. In February 2024, the Dutch government was ordered by the Court of Appeals to stop supplying Israel with F35 fighter jet parts, because of the risk that exported equipment would be used in serious violations of IHL, under the Arms Trade Treaty, in a decision under appeal to the Supreme Court,[23] in addition to being currently sued for failure to prevent genocide in Gaza and uphold international law.[24] In the UK, legal professionals addressed the prime minister, calling for weapons' exports to Israel to cease, claiming that the current policy risked breaking international law,[25] and an arms export challenge was granted full judicial review for October 2024[26] leading to the supply of some armaments being suspended.

It is up to States to pursue more vigorously enforcement of the LOAC and to react to its violations, according to their international law responsibility, through pressure on belligerents, suspension of financial support or armaments' delivery, the alternative being "as Grotius understood . . . to the degree conflict is unfettered by the restraints of war and minimum morality we really have entered into a barbaric phase in the relation of societies that are locked in conflict."[27] Responsibility and reparation must be imposed on States for their LOAC violations, including damage to the environment and its natural resources. Justice is fundamental for peace. That should be the goal of the international community.

Bibliography

Treaties

Geneva Convention IV Relative to the Protection of Civilian Persons in Time of War, 12 August 1949

22 Richard A. Falk, Eugene V. Rostow, Francis A. Boyle, W. Michael Reisman, Frits Kalshoven, and Robbie Sabel, 'Problems of the Law of Armed Conflict in Lebanon' 77 ASIL Proceedings of the Annual Meeting, 14–16 April 1983, 214

23 León Castellanos-Jankiewicz, 'Dutch Court Halts F-35 Aircraft Deliveries for Israel: A "Clear Risk" of Abuse' VerfBlog (14 February 2024)

24 SOMO (Centre for Research on Multinational Corporations), Lydia de Leeuw 'We are suing the Dutch state for failing to prevent genocide in Gaza and uphold international law, 10 October 2024'

25 Eduardo Reyes, 'Three Former Supreme Court Judges and 240 Solicitors among Signatories of Israel Sanctions Letter' The Law Society Gazette (4 April 2024)

26 Louisa Brooke-Holland, *Research Briefing, UK Arms Export to Israel, 22 May 2024, Number 9964, 22 May 2024* (House of Commons Library) par.3

27 Richard A. Falk 215

International organisations documents

Council of Europe, *Resolution CM/Res(2023)3 establishing the Enlarged Partial Agreement on the Register of Damage Caused by the Aggression of the Russian Federation against Ukraine* (12 May 2023)

ICRC, *Commentary on the Fourth Geneva Convention* (1958)

ILC, *Responsibility of States for Internationally Wrongful Acts* (ILC YB 2001, vol II (Part Two))

———, *Draft Conclusions on Identification and Legal Consequences of Peremptory Norms of General International Law (jus cogens) 2022*

UNHR, Office of the High Commissioner, *Commissions of Inquiry and Fact-finding Missions on International Human Rights and Humanitarian Law: Guidance and Practice* (2015)

National institutions documents

Brooke-Holland L, *Research Briefing, UK Arms Export to Israel, Number 9964 22 May 2024* (House of Commons Library)

International Tribunals Decisions

Legal Consequences arising from the Policies and Practices of Israel in the Occupied Palestinian Territory, including East Jerusalem, ICJ Advisory Opinion, 19 July 2024 (ICJ)

Military and Paramilitary Activities in and against Nicaragua (Nicaragua v. United States of America). Merits, Judgment ICJ Rep 1986, p. 14

Journal Articles

Castellanos-Jankiewicz L, 'Dutch Court Halts F-35 Aircraft Deliveries for Israel: A "Clear Risk" of Abuse' VerfBlog, 14 February 2024

Falk RA and others, 'Problems of the Law of Armed Conflict in Lebanon' 77 ASIL Proceedings of the Annual Meeting, 14–16 April 1983 214

Foy H and others, 'G7 and EU to Heap Pressure on Russia with Ban on Reopening of Gas Pipelines' FT 2023 1

Gerson A, 'Off-Shore Oil Exploration by a Belligerent Occupant: The Gulf of Suez Dispute' 71 AJIL 4, October 1977 725

International Law and the Israeli-Palestinian Conflict, a Rights-Based Approach to Middle East Peace (Susan M. Akram and others eds, Routledge 2011)

Kellenberger J, 'Strengthening Legal Protection for Victims of Armed Conflict, the ICRC Study on the Current State of International Humanitarian Law, Address by Dr Jakob Kellenberger, President of the International Committee of the Red Cross' 92 IRRC 879, 21 September 2010 799

Malksoo L, 'State Responsibility and the Challenge of the Realist Paragdim: The Demand of Baltic Victims of Soviet Mass Repression for Compensation from Russia' 3 Baltic YB Int'l L 2003 57 57

Reuters, 'Israel Says It Has Secured $8.7 Billion U.S. Aid Package' 26 September 2024

Reyes E, 'Three Former Supreme Court Judges and 240 Solicitors among Signatories of Israel Sanctions Letter' The Law Society Gazette, 4 April 2024

SOMO (Centre for Research on Multinational Corporations), Lydia de Leeuw 'We Are Suing the Dutch State for Failing to Prevent Genocide in Gaza and Uphold International Law, 10 October 2024'

Stephens T, *International Courts and Environmental Protection* (CUP 2009)

Stone M and others, 'US Prepares $8 Billion in Arms Aid Packages for Zelenskiy Visit, Sources Say' Reuters, 25 September 2024
Stuenkel O, 'Why the Global South Is Accusing America of Hypocrisy' FP, 2 November 2023
Trapp KN and Robinson E, 'Extra-territorial "Fiducuary" Obligations and Ensuring Respect for International Humantarian Law' 63 McGill L J 3&4 2018 677
Wolf M, 'The West Must Recognise Its Hypocrisy' FT, 11 July 2023

Index

accountability of State 25; armed group 240; occupant 73, 101
administration: of occupied territory, (military authority 71–73, public order 75–79); of public immovable property 92–97
armed conflict 10–16; classification, disputed 13–16; effects of 16–17; environmental impact of 3–6; international 11; non-international 11–13
army needs, requisitions for 90–92
attack: against civilian objects 34–38, 40; against environment 38–39; against forests 61; against military objects 34; against objects indispensable for survival 57; against works containing dangerous forces 59; impact of 41–42; indiscriminate 35, 40; precautions in 40–41, 59–60; proportionality principle 40; reprisal 37–38

Bridge: destruction of 39; military objective 36–38; seizure in occupation 84–85
British Mandate over Palestine: legal regime of land 195–196, 206; of water 215–216

civilian objects *see* objects, civilian
cluster munitions: Convention on Cluster Munitions 3, 61; determination 159–160
confiscation: natural resources 88; property 90; raw material 87
conflict, armed *see* armed conflict; of norms 98–101, 128–130
customary international law 20–22; Hague Regulations as 7, 21–22; international organizations 21; law of State responsibility as 24; VCLT as 23

damage to environment *see* environmental damage
destruction: bridge 37, 39; ENMOD 46–47; environment 3, 5, 44; 1st Gulf War 53; military advantage 36–37; military necessity 41, 44,; military objective 36; natural resources 39; objects indispensable to survival 57–58; occupied territory 82–83; power station 37, 41; property 57, 82–83;; proportionality 39–41; UNCHE Declaration 2; Vietnam war 39; village 5, 40–41; water reservoir 58; works containing dangerous forces 59
development, sustainable 123–124
discrimination principle *see* distinction principle
distinction principle 33–38; application to environment 38–40; Israel-Hezbollah conflict 2006 161–164; and proportionality 40; US doctrine 169
due diligence 52, 117–119; customary rule 116; ILC Articles on Prevention of Transboundary Harm from Hazardous Activities 117–119; lack of 134; norms' conflict 130; objective responsibility 135, 142; precautionary approach 122; standard of 136

East Jerusalem: Absentee property 203; annexation 214; Israeli law 220; occupation 189; population 190; requisitions 203–204; settlements 205, 207–208; the Wall 210–211
ENMOD Convention 4; environmental damage threshold 55–56; intergenerational equity 123; obligations under 46–47; proponents of 52

environment 17–20; civilian object 38–39; cultural heritage 18–20; historical perspective 1–6; marine 170–175; military objective 38–39; natural 17; protection of (*see* environmental protection)
environmental damage 139–142; *Armed Activities* case 76–77; collateral 39, 49–51; compensable 77, 141–142; conflict of norms 130; distinction principle 42–43; *Eritrea-Ethiopia* case 83; excessive 40, 43, 60, 119–120; historical perspective 3–6; intergenerational equity 123–124; long-term 54–55, military necessity 44; notion and threshold (under API 47–49, 52–54, under ENMOD 46–47, under IEL 139–142); precautionary principle 120–123; precautions in attacks 59–60; prevention of 114–120; severe 55; State liability for 137–139; State responsibility for 133–136; transboundary 52, 114–120; UNCC claims for 19–20; widespread 55–56
environmental impact assessment 118; and armed conflict 141; of marine pollution 171–175; *South China Sea Case* 117
environmental protection 1–4, 8, 35; anthropocentric perspective 47–48; AP/I 17, 37–38; applicability of treaties 125; *Dispute regarding navigational and related rights (Costa Rica v. Nicaragua)* case 101; due regard for 60; humanity principle 44–46; human rights jurisprudence 101; intrinsic perspective 47–48; Rio Declaration 79; sustainable development 123
equity: equitable allocation of natural resources 97; equitable use of water 132–133; intergenerational 123–124

Gaza: area 190; history 187–190; Israeli withdrawal from 191–192; population 190; *see also* Occupied Palestinian Territory
general principles of law 22–23; IEL principles as 110; liability standard under 138

Hague Regulations 6–7; application in armed conflict 16; customary international law 7, 21–22; occupation law 68; relevance 69–70
Hezbollah: armed conflict with Israel 2006 (*see* Israel-Hezbollah armed conflict 2006); history and role of 150–153; military organization 154; political party 154
humanity principle 44–46
human rights or international human rights *see* international human rights law

immovable: administration of public property 92–97; confiscation 90; crude oil 86–87; destruction 57, 82; Hague Regulations 85; land 80; natural resources 80–81; requisition 91; seizure 57, 83–85; title to 94; water 80, 89
intergenerational equity principle 123–124
international armed conflict *see* armed conflict, international
International Covenant on Civil and Political Rights (ICCPR) 79, 98; extraterritoriality 98
International Covenant on Economic Social and Cultural Rights (ICESCR) 79, 98; extraterritoriality 98
International Environmental Law (IEL) 8–10; applicability in armed conflict 6, 17, 71; applicability of IEL principles in armed conflict 110–112; applicability of treaties in armed conflict 124–125; application 237–240; conflict of norms 128–130; customary law 22; intergenerational equity 123–124; interpretation of usufruct 97; liability of State 137–139; in occupation 71, 97; precautionary principle 120; prevention of harm and transboundary damage 114–116; sovereignty over natural resources 112–113; State responsibility 133–136; sustainable development 123–124
International Human Rights Law (IHRL) 98; applicability in armed conflict 71, 98, 125; conflict of norms 98–101, 128–130; Covenants 79, 98; duty of occupant 75–77; right to water 55; sovereignty over natural resources 112
international law *see* public international law
International Water Law (IWL) 131; applicability during armed conflict 6, 71, 142, 237–238; determination of 131; Occupied Palestinian Territory 220–222, 226

Israel-Hezbollah armed conflict 2006: air pollution 178–179; attack on Jiyeh power station 168–170; Barcelona Convention 170–171, 175–178; cluster munitions 159–160; damage to forests 158–159, 167–168; damage to land 158–159, 162–163, 168–170; damage to Mediterranean Sea 172–175; EIA marine pollution 171–175; IEL principles 170–171, 175–178; indiscriminate attacks 162–164; indiscriminate weapons 161–162; proportionality principle 165–166; qualification of 153–156; UNCLOS 170–171, 175–178

Jerusalem, international trusteeship 188; annexation 114; *see also* East Jerusalem
Jordan, Jordan river 214, 216, 219; Jerusalem 214; Jordanian land law 196, 202, 206; Jordanian property 202; Jordanian rule over West Bank 196; Jordanian water law 216–218, 222

land: confiscation of 90; exploitation of 96; immovable 80, 89; land rights 81; requisition of 85, 91–92; seizure of 76, 83–85, 89; sovereignty over 112, 114; usufruct 95; water rights on 81–82
Law of Armed Conflict (LOAC) 5–8; applicability of 10–17
law of occupation 68; administration of public immovable property 92–97; applicability 68–69; army needs 91–92; confiscation 90; destruction 82; Hague Regulations 69–70; legislative change 77–79; military needs 75; natural resources, exploitation of 93–97, permanent sovereignty over 113–114; objects indispensable for survival 83; pillage 89–90; property of military use 85–89; protected persons 96; public order 75–76; requisition 90–92; security, (of occupying forces 78–79, 92, 97; of protected population 76;) seizure 83–85; sustainable use 123; war munitions (*munitions de guerre*) 85–88; *see also* occupation
Lebanon, 2006 conflict *see* Israel-Hezbollah conflict 2006
legislative change 77–79
liability 25, 133; absolute 135, 137–138; civil 137; compensation 61, 114; criminal 240–241; enforcement 61, 101, 239–240; environmental damage, compensable 141–142; fault 137–139; hazardous activities 137–139; Iraq in 1st Gulf War 5; jurisprudence 134–135; notion and threshold 139–141; nuclear activities 137–139; objective 138; oil pollution at sea 137–139; operator 137–138; reparation 61, 114, 134, 241; restitution 114; risk 138; sanctions 241; standard of liability (conflict of norms 130; due diligence obligation 119, 136; environmental damage under AP/I 49–52; general principles of law 138; objects indispensable for survival of population 57, 83; *Trail Smelter* case 134); State 137–139; strict 135, 137–138

military advantage: attacks, cancellation and suspension of 60; distinction principle 36–37, 39; evaluation 36–37; military necessity 44, 53; proportionality principle 40–43
military necessity 44; destruction in occupation 82–83; pillage, destruction and seizure during hostilities 57–58; security 92; seizure in occupation 83–85; temporary use of immovable 91
military objective 35–38; bridge as 36–38; among civilian population 40–41; Convention on Conventional Weapons 61; distinction principle 34; environment as 38–39, 47–48; nuclear submarine 50; precautions in attack 59–60, proportionality principle 39–43; supertanker 50; works containing dangerous forces 59
military operations: armed group 12; destruction, in occupation 82; end of 74; military advantage 41–42; natural resources' exploitation 96–97; occupation army needs 91; precautions in attacks 59–60; public immovable property 84–85; seizure of property of military use 85; water installations 58
military use, property of 85–89; temporary 91
mines 94–95
munitions de guerre 85–88

natural resources: civilian object 38–39; classification 80–82; commercial value

141; compensation for damage to 61; damage to 55, 139, 141; destruction 44, 57; East Timor 74–75; environment 17–20, 38–39; exploitation (purpose of 96–97, benefit of 96, rate of 93–94); human rights 100–101; immovable and movable 80–81; object indispensable for survival 57–58; obligation of occupying power 76; pillage 57, 89; private and public 81–82; property 79; public property of military use 88–89; raw material 86–87; seizure 57, 83–85; shared, water 130–133; sovereignty over 112–114; sustainable development 123; sustainable use 97, 123; UNCC claims 5, 140; use by settlers 96; war munition 86–87; WTO interpretation 129; *see also* permanent sovereignty over natural resources
non-international armed conflict 11–13

objects: civilian 34–39; cultural 19; dual-use 41, 83; environment as 38–39, 47–48, 93; indeterminate attack 40–41; indispensable to survival of the population 57–59, 83; livelihood 166–168; military 34–39; precautions in attack 59–60; works containing dangerous forces 59
obligations of conduct: AP/I obligation not to cause environmental damage 51–52; due diligence obligation 135, 142; prevention of transboundary harm 119, 135
obligations of result 51–52, 135–136
occupation 71–73; administration of territory 75–79; annexation 75; applicable laws 71; effective control 73–74; end of 74; human rights 98–101; military authority, establishment and exercise 72–73; sovereignty, inalienability 74–75; temporary 74–75; *see also* law of occupation
occupation of Palestinian Territory *see* Occupied Palestinian Territory
Occupied Palestinian Territory (OPT): Annexation (de facto 206, 210; of Jerusalem 199, 214; of Palestinian territory of 1948 189; of West Bank by Jordan 189); applicable laws 190–191 Bedouins 200; buffer zones 209–210; closed area 197–200, 205, 207 (Jordan River basin 218, West Bank 209–210); Custodian of Government and Abandoned Property 207; effective control 192; environmental damage 213, 217, 221; land, access to 209–211 (confiscation 199–201, 203, 206; expropriation 200, 205, 211; requisition 201, 203–204; seizure 197–199, 205, 220; title to 195–196, 199, 202, 206); land legal regime pre-1967 (Absentee Property Law 197–200; British Mandate 195–196; Jordanian rule 196; Land Acquisition Law 198–200; Ottoman Empire 193–195; Requisition Law 201; Uncultivated Lands Regulations 197); land legal regime post-1967; (Abandoned Property 202–203; Government Property 202–203); military administration 193; Oslo Agreement 191–192, 219–220; population 190; property, abandoned and absentee 197–201, 202–203, 204, 207; quarries 212–213; sanitation 224–226; settlement 203–204, 207–209; sovereignty over natural resources 201, 203, 206, 221, 226; State land classification 204–205; water, confiscation 220 (consumption 225, control and management 222–224; customary law water right 222; equitable use 221, 226; exploitation 217–218; human rights 222–224; Israel obligations 221; nationalization 220; ownership and use rights 215, 219–220; sanitation 224–226; sources 214–215); water legal regime pre-1967 (British Mandate 215–216; Jordanian rule 216–217; Ottoman Empire 215; Water Law (1959) 216); water legislation post-1967 (Military Order 498 (1974), Military Order 291 (1968) 218))
occupied territory 71–74; administration of 75–79
Oslo agreement 191–192, 219–220

permanent sovereignty over natural resources 112; application in armed conflict 71, 74–75, 113–114; customary international law 80, 111, 113; human rights 112; responsibility under 142; Rio Declaration 79; UNCLOS 124; UNGA Resolution 21
pillage: hostilities 57; natural resources exploitation 94; occupation 89; sovereignty over natural resources 113
pollution: air 178–179; marine 181

power station: attack on Jiyeh, Lebanon 168–178, 179; military objective 37, 39, 41
precautionary principle 120; applicability in armed conflict 122; *Beef Hormones* case 112, 120–121; environmental damage 60; Israel-Hezbollah conflict 2006 175–176; precautions in attacks 122, 142, 238; *Southern Bluefin Tuna* case 121; status 120–123
precautions in attacks 59–60; under AP/I 40; due diligence 130; precautionary principle 122, 142; prevention of transboundary harm 119–120
prevention of transboundary harm and environmental damage 114–115; applicability in armed conflict 119–120; due diligence obligation 117–119; significant harm 140; status 116; water resources 133
principles of law *see* general principles of law
property: administration of public immovable 92–97; classification, public or private 79–82; confiscation 84–85, 90; destruction (hostilities 40–41, 44, 57, occupation 82–83); immovable 91; of military use 85–89; natural resources as 79–82; occupation 82–90; pillage (hostilities 57 occupation 89–90); requisition 84, 86–87, 90–92; right to 101; seizure (hostilities 57, occupation 83–89); temporary use 91
proportionality principle 39–43; application to environment 43; indiscriminate attack 35; Israel-Hezbollah conflict 2006 165–166; status 33–34; US doctrine 53
protected persons 96; attacks on property of 38; security of 92
public international law 20–25; applicability of treaties in armed conflicts 124–128; conflict of norms 128–130; customary international law 20–22; evolutionary 54, 130; general principles of law 22–23; intertemporal 53; liability 24–25; responsibility 24–25; sources 20–24; treaties (notion 23, interpretation 23–24)

quarry: authorization to exploit 95; exploitation under usufruct 93, 95–96

requisition: army needs 90–92; crude oil 86; GC IV 90; Hague Regulations 90; jurisprudence 88; movable or immovable 84–85, 91, 97; private property 84; raw material 86
responsibility of State *see* State responsibility

seizure: of land 83–84; for military operations or necessity 82–85; of oil installations 91–92; of property 57, 83; of property of military use 85–89
sovereignty 73–74; absolute territorial 131–132; inalienability 74–75; *see also* permanent sovereignty over natural resources
State liability *see* liability, State
State responsibility 24; act of State 111; due diligence obligation 135; inadequate 137; ILC Articles on State Responsibility 25; jurisprudence 134–135; objective 133–135, 139; primary rules 24–25, 133; secondary rules 24–25,133; standard of conduct 24–25, 133–135, 142, (under AP/I 49–52); subjective 133–135; *ultra vires* act 33; wrongful act 24–25; 133–136 (and causality of damage 136, and obligation of result and conduct 135–136)
sustainable: development 123–124; use 93, 97

threshold of environmental damage *see* environmental damage threshold
transboundary harm: disastrous 117; EIA requirement 118; jurisprudence 117–118; liability of operator 138–139; prevention of 114–116; risk 117–120, 136, 138, 140–141; significant 117
treaties 23; applicability during armed conflict 124–125; civil liability treaties 137–139; conflict of norms 128–129; interpretation 23–24, 129–130; sources of law 23–24; suspension 125–127; systemic integration 129–130; termination 127–128

UNCLOS *see* United Nations Convention on the Law of the Sea
United Nations Convention on the Law of the Sea (UNCLOS): applicability during armed conflict 124; customary international law 157; damage 140; obligation of cooperation 117; pollution 171; prevention of transboundary harm

and environmental damage 170–171; treaty interpretation 129–130
usufruct 93; benefit of protected population 96; exploitation right 94–95; public immovable property 92–97; safeguarding the capital 93–94; sustainable use 97; water usufructuary rights 80–81

war munitions 86–88; water as 220
water: damage 41, 55; environment 17–20; exploitation of 94; human right 100–101; International Water Law 130–133; movable and immovable 80–81, 89; object 38–39; object indispensable to survival, drinking installations 57–58, 83; pollution 39, 53; public and private 82–83; threshold of environmental damage 56; transboundary resources 81; State right and obligation 131–132; use by settlers 96
weapons conventions 60–61
West Bank area 190; administrative areas 191–192; Interim Agreement on the West Bank and Gaza Strip 189; Israeli civil administration 193; Israeli occupation 189, 192; Jordan, annexation, disengagement 189; population 190; *see also* Occupied Palestinian territory
works containing dangerous forces 59

FSC
www.fsc.org
MIX
Papier | Fördert gute Waldnutzung
FSC® C083411

Kolibri 360 GmbH
Ferdinand-Jühlke-Straße 7
99095 Erfurt, Deutschland
produktsicherheit@kolibri360.de